The Reform of International Economic Governance

The second half of the twentieth century saw the emergence of international economic law as a major force in the international legal system. This force has been severely tested by the economic crisis of 2008. Unable to prevent the crisis, the existing legal mechanisms have struggled to react against its direst consequences. This book brings together leading experts to analyse the main causes of the crisis and the role that international economic law has played in trying to prevent it, on the one hand, and worsening it, on the other. The work highlights the reaction and examines the tools that have been created by the international legal field to implement international cooperation in an effort to help put an end to the crisis and avoid similar events in the future. The volume brings together eminent legal academics and economists to examine key issues from the perspectives of trade law, financial law, and investment law with the collective aim of reform of international economic governance.

Antonio Segura Serrano is Associate Professor, Coordinator of the Official Master of International Law and International Relations, and Vice-Secretary of the Euro-Arab Foundation of Graduate Studies at the University of Granada, Spain. He has published widely on aspects of international law both in English and Spanish.

Global Law and Sustainable Development
Series editor:
Paolo Davide Farah, West Virginia University, USA and
gLAWcal – Global Law Initiatives for Sustainable Development, UK

This series provides a new focus on the relationship between international law, economy and trade, with special attention to what are commonly referred to as non-trade-related values and concerns. Through research and policy analysis the series sheds new light on a range of issues relating to good governance and human rights in the widest sense. It is held that the values supporting these issues are directly affected by the global expansion of world trade and need to be upheld in order to balance the excesses of globalization. Multidisciplinary in approach, the series integrates studies from scholars and researchers with a range of different backgrounds and interdisciplinary expertise from law, economics, political science, and sociology through to history, philosophy and natural science.

Other titles in this series:

China's Influence on Non Trade Concerns in International Economic Law
Paolo Davide Farah and Elena Cima (forthcoming)

The Reform of International Economic Governance

Antonio Segura Serrano

Routledge
Taylor & Francis Group

LONDON AND NEW YORK

First published 2016
by Routledge
2 Park Square, Milton Park, Abingdon, Oxon OX14 4RN

and by Routledge
711 Third Avenue, New York, NY 10017

First issued in paperback 2017

Routledge is an imprint of the Taylor & Francis Group, an informa business

British Library Cataloguing in Publication Data
A catalogue record for this book is available from the British Library

Library of Congress Cataloging-in-Publication Data
The reform of international economic governance / edited by Antonio Segura Serrano.
    pages cm. — (Global law and sustainable development)
    Includes bibliographical references and index.
  ISBN 978-1-4724-7140-6 (hardback : alk. paper) — ISBN 978-1-4724-7141-3 (ebook) — ISBN 978-1-4724-7142-0 (epub)   1. International law—Economic aspects.   2. Corporate governance—Law and legislation.   3. Law reform.   4. International economic relations.   5. World Trade Organization.   6. Financial institutions, International—Law and legislation.   7. Global Financial Crisis, 2008–2009.   I. Segura Serrano, Antonio, editor.
    KZ1252.R44 2016
    343.07—dc23
    2015030412

ISBN 13: 978-1-138-48388-0 (pbk)
ISBN 13: 978-1-4724-7140-6 (hbk)

Typeset in Times New Roman
by Apex CoVantage, LLC

Contents

Abbreviations

AB	Appellate Body
ADA	Anti-Dumping Agreement
AFSI	L'Aquila Food Security Initiative
AML	Anti-Money Laundering
AoA	Agreement on Agriculture
ASCM	Agreement on Subsidies and Countervailing Measures
ASEAN	Association of Southeast Asian Nations
ASRIWA	Articles on State Responsibility for Internationally Wrongful Acts
ATC	Agreement on Textiles and Clothing
BCBS	Basel Committee on Banking Supervision
BCCI	Bank of Credit and Commerce International
BHC	Bank Holding Company
BIS	Bank of International Settlements
BIT	Bilateral Investment Treaty
BoE	Bank of England
BRRD	Bank Recovery and Resolution Directive
CAP	Common Agricultural Policy
CETA	EU-Canada Comprehensive Economic and Trade Agreement
CET1	Core Equity Tier 1 capital
CFS	Committee on Food Security
CFT	Countering the Financing of Terrorism
CGG	Commission on Global Governance
CGIAR	Consultative Group for International Agricultural Research
CJEU	Court of Justice of the European Union
CoCos	Contingent Convertible Capital Instruments
CONARROZ	Corporación Arrocera Nacional, Costa Rica
CVA	Credit Valuation Adjustment
DFA	Dodd–Frank Act
DR-CAFTA	Free Trade Agreement between the Dominican Republic, Central America and the United States of America
DSB	Dispute Settlement Body
DSG	Deposit Guarantee Scheme
DSU	Dispute Settlement Understanding
EA	Energy Agreement
EBU	European Banking Union
EC	European Community

ECHR	European Convention on Human Rights
EEC	European Economic Community
EFTA	European Free Trade Association
ESCAP	UN Economic and Social Commission for Asia and the Pacific
ESM	European Stability Mechanism
FAC	Food and Agriculture Council
FAO	Food and Agriculture Organization
FATF	Financial Action Task Force
FCN	Friendship, Commerce and Navigation
FDIC	Federal Deposit Insurance Corporation
FIU	Financial Intelligence Units
FRB	Federal Reserve Board (USA)
FSAP	Financial Sector Assessment Program
FSB	Financial Stability Board
FSF	Financial Stability Forum
FTA	Free Trade Agreement
FTC	Free Trade Commission
GATT	General Agreement on Trade and Tariffs
GFC	Global Financial Crisis
GFS	Global Food Security
GHG	Green House Gas
GPA	Global Partnership on Agriculture, Food Security and Nutrition
GPA	Government Procurement Agreement
G-SIFI	Global Systemically Important Financial Institutions
HLTF	United Nations High-Level Task Force
IAIS	International Association of Insurance Supervisors
IAS	International Accounting Standards
ICESCR	International Covenant on Economic, Social and Cultural Rights
ICSID	International Centre for Settlement of Investment Disputes
IDE	Institute of Developing Economies
IEL	International Economic Law
IFAD	International Fund for Agricultural Development
IHC	Intermediate Holding Company (USA)
ILC	International Law Commission
ILO	International Labour Organisation
IMF	International Monetary Fund
IMM	Internal Model Method
IOSCO	International Organization of Securities Regulation
IPCC	Intergovernmental Panel on Climate Change
IRB	Internal Ratings Based Approach
IRC	Incremental Risk Charge
ISDA	International Swaps and Derivatives Association
ITO	International Trade Organisation
JETRO	Japan External Trade Organization
LDC	Least-Developed Countries
MEA	Multilateral Environmental Agreement
MFA	Multi-Fiber Agreement
MFN	Most-Favoured Nation

MIWI	Made in the World Initiative
MOU	Memorandum of Understanding
MPE	Multiple Point of Entry
NAFTA	North American Free Trade Agreement
NCWO	No creditor worse off
NFIDC	Net Food-Importing Developing Countries
NPM	Non Precluded Measures
OECD	Organization for Economic Co-operation and Development
OLA	Orderly Liquidation Authority
OLF	Orderly Liquidation Fund
OTC	Over-the-Counter
PCIJ	Permanent Court of International Justice
PRA	Prudent Regulation Authority
PTA	Plurilateral Trade Agreement
ROSC	Reports on the Observance of Standards and Codes
RTA	Regional Trade Agreements
SBN	Sustainability Banking Network
SCM	Subsidies and Countervailing Measures
SDRM	Sovereign Debt Restructuring Mechanism
SEPSA	Secretaria Ejecutiva de Planificación Sectorial Agropecuaria
SIFI	Systemically Important Financial Institution
SME	Small and Medium Enterprise
SPOE	Single Point of Entry
SPS	Sanitary and Phytosanitary Measures
SRM	Single Resolution Mechanism
SSM	Single Supervisory Mechanism
TARP	Troubled Asset Relief Programme (USA)
TBT	Technical Barriers to Trade
TBTF	Too-Big-to-Fail institution
TFEU	Treaty on the Functioning of the European Union
TPRM	Trade Policy Review Mechanism
TRIPS	The Agreement on Trade-Related Aspects of Intellectual Property Rights
TRN	Transnational Regulatory Networks
TTIP	Transatlantic Trade and Investment Partnership
UN	United Nations
UNCITRAL	United Nations Commission on International Trade Law
UNCTAD	United Nations Conference on Trade and Development
UNDP	United Nations Development Programme
USTR	United States Trade Representative
VaR	Value-at-risk
VCLT	Vienna Convention on the Law of Treaties
WB	World Bank
WFA	World Financial Authority
WFC	World Food Council
WFO	World Financial Organisation
WFP	World Food Program
WFS	World Food Summit
WTO	World Trade Organization

Contributors

Kern Alexander holds the Professorial Chair in Banking and Financial Market Law at the University of Zurich. Professor Alexander is an internationally recognized expert in international financial regulation and European Union and British banking law. He is co-author of *Global Governance of Financial Systems: the International Regulation of Systemic Risk* (OUP, 2005). This work identified weaknesses in bank capital regulation and systemic risk in the derivatives markets before the 2007/2008 financial crisis. In 2014, he authored a research report for the United Nations on international banking regulation and environmental sustainability. He also served as a Specialist Adviser to the UK Parliament's Joint Select Committee on the Financial Services Act 2012 and as a Member of the Expert Panel on Financial Services of the European Parliament (2009–2014). His research interests focus on the legal regulation of macro-prudential financial risks.

Emilios Avgouleas is the inaugural holder of the International Banking Law and Finance Chair at the University of Edinburgh where he heads the Commercial Law subject area. He is also an elected member of the Stakeholder Group of the European Banking Authority (top-ranking academics section). He has published extensively in the wider field of International and European finance law and economics and behavioural finance. He is the author of a number of scholarly articles and of two monographs: *Governance of Global Financial Markets: The Law, the Economics, the Politics* (Cambridge, 2012); *The Mechanics and Regulation of Market Abuse: A Legal and Economic Analysis* (Oxford, 2005). He co-authors with Sir Ross Cranston and others the third edition of *Principles of Banking Law* (Oxford, 2016).

Chios Carmody is Associate Professor at Western University Faculty of Law in London, Ontario, Canada. He currently teaches courses in Contracts, International Trade Law and International Business Transactions. Since 2002 he has been Canadian National Director of the Canada-United States Law Institute. Professor Carmody has been a Visiting Professor at Université Montpellier I (June 2000), Visiting Adjunct Professor at Georgetown University Law Center in Fall 2001, Emile Noël Fellow at the Jean Monnet Center for International & Regional Economic Law & Justice, NYU Law School (2005–2006) and Université de Reims (June 2011). His current work focuses on developing a general theory of WTO law, which is the subject of his forthcoming monograph, *A Theory of WTO Law: A Theory of Law* (Cambridge University Press).

Elena Cima is a PhD candidate at the Graduate Institute of International and Development Studies, Geneva (Switzerland), after qualifying as LLM 2014, Yale Law School (USA);

LLB 2010, University of Milan (Italy). She was EU Commission Marie Curie Fellow at Tsinghua University School of Law, THCEREL – Center for Environmental, Natural Resources & Energy Law in Beijing (China) and Research Fellow at Università del Piemonte Orientale 'Amedeo Avogadro', DiseI – Dipartimento di Studi per l'Impresa e il Territorio (Italy).

Paolo Davide Farah is at West Virginia University, Department of Public Administration within the Eberly College of Arts and Sciences and College of Law (WV, USA). He is Research Scientist and Principal Investigator at gLAWcal – Global Law Initiatives for Sustainable Development (United Kingdom). He has a dual PhD in International Law at Aix-Marseille University (France) and at Università degli Studi di Milano (Italy), LLM from the College of Europe, Bruges (Belgium), and JD (Maitrise) in International and European Law, Paris Ouest La Defense Nanterre (France). He has been a Visiting Scholar (2011–2012) at Harvard Law School, EALS – East Asian Legal Studies (USA), EU Commission Marie Curie Fellow (2009–2011) at Tsinghua University School of Law, THCEREL – Center for Environmental, Natural Resources & Energy Law in Beijing (China) and at the CRAES – Chinese Research Academy on Environmental Sciences in Beijing (China). He was Fellow at the IIEL – Institute of International Economic Law (2004–2005) at Georgetown University Law Center (USA).

Charles Goodhart, CBE, FBA, is Emeritus Professor of Banking and Finance with the Financial Markets Group at the London School of Economics, having previously, 1987–2005, been its Deputy Director. Until his retirement in 2002, he had been the Norman Sosnow Professor of Banking and Finance at LSE since 1985. Before then, he had worked at the Bank of England for 17 years as a monetary adviser, becoming a Chief Adviser in 1980. In 1997 he was appointed one of the outside independent members of the Bank of England's new Monetary Policy Committee until May 2000. Earlier he had taught at Cambridge and LSE. Besides numerous articles, he has written a couple of books on monetary history; a graduate monetary textbook, *Money, Information and Uncertainty* (2nd edn, 1989); two collections of papers on monetary policy, *Monetary Theory and Practice* (1984) and *The Central Bank and The Financial System* (1995); and a number of books and articles on Financial Stability, on which subject he was Adviser to the Governor of the Bank of England, 2002–2004. His latest books include *The Basel Committee on Banking Supervision: A History of the Early Years, 1974–1997* (2011) and *The Regulatory Response to the Financial Crisis* (2009).

Jenya Grigorova is a doctoral researcher in Public international Law and International Economic Law at Sorbonne Law School (Paris 1 Pantheon Sorbonne University) and a junior lecturer (ATER). Her PhD thesis on 'The international regulation of trade in energy resources' is to be defended in 2016. Jenya holds master's degrees from Paris 1 University and Sofia University. She was a teaching fellow at Paris 1 University, a fellow at the Energy Charter Secretariat and worked as an intern at the European Court of Justice. Jenya's research interests include international trade law, issues related to energy regulation, environmental law and general public international law. Jenya has published in French, English and Bulgarian, on pressing issues in international trade relations and European law. She also regularly serves as judge for Moot court competitions (ELSA Moot court competition on WTO law, Jessup Moot Court).

Rosa Maria Lastra is Professor in International Financial and Monetary Law at the Centre for Commercial Law Studies (CCLS), Queen Mary University of London. She is a member of the Monetary Committee of the International Law Association (MOCOMILA), of the European Shadow Financial Regulatory Committee (ESFRC) and of the International Insolvency Institute. She is an observer at the ILA Sovereign Bankruptcy Group and a senior research associate of the Financial Markets Group of the London School of Economics. She has consulted with various governmental and intergovernmental institutions, including the International Monetary Fund, the European Central Bank, the World Bank, the Asian Development Bank, the Federal Reserve Bank of New York and the House of Lords. Prior to coming to London, she was Assistant Professor at Columbia University in the City of New York and she also worked at the Legal Department of the International Monetary Fund. She studied at Valladolid University, Madrid University, London School of Economics and Political Sciences and Harvard Law School. She has published extensively in the fields of international monetary law, financial regulation, central banking, EU Law and cross-border resolution of banking and sovereign debt crises.

Gregory Messenger is Lecturer in Law at the University of Liverpool. He was previously Junior Research Fellow in Law at the Queen's College, Oxford where he also completed his BCL and DPhil degrees. He has taught public international law, world trade law and international investment law at the universities of Oxford and Durham as well as introductory courses in English law at the University of Granada. Greg's research examines conceptual issues arising from the development and application of international economic law. His research interests are principally in public international law, international economic law, trade-related aspects of US and EU constitutional law and theoretical approaches to international economic law. He has published on trade and legal theory, and his monograph *The Development of WTO Law: Examining Change in International Law* is to be published by Oxford University Press in 2016.

Vassilis Paliouras is a PhD candidate at Queen Mary University of London. He holds degrees in law from the Aristotle University of Thessaloniki (LLB) and Washington College of Law, American University (LLM). He is a member of the Athens Bar Association and has practised briefly with a commercial law firm in Athens. His research interests include public international law, international economic and financial law and the legal aspects of sovereign debt restructuring.

Carolina Palma holds a degree in Law from the University of Costa Rica, an LLM in International Law from the LMU Munich, a master's degree in Trade Law and she is currently a PhD researcher at the World Trade Institute in Bern. Moreover, she has taught Multilateral Trade and International Public Law at the University of Costa Rica and she has been a judge for Jessup and OEA international public law competitions in China and Costa Rica. She was a former trade negotiator at the Ministry of Trade and a contributor to the Costa Rican Embassy in China. Her research focuses on agriculture, food security, dispute resolution, investment law and regional trade agreements such as the Pacific Alliance, DR-CAFTA and the Central American – European Union Agreement, and she has published a number of articles on those topics.

Antonio Segura Serrano is Associate Professor of International Law and European Law at the University of Granada, Spain. He currently teaches courses on Public International Law and Institutional European Law, and has also taught courses on International Economic

Law and the EU Internal Market. He has been Research Fellow at the London School of Economics, Harvard University, New York University and University Paris I-Pantheon Sorbonne. His current work focuses on global economic governance, EU trade policy and Internet regulation. Moreover, he has published on other issues such as intellectual property law, humanitarian law, and the theory of international law. He presently is Coordinator of the Official Master of International Law and International Relations and Vice-Secretary of the Euro-Arab Foundation of Graduate Studies at the University of Granada. He is also an Editorial Board Member of the *Revista de Derecho Comunitario Europeo*.

Catharine Titi is a Research Scientist for the French National Centre for Scientific Research (CNRS) and a member of the CREDIMI, Law Faculty of the University of Bourgogne. She holds a PhD in Law from the University of Siegen, Germany. Catharine has previously worked as a consultant for the United Nations Conference on Trade and Development (UNCTAD). She has published in a variety of academic journals and edited volumes in English and French, such as in the *European Journal of International Law*. Her monograph on *The Right to Regulate in International Investment Law* was published by Nomos and Hart Publishing in 2014 and she is co-editor (with Katia Fach) of the *Journal of World Investment & Trade* special issue on *The Latin American Challenge to the Current System of Investor-State Dispute Settlement* (2016).

Valentina Vadi is a Professor in International Economic Law at Lancaster University, United Kingdom. She formerly was a Reader in International Business Law at the same university (2013–2015), an Emile Noël Fellow at the Jean Monnet Centre for International and Regional Economic Law, at New York University (2013–2014), and a Marie Curie Postdoctoral Fellow at Maastricht University (2011–2013). She has published more than 80 articles in various areas of public international law in top journals, including the *Vanderbilt Journal of Transnational Law*, the *Stanford Journal of International Law*, the *European Journal of International Law* and others. Valentina Vadi is the author of *Public Health in International Investment Law and Arbitration* (Routledge, 2012), *Cultural Heritage in International Investment Law and Arbitration* (Cambridge University Press, 2014) and *Analogies in International Investment Law and Arbitration* (Cambridge University Press, forthcoming).

Mika Viljanen (LLD) works as a collegium researcher at the Turku Institute for Advanced Studies, University of Turku, Finland. His main research interests include banking and financial regulation, money, private law theory, regulatory theory and actor-network theory.

Friedl Weiss is Professor Emeritus in the Department of European, International and Comparative Law at the University of Vienna. Previously he was lecturer at the London School of Economics and Political Science and held the Chair of International Economic Law and International Organizations at the University of Amsterdam as well as various Visiting Professorships in European, Asian and American universities. His research and publications cover a wide range of topics of European and international (economic) law, international organizations, including those of international economic governance and European Union law. He has served as legal adviser in the EFTA Secretariat as well as legal consultant in the GATT Secretariat. He is member of the ILA Committee on the role of sustainable development in resource management for development and was member as well as former rapporteur of the ILA Committee on International Trade Law, as well as a member of the ILA Committees on International Law on Sustainable Development and on Foreign Investment.

Foreword

The editor of this volume has brought together an impressive range of leading scholars, asking them to think ambitiously about contemporary global economic governance – its weaknesses, foremost challenges, and prospects for reform. The result is an impressive book which ranges across the fields of international trade, finance and investment law, and which offers a unique snapshot of the state of the art of thinking in these fields, close to two decades into the twenty-first century.

A striking characteristic of the contributions to this collection, taken as a whole, is their healthy and clear-eyed ambivalence about the possibilities of international law as a technology of governance in the contemporary moment. On one hand, the reader is confronted with a powerful and deeply pragmatic optimism about the ability of international law and institutions to solve pressing global problems. The chapters from both Segura Serrano and Lastra, for example, make compelling cases for the need of new rules and institutions at the global level to ameliorate the lack of coordinated and coherent regulation of transnational financial services markets. Paliouras, too, explores the potential for the classical doctrine of necessity in public international law to address instances of state insolvency and public debt restructuring. More generally, virtually all contributions proceed from the common premise that international law remains one of the most important potential tools we have in our arsenal to address the complex problems thrown up by globalization.

At the same time, this optimism is tempered with an equally important dose of caution and modesty, as the limits of international law, and the problems associated with its exercise, are at times put front and centre by the contributors to this volume. Messenger's discussion of the unexpected consequences or certain aspects of the law of the World Trade Organization is an important reminder of the fact that the trajectories of international legal projects are rarely as clear as we might imagine at their inception, and that the dynamics of international legal orders often confound the expectations of their architects over time. Avgouleas' and Goodhart's exhortation to consider the disadvantages of currently favoured 'bank bail-ins' recalls also the general inability of legal projects to deliver fully on their promised benefits (here, the promise to remove once and for all the reliance on public money in future banks). And, crucially, virtually all of the authors in this book place emphasis on the fact that some of our most pressing global challenges are in part the product of international law, not merely the consequence of international law's absence. International law, this volume reminds us, is virtually always present as part of the problem before it emerges as a potential solution – so that the choice is never simply between 'more' or 'less' law, 'greater' or 'lesser' judicialization.

To some extent this ambivalence probably reflects the state of the discipline of international law itself in the present moment, as it continues to struggle with the complex legacy of the global turn to international law during the 1990s. For many international lawyers, it is hard to tell whether our current global problems are best understood as the result of the international legal hubris of the immediate aftermath of the end of the Cold War – or are instead in reality the consequence of a failure to carry through international legal projects, to extend them, secure them, and ensure their successful implementation.

Perhaps as a result of this, the overriding approach to legal change which emerges from this volume is one of incrementalism. Lastra, for example, argues powerfully for the need for a World Financial Organization, but seeks to operationalize its various functions within existing institutions, primarily the International Monetary Fund. Weiss calls for a programme of 'incremental systemic improvements' to the WTO, which in his view must 'remain rooted in the fundamentally unchanged commitment to the shared common value[s]' of the present institution. And, in a different context, Grigorova rejects calls for a new energy agreement in the WTO, in favour of the less conflictual path of creative reinterpretation of existing texts, to take account of new realities in the energy sector. Given the complexities of contemporary problems, it is both understandable and in many ways attractive for international legal projects to be so deeply informed by the values of modesty and caution – even if Viljanen's chapter on the Basel III reforms may prompt us at the same time to reflect more deeply on its dangers.

It is, in addition, a great strength of this book – and a testament to the vision of its editor – that it so successfully cuts across traditional boundaries within the discipline of international law, and seamlessly integrates divergent themes. In this respect it is an example for international lawyers generally who, over the coming decade, will be faced with the twin tasks of defining a list of salient challenges to be the focus of international legal attention, and of identifying the full range of bodies of international law relevant to them. Crossing boundaries between sub-fields in international law, as this volume does, should not only contribute to greater coherence and international legal integration, but also, and equally importantly, help us to discover causal and structural connections between different bodies of international and transnational law which are presently hidden in plain sight by our current intra-disciplinary boundaries. In this context, this volume impressively sets apparently disparate projects, themes and approaches next to one another in ways which facilitate connected thinking about the most important global challenges of our time. For this reader, and no doubt many others, there are a wealth of lessons in its pages to be learnt.

Andrew Lang
London, July 2015

Part I

Introduction

1 Reforming the Trading and Financial Systems

Antonio Segura Serrano *

Introduction

International Economic Law (IEL) is in need of reform. In the aftermath of the recent economic and financial crisis there is a growing consensus regarding the need to reconfigure the international economic order. However, trade law and finance display very different features and demand distinctive approaches.

On the one hand, it is evident the success of the multilateral trading system through the GATT-1947, later reinforced by the World Trade Organization (WTO) and its very advanced dispute settlement system, which has provided security and predictability in the trade area. The WTO has been praised as a major achievement within IEL and International Law in general. It has become a very solid institution, itself the product of hard law, with the power to authorize the imposition of stiff economic sanctions to those infringing the agreed trade norms. According to the prevailing accounts, the 2008 economic crisis, already termed as the Great Recession,[1] has confirmed that the WTO has performed as expected and so it can be acclaimed as the most suitable institutional dike against the adoption of restrictive trade measures among states. On the other hand, in the monetary and financial arenas IEL shows a very different record. Since their inception, the World Bank (WB) and especially the International Monetary Fund (IMF) have been unable to achieve a similar status as their role and legitimacy in the regulation and sanction of economic behaviour in these fields had diminished over time.[2] Moreover, the Global Financial Crisis (GFC) and the ensuing Great Recession have placed IEL regulating the financial system centre stage. Governments and civil society have turned to IEL in search of an international coordinated answer. While in the trading system the WTO has been instrumental for an institutional answer, in the financial system this reaction has come mainly through G20 meetings, together with a timid response by the IMF, which has adopted decisions in the form of traditional soft law. The question is why IEL has performed so unevenly in these two areas as if there was fundamental difference between the regulation of trade, on the one hand, and the regulation of money and finance, on the other, or the regulatory functions accomplished by IEL were so distinctively disconnected in these two areas of economic activity.

---

* Associate Professor of International Law and European Law, University of Granada. This chapter is a modified and updated version of the following journal article: Antonio Segura Serrano, 'International Economic Law at a Crossroads: Global Governance and Normative Coherence' (2014) 27 *Leiden Journal of International Law* 677.

1 RB Ahdieh, 'After the Fall: Financial Crisis and the International Order' (2010) 24 *Emory International Law Review* 1, 4.
2 HR Torres, 'Reforming the International Monetary Fund – Why it's Legitimacy is at Stake' (2007) 10 *Journal of International Economic Law* 443, 447.

The WTO and Global Governance

As against the more diplomatic-oriented approach of the trading system in its origins,[3] the establishment of the WTO in 1995 reconfigured this system into a more legally oriented regime. The current trade regime based on the workings of the WTO system has been best explained as the intellectual triumph of the model purporting 'economic efficiency'.[4] This efficiency model, and the economic liberalization that it promotes, has operated as the normative benchmark of the trading system for the last three decades approximately, to the detriment of the collective action model and, above all, the embedded liberalism model.[5] The legalization of the trade regime poses at least two questions: (1) whether the WTO system has been up to the promise of the compliance with legal obligations agreed by WTO members in the face of the crisis; and (2) whether the WTO legal system is in need of material reform regarding the Doha Round stalemate and the continuing challenges stemming from the 'trade and . . .' debate.

The WTO vis-à-vis the Economic Crisis

One of the most debated questions among trade policy officials and international trade lawyers since the outbreak of the economic crisis in 2008 has been whether WTO rules have worked as an actual deterrent for the adoption of trade barriers by members. In other words, the success of the current multilateral trade regime should be measured in terms of its ability to avoid the across-the-board tariff increases similar to those adopted by states in the aftermath of the Great Depression, in the interwar period. One should remember that the enactment of the Smoot–Hawley Tariff Act of 1930 by the US was at the origin of the most devastating trade wars among developed countries[6] that resulted in the doubling of the tariff rates from 1929 to 1930.[7]

According to the reports prepared by the WTO Secretariat, WTO members have achieved a good record during the recent crisis, as they have avoided adopting protectionist measures, on average, that would have led to a situation comparable to that of the Great Depression. Specifically, these reports[8] have been produced in response to the request by the G20 to the WTO, together with the OECD and the UNCTAD, 'to monitor and report publicly on G20 adherence to their undertakings on 'Resisting protectionism and promoting global trade and investment''.[9] Furthermore, the information about the measures which are the object of the

---

3   RE Hudec, 'The GATT Legal System: A Diplomat's Jurisprudence' (1970) 4 *Journal of World Trade Law* 615; JHH Weiler, 'The Rule of Lawyers and the Ethos of Diplomats: Reflections on the WTO Dispute Settlement' in RB Porter et al (eds), *Efficiency, Equity and Legitimacy: The Multilateral Trading System at the Millennium* (Brookings 2001) 334.

4   JL Dunoff, 'The Death of the Trade Regime' (1999) 10 *European Journal of International Law* 733, 752.

5   J Ruggie, 'International Regimes, Transactions and Change: Embedded Liberalism in the Postwar Economic Order' (1982) 36 *International Organization* 379, 393.

6   See some of the most illustrative examples in DA Irwin, *Peddling Protectionism: Smoot–Hawley and the Great Depression* (Princeton 2011) 159.

7   JB Madsen, 'Trade Barriers and the Collapse of the World Trading System during the Great Depression' (2001) 67 *Southern Economic Journal* 848, 848.

8   There have been already 12 reports, issued on 14 September 2009, 8 March 2010, 14 June 2010, 4 November 2010, 24 May 2011, 25 October 2011, 31 May 2012, 31 October 2012, 17 June 2013, 18 December 2013, 16 June 2014 and 5 November 2014. From the third report on, there is a Joint Summary only and, separately, a Trade Report prepared by the WTO and an Investment Report prepared by the OECD and the UNCTAD.

9   OECD/WTO/UNCTAD, Report on G-20 Trade and Investment Measures, 14 September 2009, 5 <www.wto.org/ english/news_e/news09_e/trdev_14sep09_e.htm> accessed 15 January 2015.

analysis in the report has been collected from formal notifications submitted by G20 members and from other official and public sources.[10] The trade measures covered by the reports are what might be called traditional trade measures,[11] that is, border measures, behind-the-border measures and trade defence measures, although in subsequent reports the coverage has been expanded, including Sanitary and Phytosanitary Measures (SPS) and Technical Barriers to Trade (TBT).

The picture described by these reports may look uneven. The initial reports produced by the WTO/OECD/UNCTAD showed that there was 'no indication of a descent into high-intensity protectionism as a reaction to the crisis, involving widespread resort to trade or investment restriction or retaliation'.[12] However, the Sixth Report of October 2011 indicated that 'there is a growing perception that trade protectionism is gaining ground in some parts of the world as a political reaction to current local economic difficulties'.[13] Moreover, the Seventh Report insists on the 'revival of protectionist rhetoric in some countries'[14] which, together with the continuing implementation of new trade restrictions, the accumulation effect of trade restrictions since the outbreak of the crisis, and the very slow pace of removal of existing restrictions,[15] all add to depict a worrying situation in terms of free trade and open markets.

As well as the WTO, the EU produces its own reports devoted to evaluating the trade restrictive measures 'identified in the context of the economic crisis' (as stated in the subtitles of these reports). The EU has published already 11 reports, the first one being in February 2009[16] and prepared in the aftermath of the November 2008 G20 summit in Washington, DC. The EU reports evaluate trade measures which are potentially trade restrictive, including border measures (import and export restrictions), behind-the-border measures (TBTs, government procurement, services and investment restrictions), stimulus packages and export support measures, and trade defence instruments.[17] There is also an annex at the end of the report which collects potentially trade restrictive measures adopted or planned since October 2008.[18] Whereas the first EU report highlighted that there was no generalized race towards protectionism,[19] the

10 ibid.

11 B Ruddy, 'The Critical Success of the WTO: Trade Policies of the Current Economic Crisis' (2010) 13 *Journal of International Economic Law* 475, 481.

12 OECD/WTO/UNCTAD, Report on G-20 Trade and Investment Measures, 14 September 2009 (n 9) 6.

13 WTO, Report on G-20 Trade Measures (May to mid October 2011), 25 October 2011, 1 <www.wto.org/english/news_e/news11_e/igo_26oct11_e.htm> accessed 15 January 2015. This Report also conveys a strong concern regarding the possible revival of industrial policies by G20 members, oriented to help national champions. Similarly, there are indications on the use of import substitution measures to back up those policies. All combined may make the situation worsen the crisis 'by triggering a spiral of tit-for-tat reactions in which every country will lose.'

14 WTO Report on G-20 Trade Measures (mid October 2011 to mid May 2012), 31 May 2012, 1–2 <www.wto.org/english/news_e/news12_e/igo_31may12_e.htm> accessed 15 January 2015.

15 The trade coverage of the restrictive measures put in place since October 2008 hit 3.9% of world merchandise imports, see WTO Report on G-20 Trade Measures (mid May 2013 to mid November 2013), 18 December 2013, 2 <www.wto.org/english/news_e/news13_e/g20_wto_report_dec13_e.pdf> accessed 15 January 2015.

16 European Commission, Directorate-General for Trade, Early Warning Report on potentially protectionist measures, February 2009 (Report to the 133 Committee) <www.rijksoverheid.nl/bestanden/documenten-en-publica ties/kamerstukken/2009/03/03/early-warning-report-on-potentially-protectionist-measures/9035715-bijlage3. pdf> accessed 15 January 2015.

17 European Commission, Directorate-General for Trade, 11th Report on Potentially Trade-Restrictive Measures, 1 June 2013–30 June 2014, 20 <http://trade.ec.europa.eu/doclib/docs/2014/november/tradoc_152872.pdf> accessed 15 January 2015.

18 ibid 46.

19 European Commission, Directorate-General for Trade, Early Warning Report on potentially protectionist measures (n 16) 3.

latest reports stress the danger accruing from the rising number of potentially trade restrictive measures.[20] Other reports come from private organizations. For instance, Global Trade Alert – which is coordinated by the think-tank called Centre for Economic Policy Research – elaborates the GTA Database collecting national government measures taken during the current global economic downturn that are likely to discriminate against foreign commerce.[21] GTA has produced several very critical reports so that it has warned that worsening macroeconomic prospects have already prompted more protectionism and more protectionism of the most harmful kind, that is, across-the-board.[22] Moreover, the evidence presented in one of its latest reports 'casts doubts on the strength of international restraints on the resort to protectionism by governments, in particular by G20 governments'.[23]

Nevertheless, from an economic point of view, there is a strong feeling and evidence that G20 members and other governments have been able to succeed in overall management of the political process of keeping domestic protectionist pressures under control. WTO reports have shown that, although trade restrictive measures have been adopted and are even on the rise to this day, it is however true that 'the multilateral trading system has acted as an effective backstop against protectionism'.[24] This is so because the identified trade restrictive measures apply to a narrow range of trade and for a short period of time, which means that they have a limited economic effect.[25] As the EU Ninth Report states, the past years show that overall recourse to trade protectionism has been sidestepped, and trade openness preserved.[26]

However, from a legal point of view, the assessment might be very different. There have been many instances of adoption of trade barriers and subsidization in the form of bail-outs or otherwise[27] that the system is not addressing, as WTO members have not decided to initiate proceedings before the DSS.[28] This might be interpreted as if there were a concealed consensus between the main players towards various forms of government intervention in the presence of a big market failure like the economic crisis of 2008. This non-compliance phenomenon might be avoided if the DSS were open to complainants other than WTO members (even with the help of a prosecutor or otherwise)[29], or if individuals could resort directly to their domestic courts to enforce their trade rights, but of course that would imply a very different world trading system.

20 European Commission, Directorate-General for Trade, Ninth Report on Potentially Trade Restrictive Measures, September 2011–1 May 2012, 3 <http://trade.ec.europa.eu/doclib/docs/2012/june/tradoc_149526.pdf.> Particularly, the EU points to the use of restrictive measures as part of new industrialization policies, aimed at shielding domestic markets from international competition, ibid 10.

21 SJ Evenett (ed), *Resolve Falters as Global Prospects Worsen: The 9th GTA Report* (Global Trade Alert, July 2011) iv <www.globaltradealert.org/9th_GTA_Report> accessed 15 January 2015.

22 SJ Evenett (ed), *Trade Tensions Mount: The 10th GTA Report* (Global Trade Alert, November 2011), 7 <www.globaltradealert.org/gta-analysis/trade-tensions-mount-10th-gta-report> accessed 15 January 2015.

23 SJ Evenett (ed), *Débâcle: The 11th GTA Report on Protectionism* (Global Trade Alert, June 2012) at 1 <www.globaltradealert.org/sites/default/files/GTA11_0.pdf> accessed 15 January 2015.

24 WTO, Report on G-20 Trade Measures (mid May 2014 to mid October 2014), 5 November 2014 <www.wto.org/english/news_e/news14_e/g20_wto_report_oct14_e.pdf> accessed 15 January 2015.

25 Ruddy (n 11) 485–86. However, the stock of restrictive trade measures introduced by G-20 economies since 2008 continues to rise in the latest period under examination by the WTO, see WTO Report (n 15) 4.

26 European Commission (n 20) 2.

27 R Baldwin and SJ Evenett (eds), *The Collapse of Global Trade, Murky Protectionism, and the Crisis: Recommendations for the G-20* (VoxEu.org 2009).

28 But see P Delimatsis, 'Transparent Financial Innovation in a Post-Crisis Environment' (2013) 16 *Journal of International Economic Law* 159, 197, warning that complaints may still rise in the near future.

29 T Cottier, 'The Common Law of International Trade and the Future of the World Trade Organization' (2015) 18 *Journal of International Economic Law* 3, 14.

The Future of the Trading System

Even if we assume that the trade regime has ably performed during the recent economic crisis, there are many open questions regarding the future of the multilateral trading system. The Doha Round deadlock for more than 10 years reveals in a stark way the exhaustion that the model is experiencing. Setting aside other possible explanations,[30] developing countries are nowadays willing to resist pressures unless they see their demands satisfied in the marketplace for a bigger part of the pie.[31] But the biggest loser of the Doha Round fiasco might be the WTO system itself as its credibility may suffer irreparable damages.[32] However, the Bali Package recently agreed at the Ninth Ministerial Conference in December 2013, specially the Agreement on Trade Facilitation,[33] has been praised as the 'first major agreement among WTO members since it was formed in 1995'.[34] Therefore, the bargain struck in Bali might be considered as a relief taking into account the previous lack of progress.[35] Nevertheless, the Bali Package does not solve the heart of the 2001 agenda[36] and has actually been regarded as a *small deal*.[37] Even if we assume that the Doha Development Agenda was already dated by the time negotiators met in 2001,[38] the WTO cannot move on new issues until it achieves the Doha political goals of 'rebalancing' the trading system from the point of view of developing countries.[39]

Perhaps, the WTO should make fewer efforts for the periodic negotiations towards new commitments to further liberalize trade, and focus more on the actual enforcement of the existing agreements. The most pressing concerns faced by the world trading system today are therefore the efficacy and fairness of the dispute settlement mechanism together with the integration of other 'flanking policies' within the WTO system, i.e. industrial policies or development, on the one hand, and environmental, human rights and labour policies, on the other.[40] Both kinds of issues are linked together.

---

30 R Wolfe, 'First Diagnose, Then Treat: What Ails the Doha Round?' (2015) 14 *World Trade Review* 7.

31 F Ismail, 'An assessment of the WTO Doha Round July–December 2008 Collapse' (2009) 8 *World Trade Review* 579, at 581, underlining that the main reason for the failure of the Doha Round in 2008 was the persistence of protectionism in the major developed country markets together with the marginalization of developing country interests.

32 S Cho, 'Is the WTO Passé?: Exploring the Meaning of the Doha Debacle' (2009) 29 <http://papers.ssrn.com/sol3/papers.cfm?abstract_id=1403464> accessed 15 January 2015.

33 BJ Taylor and JS Wilson, 'Doha and Trade Facilitation: Lending Specificity to the Multilateral Trade and Development Agenda' in W Martin and A Mattoo (eds), *Unfinished Business? The WTO's Doha Agenda* (CEPR and World Bank 2011) 213.

34 WTO, 'Days 3, 4 and 5: Round-the-clock consultations produce "Bali Package"', 2 <www<www.wto.org/english/news_e/news13_e/mc9sum_07dec13_e.htm> accessed 15 January 2015. See also 'WTO Reaches First Global Trade Deal', *New York Times* (New York, 7 December 2013) <www.nytimes.com/2013/12/08/business/international/wto-reaches-first-global-trade-deal.html?_r=0> accessed> accessed 15 January 2015.

35 B Hoekman, W Martin and A Mattoo, 'Conclude Doha. It Matters!' (2010) 9 *World Trade Review* 505, 506, submitting that the liberalization that the Doha Round implies is very important in the present context of economic crisis, as it would provide an improvement to world demand in a period in which many countries will be seeking to diminish fiscal stimulus measures.

36 R Baldwin, 'WTO Agreement: The Bali Ribbon' 1 <www.voxeu.org/article/wto-agreement-bali-ribbon> accessed 15 January 2015.

37 C Boonekamp, 'Simplify and Complete the DDA' in SJ Evenett and A Jara (eds), *Building on Bali: A Work Programme for the WTO* (CEPR 2013) 37.

38 G Aldonas, 'Trade, Global Value Chains and the World Trade Organization' in SJ Evenett and A Jara (eds), *Building on Bali: A Work Programme for the WTO* (CEPR 2013), 53.

39 Baldwin (n 36) 1.

40 J Pauwleyn, 'New Trade Politics for the 21st Century' (2008) 11 *Journal of International Economic Law* 559, 565 and 571, who stresses the need to adopt an 'embedded liberalism' (that combines economic globalization

First, the suggestion regarding the incorporation of these other policies within the WTO is of course not new. In fact, the 'trade and . . .' debate has been with us for quite a few years, pointing to the need to overcome the persistent trade bias found in the multilateral trading system.[41] This trade bias stems from the non-consideration of the non-trade issues linked to trade, a result that should be attributed to the fragmentation of international trade law.[42] The first suggested approach to solve the mentioned trade bias would be through the use of the WTO dispute settlement system. Commentators generally purport that the WTO dispute settlement system should embrace public international law in order to bring in a broader legal and normative order, hence amplifying the WTO narrow mandate exclusively focused on the trade regime.[43] Contrary to other opinions,[44] this view submits that the WTO does not constitute a self-contained regime, but must be open to other sources of public international law,[45] which gives the WTO more legitimacy.[46] If the WTO's Appellate Body was apparently willing to apply this expanded or coordinated approach in some of the already key cases decided in the 1990s, like the *Gasoline* or the *Shrimp* cases,[47] however, in the 2000s the Appellate Body has adopted a more restrained approach, like in the *Hormones* and the *Biotech* cases,[48] a result very much criticized.[49] Possibly, the Appellate

---

with the 'flanking policies') and the need to abandon the 'economic straight-jacket' of the Washington consensus in the 1990s (free trade, fiscal austerity, no capital controls). See also A Mattoo and A Subramanian, 'Multilateralism Beyond Doha' in W Martin and A Mattoo (eds), *Unfinished Business? The WTO's Doha Agenda* (CEPR and World Bank 2013) 393, submitting that the international trade architecture cannot ignore critical international policy areas such as environmental protection or financial security.

41   *Contra* JO McGinnis and ML Movsesian, 'Against Global Governance in the WTO' (2004) 45 *Harvard International Law Journal* 353, 354.

42   T Cottier et al, 'Fragmentation and Coherence in International Trade Regulation: Analysis and Conceptual Foundations' in T Cottier and P Delimatsis (eds), *The Prospects of International Trade Regulation: From Fragmentation to Coherence* (CUP 2011) 1, 12.

43   J Pauwelyn, 'The Role of Public International Law in the WTO: How Far Can We Go?' (2001) 95 *American Journal of International Law* 535; J Pauwelyn, *Conflict of Norms in Public International Law: How WTO Relates to Other Rules of International Law* (CUP 2003).

44   JP Trachtman, 'The Domain of WTO Dispute Resolution' (1999) 40 *Harvard International Law Journal* 333, 342; JP Trachtman, 'Institutional Linkage: Transcending "Trade and . . ."' (2002) 96 *American Journal of International Law* 77, 88, highlighting the limited role of the WTO dispute settlement system.

45   D Palmeter and PC Mavroidis, 'The WTO Legal System: Sources of Law' (1998) 92 *American Journal of International Law* 398, 399; T Schoenbaum, 'WTO Dispute Settlement: Praises and Suggestions for Reform' (1998) 47 *International and Comparative Law Quarterly* 647; L Bartels, 'Applicable Law in WTO Dispute Settlement Proceedings' (2001) 35 *Journal of World Trade* 499.

46   R Howse and K Nicolaïdis, 'Legitimacy and Global Governance: Why Constitutionalizing the WTO Is a Step Too Far' in RB Porter et al (eds) *Efficiency, Equity and Legitimacy: The Multilateral Trading System at the Millennium* (Brookings 2001) 227, 244, 'stating that '[r]eference to interpretative norms of general public international law enhances the legitimacy of the dispute settlement organs in adjudicating competing values'; R Howse, 'From Politics to Technocracy – and Back Again: The Fate of the Multilateral Trading Regime' (2002) 96 *American Journal of International Law* 94, 110.

47   Appellate Body Report, United States – Standards for Reformulated and Conventional Gasoline, 20 May 1996, WT/DS2/AB/R at 17; Appellate Body Report United States – Import Prohibition of Certain Shrimp and Shrimp Products, 6 November 1998, AB-1998–94, WT/DS58/AB/R, para 130; Appellate Body Report Korea – Measures Affecting Government Procurement, 19 June 2000, WT/DS163/R, para 7.96.

48   See Appellate Body Report, EC – Measures Concerning Meat and Meat Products (Hormones), 13 February 1998, WT/DS26/AB/R and WT/DS48/AB/R, para 123; Panel Report, European Communities – Measures Affecting the Approval and Marketing of Biotech Products, 21 November 2006, WT/DS291–3/R, paras 7.88–87.89.

49   B McGrady, 'Fragmentation of International Law or 'Systemic Integration' of Treaty Regimes: EU – Biotech Products and the Proper Interpretation of Art 31(3)(c) of the Vienna Convention on the Law of Treaties' (2008) 42 *Journal of World Trade* 589; Cottier (n 42) 18.

Body has implicitly sent out the message that, even though non-WTO law must be resorted to where technical questions are at stake, other issues of political or constitutional bearing may only be solved at the political level.[50]

The second approach to articulate trade and non-trade issues would be through treaty or policy-making. First, the introduction of a 'social clause' has been proposed already since the mid 1990s.[51] However, the Singapore Ministerial Declaration in 1996 reached a compromise between supporters and those against the integration of a social clause, which has resulted in the practical abandonment of this approach within the WTO, though the US and the EU are pursuing this path in their bilateral and regional trade agreements.[52] Second, another venue could be the establishment of some kind of primacy or hierarchy among trade rules, on the one hand, and human rights, environmental or labour rules, on the other.[53] Nevertheless, neither the strategy consisting of setting conflict clauses in subsequent multilateral agreements (e.g. the Biosafety Protocol), nor the articulation of solutions within the WTO itself (whether in the form of general decisions, authoritative interpretations or waivers as provided for by Article IX of the WTO Agreement)[54] has led to a working solution (the work of the Committee on Trade an Environment has shown itself devoid of any clear resolve).[55]

In spite of the above mentioned difficulties, there is, however, a growing consensus within the discipline towards the need to address from within the WTO the 'trade and . . .' question. If it is assumed that nowhere in the WTO Agreements is stated that free trade is the objective to be pursued by the organization,[56] then WTO law could serve as a vehicle for global governance, where liberal trade would be on an equal footing vis-à-vis other societal values.[57] After all, 'there is no persuasive overarching rationale to explain the choice for embodying intellectual property rights in a trade agreement but not labour rights, for instance'.[58] A material reform of the WTO architecture to integrate those areas is the most practical solution, which could take the form of plurilateral agreements or codes for adherence to which WTO members would progressively adhere to.[59] Furthermore, the plurilateral

---

50 A Lang, *World Trade Law after Neoliberalism: Re-Imagining the Global Economic Order* (OUP 2011) 150–53.

51 R Wilkinson and S Hughes, 'International Labour Standards and World Trade: No Role for the World Trade Organization?' (1998) 3 *New Political Economy* 375; *Contra* S Charnovitz, 'Triangulating the World Trade Organization' (2002) 96 *American Journal of International Law* 28.

52 SA Aaronson and JM Zimmerman, *Trade Imbalance: The Struggle to Weigh Human Rights Concerns in Trade Policymaking* (CUP 2008) 133–35 and 163 ff.

53 JE Alvarez, 'How Not to Link: Institutional Conundrums of an Expanded Trade Regime' (2001) 7 *Widener Law Symposium Journal* 1, 4, opting for explicit provisions in order to clarify the question of the status of WTO Agreements vis-à-vis other conventions.

54 For example B Choudhury et al, 'A Call for a WTO Ministerial Decision on Trade and Human Rights' in T Cottier and P Delimatsis (eds), *The Prospects of International Trade Regulation: From Fragmentation to Coherence* (CUP 2011) 323.

55 R Tarasofsky, 'The WTO in Crisis: Lessons Learned from the Doha Negotiations on the Environment' (2006) 82 *International Affairs* 899, 916.

56 BM Hoekman, PC Mavroidis, *The World Trade Organization* (Routledge 2007) 14, stating that the formal objective of the WTO is not free trade (trade is a means to achieve the objectives listed in the Preamble of the WTO Agreement); A. von Bogdandy, 'Law and Politics in the WTO – Strategies to Cope with a Deficient Relationship' (2001) 5 *Max Planck Yearbook of United Nations Law* 609, 659.

57 M Bronckers, 'More Power to the WTO?' (2001) 4 *Journal of International Economic Law* 41, 53.

58 Howse and Nicolaïdis (n 46) 235; see also C Thomas, 'The WTO and Labor Rights: Strategies of Linkage' in S Joseph, D Kinley and J Waincymer (eds), *The World Trade Organization and Human Rights: Interdisciplinary Perspectives* (Edward Elgar 2009) 257, 276.

59 Howse (n 46) 113–14.

path is preferable to the bilateral approach that the US and the EU have adopted in their recent trade agreements.[60] Therefore, as long as the world trading system is dominated by economic liberalism,[61] the incorporation of social and related issues into the WTO could probably help solve the questions of global governance and coherence among regimes in the meantime, if only in an incomplete manner.[62]

Second, development issues[63] must also be addressed by the WTO more intensely. As a general criticism, it has been submitted that IEL has taken developing countries as 'objects' rather than 'subjects'.[64] However, the adoption of the Doha Development Agenda in the current Doha Round reveals the importance and the agreement attached to the need of solving the question of economic and social development. To a large extent, the stalemate that this Doha Round is experiencing is due to the major differences expressed by developed and developing countries on the approaches and expectations of each group on this issue.[65] As noted, the concerns voiced by developing countries after the Uruguay Round are very similar to those articulated three or four decades ago.[66] Moreover, the proposals submitted during the first years of the Doha Round are similarly based on the current special and differential treatment that has by now shown its limits.[67] However, the recent Bali Package agreed in December 2013 has adopted several Decisions on development issues.[68] In addition to the 'Aid for Trade' and 'Cotton' Decisions, the Bali Package includes four Decisions affecting Least-Developed Countries.[69] But, in the long run, what is needed is an approach that not only addresses development as an incidental issue that needs to be fixed on an ad hoc basis, but that embraces development as a normative project that 'is grounded in an affirmative understanding of the balancing between trade liberalization objectives and

60 BM Hoekman and PC Mavroidis, 'Embracing Diversity: Plurilateral Agreements and the Trading System' (2015) 14 *World Trade Review* 101.

61 R Howse, 'Adjudicative Legitimacy and Treaty Interpretation in International Trade Law: The Early Years of WTO Jurisprudence' in JHH Weiler (ed), *The EU, The WTO and the NAFTA: Towards a Common Law of International Trade* (OUP 2000) 36, 37, stating that values other than liberal trade have not been privileged by legal and institutional arrangements of globalization.

62 Lang (n 50) 135, 347, according to this author, the several reform projects aimed at achieving the proper balance between trade values and other social values do not serve to the objective of re-imagining the world trading system in terms of a new legitimating collective purpose; see also D Kennedy, 'The Politics of the Invisible College: International Governance and the Politics of Expertise' (2001) *European Human Rights Law Review* 463, 467 ff.

63 Asif H Qureshi, 'Distinguished Essay: Reflections on the Global Trading Order Twenty Years after Marrakesh: A Development Perspective' (2014) *European Yearbook of International Economic Law* 93, 97, stating that the 'development dimension, although trade related, is acknowledged as being within the scope of the competence of the WTO'; see also Nicolas Lamp, 'The "Development" Discourse in International Trade Lawmaking' (2015) Queen's University Legal Research Paper No 057 <http://papers.ssrn.com/sol3/papers.cfm?abstract_id=2608198> accessed 25 May 2015.

64 J Faundez and C Tan, 'Introduction' in J Faundez and C Tan (eds), *International Economic Law, Globalization and Developing Countries* (Edward Elgar 2010) 1, 2.

65 S Cho, 'The Demise of Development in the Doha Round Negotiations' (2010) 45 *Texas International Law Journal* 573, 574.

66 SE Rolland, *Development at the WTO* (OUP 2012), 59.

67 ibid 251.

68 WTO, 'Days 3, 4 and 5: Round-the-clock consultations produce "Bali Package"' (n 34) 3.

69 The Bali Ministerial Declaration refers to four Decisions whose texts remained unchanged from their Geneva versions: Preferential Rules of Origin for Least-Developed Countries; Operationalization of the Waiver Concerning Preferential Treatment to Services and Service Suppliers of Least-Developed Countries; Duty-Free and Quota-Free Market Access for Least-Developed Countries; and Monitoring Mechanism on Special and Differential Treatment, ibid 2–3.

development priorities'.[70] Some authors have suggested institutional reforms in order to advance the development agenda within the WTO.[71]

The Coherence of the Global Financial System

The financial crisis recently witnessed in Western countries from 2007 to 2010 onwards (the European countries are still dealing with a huge sovereign debt crisis) is not a unique event. In fact, there have been several recurrent financial crises like the Latin America debt crisis in the 1980s; the South-East Asian financial crisis in 1997–1998; the Russian crisis in 1996–1999; or the sovereign default crisis of Argentina in 2002.[72]

The question arises whether IEL was and is normatively well equipped to prevent or even deal with these crises. International financial stability is a very contemporary concept that, in any case, can be considered as a public good[73] consisting of the avoiding of systemic risk from unfolding uncontrollably in the market.[74] It is true that monetary and financial stability was difficult to achieve taking into account the huge changes the international economy has gone through since the end of the system based on fixed exchange rates in the 1970s. Open markets in trade and finance favoured by loose or tolerant national regulation (due to neoliberal policies) has led to ever increasing volumes of capital flows. Financial transactions have grown exponentially thanks to financial innovation combined with quick telecommunications technologies (Internet). Most importantly, in the absence of an international strategy, this openness and interconnectedness have led to global imbalances in the financial markets which are in the origin of the crisis.[75]

Soft Law Standards

The main international organizations in the field, i.e. the IMF and the WB, are based on hard-law rules, specifically international treaties, have international institutions or organs proper within their structure, and are endowed with a large and permanent staff. However, they have not played a significant role in the administration of the financial system. This is due to the fact that they are devoid of the necessary regulatory powers (and maybe expertise) to adequately perform as financial regulators.[76] As has been pointed out, the IMF and the WB do not normally create regulatory standards.[77]

---

70 Rolland (n 66) 331; see also F Ismail, 'Mainstreaming Development in the World Trade Organization' (2005) 39 *Journal of World Trade* 11.

71 Y-S Lee, 'World Trade Organization and Developing Countries – Reform Proposal' in Y-S Lee et al (eds), *Law and Development Perspective on International Trade Law* (CUP 2011) 105 108, submitting the creation of a Council for Trade and Development within the WTO; see also JP Trachtman, 'Legal Aspects of a Poverty Agenda at the WTO: Trade Law and "Global Apartheid"' (2003) 6 *Journal of International Economic Law* 3, 19–20, advising the assessment of poverty reduction within the Trade Policy Review Mechanism, although this author warns that this proposal could be regarded as a form of interventionism or even neo-colonialism.

72 C Reinhart and KS Rogoff, *This Time is Different: Eight Centuries of Financial Folly* (Princeton 2011).

73 G20, *Declaration of the Summit on Financial Markets and the World Economy*, Washington DC, November 15, 2008, para 8 <www.g20.utoronto.ca/2008/2008declaration1115.html> accessed 15 January 2015.

74 C Ohler, 'International Regulation and Supervision of Financial Markets after the Crisis' (2010) *European Yearbook of International Economic Law* 3, 16.

75 Reinhart and Rogoff (n 72), stating that most of the historical crises were preceded by financial liberalization by which financial entities or instruments were under-regulated or not regulated at all.

76 E Pan, 'Challenge of International Cooperation and Institutional Design in Financial Supervision: Beyond Transgovernmental Networks' (2010) 11 *Chicago Journal of International Law* 243, 244.

77 C Brummer, 'Why Soft Law Dominates International Finance – And not Trade' (2010) 13 *Journal of International Economic Law* 623, 627.

Instead, the standard-setting function has been assumed in this area by several international bodies, which in turn have produced soft-law rules aimed at protecting the stability of the financial system. Political bodies like the G10 or the G7, then the G8, assumed progressively since the 1970s the task to create those international bodies that would be entrusted with the job of providing the standards needed to cope with the increasing globalization in the financial domain. As a result, the Basel Committee on Banking Supervision (BCBS), the International Association of Insurance Supervisors, and the International Organization of Securities Commission were created and rank among the most prominent bodies.[78] These heterogeneous bodies were progressively created as a way to fill the gap left after the demise of the Bretton Woods System in the 1970s. They are not formal international organizations and do not have law-making powers. The latter feature makes them rely on the adoption of Principles, Codes, Guidelines, etc. which in turn are to be implemented at the national level, thereby setting up a decentralized enforcement mechanism.[79] These bodies are generally known as Transnational Regulatory Networks (TRN), and bear many differences among them regarding their quality or composition (from central bank officials to private nongovernmental actors).[80] As a way to achieve coordination among these different bodies, the Financial Stability Forum was established in 1999 by the G7.[81]

The soft-law standard-setting method used by these bodies over the years has been described as 'an alternative form of international law-making without the burden of cumbersome treaty formation rules'.[82] Furthermore, the resulting international financial soft-law regulatory framework has been regarded as 'more coercive than traditional theories of international law predict',[83] because they 'are more than 'soft law'; they reflect mutual commitments made after intense negotiations, and taken together, they contain both incentives for compliance and at least the suggestion of meaningful sanctions for non-compliance'.[84] Among these international financial standards, the main regulatory outcome has been produced by the BCBS which adopted in 1988 the 'Basel Accord' establishing minimum capital requirements for banks (Basel I), subsequently substituted by the Basel Accord II in 2004.

However, the soft-law making process carried out by these TRNs and the resulting international financial standards have also raised much criticism as they present several limitations. First, the process has been condemned because of a lack of political legitimacy and

---

78 Other bodies are the Committee on the Global Financial System, the Committee on Payment and Settlement Systems, the International Association of Insurance Supervisors, and the International Accounting Standards Board. See M Giovanoli, 'The Reform of the International Financial Architecture after the Global Crisis' (2009) 42 *New York University Journal of International Law and Politics* 81, 100, that provides a table with the bodies that make up the international financial architecture.

79 A Viterbo, *International Economic Law and Monetary Measures* (Edward Elgar 2012), 107.

80 D Zaring, 'International Law by Other Means: The Twilight Existence of International Financial Regulatory Organizations' (1998) 33 *Texas International Law Journal*, 281; see also the seminal work AM Slaughter, *A New World Order* (Princeton 2004), on 'government networks'.

81 M Giovanoli, 'The International Financial Architecture and Its Reform after the Global Crisis' in M Giovanoli and D Devos (eds) *International Monetary and Financial Law* (OUP 2010) 3, 5; J Liberi, 'The Financial Stability Forum: A Step in the Right Direction . . . Not Far Enough' (2003) 24 *University of Pennsylvania Journal of International Economic Law* 549.

82 K Alexander, 'Global Financial Standard Setting, G10 Committees, and International Economic Law' (2009) 34 *Brooklyn Journal of International Law* 861, 879.

83 C Brummer, 'How International Financial Law Works (and How It Doesn't)' (2011) 99 *The Georgetown Law Journal* 257, 262.

84 A Lowenfeld, *International Economic Law* (2nd edn, OUP 2008) 845.

accountability,[85] as developing countries are not given a voice within the bodies that produce those standards, later imposed on them by developed countries.[86] Second, the TRNs' effectiveness in solving concrete international regulatory problems is doubtful when cooperation involves distributive implications and enforcement problems.[87] Certainly, soft-law financial regulation as a product has been disregarded because of the absence of mechanisms to ensure its enforcement.[88]

Financial Crisis and Regulatory Failure

Recent studies have tried to ascertain the main causes of the financial crisis[89] so that today they can be classified between macro- and micro-causes or failures.[90] As has been suggested, from a legal point of view it may seem surprising that the 2008 financial crisis happened despite the existence of a 'comprehensive' corpus of international financial standards that had been developed over the last 35 years.[91] However, this crisis may be largely explained by the ineffective implementation and enforcement of existing regulations,[92] overreliance on self-regulation by the market (due to neoliberal and deregulation policies),[93] and the lack of macro-stability surveillance, i.e. supervision of the whole financial system. Furthermore, multilateral surveillance (through IMF) did not function efficiently.

---

85 K Alexander, R Dhumale and J Eatwell, *Global Governance of Financial Systems: The International Regulation of Systemic Risk* (OUP 2005), 153.

86 SJ Toope, 'Emerging Patterns of Governance and International Law' in Michael Byers (ed), *The Role of Law in International Politics: Essays in International Relations and International Law* (OUP 2000) 91, 96–97; K Raustiala, 'The Architecture of International Cooperation: Transgovernmental Networks and the Future of International Law' (2002) 43 *Virginia Journal of International Law* 1, 24–25. See also P Alston, 'The Myopia of the Handmaidens: International Lawyers and Globalization' (1997) 8 *European Journal of International Law* 435, 446; D Kennedy, 'When Renewal Repeats: Thinking against the Box' (2000) 32 *New York University Journal of International Law and Politics* 335, 412. More recently, J Black, 'Constructing and Contesting Legitimacy and Accountability in Polycentric Regulatory Regimes' (2008) *LSE Law, Society and Economy Working Papers* 2/2008, 13 <http://eprints.lse.ac.uk/23040/1/WPS2008–02_Black.pdf> accessed 15 January 2015.

87 PH Verdier, 'Transnational Regulatory Networks and Their Limits' (2009) 34 *The Yale Journal of International Law* 113, 120–30. Verdier stresses that regulators participating in TRNs are accountable to their domestic political interests which makes TRNs effective only when there are pure coordination games. However, when international regulatory cooperation encompasses distributive and enforcement problems (the most likely scenario) it is very unlikely that TRNs would promote international cooperation for its own sake: dominant national interests within TRNs 'may clash over alternative rules, attempt to resist or dilute international standards, and resist compliance', ibid 121. See also the critique made by K Anderson, 'Squaring the Circle? Reconciling Sovereignty and Global Governance through Global Government Networks' (2005) 118 *Harvard Law Review* 1255, 1276.

88 Report of the Commission of Experts of the President of the United Nations General Assembly on Reforms of the International Monetary and Financial System (Stiglitz Report), New York, 21 September 2009, 96.

89 See among others: RM Lastra and G Wood, 'The Crisis of 2007–09: Nature, Causes, and Reactions' (2010) 13 *Journal of International Economic Law* 531, 537–38; N Roubini and S Mihm, *Crisis Economics: A Crash Course in the Future of Finance* (Penguin 2010); S Charnovitz, 'Addressing Government Failure through International Financial Law' (2010) 13 *Journal of International Economic Law* 743, 746.

90 E Avgouleas, *Governance of Global Financial Markets* (CUP 2012) 89; Viterbo (n 79) 6; Ohler (n 74) 6; J de Larosière, *High-Level Group on Financial Supervision in the EU* (2009) 11–12 <http://ec.europa.eu/internal_market/finances/docs/de_larosiere_report_en.pdf> accessed 15 January 2015.

91 Giovanoli (n 81) 6.

92 P Troberg, 'Global Capital Markets and National Reporting: International Regulation but National Application?' in J Klabbers and T Piiparinen (eds), *Normative Pluralism an International Law* (CUP 2013) 301, providing a recent empirical assessment regarding International Financial Reporting Standards.

93 Avgouleas (n 90) 110; Stiglitz Report (n 88) 48.

Once the crisis erupted, the international financial architecture based mainly on the activity of TRNs has been useless in order to cope with the financial meltdown witnessed in 2007–2010[94] and still present in many countries, especially the European countries. In the absence of a centralized international mechanism to address the challenge, the reaction to the financial crisis has mainly come from unilateral measures taken individually by states with no coordination and even at the cost of originating important inconsistencies among them.[95]

From an institutional point of view, the answer to the crisis has been in the form of a revitalization of the G20. The G20 has acted as a coordinating executive, as a mega-network,[96] and the several G20 meetings held after the eruption of the crisis have produced two changes: the establishment of the Financial Stability Board (FSB), previously the Financial Stability Forum (FSF), and the pledge to strengthen the IMF. The FSB has an undefined legal status from an international law point of view[97] and may be deemed as another example of a TRN with the aim of supervising regulatory policies and standards. Together with other standard-setting bodies (like the BCBS), the FSB has tried to solve the problems regarding legitimacy and accountability through the broadening of its membership to include emerging economies from the G20. However, governance problems are not completely solved as the FSB remains a TRN with no binding powers or meaningful tools to accomplish its function. Commitments undertaken by FSB member states are still of a soft-law nature.[98] As to the IMF, its primary surveillance role has been recognized by an IMF/FSF Joint Letter in 2008 and reinforced by the 2010 Executive Board Decision to integrate FSAP stability valuations within the IMF ability to carry out bilateral assessments (Article IV, Section 1).[99] Nevertheless, there is still an important gap concerning surveillance as IMF Art. VII, Section 5 allows member states not to disclose data regarding individuals or corporations.[100] But then again what would be needed precisely is the mandatory international supervision of private financial entities.[101] From a substantive point of view, there has been an effort to harden the 'soft-law' financial standards. A new Basel Accord (Basel III) has been adopted in 2010 by the BCBS and will be fully implemented at national level by 2019.[102] Other standards have also been revised.[103]

---

94 D Zaring, 'International Institutional Performance in Crisis' (2010) 10 *Chicago Journal of International Law* 475, 478; see also Pan (n 76) 244.

95 Pan (n 76) 264.

96 S Cho and CR Kelly, 'Promises and Perils of New Global Governance: A Case of the G-20' (2012) 12 *Chicago Journal of International Law* 491, 553.

97 L Catá Backer, 'Private Actors and Public Governance beyond the State: The Multinational Corporation, the Financial Stability Board and the Global Governance Order' (2011) 18 *Indiana Journal of Global Legal Studies* 751.

98 Art 16 FSB Charter, stating that the Charter does not create any legal rights or obligations. *Contra* Viterbo (n 79) 120, who considers FSB member state obligations as 'unilateral promises'.

99 Although limited to those 25 jurisdictions deemed to host systemically important financial institutions.

100 S Hagan, 'Enhancing the IMF's Regulatory Authority' (2010) 13 *Journal of International Economic Law* 955, 963.

101 Pan (n 76) 246.

102 M Hellwig, 'Capital Regulation after the Crisis: Business as Usual?' (2010) Max Planck Institute for Research on Collective Goods Pre-print, No 2010/31 <http://papers.ssrn.com/sol3/papers.cfm?abstract_id=1645224##> accessed 15 January 2015, providing a criticism of the new Basle Accord because, as the previous Basel II, it is based on risk-calibrated capital requirements, in particular under the model-based approach which may again lead to the undercapitalization of banks witnessed in the 2008 financial crisis. That is why Basel II has been qualified as a new failure of TRNs, Cho and Kelly (n 96) 532.

103 <www.financialstabilityboard.org/what-we-do/about-the-compendium-of-standards/key_standards/> accessed 15 January 2015.

To sum up, although some steps have been taken in order to make the international financial system more integrally coordinated (like the Non-Cooperative Jurisdictions Initiative),[104] the truth is that the soft-law approach and the voluntary, non-binding character of international financial obligations still prevails.[105] In other words, the post-crisis reforms have shown a preference for a model of governance based on more or less informal government networks over more formal intergovernmentalism of the Bretton Woods Conference.[106] In doing so, they perpetuate pre-crisis patterns as they 'do not fundamentally replace TRNs and soft law, but rather attempt to expand, rationalize, and strengthen the existing system in various ways'.[107]

In Search of a New Financial System

The reaction to the financial meltdown of 2008 at the international level has mainly come through the response of an invigorated G20, which means more a strengthening of the existing regulatory apparatus, based on TRNs, than a radical transformation of it. However, the reinforcement of this kind of trans-governmental regulatory network seems to fall very short of what is needed within the international financial system. The G20 speedy reaction of 2008 will very likely blur overtime as the urgent needs of the day dissipate and there is some recovery from the financial and economic crises.[108] Reinforced international cooperation through the G20 is doomed to lose political momentum and seems to be only a temporary solution.[109] If the aim consists of establishing an international framework to avoid a new financial crisis such as the one recently witnessed then there are other choices available in international law based on a more supra-national attitude.

The alternative options which transmit a hard-law regulation approach and a more vertical or institutionalized financial system at the international level have already been advanced. All of them revolve around the idea that a formal international treaty establishing some kind of supra-national body would be the most effective solution to the problems posed by international finance. First, there is a proposal to craft a formal international organization that could be termed the World Financial Authority (WFA)[110] or the World Financial Organization

---

104 The Non-Cooperative Jurisdictions Initiative promoted by the G-20 and carried by the FSB in order to oblige those jurisdictions to comply with prudential standards raises some problems of legitimacy, ie the legal basis of G-20 members to force third countries to abide by standards not legally binding on G20 member states in the first place, Giovanoli (n 78) 122.

105 Viterbo (n 79) 128.

106 E Helleiner, 'A Bretton Woods Moment? The 2007–2008 Crisis and the Future of Global Finance' (2010) 86 *International Affairs* 619, 632.

107 PH Verdier, 'The Political Economy of International Financial Regulation' (2013) 88 *Indiana Law Journal* 1405, 1461–62. According to Verdier, in the post-crisis reform scenario regulators retain considerable control over the process of raising prudential standards; great powers maintain their discretion to address failures on an ad hoc basis; and surveillance is reinforced only in a formal not a substantive way, ibid 1463–1470.

108 Cho and Kelly (n 96) 526, highlighting that the G20 initial political impetus appears to be waning. Moreover, at the outbreak of the financial crisis in 2008, there were two meetings of the G20 per year. Nowadays, these meetings have been reduced to one per year, see <www.g20.utoronto.ca/summits/index.html> accessed 15 January 2015.

109 Pan (n 76) 245.

110 J Eatwell and L Taylor, *Global Finance at Risk: The Case for International Regulation* (New Press 2000), 208 ff. According to these authors, the WFA could be created from an expanded Bank for International Settlements (BIS) (expanded authority, remit, role and membership); an alternative could be to place the WFA function within the IMF, ibid 235–37.

(WFO), maybe even in the image of the WTO.[111] This WFO would produce compulsory international financial standards for those states seeking market access for home financial entities in foreign countries. This international organization should also be invested with the power to sanction members whose national regulatory policies fail to comply with those international standards,[112] by way of authorized countermeasures or otherwise.[113] A very similar scheme introduces the setting-up of a treaty-established *Governing Council* that would probably delegate to other bodies the authority to develop those standards and even the tasks of surveillance and enforcement.[114] The rationale of this proposal follows very closely the one that the Stiglitz Report advises for the whole economic area.[115] Other authors, building on the 'Global Administrative Law' project,[116] have suggested the setting-up of an international administrative body in the form of an independent college of supervisors that would be entrusted with financial regulatory, but most importantly, supervisory powers.[117] This administrative agency should also have the means to impose sanctions when national financial institutions do not conform to the legal standards.[118]

Second, a very similar result could be achieved through a strengthening of the IMF.[119] The financial crisis of 2008 has demonstrated how necessary a world financial authority is for the smooth functioning of global markets. Therefore, it would be wise to have recourse to the IMF because it 'is not only the international monetary institution *par excellence*; the IMF is also at the centre of the international financial system'.[120] Within this alternative, there are different degrees: on the one hand, as the IMF has statutory responsibility for surveillance of international economies and has the power and responsibility of an international lender, incorporating the function of a WFA would be like combining the 'roles of a quasi-central bank and a quasi-regulator'.[121] On the other hand, a less ambitious scheme would only attribute

111   Rosa M Lastra, 'Do We Need a World Financial Organisation?' Ch 3 of this book. See also C Reinhart and K Rogoff, 'Regulation should be International' *Financial Times* (London 18 November 2008) 13; B Eichengreen, 'Not a Bretton Woods, but a New Bretton Woods Process' in B Eichengreen and R Baldwin (eds), *What G-20 Leaders Must Do to Stabilise Our Economy and Fix the Financial System* (VoxEu.org 2008) 25; L Garicano and RM Lastra, 'Towards a New Architecture for Financial Stability: Seven Principles' (2010) 13 *Journal of International Economic Law* 597, 619; P Boone and S Johnson, 'Will the Politics of Global Moral Hazard Sink Us Again?' in A Turner et al, *The Future of Finance* (LSE 2010) 247, 269.

112   Independent panels of experts would have the task of determining whether countries are in compliance with their obligations as members of the new organization, B Eichengreen, 'International Financial Regulation after the Crisis' (2010) *Daedalus* 107, 113–14.

113   B Eichengreen, 'Out of the Box Thoughts about the International Financial Architecture' (2009) IMF Working Paper No 09/116, 19 <http://papers.ssrn.com/sol3/papers.cfm?abstract_id=1415173> accessed 15 January 2015.

114   Alexander et al (n 85) 163, speaking of a Global Financial Governance Council; Avgouleas (n 90) 429 ff.

115   Stiglitz Report (n 88) 87, discussing the advantages of establishing a Global Economic Coordination Council.

116   B Kingsbury, N Krisch and RB Stewart, 'The Emergence of Global Administrative Law' (2005) 68 *Law and Contemporary Problems* 15.

117   Lord Adair Turner, *The Turner Review: A Regulatory Response to the Global Banking Crisis* (Financial Services Authority 2009), 9, Recommendation 25 <www.fsa.gov.uk/pubs/other/turner_review.pdf> accessed 15 January 2015.

118   Pan (n 76) 273–75. See also D Aldford, 'Supervisory Colleges: The Global Financial Crisis and Improving International Supervisory Coordination' (2010) 24 *Emory International Law Review* 57.

119   *Cf.* Jean-Marc Sorel, 'Système ou non système monétaire international? Du système a la tectonique des plaques en passant par la dérive des continents' in Habib Gherari (ed), *Les dérèglements économiques internationaux: crise du droit ou droit des crises* (Pedone 2014) 43, 57, stating that the IMF cannot expect nowadays to find a role comparable to the one it had between 1944 and 1971.

120   RM Lastra, 'The Role of the IMF as a Global Financial Authority' (2011) *European Yearbook of International Economic Law* 121, 122.

121   Eatwell and Taylor (n 110) 236.

supervisory tasks to the IMF, but not a regulatory or a dispute settlement role. Although it would be advisable to expand the IMF powers through an amendment of its Articles of Agreement, a creative interpretation of Article I and Article IV would be enough to reinforce its surveillance function over issues of financial stability.[122]

Finally, other less ambitious approaches, even admitting the superiority of a proposal based on hard law, put forward some intermediate steps which would serve to harden specific features of the soft-law model strengthened in the post-crisis reforms.[123] One of those steps would consist of the establishment of a dispute settlement mechanism close to the one existing within the WTO in order to solve differences over international burden sharing in the event of trans-border financial institution failures.[124]

These alternative frameworks for introducing some degree of institutionalization regarding the international financial structure have been qualified as politically unfeasible.[125] We are reminded that there is no consensus among states regarding the establishment of an international framework of a mandatory type in this realm. Truly, developed countries which are home to the largest private international institutions or are in control of the most important financial centres (New York, London) will be reluctant to risk the political weight they currently enjoy.[126] For sure, creating an international financial organization goes against their national interests and those of their domestic financial champions[127] in areas like investment banking or credit rating. However, normatively speaking, the solution consisting of building an international financial framework based on a formal international organization with legal powers is superior to the one chosen after the 2008 crisis. If crises are recurrent, it might be wise to try to avoid them or limit their negative effects as much as possible through more, not less, hard-law/formal regulation of the kind suggested in this chapter. As has been stated, '(t)he key to effectively managing systemic risk is having regulatory authorities who operate in the same domain as the institutions they regulate'.[128] If 'informal cooperation has reached the limits of effectiveness' then the optimal solution from a normative point of view is a WFA that performs the same tasks that are performed today by efficient national regulators, 'namely information, authorisation, surveillance, guidance, and policy' (including the macroeconomic

---

122 Lastra (n 120) 122–23.

123 DW Arner and MW Taylor, 'The Global Financial Crisis and the Financial Stability Board: Hardening the Soft-Law of International Financial Regulation?' (2009) 32 *University of New South Wales Law Journal* 488. According to these authors, both supervision and crisis management arrangements for cross-border international financial institutions are issues that truly demand hard-law regime answers, ibid 490, 496. See also MC Turk, 'Reframing International Financial Regulation after the Global Financial Crisis: Rational States and Interdependence, not Regulatory Networks and Soft Law' (2014) 36 *Michigan Journal of International Law* 59.

124 Arner and Taylor (n 123) 490. See also D Schoenmaker and A Siegmann, 'Can European Banks Bailouts Work?' (2014) *Journal of Banking and Finance* 334, analysing the European context and submitting that, after a supra-national approach, a second best solution would be a binding rule among national governments to share the burden of failing banks in order to maintain financial stability.

125 LG Baxter, 'Exploring the WFO Option for Global Banking' in L Boulle (ed), *Globalisation & Governance* (Siber Ink 2011) 113, 116, stating that the WFO idea is misconceived and doomed to failure. See also Brummer (n 83) 312.

126 Avgouleas (n 90) 431, highlighting the expected opposition of big stakeholders like the US and the EU to a supra-national governance system.

127 S Gadinis, 'The Politics of Competition in International Financial Regulation' (2008) 49 *Harvard International Law Journal* 447, 450, highlighting that domestic interest groups' preferences have a direct influence on national policies, especially in a dominant state like the US, towards international coordination in financial regulation.

128 Eatwell and Taylor (n 110) 219.

and microeconomic level).[129] Moreover, from a political theory point of view, an institutionalized international organization would be in a better position to resist the domestic political pressures that government networks and national regulators currently face.[130] Finally, it is true that this proposal entails some dangers regarding over-integration in economic life.[131] But, firstly, only those states wanting to engage in deeper financial integration should commit to new and more elaborated institutional frameworks.[132] Second, the proposed institutional reconfiguration does not rule out other tools like the dynamic management of a country capital account,[133] thus enhancing policy space and national regulatory autonomy.

Concluding Remarks

International trade law and international financial law have similar functions in that both aim to achieve system stability (whether in trade or financial trans-border operations).[134] The multilateral trading system has developed a higher level of institutionalization and legalization but at some cost. First, as we have seen, the trade system allows the main players to adopt protectionist measures if there is a big market failure (the 2008 economic crisis). Second, the 'trade and . . .' debate shows that the trade regime is not complete as long as other societal values are not incorporated. The protection of human rights, labour rights, the environment, and the real promotion of development must be addressed at the WTO system if we want to preserve it from irrelevance in the near future. After all, it is not at all clear that the world trading system is only about free trade. The Preamble to the WTO Agreement encompasses other objectives together with trade liberalization (like raising standards of living, ensuring full employment, sustainable development, and the preservation of the environment). In the end, it is only a question of enabling the trading system to get rid of the pervasive economic liberalism that has been dominating it during the last decades and adopting a true global governance stance that accords with the goals stated and needs observed within the trade regime.

With respect to finance, there is a real need to change the structure of the financial architecture. Soft-law standards produced by TRNs were once acclaimed because they could solve the globalization paradox. However, these government networks have been unable to cope with the tasks once assumed, that is, the stability of the international financial system. As attested by the recent crises, those financial standards convey important problems regarding effectiveness and enforcement. They do not solve the crucial issues related to international banking regulation like the supervision of prudential regulation and the application of bank-resolution mechanisms for cross-border financial institutions. Moreover, their lack of

---

129 ibid 220.
130 Reinhart and Rogoff (n 111) 13.
131 D Kennedy, 'Law and the Political Economy of the World' (2013) 26 *Leiden Journal of International Law* 7, 20.
132 D Rodrik, 'A Plan B for Global Finance' *The Economist* (London, 12 March 2009) 3 <www.economist.com/node/13278147> accessed 15 January 2015.
133 Stiglitz Report (n 88) para 204. See also JD Ostry et al, 'Capital Inflows: The Role of Controls' (2010) IMF Staff Position Note No 10/04, conveying a real change in the IMF's stance towards the use of capital controls; Adam Feibelman, 'The IMF and Regulation of Cross-Border Capital Flows' (2015) 15 *Chicago Journal of International Law* 409.
134 PC Mavroidis, 'Free Lunches? WTO as Public Good, and the WTO's View of Public Goods' (2012) 23 *European Journal of International Law* 731, underlining the idea that the public good is not free trade but instead the WTO understood as a forum that is necessary to address (negative) external effects stemming from the unilateral definition of trade policies.

accountability and inclusiveness make them an instrument for developed countries to impose their standards on non-participating countries, mostly developing countries. A proposal for reform would consist of the establishment of a WFO, although there are more modest approaches that may serve as an intermediate step. The current unfeasibility of this approach predicated by its critics may not change its normative coherence weight: collective problems may only be solved through the most appropriate coordinated responses which in this case require an institutional or vertical articulation in the form of an international organization.[135]

As this chapter has tried to demonstrate, the recent economic and financial crisis has put IEL at a crossroads in the two areas under scrutiny, trade law and financial law. Global governance and normative coherence have been used as the theoretical tools to unveil the similarities stemming from the functions performed and the need for transformation that both areas of IEL have in common. Trade law and financial law are in need of reform at the international plane, be it a substantive reform in the first case or an institutional reform in the second. Of course, this change in both areas of law would introduce a meaningful step from negative regulation towards a more positive approach to regulation (an outcome already achieved with the TRIPS Agreement).

---

135 G Shaffer, 'International Law and Global Public Goods in a Legal Pluralist World' (2012) 23 *European Journal of International Law* 669, 683, who highlights the role of international organizations in the provision of global public goods. See generally 'Symposium: Global Public Goods and the Plurality of Legal Orders' in the same issue.

Part II

Finance

2   Global Economic Governance and Banking Regulation

Redesigning Regulation to Promote Stakeholder Interests

*Kern Alexander**

Introduction

The global financial crisis of 2007–2008 demonstrated serious weaknesses in global financial governance and has led to comprehensive reforms of international financial regulation. The G20 and the Financial Stability Board have taken the lead post-crisis with efforts to make international financial standard-setting more accountable and legitimate by involving more countries in the standard-setting process and by making deliberations more transparent and reflecting the views of a broader number of stakeholders. Moreover, the G20 initiated at the Pittsburgh Heads of State Summit in September 2009 an extensive reform of international financial regulation with the overall aim 'to generate strong, sustainable and balanced global growth'. An important feature of the international regulatory reforms has been the G20s stated objective to make financial regulation more 'macro-prudential', that is, to address risks and vulnerabilities across the financial system and broader economy that might threaten the stability of the financial system – and hence imperil the stability and sustainability of the economy.

Since the 1970s, increasing liberalization of financial markets and cross-border capital flows have brought more liquidity to financial markets during periods of market confidence, but have proved to be a channel for contagion during periods of fragility and crisis. These cross-border linkages between national financial systems have led to the emergence of a globalized financial market in banking, wholesale securities, and asset management. Indeed, the move from segmented national financial systems to a liberalized and globalized financial system has posed immense challenges to financial regulators and supervisors, including the need to adopt more effective regulation and supervision across financial systems and to enhance coordination between states in supervising on a cross-border basis and internationally.

The crisis demonstrates the need to adopt a more holistic approach to financial regulation and supervision that involves linking micro-prudential supervision of individual institutions with broader oversight of the financial system and to macro-economic policy. This chapter argues that the 'macro-prudential' dimension of financial regulation will have important implications for global financial governance and will require more accountability and legitimacy in the international financial standard-setting process. First, the chapter traces the development of international financial standard-setting from the 1960s to the reforms

* Chair for Law & Finance, University of Zurich & Former Member of the European Parliament's Expert Committee on Financial Services (2009–2014) and Head of the United Nations Environment Programme's Research Project and Report Author: 'Stability and Sustainability in Banking Reform: Are Environmental Risks Missing in Basel III' (UNEP, 2014).

following the 2007–2008 crisis. Second, the chapter considers the post-crisis international regulatory reforms and whether they adequately address regulatory weaknesses and represent relevant stakeholder interests. Third, the chapter suggests that although international reforms have addressed the interests of wider stakeholder groups through macro-prudential regulation, more work should be done to address stakeholder concerns regarding the impact of environmental and social risks on financial stability.

Global Financial Governance and the Rise of G10 Committees

In international finance, the globalization of financial services has necessitated that regulators develop cooperative relations to facilitate their oversight and regulation of banking and financial services. Beginning in 1962, the central banks of the 10 leading industrialized nations began to meet regularly at the Bank for International Settlements[1] and other venues to coordinate central bank policy and to organize lending to each other through the General Arrangements to Borrow.[2] These 10 countries (plus the Swiss National Bank) became known as the Group of Ten or G10.

It is important to emphasize that the central bank governors of the world's advanced industrialized countries were responsible for setting the agenda of the G10 committees and that in the G10s early years much of their activity – central bank operations and lending to one another – concerned the maintenance of each country's currency exchange rate parity within the International Monetary Fund's (IMF) fixed exchange rate regime. In the 1960s, the G10 central bank governors established two committees whose secretariats were based at the BIS. The first of these committees was the Eurocurrency Standing Committee (also, known as the Markets Committee). Founded in 1962, it was formed to monitor and assess the operations of the then newly established euro currency markets. This Committee later became the Committee on the Global Financial System in 1971. It now deals with broader issues of systemic risk and financial stability. And the Committee on Payment and Settlement Systems was formed in 1990 to negotiate and set standards to support the continued functioning of payment and settlement systems.[3]

In the early 1970s, after the IMF exchange rate regime collapsed, the G10 was confronted with extreme volatility in the foreign exchange markets and imbalances caused by 'petro dollar' flows from oil producing countries following the Arab oil embargo. These market developments led the G10 to establish the Basel Committee on Banking Regulation and Supervisory Practices in December 1974, which is today known as the Basel Committee on Banking Supervision, to address cross-border coordination issues between central banks and

---

1 The Bank for International Settlement (BIS) is an international organization created under The Hague Agreements of 1930 and the Constituent Charter of the Bank for International Settlements of 1930. It was established in the context of the Young Plan, which dealt with the issue of the reparation payments imposed on Germany by the Treaty of Versailles following the First World War. The BIS served as the payment agent for the European Payments Union (EPU, 1950–1958), which facilitated the restoration of currency convertibility for the Western European countries following the Second World War. See Daniel Gros and Niels Thygesen *European Monetary Integration* (2nd edn, Macmillan 1998) 4–8.

2 See discussion of the General Arrangements to Borrow (the 'GAB') in Kern Alexander 'The Fund's Role in Sovereign Liquidity Crises' in *Current Issues in Monetary and Financial Law*, vol 5 (International Monetary Fund 2008) 131, 140–46.

3 See James C Baker, *History of the Bank for International Settlements* (CUP 2002) 32. Three other secretariats operate out of the BIS: the Financial Stability Forum, the International Association of Deposit Insurers and the International Association of Insurance Supervisors.

bank supervisors in overseeing cross-border banking activity.[4] The Basel Committee was formed in response to a serious threat to banking stability caused by collapse of the German bank Herstatt, which had created significant problems in the foreign exchange settlement markets between US and European banks. In the same year, the US Franklin National Bank became insolvent and posed a risk to counterparty banks because of its miscalculations of foreign exchange risk in the wholesale loan market. These bouts of financial instability exposed substantial gaps in the ability of central bankers and national regulators to control and manage banking sector instability with cross-border effects.

Since the 1970s, the three main G10 committees – the Basel Committee on Banking Regulation, the Committee on Payment and Settlement Systems and the Committee on the Global Financial System – have become the most influential international standard-setting bodies by exercising either direct or indirect influence over the development of banking, currency and market operations, and payment system law and regulation for all developed countries and most developing countries.[5] Specifically, the Basel Committee has produced a number of important international agreements that regulate the amount of capital that banks must set aside against their risk-based assets and the allocation of jurisdictional responsibility for bank regulators in overseeing the international operations of banks. Although the Committee's early agreements in the 1970s and 80s were viewed by policymakers and commentators to be necessary to stabilize international banking markets, its efforts in the early 2000s to adopt Basel II and to extend its application to all countries where international banks operate attracted significant critical comment and brought its work under close scrutiny by leading policy-makers and regulators.

The Committee on Payment and Settlement Systems has produced important agreements setting forth principles and recommendations for the regulation of bank payment systems and have worked with the International Organization of Securities Commissions (IOSCO) to adopt principles and standards for the regulation of clearing and settlement of securities and derivatives trading. The Committee on Global Financial Systems, though it has not adopted

---

4 Indeed, Goodhart described the relationship of the G10 with one of its standard-setting committees – the Basel Committee – as one of delegated authority to engage in regulatory standard-setting: 'Having established a standing committee of specialists in this field, the G10 Governors would find it difficult to reject a proposal from them, especially on a technical matter. The relationships between the G10 Governors and the BCBS emerge from the analysis of what the BCBS actually did and were quite complex. The G10 Governors set priorities for work, and frequently required papers to be revised and reconsidered. But at the same time they often gave the BCBS considerable freedom to decide its own agenda, and frequently rubber-stamped the papers emerging; basically the Governors did not have the time or the desire for textual criticism. They had a general oversight role; the detail was to be hammered out in the BCBS', Charles AE Goodhart, *A History of the Basel Committee on Banking Supervision* (CUP 2011) ch 14.

5 Walker observes that 'International standards have become of particular importance in recent years due to the need to develop some common or, at least, minimum level of rules and regulations in various core areas of modern financial and economic practice. In light of the difficulties that naturally arise in attempting to agree any formal treaty, convention or similar formal prescriptive solution at the international level, a more informal consensus based approach has to be attempted, at least, during the early stages until some basic common agreement (and supporting sense of self-interest and commitment) may be achieved. This will certainly be the case in many such sensitive and complex areas as international bank and financial market control. A standards based approach also has the obvious advantage of flexibility and informality although this necessarily means that it suffers from the associated operational limitations of weak adoption and compliance. The key issues that then arise with international standards are not with regard to legal classification and formal enforcement but with national adoption and implementation and implementation review', George Alexander Walker, *International Banking Regulation: Law, Policy, and Practice* (Kluwer 2001) preface, xxiii.

regulatory principles or recommendations, has produced a number of influential reports that have influenced the debate over macro-prudential financial reforms post-crisis to control systemic risk across financial systems and the interrelationship with monetary policy.

These committees have examined many important central banking and financial regulatory issues, as well as attempted to elaborate and promulgate best practices in supervision and regulation, the functioning of payment and settlement systems, and the overall operation of financial markets. The committees are usually chaired by senior officials of member central banks and are composed of experts from central banks, regulatory authorities and finance ministries. In the case of the Basel Committee on Banking Supervision, members also include non-central bank supervisory authorities and other regulatory and economic policy experts. Members of the committees have voting power and decision-making authority, while non-G10 country representatives were often consulted for their views on a variety of regulatory and economic issues. Frequently, special initiatives are undertaken to share experience with, and invite the opinions of, those not directly involved in the work of the committees. In promoting cooperation in their respective areas, the committees determine their own agenda and, within their mandate, operate independently from their host organization, the BIS, which only provides its good offices for meetings as well as administrative and research support. Significantly, these committees have resolved not to adopt legally binding international standards in a public international law sense, but rather to influence domestic regulatory practices and standards by adopting what has become known as 'international soft law'.[6]

The Basel Committee has been the most influential of the G10 committees with respect to its impact on developing legally non-binding international financial norms of banking regulation standards, especially through the adoption of the *Capital Accord, the Concordat,* and *the Core Principles for Effective Banking Supervision* and their impact on domestic regulatory and supervisory practices. For instance, the Basel Committee's Concordat – adopted in February 1975 – established principles of information exchange and cross-border coordination for the oversight of the international banking operations. The 1983 Revised Concordat[7] contained the principle of consolidated supervision; this principle provides that home country regulators shall have responsibility for ensuring that the transnational operations of their home country banks are sound regarding credit risk exposure, quality of assets, and the capital adequacy of the banking group's global operations, while the host country authority will mainly be responsible for the provision of local liquidity to foreign banks.[8]

Following the Latin American debt crisis of the early 1980s and the near collapse of several major US banks, the Basel Committee adopted the 1988 Capital Accord, which established a minimum 8 per cent capital adequacy requirement on internationally active banks within G10 country jurisdictions.[9] The Capital Accord was originally calculated based on

---

6 See Kern Alexander, Rahul Dhumale and John Eatwell, *Global Governance of Financial Systems: The International Regulation of Systemic Risk* (OUP 2006) ch 3 discussing international soft law. As an international legal matter, the Basel Capital Accord and its amended versions, Basel II and III, are not legally binding in any way for G10 countries or other countries that adhere to it. The Capital Accord has been analysed and classified as a form of 'soft' law, ibid 135–37.

7 The 1975 Concordat was amended in 1983 in response to the collapse and insolvency of the Italian bank Banco Ambrosiano. The 1983 Revised Concordat was entitled Principles for the Supervision of Banks' Foreign Establishments.

8 See Kern Alexander and others (n 6) 47–48.

9 The 1988 Capital Accord's original purpose was to prevent the erosion of bank capital ratios resulting from aggressive competition for market share by the leading banks during the 1980s. The Accord also hoped to harmonize the different levels and approaches to capital among the G10 countries. In adopting the 1988 Accord, banking

a bank's credit risk exposure, but was later amended in 1996 to include a bank's market risk exposure (i.e., trading book exposure), thereby extending the 8 per cent capital adequacy requirement to a bank's trading book activities.[10] Between 1999 and 2004, the Committee engaged in a lengthy and radical revision of the Accord known as 'Basel II.' The final text was concluded in 2004, and resulted in radical changes in how the largest and most sophisticated banks calculated their regulatory capital: Basel II would permit them to use their own historic loan loss and trading book data as a basis to estimate the riskiness of their assets and hence to determine their regulatory capital.

In doing so, Basel II aimed to make regulatory capital more sensitive to the risks which banks face in the marketplace. In doing so, it allowed banks, under most conditions, to hold less regulatory capital for their credit, market and operational risk exposures than what was required under Basel I. The global credit crisis of 2007–2008, however, revealed that banks are also exposed to significant liquidity risks, especially in their off-balance sheet exposures, and that banks should hold more loss-absorbent capital. Basel II failed to address the liquidity risks to which banks are exposed and also did not require banks to hold adequate levels of loss-absorbent capital. Moreover, Basel II's excessive reliance on risk-weighting of assets to calculate regulatory capital resulted in procyclicality – that is, banks holding too little capital during market upturns and too much capital during downturns.[11] It also favoured large banks with sophisticated data bases over small banks with less data in that it allowed larger banks to hold less capital as a percentage of risk-weighted assets compared to medium-sized and smaller banks. It also advantaged the banking systems of advanced economies at the expense of less-developed and emerging market economies, as banks in advanced economies had access to large amounts of default data on borrowers and counterparties, therefore were in a better position to devise risk models based on this data that would qualify the bank for a lower capital requirement. Moreover, the procyclicality of Basel II had pernicious effects on economies that were more prone to volatility and booms and busts – specifically, developing and emerging market economies.

The Basel Committee responded to the 2007–2008 financial crisis by adopting further amendments to Basel II, which became known as Basel III. Basel III requires an increased level of Tier One regulatory capital to 4.5 per cent from 2 per cent plus a 2.5 per cent capital conservation buffer, a tighter definition of Tier One capital to include mainly ordinary common shares and retained earnings, and up to an additional 2.5 per cent counter-cyclical capital ratio that will be adjusted across the economic cycle.[12] Basel III also contains liquidity requirements that include a ratio for stable wholesale funding, liquidity coverage ratios, and

---

regulators wanted to establish an international minimum standard that would create a level playing field for banks operating in the G10 countries and that banking regulators wanted capital requirements to reflect accurately the true risks facing banks in a deregulated and internationally competitive market. The 1988 Capital Accord required banks actively engaged in international transactions to hold capital equal to at least 8 per cent of their risk-weighted assets. This capital adequacy standard was intended to prevent banks from increasing their exposure to credit risk by imprudently incurring greater leverage. The 1988 Capital Accord was entitled 'International Convergence of Capital Measurement and Capital Standards' and it applied based on the principle of home country control to banks based in G10 countries with international operations (Basel 1988).

10 This was known as the Market Risk Amendment 1996, see Alexander and others (n 6) 38–39.

11 Kern Alexander, John Eatwell, Avinash Persaud and Robert Reoch 'Financial Supervision and Crisis Management in the EU', Commissioned Report for the EU Parliament Committee on Economic and Monetary Affairs (EU Parliament 2007) <www-cfap.jbs.cam.ac.uk/publications/downloads/2007_alexander_eatwell_persaud_reoch_financial.pdf> accessed 24 April 2015.

12 See Basel Committee on Banking Supervision 'Basel III Regulatory Consistency Assessment Program (RCAP) (2013) <www.bis.org/publ/bcbs264.pdf> accessed 14 June 2014.

an overall leverage ratio. Also, an additional capital charge of up to 2.5 per cent regulatory capital will be required for large and interconnected systemically important financial institutions (SIFIs).

Despite significant increases in capital and liquidity requirements, Basel III essentially builds on the edifice of Basel II by leaving in place the Basel II risk-weighting regime. However, Basel III requires regulators to challenge banks more in the construction of their models and broadens regulatory authority to require banks to undergo more frequent and demanding stress tests. The Pillar 2 review also consists of a supervisory review enhancement process (SREP) that includes separate assessments of bank capital and governance. The SREP can be utilized to forecast the bank's exposure to systemic risks and related macro-prudential risks. The SREP is also designed to address bank corporate governance and risk management. The corporate governance dimension of Pillar 2 is important for assessing the effect of Basel III on broader stakeholders who are affected by the regulation and supervision of banks. Enhanced bank corporate governance is designed not only to promote bank shareholder value but also to control and limit the potential social costs of weak bank management and the deleterious effect on the broader economy. In other words, Pillar 2 of Basel III – especially through the SREP process – is concerned with the effect of bank governance and risk management on stakeholders – those in the economy who are directly and indirectly affected by banks. As discussed below, a significant part of Basel III (and of Basel II) can be utilized to address environmental and social governance issues.

Other international supervisory bodies have also played a key role in developing international standards and rules for the regulation of financial markets. The International Association of Deposit Insurers meets at the BIS and discusses and adopts international principles and standards that govern deposit insurance regulation. In the area of money laundering and terrorist financing, the OECD's Financial Action Task Force ('FATF') has attained a high profile role in setting international standards (so-called recommendations) of disclosure and transparency for the regulation of banks, financial service providers, and other businesses in order to combat the global problem of financial crime.[13] The FATF and the Basel Committee have each played a much more prominent role in their respective international regulatory standard-setting functions as compared to the International Organization of Securities Commissions ('IOSCO') and the International Association of Insurance Supervisors ('IAIS'). In recent years, however, IOSCO and the IAIS have attracted much more policy attention since their standards and recommendations have been recognized by the IMF and World Bank as international benchmarks against which IMF and World Bank member countries are assessed for compliance in their financial sector assessment programmes.

As discussed above, these international standard-setting bodies have been characterized as 'networks' of international technical experts, which are not concerned with broader public policy or international political economy issues. Rather, they are at the 'coal face' of technical and regulatory standard-setting. The goal of these regulatory technicians in international bodies is to coordinate regulatory and supervisory oversight of international banks and financial conglomerates with operations across financial sectors. These networks are composed of national regulators and supervisors – mainly from developed countries – who

---

13 The International Accounting Standards Board (IASB) and the International Federation of Accountants (IFAC) are bodies composed of professional accountants and academics who devise international accounting standards for the accounting industry. Similarly, the International Auditing and Assurance Standards Board (IAASB) sets standards for international financial reporting. See <www.ifac.org/> accessed 15 January 2015.

have established several international bodies to coordinate communication and the exchange of ideas among regulators on common issues of concern. These regulatory networks play an important role in disseminating information among regulators across financial sectors in different jurisdictions.

Before the 2007–2008 crisis, the Financial Stability Forum (FSF) coordinated activities relating to issues common to the banking, securities, and insurance sectors. As the common body of three international financial standard setters, the BCBS, the IAIS, and the IOSCO and the Joint Forum on Financial Conglomerates set soft law in the form of guidance[14] and reports in the form of broad principles, which serve to establish a minimal standard.[15] Crucially, it involved representatives of the banking and financial services industry in its deliberations and they played an important role on FSF working groups that published papers on regulatory reform that had significant influence on the work of the BCBS, the IAIS, and the IOSCO.

The Legitimacy of International Financial Standard-Setting

The international financial bodies lack the requisite attributes of an international organization, namely, they are not subject to international law, and do not have international personality, the capacity to conclude treaties, or international legal immunities. Insofar as these organizations are neither composed of states nor founded upon an international treaty, they also do not meet the traditional legal definition of an international organization and therefore are not subject to minimum rules of transparency regarding, for example, the keeping of meeting minutes and other records concerning decision-making and deliberations. It is argued in some quarters that this lack of accountability in decision-making and operational processes can potentially undermine the effectiveness and legitimacy of the IFIs. On the other hand, other commentators suggest that precisely because these international standard-setting bodies are devoid of legal personality and excluded from the potential discipline of international law, they gain in flexibility and enhanced coordination benefits by not being subject to formalistic rules of decision-making process and consultation, and therefore are in a position to devise international norms that turn out to be more effective in influencing state practice than traditional methods and procedures of public international law-making.[16] The worldwide credit crisis of 2007–08, however, called into question the efficacy of this flexible and unstructured decision-making framework and in particular raised concerns regarding the accountability and legitimacy of the IFI standard-setting processes.

In assessing whether the Basel Committee's standard-setting process complies with the principle of legitimacy as discussed above, a closer look at the Basel Committee's deliberation

---

14 See Alexander and others (n 6) 74–76.

15 The Financial Stability Forum (FSF) was established in 1999 in response to the Asian financial crisis and is composed of regulatory officials from leading developed countries and some large developing countries. It relies on the work of the other international financial standard-setting bodies and the central banks and the various departments of the OECD. The FSF has compiled a Compendium of Standards (CoS) with a summary and classification of the most significant rules, best practices, principles and guidelines of international financial regulation. They are categorized according to the sector they pertain to, such as government and central bank, banking, securities, and insurance industries, and the corporate sector, and functionally, such as to governance, accounting, disclosure and transparency, capital adequacy, regulation, and supervision, information sharing, risk management, payment and settlement, business ethics, etc, and according to their specificity in principles, practices and guidelines.

16 See Alexander and others (n 6) 136–39.

and decision-making process is necessary. The Basel Committee addresses issues that are of global concern to regulators and supervisors through a set of committees established to address particular issues of concern to bank regulators. After committees deliberate they issue recommendations to the Basel Committee Secretary General and Deputy Secretary General who are in position to table recommendations or issues of concern (including reports by external bodies) to the Basel Committee's Committee. Its decision-making operates on a consensus basis. Although the Committee's decision-making has traditionally been secretive and substantially relied on personal contacts, it has become more formalized in recent years because of the considerable attention given to the deliberations over Basel II.[17] As discussed above, the Committee's decisions are *legally non-binding* in a traditional public international law sense and place a great deal of emphasis on decentralized implementation and informal monitoring of member compliance.[18] The Committee has sought to extend its informal network with banking regulators outside the G10 through various consultation groups.[19] Most recently, it has conducted seminars and consultations with banking regulators from over 100 countries as part of the deliberations over adopting the Basel II agreement.

Although some have viewed the informality of the Committee's decision-making process as effective for developing international banking regulatory standards,[20] others have considered it a constraint on effective implementation.[21] As Goodhart has observed, 'The way that the BCBS, under its various Chairmen, interpreted this constraint was that all proposals for forward transmission to the G10 Governors, and thence to the wider community of regulators/supervisors around the world, had to be accepted consensually by all country members of the Committee.'[22] As a consensus of all Committee members was required to adopt any standards or agreement, each country had a veto. According to Goodhart, however, this was in practice 'somewhat less of a constraint than it might seem at first sight'.[23] The smaller countries, for example, Benelux, Canada, Italy, Sweden and Switzerland, were reluctant to object to proposals by the United States and United Kingdom and rarely took a minority position, 'except on a matter of extreme national importance, an example of [which is] . . . banking secrecy for Switzerland'.[24] Despite Japan's substantial economic and financial influence,

---

17 For instance, during the Basel II negotiations, the Committee put a number of issues for consultation on its website and engaged in a public dialogue on its website through the publication of its quantitative impact studies which measured the impact of Basel II on a hypothetical basis based on the reports of a number of banks in both G10 and non-G10 countries.

18 Indeed, the Basel Committee states on the BIS website the following: 'The Committee does not possess any formal supranational supervisory authority, and its conclusions do not, and were never intended to, have legal force. Rather, it formulates broad supervisory standards and guidelines and recommends statements of best practice in the expectation that individual authorities will take steps' to implement them through detailed arrangements – statutory or otherwise – which are best suited to their own national systems. In this way, the Committee encourages convergence towards common approaches and common standards without attempting detailed harmonisation of member countries' supervisory techniques' <www.bis.org/bcbs/aboutbcbs.htm> accessed 24 April 2014.

19 The Core Principles Liaison Group remains the most important forum for dialogue between the Committee and systemically relevant non-G10 countries. Moreover, the BIS established the Financial Stability Institute to conduct outreach to non-G10 banking regulators by holding seminars and conferences on implementing international banking and financial standards.

20 Patricia Jackson, 'Amending the Basel Capital Accord' (unpublished paper, Cambridge Endowment for Research in Finance Seminar, 22 January 2000).

21 Charles Goodhart (n 4).

22 ibid.

23 ibid.

24 ibid.

Goodhart notes that Japanese representatives on the Committee 'usually remained quiet and withdrawn . . . partly due to their rapid turn-over of personnel, so they had little opportunity to build up expertise'.[25]

Monitoring noncompliance has generally been a decentralized task that is the responsibility of member states themselves, not international organizations, such as the BIS, or other international bodies.[26] Nonetheless, the Committee monitors and reviews the Basel framework with a view to achieving greater uniformity in its implementation and convergence in substantive standards. Moreover, the Committee claims that the legitimacy of the international standards it adopts derives from a communiqué issued by the G7 heads of state in 1998 that encouraged emerging economies to adopt 'strong prudential standards' and 'effective supervisory structures'.[27] To ensure that its standards are adopted, the Committee expects the IMF and World Bank to play a surveillance role in overseeing Member State adherence through its various conditionality and economic restructuring programs. In addition, because most G10 countries are members of the European Union, they are required by EU law to implement the Capital Accord into domestic law.[28] In fact, the only G10 countries not required by local law to implement the Capital Accord are Canada, Japan and the United States.[29] This extended application of the Basel Committee's standards to non-G10 countries has raised questions regarding the accountability of its decision-making structure and its suitability for application in developing and emerging market economies.

In addition, the Basel Committee's capital adequacy standards and rules on consolidated supervision were originally intended to apply only to credit institutions based in G10 countries that had cross-border operations. But this changed in 1998 during the Asian financial crisis when, at the urging of the G7 finance ministers and the world's largest financial institutions, which were lobbying for more market-sensitive capital standards, the Basel Committee stated its intent to amend the Capital Accord and to begin working on Basel II with a view to making it applicable to all countries where banks operate on a cross-border basis. Many non-G10 countries have incorporated the Basel standards into their regulatory frameworks for a variety of reasons, including strengthening the soundness of their commercial banks, raising their credit rating in international financial markets, and achieving a universally recognized international standard. The IMF and World Bank have also required many countries

---

25 ibid.

26 See generally Joseph Norton, *Devising International Standards of Banking Supervision* (Kluwer 1995).

27 ibid.

28 See Capital Requirements Directive (CRD) IV which consists of the Directive 2013/36/EU of the European Parliament and of the Council of 26 June 2013 on access to the activity of credit institutions and the prudential supervision of credit institutions and investment firms, amending Directive 2002/87/EC and repealing Directives 2006/48/EC and 2006/49/EC [2013] OJ L 176/338, and Regulation (EU) No 575/2013 of the European Parliament and of the Council of 26 June 2013 on prudential requirements for credit institutions and investment firms and amending Regulation (EU) No 648/2012 [2013] OJ L 176/1. The states that are required to implement the CRD IV are the 31 member states of the European Economic Area (EEA) consisting of the 28 EU member states and three other states – Iceland, Liechtenstein and Norway – not in the EU but which are required to adopt most EU economic and financial legislation.

29 In fact, a major obstacle in negotiations over Basel II had been the initial reluctance of US Congress and refusal of some US bank regulators to apply Basel II to most US banks. The Federal Reserve, which has been an important supporter of Basel II and has authority to apply it to US Financial Holding Companies, has begun applying it to the largest US financial holding companies, while all other US credit institutions will follow a different implementation schedule that will result in Basel II being fully adopted by US banks around 2013–2015. See Federal Reserve, 'Risk-based Capital Guidelines; Capital Adequacy Guidelines; Capital Maintenance; Domestic Capital Modifications, Advanced Notice of Proposed Rule-making' 12 CFR part 3 (6 October 2005).

to demonstrate adherence or a realistic effort to implement the Basel Accord in order to qualify for financial assistance as part of IMF Financial Sector Assessment Programs and World Bank Financial Sector Adjustment Programs. Moreover, as a condition for obtaining a bank licence, all G10 countries require foreign banks to demonstrate that their home country regulators have adopted the Capital Accord and other international agreements. International reputation and market signals are also important in creating incentives for non-G10 countries to adopt the Capital Accord. Many non-G10 countries (including developing countries) have found it necessary to require their banks to adopt similar capital adequacy standards in order to attract foreign investment as well as to stand on equal footing with international banks in global financial markets.

Regulatory Capture in Global Financial Governance

Although the flexible and secretive manner in which the G10 international financial standard-setting bodies conducted their deliberations and standard-setting was generally considered a strength in the effectiveness of their governance structures and decision-making processes,[30] it also had the unfortunate result of exposing them to special interest group pressure from major banks and international finance associations.[31] For example, most of the major international banks and their advocates pressured the Basel Committee to incorporate weaker capital adequacy measurement processes into Basel II; allowing banks to use more market-sensitive risk-measurement models, these processes resulted in lower levels of regulatory capital being held by banks.[32] This left the banking system seriously exposed to liquidity risk and subsequently deteriorated the credit risk exposure of bank balance sheets, a development that began in the summer of 2007 and later intensified with the worldwide credit crisis of 2008–2009.[33] Consequently, Basel II permitted regulators to approve more market-risk sensitive capital models, which led to lower levels of regulatory capital and created an incentive for banks to increase their leverage levels in the structured finance and securitization markets.[34] The Basel Committee's failure to adopt regulatory capital standards that would protect the global financial system from systemic risk contributed significantly to the regulatory failings that caused the worst financial crisis since the Great Depression of the 1930s. In other words, the lack of transparency, accountability and legitimacy in the Committee's decision-making structure and the bank's excessive influence on the regulators who were members of the Committee resulted in the leading G10 countries adopting weak bank capital standards, thereby significantly contributing to the largest global financial crisis since the 1930s that resulted in a worldwide economic recession, from which the global economy has not fully recovered.

30 The unstructured and secretive deliberations process has been praised because it allows regulators to respond quickly to rapidly changing developments in financial markets: see Jackson (n 21).

31 For example, the Institute for International Finance in Washington DC.

32 Indeed, a major impetus for Basel II was the lobbying of major multinational banks and their trade associations who wanted the 8 per cent capital adequacy standard of the 1988 Capital Accord lowered significantly to reflect more approximately the economic capital levels which bank risk models suggested that they hold to protect the investment capital of bank shareholders.

33 As the financial crisis of 2007–2009 has unfolded, it has been demonstrated that the market-sensitive regulatory capital measurement processes approved by the Basel Committee in 2004 have undermined financial stability and put the global financial system at serious risk, see Kern Alexander, John Eatwell, Avinash Persaud and Robert Reoch, 'Financial Supervision and Crisis Management in the EU', Commissioned Report by the EU Parliament Committee on Economic and Monetary Affairs (EU Parliament, December 2007) 2–7.

34 ibid.

The implications for global financial governance of the international financial standards produced by the international bodies discussed above have raised important questions regarding the accountability and legitimacy of global financial governance. The growing importance of international financial standards, such as the Basel Capital Accord, and their acceptance by most countries for their domestic regulatory systems demonstrated the importance of international financial soft law in influencing state regulatory practice. Nevertheless international financial soft law and its development through global financial governance structures failed to produce effective regulations and supervisory standards because the countries and the banking industry that developed the standards did not consult countries that were not members of the Basel Committee (mainly developing and emerging market economies), including their banking industries, and did not consider the interests of broader stakeholders in society who were affected by the operations of the banking and financial system. As a result, Basel II was inadequate for the needs of most countries' economies and their banking sectors and broader financial systems. In particular, it demonstrated a lack of accountability and legitimacy for the non-members of the Basel Committee and their banking sectors who were subject to these international financial norms. Also, because the standard-setting process was opaque and subject to excessive influence by some stakeholder groups (e.g., the large banking groups) it failed to adopt efficient regulatory standards that would promote regulatory objectives for the countries that were members of the Basel Committee.

Post-Crisis International Institutional Reforms

The global financial crisis that began in 2007 and intensified in 2008 with the collapse of Lehman Brothers bank and which resulted in the largest global economic slowdown since the 1930s has demonstrated serious weaknesses in global financial governance. Financial markets in the United States and many developed countries had moved away from a bank-based model of finance to a wholesale capital market model of finance which had brought diversification and increased liquidity to financial markets, but also had introduced systemic risks to the financial system which regulators had failed to identify and control. Specific types of financial innovation – such as securitization and credit default swaps – that began in the early 1990s partially in response to regulatory requirements such as Basel I had changed the nature of financial risk-taking and systemic risk.

The G20 Response

The financial crisis has triggered intense efforts internationally, regionally and nationally to enhance the monitoring of systemic stability and to strengthen the links between macro- and micro-prudential oversight, supervision and regulation. One such response is the widening of the international forum in which worldwide economic and financial policy issues are discussed from G8, the group of eight leading industrialized countries, to G20 in 2008. The transition from G8 to G20/Financial Stability Board (FSB) is of great importance because at all G20 meetings of 2008 to 2010, notably those in London (2009), Pittsburgh (2009) and Seoul (2010), the financial crisis and the international response to it were the dominant topics. And it were indeed decisions taken by the assembled 20 heads of state which kick-started many of the national and regional responses to the crisis that are discussed in this section of the chapter. For instance, in motivating the steps it has taken to avoid a repetition of the crisis or at least to mitigate the negative effects that a new financial crisis might have, the EU authorities regularly referred to commitments made at G20 meetings. Through this stimulating function of the G20 meetings alone the mid-term reactions have an international dimension.

Since the crisis, the philosophy of prudential financial regulation has shifted away from a sole focus on micro-prudential regulation and supervision – the regulation of individual banks and financial firms – to a broader focus on the whole financial system and how it relates with the broader economy. This is called macro-prudential regulation. The redesign of international financial regulation – and the main objective of global financial governance – is regulatory challenge posed by the financial crisis will be how regulators and central bankers can strike the right balance between micro-prudential regulation and supervision with macro-prudential controls on the broader financial system and economy. The overriding theme of the international financial reform initiatives (for example, the G20, the Financial Stability Board and Basel Committee) that began with the G20 Summits in Washington DC in November 2008 and London in April 2009[35] has been how to devise effective regulatory frameworks that durably link micro-prudential supervision with broader macro-prudential systemic risk concerns. Indeed, a major reform of global financial governance has been the shift in regulatory and supervisory focus from micro-prudential to macro-prudential regulation.

The focus on macro-prudential regulation has involved, for instance, devising regulatory standards to measure and limit leverage levels in the financial system and to require financial institutions to have enhanced liquidity reserves against short-term wholesale funding exposures. Macro-prudential regulation will also involve capital regulation that is counter-cyclical – requiring banks to hold more regulatory capital during good times and permitting them to hold less than what would be usually required during bad times. Counter-cyclical capital requirements would link capital charges to points in the macro-economic and business cycle. For example, this would involve dividend restriction policies during a crisis or recession so that banks will lend more.[36] This will necessarily involve banks using more forward-looking provisions based on expected losses. Moreover, a more effective macro-prudential capital regime requires enhanced quality and transparency of Tier One capital that allow shareholders to absorb losses more readily and to impose losses on certain creditors and bondholders before a bank becomes insolvent.

The Financial Stability Board

The Financial Stability Board[37] is the international body that has been given the responsibility by the G20 to develop international financial standards that control systemic risk and provide more effective oversight of the global financial system.[38] The FSB was created at the G20 London Summit in 2009 and was later established with legal personality by

---

35 The G20 Washington Action Plan and the London and Pittsburgh Summit Statements on strengthening the financial system reaffirm the policy recommendations of the FSF's April 2008 and 2009 Reports that provided a roadmap on financial supervision and regulation, and set forth principles for a more robust supervisory and regulatory framework based on new rules not only for financial institutions but also other actors, markets and supervisors.

36 The Basel Committee has introduced a framework for national authorities to consider how to implement counter-cyclical capital buffers. The Committee is reviewing the appropriate set of macro-economic indicators (eg, credit variables) and micro-indicators (banks' earnings) to determine how and when counter-cyclical regulatory charges and buffers should be imposed.

37 The Financial Stability Board is an institutional continuation of the FSF and has continued more or less to follow similar financial policies and regulatory approaches that are market-based and sensitive to the needs of the major international banks.

38 The FSB was formally created in April 2009 by the G20 Heads of State, see G20, 'London Statement' (2 April 2009) para 15. The FSB consists of 26 member countries, the European Central bank and the International

the G20 in the Cannes 2010 Summit Communiqué that stated that the Financial Stability Board will have 'legal personality', which could dramatically change the present system of legally non-binding international financial soft law standards. The Cannes Communiqué also provided for enhanced G20s/FSB's coordination with the International Monetary Fund on macro-prudential financial regulation and oversight of the global financial system. This raises important issues regarding the binding nature of G20/IMF macro-economic policy regulatory objectives and their decision-making and standard-setting processes.

The FSB has adopted 12 key standards for sound financial systems, all of which are legally non-binding soft law but nevertheless are expected to be incorporated into the national regulatory regimes of all countries.[39] Since its establishment, the FSB has been addressing a diverse range of regulatory issues.[40] For example, it has taken some of the work of the Financial Stability Forum forward by overseeing reviews of the system of supervisory colleges to monitor each of the largest international financial services firms.[41] It has developed guidance notes and draft bank recovery and resolution plans to assist with its advice to national authorities for implementing the FSB *Principles for Cross-Border Cooperation on Crisis Management*.[42] It has established *Principles for Sound Compensation Practices*,[43] and has coordinated with other international financial bodies such as IOSCO to develop a consistent regulatory framework for the oversight of hedge funds.[44] It is also overseeing the emergence of national and regional frameworks for the registration, regulation and oversight of credit rating agencies and encouraging countries to engage in bilateral dialogues to resolve home–host country issues, involving inconsistencies and disagreements that may arise because of different regulatory approaches.

To enhance the legitimacy of the FSB standard-setting, the G20 and FSB increased their membership to include 12 additional member countries compared to the previous membership of the Financial Stability Forum and the G10 standard-setting committees. The additional membership includes large developing and emerging market countries, such as China, South Africa, India and Brazil.

Regarding the Basel Committee, when the crisis hit, it started almost immediately to adopt Basel III, a fundamental overhaul of the Basel II capital requirement rules. The G20 London Summit communiqué put the work of the Basel Committee under the oversight of the Financial Stability Board.

Monetary Fund. The representatives of FSB member countries are the same as that of the Basel Committee <www.financialstabilityboard.org/about/overview.htm> accessed 15 January 2015.

39 The list is published at <www.financialstabilityboard.org/cos/key_standards.htm>.

40 Initially, the FSB addressed the significant regulatory gaps in overseeing the failure of banks with cross-border establishments and operations by introducing resolution principles in late 2009 that aimed primarily at controlling systemic risk when a bank fails. Also, banks were required under Basel III to 'move expeditiously' to raise the level and quality of capital, but in a manner that 'promotes stability of national banking systems'.

41 See G20/FSB protocol to establish colleges of supervisors for all major cross-border financial institutions. Reports of the Financial Stability Board to G20 Finance Ministers and Governors, *Overview of Progress in Implementing the London Summit Recommendations for Strengthening Financial Stability* (FSB September Report 2009) 2–3 and (FSB November Report 2009), 13. Other FSB initiatives include its *Principles for Cross-Border Cooperation on Crisis Management* (2 April 2009) <www.financialstabilityboard.org/2009/04/princi ples-for-cross-border-cooperation-on-crisis-management/> accessed 15 January 2015. The Basel Committee and FSB have also established a task force to review the practices of colleges.

42 FSB November 2009 Report (n 42) 14.

43 FSB *Principles for Sound Compensation Practices: Implementation Standards* (25 September 2009) <www. financialstabilityboard.org/wp-content/uploads/r_090925c.pdf?page_moved=1> accessed 15 January 2015.

44 FSB November 2009 Report (n 42) 11–12.

The EU response to the crisis: changes in substantive regulatory reform to implement revised international standards (e.g., Basel III) and a fundamental change in the institutional structure of EU regulation and supervision with the creation of three European Supervisory Authorities, prompted by the experience of the crisis, along with further institutional reforms related to the European Banking Union and the European Central Bank's new power to supervise banks in the euro area. At the national level, most countries reacted unilaterally to the crisis by adjusting their financial regulatory rules and supervisory practices and in the case of the United Kingdom changing the institutional structure of financial regulation.

The design and implementation of macro-prudential oversight and regulation at the international level concerns practical policy and legal issues involving the operation of the newly created FSB and the need for it to adopt effective standards of macro-prudential regulation. The creation of the FSB has not yet demonstrated that it is a meaningful institution for enhancing the macro-prudential focus of international financial regulation. Although the FSB has been engaged with micro-prudential reform issues, its efforts so far do not inspire confidence that more adequate macro-prudential measures are being adopted at the international level.

Consequences of Global Financial Governance Reform

International Reforms

The crisis has led to significant changes in regulatory standards, stricter supervisory practices, and institutional restructuring of financial regulation. Nevertheless, weaknesses remain. Basel III continues to allow global banking groups to use risk-weighted internal models to calculate credit, market and liquidity risks that rely on historic data and risk parameters that are based on individual bank risk exposures and not to systemic risk across the financial system. Although Basel III contains higher core Tier One and Tier One capital requirements, liquidity requirements and a leverage ratio, it remains essentially dependent on risk-weighted models that were proven to be unreliable prior to the crisis because of their disproportionate focus on risk management at the level of the individual firm. As discussed above, the G20 and the Financial Stability Board have adopted the overall objective of reconstructing financial regulation along macro-prudential lines. This requires not only stricter capital and liquidity requirements for individual institutions, but also monitoring risk exposures across the financial system, including the transfer of credit risk to off-balance sheet entities and the general level of risk across the financial system. For example, the G20/FSB objective of requiring systemically significant financial instruments (that is, OTC derivatives) to be traded on exchanges and centrally cleared with central counterparties is an important regulatory innovation to control systemic risk in wholesale securities markets. Also, systemically important financial institutions will be subjected to more intensive prudential regulatory requirements, including higher capital requirements and more scrutiny of their cross-border operations.

In addition, the wide scope of macro-prudential regulation will require a broader definition of prudential supervision to include both *ex ante* supervisory powers, such as licensing, authorization and compliance with regulatory standards, and *ex post* crisis management measures, such as recovery and resolution plans, deposit insurance and lender of last resort. Indeed, the objectives of macro-prudential regulation – to monitor and control systemic risks and related risks across the financial system – will require greater regulatory and supervisory intensity that will necessitate increased intervention in the operations of cross-border banking and financial groups and a wider assessment of the risks they pose. The broad area of recovery and resolution will necessarily involve authorities in restructuring and disposing of banking assets and using taxpayer funds to bail out and provide temporary support for ailing financial institutions.[45]

The exercise of macro-supervision and regulation along with overseeing recovery and resolution programmes will require a greater role for host country authorities to ensure that the risk-taking of cross-border financial groups complies with the host country's macro-prudential objectives. Most host countries will be able to achieve macro-prudential objectives in part by utilizing traditional tools of macro-economic policy – exchange rates, interest rates and fiscal policy – and by applying under certain circumstances, tools of micro-prudential supervision, such as the use of counter-cyclical capital requirements, loan-to-value ratios, and debt-to-income ratios. Moreover, under the FSB/G20 proposals, countries will be expected to intervene in a bank's or financial firm's business practices at an early stage to require prompt corrective action to comply with regulatory requirements and if necessary to alter the organizational structure of the institution by requiring, for instance, that the local operations of a cross-border bank be placed in a separately capitalized subsidiary or independent legal entity so that the local operations of a large systemically important institution could be compelled to undergo a restructuring and/or recapitalization by local authorities. Indeed, a key element of any bank resolution regime is that the local authority can have tools at its disposal to intervene in bank management (ie., restrict dividends), restructure creditor claims or use taxpayer funds to recapitalize a systemically important institution or facilitate the transfer of assets to a private purchaser in a bank insolvency.

Environmental Risks and Banking Stability

An important question arises whether international financial regulation adequately addresses systemic environmental risks – for example, the macro-prudential economic risks associated with the banking sector's exposure to high carbon and other fossil fuel assets.[46] As discussed above, Basel III has already taken important steps to address both micro-prudential and macro-prudential systemic risks in the banking sector by increasing capital and liquidity requirements and requiring regulators to challenge banks more in the construction of their risk models and for banks to undergo more frequent and demanding stress tests. Moreover, under Pillar 2, banks must undergo a supervisory review of their corporate governance and risk management practices that aims, among other things, to diversify risk exposures across asset classes and to detect macro-prudential risks across the financial sector. Regarding environmental risks, Basel III already requires banks to assess the impact of specific environmental risks on the bank's credit and operational risks exposures, but these are mainly transaction-specific risks

---

45 Indeed, the FSB has stated in its *Key Attributes of Effective Resolution Regimes for Financial Institutions* that: '[t]o improve a firm's resolvability, supervisory authorities or resolution authorities should have powers to require, where necessary, the adoption of appropriate measures, such as changes to a firm's business practices, structure or organisation . . . To enable the continued operations of systemically important functions, authorities should evaluate whether to require that these functions be segregated in legally and operationally independent entities that are shielded from group problems' FSB Key Attribute 10.5 <www.financialstabilityboard. org/2014/10/r_141015/> accessed 15 January 2015.

46 The challenge of addressing environmental systemic risks was first introduced in the literature by an empirical report authored by Kern Alexander entitled 'Stability and Sustainability in Banking Reform: Are Environmental Risks Missing in Basel III?' (UNEP/CUP September 2014).

that affect the borrower's ability to repay a loan or address the 'deep pockets' doctrine of lender liability for damages and the cost of property clean-up. These transaction-specific risks are narrowly defined and do not constitute broader macro-prudential or portfolio-wide risks for the bank that could arise from its exposure to systemic environmental risks.

Recent research suggests that Basel III is not being used to its full capacity to address systemic environmental risks and that such risks are in the 'collective blind spot of bank supervisors'.[47] Despite the fact that history demonstrates direct and indirect links between systemic environmental risks and banking sector stability and that evidence suggests this trend will continue to become more pronounced and complex as environmental sustainability risks grow for the global economy, Basel III has yet to take explicit account of, and therefore only marginally addresses, the environmental risks that could threaten banking sector stability.

Nevertheless, some international standard-setting groups are taking the lead in addressing environmental and social risks in the banking and other financial sectors. The Sustainability Banking Network (SBN) of the International Finance Corporation – consisting of bank regulators of developing and emerging market countries, China, Brazil and Peru, and a number of large banking groups and financial institutions – have adopted standards of bank corporate governance that incorporate environmental and social risk controls into the institution's risk governance strategy. Under the SBN guidelines, bank supervisors in participating jurisdictions have engaged in a variety of innovative regulatory and market practices to control environmental systemic risks and to adopt practices that mitigate the banking sector's exposure to environmentally unsustainable activity and related social risks. A defining feature of the SBN is that its membership largely consists of regulatory officials and financial institution representatives from developing and emerging market countries and that none of their members are from central banks or other regulatory authorities of the G10 advanced industrial countries. This has allowed the SBN to define itself in a unique way by emphasizing innovative and forward-looking regulatory approaches that address in many instances broader stakeholder interests related to the environmental and social drivers of risk in the financial sector and the relationship with financial stability and sustainability.

SBN regulatory members – including Brazil, China and India – have been concerned with how prudential bank regulation affects the green economy and inequality in society. Their regulatory initiatives have been based on existing regulatory mandates in Basel III to promote financial stability by identifying, monitoring and managing banking risks both at the transaction-specific level and at the broader portfolio level. What is significant about these various country and market practices is that the regulatory approaches used to enhance the bank's risk assessment fall into two areas: (1) Greater interaction between the regulator and the bank in assessing wider portfolio level financial, social and political risks, and (2) banks' enhanced disclosure to the market regarding their exposures to systemic environmental risks. These innovative regulatory approaches and market practices are the result of proactive policy-makers and regulators adjusting to a changing world. Other international bodies, such as the United Nations Finance Initiative, have sought to promote further dialogue between practitioners and regulators on environmental sustainability issues and to encourage a better understanding of these issues by financial regulators.[48]

---

47 ibid.
48 See United Nations Environment Programme Finance Initiative, 'Inquiry into the Design of a Sustainable Financial System' (23 January 2014) <www.unep.org/inquiry/portals/50215/Inquiry_expanded.pdf> accessed 15 January 2015.

Although the Basel Committee has formed a committee to address certain areas of social risks, such as financial inclusion,[49] it (and other international financial bodies) has not addressed larger environmental and social risk governance concerns. China, Brazil and Peru, among others, are examples of countries, acting under the guidance of the SBN, that have embarked on innovative risk assessment programmes to assess systemic environmental risks from a macro-prudential perspective as they recognize the materiality of systemic environmental risks to banking stability. These state practices should be linked to and coordinated with the work of the traditional international financial standard-setting bodies, such as the Basel Committee.

Conclusion

The global financial crisis of 2007–2008 has called into question the efficacy of the traditional global financial governance model's flexible and unstructured decision-making framework and in particular has raised concerns regarding the accountability and legitimacy of the IFI standard-setting processes. The discussion of the international financial standard-setting bodies' efforts in this area and the need for them to be more inclusive in their membership suggests that international financial regulation should be more accountable and legitimate in how it is developed. Moreover, it suggests that the flawed economic policies and regulatory practices of the G10 advanced industrial countries do not provide sustainable models for economic and financial development. This means that the development of global financial regulation should be influenced more by countries outside the traditional G10 power structure and the regulatory standards should address broader risk factors – environmental and social risks – that can have a significant effect on financial stability thereby contributing to more sustainable economic growth and financial development. The overall message – welcomed in many reform circles – is that economic policy-makers should consider building institutional mechanisms that transcend national borders which establish solidarity between the financial sector and all parts of society that are affected by financial risk-taking.

---

49 See generally, Basel Committee on Banking Supervision, Range of practice in the regulation and supervision of institutions relevant to financial inclusion', (January, 2015) Basel: BIS.

3 Do We Need a World Financial Organization?[*]

Rosa Maria Lastra[**]

Introduction

The quest for international financial regulation looks into the future of finance by considering both the present and the past. The past, because history matters; institutions and laws are creatures of their times. [In the words of Jorge Santayana, 'those who cannot remember the past are condemned to repeat it'[1]]. Economists refer to this as path dependency. The present, because the issues surrounding banking and financial reform are no longer only the domain of the specialist: after the financial crisis, they have come to the forefront of economic and policy debate.

Confidence and trust are preconditions for a market economy to function efficiently (the term credit comes from the Latin *credere*: to trust, to believe), and such trust that underlies all transactions, that is the foundation of enterprise and development, is supported by a legal framework. That markets need rules to function well has been argued by Ronald Coase[2] and Douglass North,[3] both Nobel Laureates. But long before Coase and North, the importance

[*] This chapter was originally published as an article with the same title 'Do we need a World Financial Organization?' by the *Journal of International Economic Law* (2014) 17(4) 787–805.

[**] Rosa M Lastra is Professor of International Financial and Monetary Law at Queen Mary University of London. The first draft of this chapter was prepared for the Symposium held in Washington DC on 16 November 2012 in honour of Professor John H Jackson. The chapter draws on the ideas that led to the Special Issue of the Journal of International Economic Law (September 2010), published by OUP in 2012 as a book edited by John Jackson, Thomas Cottier and myself, entitled *International Law in Financial Regulation and Monetary Affairs* and upon the ideas presented in my Inaugural Lecture on 23 March 2011. Some of these ideas have been also further developed in an edited volume with Thomas Cottier, Christian Tietje and Lucia Satragno, *The Rule of Law in Monetary Affairs*, World Trade Forum, published by CUP, 2014; and in the volume *International Financial and Monetary Law* (the second edition of *Legal Foundations of International Monetary Stability*), by OUP in 2015. I would also like to acknowledge the comments received from the participants in the Seminar on Financial and Monetary Law held at the Bank of England on 16 May 2014 and from the participants in the conference on 'The Reform of International Economic Governance' organized by the University of Granada on 9 October 2014. I admire John Jackson's vision, his fresh original approach to international economic law and his enthusiasm for exploring new legal issues; and I also greatly appreciate his humanity, friendship and the warm hospitality that he and Joan have always extended to me.

1 Jorge Santayana, *Reason in Common Sense*, vol 1 of The Life of Reason (1905, repr Charles Schribners' Sons 1920).

2 See Ronald H Coase, *The Firm, the Market and the Law* (The University of Chicago Press 1988). This book is a collection of Coase's main papers, including his two seminal articles: 'The Nature of the Firm' (1937) and 'The Problem of Social Cost' (1960).

3 See Douglass C North, *Institutions, Institutional Change and Economic Performance* (CUP 1990).

of the law for functioning markets had been recognized. Adam Smith, the founding father of economics as an autonomous subject, wrote in 1776:

> Commerce . . . can seldom flourish long in any state which does not enjoy a regular administration of justice, in which the people do not feel themselves secure in the possession of their property, in which the faith of contracts is not supported by the law, and in which the authority of the state is not supposed to be regularly employed in enforcing the payment of debts from all those who are able to pay.[4]

The law, after all, is about setting boundaries for personal and collective behaviour. But beyond the basic laws that support a market economy and provide stability, continuity and predictability of contract and property rights, the case for banking and financial regulation requires additional justification. It is the existence of market failures and deficiencies, notably negative externalities and information asymmetries that provides the rationale of regulation.[5]

The remainder of this chapter is organized as follows: first, we examine the rationale of international regulation and discuss the inadequacy of the principle of sovereignty for the regulation of cross-border financial institutions. Then, we survey the current status quo, characterized by the coexistence of national law and institutions and global financial markets. Finally, we consider the emerging *lex financiera* and debate the need for a World Financial Organization (WFO).

Why International Regulation?

The quest for international law in money and finance is a logical response to the increasing globalization of financial markets. It is also a response to the need to prevent and contain contagious systemic risk, a risk that does not respect geographic boundaries. The crisis showed that national financial markets cannot be looked at in isolation. A fragmented global regulatory and accounting regime gives rise to regulatory arbitrage ('forum shopping'), loopholes and shadow institutions and markets; it also increases transaction costs and can lead to financial protectionism. Incompatible or conflicting rules from country to country increase the regulatory costs and can create new risks. Regulatory competition can also lead to a race to the bottom. And since international problems emerged as a consequence of domestic failures, an extra argument for international regulation is that it can be a backstop to domestic regulation (a point which has been made by Howard Davies, first chairman of the now defunct FSA).

Globalization has changed the traditional understanding of financial markets and has led to the emergence of multinational banks, financial groups and new instruments and markets that

---

4 Adam Smith, *An Inquiry into the Nature and Causes of the Wealth of Nations*, Book V, III 'Of Public Debts' (repr in 2009 by Digireads.com Publishing) 546.

5 Externalities are the costs to society of banking failures. And, indeed, the costs to society of a crisis are very large – as we know from recent experience – and, by far, exceed the private costs to individual financial institutions; that is why a key aim of regulation should be to internalize these externalities. Information asymmetries or deficiencies – a feature of the services industry in general – refers to the fact that the provider of the service knows much more than the consumer of the service. In banking these problems are particularly acute and the phenomenon of bank runs is well known. The aim of banking and financial laws is to protect individuals (depositors, investors, policy-holders), to ensure the smooth conduct of the business (fair, efficient and transparent markets) and to safeguard the payment system and the stability of the financial system at large, preventing and containing systemic risk and systemic crises.

operate across jurisdictions. Financial globalization was fostered by financial innovation, the technological revolution, the integration and liberalization of markets, the mobility of people and capital and other factors.

But the global financial market is not a huge global homogeneous market. It is more like a spider's web or a radial web with multiple interconnections and linkages,[6] in which local markets permeate each other and in which a few players dominate the scene. The size or importance of some of these players (the term SIFIs or systemically significant financial institutions is now in vogue) is a source of concern globally and nationally.[7] The dangers of SIFIs remind me of the image of the baobabs in *The Little Prince*:

> There were some terrible seeds on the planet that was the home of the little prince, and these were the seeds of the baobab . . . A baobab is something you will never be able to get rid of if you attend to it too late. It spreads over the entire planet . . . And if the planet is too small and the baobabs are too many, they split it into pieces . . . After explaining how he cleaned the seeds of the baobabs everyday he added: 'Sometimes, there is no harm in putting off a piece of work until another day. But when it is a matter of baobabs, that always means a catastrophe. I knew a planet that was inhabited by a lazy man. He neglected three little bushes . . .' *So, as the little prince described it to me, I have made a drawing of that planet. I do not much like to take the tone of a moralist. But the danger of the baobabs is so little understood, and such considerable risks would be run by anyone who might get lost on an asteroid, that for once I am breaking through my reserve . . . I say plainly, 'watch out for the baobabs.'* (Antoine du Saint-Exupéry, *The Little Prince*)

Globalization has magnified the impact and geographic outreach of systemic risk. And the globalization and liberalization of financial markets have proceeded at a much faster pace than the development of an appropriate international legal and institutional framework.

Though the financial crisis was global, the solutions to the mounting problems were mostly national. Some of these solutions – including unprecedented liquidity assistance and massive government support and intervention – have been quite extraordinary and, in the absence of adequate laws, emergency legislation or new rules were expeditiously introduced in several countries. Using an analogy with fire departments, while every effort was made to extinguish the fire during the crisis, in the aftermath of the financial crisis we need to re-examine the fire regulations and to consider how well (or how badly) the institutions did. In many cases we may conclude that the adequate response is not necessarily more regulation, but better supervision and enforcement or greater transparency or better international coordination. We should also beware of the excesses of regulation and the dangers of over-regulating a given sector or type of institutions, creating incentives for businesses to move outside the regulatory framework. Any regulatory perimeter brings its own shadows and loopholes. We must also be mindful of the question of competition. Regulation and liberalization are not always companions; at times, they are antagonists.

---

6 Andrew Haldane of the Bank of England has looked at the lessons that ecology, epidemiology and genetics provide in order to understand financial networks and complex financial systems. See for example <www.bankofengland. co.uk/archive/Documents/historicpubs/speeches/2009/speech386.pdf>.

7 If banks are able to borrow at artificially low rates because creditors do not believe that they will be allowed to fail, this encourages moral hazard. See generally Rosa Lastra, 'Systemic Risk, SIFIs and Financial Stability' (2011) 6 *Capital Markets Law Journal* 197.

Sovereignty and International Financial Markets

In order to understand what making rules international means, and why such rules are needed, we should review the evolution of the notion of sovereignty.[8]

Sovereignty is the supreme power within a territory, the territory of the nation state. Thus, sovereignty has a territorial dimension, and the government is the political institution in which sovereignty is embodied. Sovereignty forms part of the fundamental principles of international law and is a key organizing concept of international relations. But it is a principle rooted in history. The modern understanding of the attributes of sovereignty was developed in the Renaissance. Indeed, politics operated without this organizing principle in the Middle Ages.

When it comes to modern financial markets, sovereignty is an inadequate principle to deal with financial conglomerates, complex groups and, generally, with cross-border institutions and markets. It is not a good principle to deal with crisis management either, nor with the home/host country divide. Indeed, like a tsunami that does not respect territorial borders, the effects of a financial crisis spread beyond geographic frontiers. You cannot fight it only with national measures. In some parts of our modern life we need to move beyond national sovereignty.

A different view is held by Dani Rodrik, who argues that we cannot have 'deep economic integration' (he uses the terms 'hyper-globalization'), national sovereignty (nation state) and democratic politics all at once.[9] We can have at most two out of three. Since democracy cannot be compromised, and he rejects the 'global governance' option, he proposes a return to national sovereignty. He considers that 'global standards and regulations are not just impractical; they are undesirable. The democratic legitimacy constraint ensures that global governance will result in the lowest common denominator, a regime of weak and ineffectual rules'.[10] Interestingly Rodrik contends (in chapter 11) that markets need other institutions to support them, notably courts of justice, legal arrangements to enforce property rights, and regulations to rein in abuse and fix market failures, since 'markets do not create, regulate, stabilize or sustain themselves' and he points out that 'what is true of domestic markets is true also of global ones'. The logical extension of his argument (which would contradict a basic tenet of the book, Rodrik's choice to solve the 'trilemma') is that if national markets need adequate national rules, international markets need adequate international rules. This would mean that national sovereignty, rather than global governance, should be sacrificed in order to solve the 'trilemma'. And, in my opinion, this is the best solution to the trilemma.

Financial markets transcend national boundaries (though in the last four years we have been experiencing a substantial de-globalization or renationalization of financial markets), and so do financial stability and systemic risk. It may actually be in the best interests of

---

8 See generally John Jackson, 'Sovereignty – Modern: A New Approach to an Outdated Concept' (2003) 97 *American Journal of International Law* 782, reprinted in Georgetown, The Scholarly Commons (2003) <http://scholarship. law.georgetown.edu/facpub/110/> accessed 15 January 2015. See also Rosa Lastra, *Legal Foundations of International Monetary Stability* (OUP 2006) ch 1; Dan Sarooshi, International Organizations and Their Exercise of Sovereign Powers (OUP 2005); and Claus Zimmermann, *A Contemporary Concept of Monetary Sovereignty* (OUP 2013).

9 See Dani Rodrik, *The Globalization Paradox: Democracy and the Future of the World Economy* (WW Norton & Co 2011) 200–201. See Rosa Lastra, 'Book Review of Dani Rodrik's *The Globalization Paradox: Democracy and the Future of the World Economy*' (2013) 11 *International Journal of Constitutional Law* 809–12.

10 Rodrik (n 9) 204.

countries to pool sovereignty in this area. Drawing on the lessons of history, it was in the context of the Second World War that countries were ready to make the sacrifices needed in terms of sovereignty by signing a number of international treaties that gave rise to international organizations such as the United Nations, the International Monetary Fund (IMF) and the World Bank. John Maynard Keynes had wisely stated that in order to win the war we needed to 'win the peace'. It was this understanding that also inspired Henry Morgenthau (then US Treasury Secretary) to proclaim in the opening remarks of the Bretton Woods conference in New Hampshire in July 1944 that 'prosperity like peace is indivisible'.[11] Neither Keynes nor Morgenthau was thinking only in territorial/national terms: they were thinking in international terms. Following John Jackson's notion of 'sovereignty-modern', we should:

> disaggregate and . . . break down the complex array of 'sovereignty' concepts and examine particular aspects in detail and with precision to understand what is actually at play. A major part of this approach is to understand the pragmatic functionalism of the allocation of power as between different levels of governance entities in the world. To the extent feasible, this should be done in a manner not biased either in favour of or against international approaches.[12]

The doctrine of multilayered governance, which discusses the allocation of powers at the national, regional and international levels, provides a template to address some of these issues. The challenge is to identify the criteria under which financial regulatory powers should be allocated (who decides what) and the different layers that are needed as well as the links between the different international and supra-national structures and spill-over effects. For example, in the context of the extraordinary measures undertaken by central banks to combat the crisis (national measures with cross-border effects) the debate about 'currency wars' has been recently rekindled.[13]

Financial markets need to rely on different levels of governance. An analogy with football (soccer) can be instructive in this regard. There are domestic leagues, ruled by national football associations, there is in Europe a Champions League governed by UEFA, and

---

11 See generally Rosa Lastra, *Legal Foundations of International Monetary Stability* (OUP 2006) ch 12. For a recent study see Ben Steil, *The Battle of Bretton Woods: John Maynard Keynes, Harry Dexter White, and the Making of a New World Order* (Council on Foreign Relations Books, Princeton University Press 2013).

12 Jackson (n 8) 801.

13 The phrase 'currency war' was coined by Brazilian Minister of Finance Guido Mantega in 2010. The issue, however, is not new. Competitive currency devaluations have pernicious effects upon the economic relations between states, in particular upon their trading relations. Through the abandonment of the par value regime (original art IV) the IMF lost the jurisdictional power over exchange rates: Since the entry into force of the Second Amendment, the Fund has no substantive legal rights with respect to the choice of exchange rate arrangements of its members. But exchange rates were and are a key focus of art IV consultations and art IV prohibits currency manipulation. Art XV of GATT provides the legal link between the IMF and WTO (and it was not amended following the collapse of the par value regime). Art XV establishes that 'the contracting parties shall not, by exchange actions, frustrate the intent of the provisions of this agreement, nor by trade action, the intent of the provisions of the Articles of Agreement of the IMF'. See generally Vera Thorstensen, Daniel Ramos and Carolina Muller, 'The "missing link" between the WTO and the IMF' (2013) 16 *Journal of International Economic Law* 353. In a working paper of 2013 entitled 'The (Mis)Alignment of the Trade and Monetary Legal Orders', Gregory Shaffer and Michael Waibel claim that 'While trade in goods, and to a lesser extent trade in services, are highly regulated by legal rules backed by an enforcement mechanism, currency valuation is now determined by the discretionary activities of central banks and treasury departments run largely by economists with little to no guidance from law'.

finally – though this is a competition among countries not clubs – there is FIFA and the World Cup. Some institutions play locally, while others compete in the European or global stage.

Banking union in the EU is a recognition of this need at a regional level. Banking union is based upon three pillars. The first pillar is 'single supervision', with the establishment of the Single Supervisory Mechanism (SSM). 'Single supervision' in the context of banking union means European supervision (conferred upon the European Central Bank, ECB) for credit institutions of eurozone Member States and of non-eurozone EU Member States that choose to become part of the SSM.[14] The second pillar is 'single resolution', with a Single Resolution Mechanism (SRM)[15] – aligned with the EU Bank Recovery and Resolution Directive (BRRD)[16] – and a Single Resolution Fund. The third pillar is 'common deposit protection'.[17] The jurisdictional area of banking union comprises the eurozone Member States and those other Member States that establish close cooperation arrangements.[18]

We need to identify the functions (or sub-functions) that require a supra-national or international structure and the functions that are best left at the national level. When it comes to financial markets, there are three key functions that are necessary to achieve the elusive goal of financial stability and these are: regulation (or rule-making), supervision (risk control, monitoring and compliance) and crisis management (lender of last resort, deposit insurance, resolution and insolvency). A global banking and financial system requires some binding international rules, efficient supervision, and an international system for the resolution of conflicts and crises. Effective enforcement though remains the greatest challenge at the international level, since enforcement mechanisms have traditionally been nationally based, a logical extension of the principle of sovereignty. But we need to seek new ways of enforcement. In the current process of globalization, the state is finding it increasingly difficult to enforce its laws against global actors such as multinational corporations and criminal organizations; tax laws are a case in point. Resolving conflicts is also diverging from the state's judicial machinery to private bodies through the increasing popularity of arbitration as an alternative dispute resolution mechanism. Even in the area of policing, the state is enlisting the private

---

14 Council Regulation (EU) No 1024/2013 of 15 October 2013 conferring specific tasks on the European Central Bank concerning policies relating to the prudential supervision of credit institutions [2013] OJ L287/63, commonly referred to as SSM Regulation.

15 Regulation (EU) No 806/2014 of the European Parliament and of the Council of 15 July 2014 establishing uniform rules and a uniform procedure for the resolution of credit institutions and certain investment firms in the framework of a Single Resolution Mechanism and a Single Resolution Fund and amending Regulation (EU) No 1093/2010 [2014] OJ L225/1.

16 Directive 2014/59/EU of the European Parliament and of the Council of 15 May 2014 establishing a framework for the recovery and resolution of credit institutions and investment firms and amending Council Directive 82/891/EEC, and Directives 2001/24/EC, 2002/47/EC, 2004/25/EC, 2005/56/EC, 2007/36/EC, 2011/35/EU, 2012/30/EU and 2013/36/EU, and Regulations (EU) No 1093/2010 and (EU) No 648/2012, of the European Parliament and of the Council, Text with EEA relevance [2014] OJ L173/190.

17 Although a single deposit guarantee scheme shall not be established for the time being (we will continue to rely upon the existing networks of national deposit guarantee schemes) a new Directive on Deposit Guarantee Schemes repealing Directive 94/19/EC was adopted by the Council and the European Parliament in April 2014, Directive 2014/49/EU of the European Parliament and of the Council of 16 April 2014 on deposit guarantee schemes (recast), Text with EEA relevance [2014] OJ L173/149.

18 For an analysis of the uneasy coexistence between banking union and single market see Rosa Lastra, 'Banking Union and Single Market: Conflict or Companionship?' (2013) 36 *Fordham International Law Journal* 1190. See also Eilis Ferran, 'European Banking Union and the EU Single Financial Market: More Differentiated Integration, or Disintegration?' (18 April 2014) University of Cambridge Faculty of Law Research Paper No 29/2014 <http://ssrn.com/abstract=2426580> accessed 15 January 2015.

sector in the fight against crime. Money laundering control systems and the reporting duties they impose on financial institutions are examples of this shift towards private policing.

The other major challenge to advance towards international solutions is, of course, the fiscal issue, in particular the establishment of adequate *ex ante* burden sharing arrangements in a crisis.

National Institutions and International Financial Markets

We still rely to a large extent upon national institutions. Amongst them, the central bank continues to play a key role in the monetary and financial system. I have written elsewhere that central banks inhabit a 'world of policy' and that the law has generally played a limited role in central bank operations.[19]

Central banking has evolved significantly throughout its relatively short history, from the time in which the Swedish Riksbank (1668) and the Bank of England (1694) were set up, to central banks in contemporary times. While the original rationale for the establishment of the first central banks was to be a bank that was awarded privileges by the government to issue currency and that was expected to finance the government needs (mostly in war time), this rationale has changed over time. The Federal Reserve System (the Fed) was founded in 1913, following the banking crisis of 1907, to safeguard the soundness of banks and to fulfil other objectives. The twin mandate of central banks has typically been stable money and sound banking (today we say monetary stability and financial stability), though the vicissitudes of history have given a greater emphasis to some functions and objectives in response to economic circumstances. The Bundesbank was set up in 1957 primarily as a monetary institution to preserve price stability (hyperinflation during the interwar period had left a long-lasting dislike for inflation amongst the German public and politicians). The advent of central bank independence as a means to achieve price stability consolidated the role of central banks as monetary institutions in the 1990s and beginning of the twenty-first century. The Bundesbank model of the central bank as a monetary policy institution became the functional model for the European System of Central Banks when it was established in 1999. The ECB was conceived in the Maastricht Treaty as a monetary authority and the treaty provisions are clear both as to the primacy of the price stability mandate and as to the independence of the institution.

The financial crisis 2007–2009 – a rude awakening in so many areas – brought the importance of the financial stability mandate of central banks back to the fore, in particular their lender of last resort role.[20] And in the European context, the events of the last few years stretched to the limit what the European Central Bank can do under the Treaty and exposed the deficiencies of institutional design.[21] For example, with the adoption in May 2010 of the controversial Securities Markets Programme to purchase government bonds, the ECB

---

19 Rosa Lastra, *International Financial and Monetary Law* (OUP 2015) ch 2 ('Central Banking'). This book is the second edition of *Legal Foundations of International Monetary Stability*.

20 The financial crisis also exposed the limitations of too narrow a focus. In line with Goodhart's law (any observed statistical regularity will tend to collapse once pressure is placed upon it for control purposes), the measurement of inflation largely ignored asset prices, in particular house prices, thus being unable to identify and combat the 'elephant in the room', that is a large asset price bubble that eventually burst in August 2007.

21 They have also exposed the deficiencies in terms of legitimacy and accountability. Institutions and laws cannot survive without societal legitimacy, without the support of the general public. This is the greatest challenge for the goal of European integration.

entered into unchartered territory. The no-bail-out clause, the sovereign debt problems in Greece and other peripheral EU Member States, fiscal constraints, uncoordinated national measures, and other banking and financial problems – from Iceland to Ireland, from Portugal to Spain – have resulted in a number of measures, reform packages and initiatives trying to address the weakness of the 'E' of EMU, the weakness of its economic/fiscal pillar.[22] These changes are also symptomatic of an underlying trend, the federalization of financial supervision and of crisis management. This process of federalization requires adequate coordination between different levels of governance and a careful analysis of which functions should remain at the national level (in accordance with the principle of subsidiarity) and which functions should be federalized.

The problems of coordination between federal and national (state) structures and organizations are not new; indeed, they have characterized the design of financial regulation and supervision in the US. Federal law prevails in securities, while insurance has traditionally been a matter of state law and banking offers a mix of federal and state powers. Over the years, however, there has been a process of federalization in the supervision and crisis management of financial institutions, with the latest addition, the Dodd–Frank Act of 2010, substantially increasing federal powers for any financial institution that is deemed to be systemically significant. Lender of last resort was federalized in 1913 with the Federal Reserve Act, while the Federal Deposit Insurance Corporation (FDIC) was established in 1933. The experience in the US offers interesting lessons for the EU, with the centralization of banking policy (via banking union) and the increasing federalization of financial supervision in other sectors of the financial system.[23]

The Emerging *Lex Financiera*

Globalization and regionalization (the latter in particular in the EU) have challenged the traditional law-making process. The financial crisis exposed the limitations of relying upon a loose network of soft-law standard-setters and an inadequate system of resolution of financial crises. In order to understand the development of the emerging *lex financiera* it is useful to offer some reflections about the evolution of law.

Formal law has often been born out of the development of informal law. This is not a new phenomenon. It is a recurrent feature in the history of law. The evolution of international law and of commercial law, to cite two relevant examples, provides clear evidence in this regard. The primary sources of international law are conventional law (treaty law), customary law and the general principles of law, as recognized by article 38 of the Statute of the International Court of Justice. Customary international law results when states follow certain practices generally and consistently. Customary law, however, can evolve into conventional law. Indeed, important principles of customary international law have become codified in the Vienna Convention of the Law of the Treaties, thus acquiring the characteristic of 'conventional law'.

The birth and development of formal commercial law was influenced by the medieval *lex mercatoria*, that is by the mercantile codes and customs which reflected the usages of

---

22 See generally Rosa Lastra and Jean Victor Louis, 'European Economic and Monetary Union: History, Trends and Prospects' (2013) *Yearbook of European Law* 1 <http://yel.oxfordjournals.org/content/early/2013/03/27/yel. yet003.full.pdf>.

23 See generally ch 4 in Thomas Cottier, Rosa Lastra, Christian Tietje and Lucia Satragno (co-edited book), *The Rule of Law in Monetary Affairs* (CUP 2014).

trade, the international maritime and commercial practice at the time. Many of the uncodified usages of trade that constituted the *lex mercatoria* eventually became formal law.[24]

The emerging *lex financiera* is similar to the *lex mercatoria* in its international character. The development of international financial law has been a slow and patchy phenomenon because of three reasons: (1) the lack of a clear legal mandate; (2) a reactive rather than a proactive character; and (3) the vested interests national governments have in the supervision and regulation of their financial sectors. The lack of a clear legal mandate raises important issues of legitimacy and accountability. The reactive nature, the fact that we appear to always be fighting the last war haunts regulation. And the national vested interests are again behind the reluctance to further liberalize and integrate financial markets.

Some may argue that certain national laws can be exported or transplanted into other jurisdictions on the basis of their intrinsic superiority (the case for common law is often made in finance). That is surely one way in which the *lex financiera* can progress. But there are other ways of achieving legislative convergence, such as rule harmonization via conventions, model laws, soft-law rules or standards, or the centralization of regulatory functions in a common authority to which responsibility in this area is transferred.

International financial regulation so far has proceeded through the harmonization route, and has done so via soft law. Soft law is law[25] though, as opposed to hard law, it is informal and does not rely on traditional mechanisms of enforcement. Typically soft law standards must be adopted into national law (or other hard law legislative instruments such as EU Directives and Regulations) in order to become enforceable. Observance is to soft law what enforcement is to hard law. Yet, the imposition of 'sanctions' in the case of non-observance remains a formidable challenge. One way of tackling this problem could be the conditioning of market access on the basis of compliance with some international rules.

Over time, though, we should also expect a degree of formalization of the emerging *lex financiera* in line with the evolution of law generally.

Do We Need a WFO?

Institutions and laws are creatures of their times. In the words of Justice Oliver Wendell Holmes, a page of history is worth a volume of logic.[26] The debate about the need for a WFO is based upon the premise that our times need a new order. We live in a family of nations and we

---

24 Sir Roy Goode recalls in his writings that the *lex mercatoria* or law merchant (which was international rather than English and which was administered by its own mercantile courts) was given full recognition by the common law courts (absorbed in the common law itself). The fertility of the business mind and the fact that a practice which begins life by having no legal force acquires over time the sanctity of law are key factors to which the commercial and financial lawyer must continually be responsive. Roy Goode, *Commercial Law* (2nd edn, Penguin Books 1995) 3.

25 As explained in ch 14 of Rosa Lastra (n 8): 'Soft law is indeed law (rules of an informal nature, but yet rules). International financial soft law is often well suited to the changing needs and rapidly evolving structures that characterize the workings of financial markets. It would be wrong to dismiss it because of its "softness" . . . Indeed, one can argue that there is hard "soft law" (eg the international standards on money laundering, ie the Forty Recommendations on Money Laundering and the Nine Special Recommendations on Terrorist Financing by the Financial Action Task Force, with specific measures that countries should have in place covering their criminal justice, law enforcement, and financial regulatory systems) and soft "hard law" (eg treaties dealing with economic integration in West Africa, such as the 1975 and 1993 ECOWAS Treaties, notorious for their lack of enforcement).'

26 New York Trust *Co v* Eisner — 256 U.S. 345 (1921).

have public international law to regulate the relations between nation states as well as a set of international organizations to govern such relations.[27] Some areas of international law are quite developed, for example the law of the sea. In the field of international economic law, the three main pillars of economic relations between states – money, trade and foreign investment – are supported by a different legal regime. The regime in trade is multilateral with the World Trade Organization (WTO) providing an adequate system of international rules and dispute settlement. The regime in foreign investment is mostly bilateral (and what glues it together is arbitration). The regime in finance still relies mostly on national law and soft law.

In finance we have a 'black hole' with few formal international rules and no adequate system to deal with cross-border crisis or conflicts. We may think there has been a proliferation of rules, but in fact we have very few formal international rules. Why this 'black hole'?[28] This is due, in part, to the belief – widespread before the crisis – that financial markets are best left to their own devices and that therefore soft law was sufficient. Indeed, the fact that the legal framework appeared to be lagging behind or even not to play a major role in the development of international finance was considered by many as a rather good state of affairs pre-2007 (even though at the national level, financial markets are heavily regulated). And this 'black hole' is also due to the reticence that nation states have to make the sacrifices that are needed in terms of national sovereignty to agree upon international solutions. Additionally, there are also serious legal and fiscal constraints, notably the lack of *ex ante* burden sharing arrangements at the international level. And lest we forget, 'he who pays the piper calls the tune'.

But things can change very rapidly. Indeed, events such as the 'Arab spring' remind us of how the wind of change can topple regimes and structures in a matter of weeks. It took a major debacle – the great financial crisis of 2007–2009 – to shatter some of the pre-existing assumptions. However, the window for change closes quickly once a crisis no longer seems acute.

In order to address the challenges of our times, we must design an appropriate international institutional framework. As stated above, a global banking and financial system requires some binding international rules (regulation), efficient supervision or surveillance, and an international system for the resolution of conflicts and crises. These are the functions for which we need a WFO.

The functional debate is particularly important because a WFO (or several WFOs) should not become some sort of global regulatory leviathan. For example, if we agree that we need rules on cross-border resolution, or rules with regard to capital movements, or guidance on remuneration, who is going to enforce such rules? We lack an effective mechanism to ensure the consistent application of global financial rules.

---

27 The 'School of Salamanca' (Salamanca being my home town in Spain) is the name applied to a group of Spanish jurists, theologians and philosophers who created a body of doctrine on natural, international and economic law, rooted in the intellectual work of Francisco de Vitoria, who started teaching in Salamanca in 1526 on the *catedra de prima*, the most important chair of theology at the university. The role of the School of Salamanca in the development of early monetary theory has been documented in the work of Marjorie Grice-Hutchinson. While at the LSE, Marjorie came under the influence of Friedrich von Hayek, who urged her to study the manuscripts of this group of Spanish scholars from the sixteenth and early seventeenth century. Her monograph, 'School of Salamanca: Readings in Spanish Monetary Theory, 1544–1605', was published by Clarendon Press, Oxford in 1952.

28 As explained in the special issue of the *Journal of International Economic Law* of 2010 (co-edited with John Jackson and Thomas Cottier) on 'The Quest for International Law in Financial Regulation and Monetary Affairs' (2010) 13(3).

The quest for international law in finance should commence with an appropriate system for cross-border resolution and insolvency of financial institutions on the one hand, and a mechanism for the resolution of sovereign debt crises. In the aftermath of Lehman Brothers, no one wishes another chaotic resolution. The alternative, a 'bail-out' package, is equally unpalatable. There is, however, a viable solution between chaos and bail-out and that is an orderly resolution, as proposed in the FSB Key Attributes of Effective Resolution Regimes for Financial Institutions of October 2011[29] and in the EU Bank Directive on Recovery and Resolution.[30]

As regards the resolution of sovereign debt crises there is no international bankruptcy court nor a transnational sovereign bankruptcy regime or code that will permit sovereign borrowers to obtain debt relief when their financial obligations outstrip their ability to pay without worrying about hostile creditor actions. In order to solve this problem, four policy options have been put forward:[31] (1) a voluntary contractual regime based on collective action clauses; (2) a limited statutory regime based on a model law/statute, a treaty or an amendment to the IMF Articles of Agreement; (3) a wider statutory regime, akin to the Sovereign Debt Restructuring Mechanism (SDRM) proposals,[32] possibly giving a role to the IMF and (4) a less protective regime strengthening creditors' positions and diluting protections for insolvency states. The eurozone debt crisis and the Argentine litigation evidenced the need for clear rules in this field.

In addition to an adequate dispute resolution to provide predictability and consistency in the management of cross-border banking crises and sovereign debt crises, we also need better macro-prudential supervision (monitoring the health of the forest and not just the health of individual trees) to identify systemic risk.[33] Such macro-prudential supervision requires effective coordination between the different regional or national committees or councils in charge of financial stability.[34]

The regulatory function at the international level is currently shared by a variety of actors, including formal international organizations (such as the IMF), informal groupings of an international character such as the Financial Stability Board, the Basel Committee on Banking Supervision, the International Organization of Securities Regulation (IOSCO) and the International Association of Insurance Supervisors (IAIS), professional associations – such as the International Swaps and Derivatives Association, ISDA – and other entities.

---

29 <www.financialstabilityboard.org/publications/r_111104cc.pdf> accessed 15 January 2015.

30 Directive 2014/59/EU (n 16).

31 See generally Rosa Lastra and Lee Buchheit, *Sovereign Debt Management* (OUP 2014) which extensively deals with all these issues. See also the Report presented by the Sovereign Insolvency Study Group – chaired by Philip Wood – to the ILA Hague Conference (August 2010) on 'State Insolvency: options for the way forward' (co-rapportuers: Michael Waibel and Brian Hunt).

32 See Ann Krueger, *International Financial Architecture for 2002: A New Approach to Sovereign Debt Restructuring* (26 November 2001) <www.imf.org/external/np/speeches/2001/112601.htm> accessed 15 January 2015; see generally, Sean Hagan, 'Designing a Legal Framework to Restructure Sovereign Debt' (2005) 36 *Georgetown Journal of International Law* 299.

33 Peter Cooke wrote: 'Outside the supervisor's window, there is a kaleidoscope of financial markets and institutions and range of services – all interlinked to a greater or lesser degree. Each regulator, national or sectoral, only sees a part of this kaleidoscope and cannot be sure he controls all that he can see.' See Peter Cooke 'Preface' in Rosa Lastra (ed), *The Reform of the International Financial Architecture* (Kluwer Law International 2001).

34 In the light of the principle of subsidiarity some micro prudential supervisory responsibilities can be best exercised at the national or regional levels, while the cross-border dimension inherent in the exercise of macro-prudential supervision suggests the need for a cross-border solution.

International financial soft-law is often a 'top-down' phenomenon with a two-layer implementation scheme. The rules (for example, the Basel capital rules) are agreed by international financial standard-setters and national authorities must implement them in their regulation of the financial industry. The financial intermediaries are the 'final' addresses of those rules. Standards and uniform rules, however, can also be designed by the financial industry itself. Self-regulation, by definition, has a 'bottom-up' character, comprising rules of practice, standards, master agreements, usages as well as rules and principles agreed or proposed by scholars and experts.[35]

We need to foster better observance of the standards to preserve competitive equality amongst nations; we need the hardening of some soft law rules (there is 'soft soft law' and 'hard soft law', with the latter paving the way for a transition towards formal hard law); we need a mechanism for ensuring the consistent application of global financial rules; we need effective macro-prudential supervision; and we need a forum to bring disputes when standards are not observed, which brings us back to the institutional debate.

Having identified the key functions, let us look at the candidates for the WFO job (or jobs) given that there are different functions which require a different 'skill set' each. In addition to this functional analysis we also need to address the issues of accountability, legitimacy, expertise (adequate personnel) and resources.

The top candidates for the WFO job (or jobs) are the IMF, the BIS, the WTO, the Financial Stability Board and other standard-setters, such as the Basel Committee on Banking Supervision, IOSCO and IAIS.

Standard-setters, as discussed above, are adept at the regulatory function, though the rules that emanate from them are of a soft-law nature. However, when it comes to the supervisory and crisis management function the IMF is uniquely qualified in my opinion.

The International Monetary Fund was conceived in the 1940s as an international monetary authority with a very particular and rather narrow remit; once the fixed exchange regime (the so-called 'par value system') was abandoned in the 1970s, the IMF lost a large part of its original role. Nonetheless, the IMF has become the 'master of reinvention'. Like a phoenix bird resurrecting out of its own ashes, following the abandonment of what had been its *raison d'être* – the par value regime – the IMF has been singularly adept at finding new roles (as arbiter in negotiations between debtor and creditor countries, as gatekeeper of stability and creditworthiness – via conditionality and surveillance – and as international lender of last resort). Why? Colloquially we would answer: 'because there is no other institution in town'. The IMF has survived because its role is indispensable when it comes to solving countries' external payments and debt problems, as the experience in the 1980s, 1990s and first 14 years of the twenty-first century have confirmed.

The challenges faced by the IMF have changed since the collapse of the Bretton Woods regime. The IMF played a leading role in the sovereign debt restructuring of the Least-Developed Countries (LDC) countries in the 1980s, in the transition to a market economy of formerly communist countries in the early 1990s and in the resolution of financial crises in Mexico and Asia, Russia and Brazil in the mid-to-late 1990s. And then there are the challenges of today, following the global financial crisis and the eurozone debt crisis. With minimum amendments to the IMF Articles of Agreement, the IMF has been called to respond to all these issues: financial reform, financial crises, financial stability and sovereign debt crises

---

35 On soft law see generally Chris Brummer, *Soft Law and the Global Financial System: Rule-Making in the Twenty-First Century* (CUP 2012).

with its array of tools, namely surveillance, conditional financial assistance and technical assistance. The IMF has become the de facto international financial authority.

The IMF is the only institution (other than the Bank for International Settlements and the World Trade Organization) that has international legitimacy, an array of tools (surveillance, conditional financial assistance and technical assistance), appropriate financial resources and staffing to assume a formal role as global financial authority.[36] Other 'informal' international standard-setters, such as the Financial Stability Board,[37] the Basel Committee on Banking Supervision or IOSCO, can continue with their rule-making role, but only the Fund can effectively contribute to the enforcement of those standards through its surveillance function.

The IMF can play a role similar to that played by the Financial Action Task Force (FATF) with regard to anti-money laundering/countering the financing of terrorism (AML/CFT) standards. In the same way as the FATF seeks partnership with the IMF, World Bank, FATF regional bodies, national financial intelligence units (FIUs) and even the financial industry itself[38] to verify the observance of AMF/CFT standards and to ensure that every country in the world is assessed using the same methodology, the IMF can also seek to further develop partnerships with other national, regional and international bodies to ensure adequate implementation of adequate standards for supervision, regulation and resolution of financial institutions.

The IMF is thus uniquely placed to monitor the compliance with standards and rules through its function of surveillance and through its assessment of the health of the financial sector (via the Financial Sector Assessment Program, FSAP, and the Reports on the Observance of Standards and Codes, ROSCs) and to provide countries with the incentive to observe those standards through the design of conditionality (carrots and sticks).

The IMF is uniquely place to exercise global macro-prudential supervision as part of its surveillance function (bilateral, regional and multilateral). Systemic risk after all does not respect geographic boundaries.

The IMF also has the know-how when it comes to sovereign debt workouts [indeed, it is now inserted in the EU process], as well as the financial capacity to act as international lender of last resort, and also has the experience in understanding the relationship between banking crises and sovereign debt crises, as well as adequate resources and personnel.

---

36 See ch 13 of Lastra (n 11). The main functions performed by the IMF in relation to its members are surveillance (art IV of the IMF Articless of Agreement), financial assistance (art V s 3) and technical assistance (art V s 2 (b)). The Fund uses surveillance, financial assistance and technical assistance as instruments to accomplish its objectives or purposes as defined in art I. From the point of view of the member states, they constitute the main 'services' that the Fund provides to them. From the Fund's perspective, its powers can be broken down into three categories: (i) regulatory (jurisdiction), comprising art VIII s 2 and art IV; (ii) financial (art V s 3), and (iii) advisory (technical assistance art V s 2(b)).

37 Since January 2013 the FSB is an association under art 60 of the Swiss Civil Code. See Financial Stability Board, 'Meeting of the Financial Stability Board in Zürich' Press Release 28 January 2013 <www.financialstability board.org/press/pr_130128.htm> accessed 15 January 2015, and 'Arts of Association of the Financial Stability Board (FSB)' 28 January 2013 <www.financialstabilityboard.org/wp-content/uploads/AoA-26-March-2015-FINAL.pdf> accessed 15 January 2015. The FSB Arts of Association complements the Charter and are binding under Swiss law and not internationally where the Charter continues as a non-binding agreement between members. For a brief summary of the functions of the FSB see ch 8 of the House of Lords' Report <www.publications. parliament.uk/pa/ld200809/ldselect/ldeucom/106/106i.pdf> accessed 15 January 2015.

38 See James Fries, 'Global Markets and Global Vulnerabilities: Fighting Transnational Crime through Financial Intelligence' prepared remarks for the MOCOMILA meeting in Salamanca on 25 April 2008 <www.mocomila. org/meetings/2008-freis.pdf> accessed 15 January 2015.

Therefore, the IMF should have an enhanced role in the prevention of future crises and in the development of appropriate tools and frameworks for the resolution of both cross-border financial crises and sovereign debt crises (often intertwined). However, from a legal perspective, under the current Articles of Agreement, the IMF cannot supervise financial institutions. The supervisory function it exercises is the 'surveillance of financial sector policies', i.e., the supervision of how countries comply with standards, and what type of procedures and tools they have in place for resolution, supervision, regulation and others. Surveillance is key to the understanding of the role of the IMF in the twenty-first century.

In February 2010, the IMF released a document entitled 'The Fund's Mandate – The Legal Framework' to accompany an earlier document, 'The Fund's Role and Mandate – An Overview', published on 22 January 2010.[39] The aim of this February 2010 document is to survey the constraints and flexibilities that exist under the current legal framework to expand the role of the Fund with regard to financial sector issues and to confer upon it a clear mandate for 'systemic surveillance', as a form of 'multilateral surveillance':

> Just as national regulatory oversight after the crisis is shifting from the risks in individual institutions to the risks in the financial system as a whole, the Fund's oversight too must shift from a sum of its parts (bilateral surveillance of countries) to the system as a whole. (multilateral surveillance)[40]

The Fund somehow appears to be struggling to try to sort out how the international financial system relates to the international monetary system (as well as differentiating between what is public and what is private).[41] The February 2010 document claims that the Articles provide sufficient flexibility to accommodate reforms (with the limits imposed by articles 31–33 of the Vienna Convention of the Law of Treaties)[42] and that the drafters of the Articles conferred upon the Fund 'enabling authority' in key areas that can facilitate an updated or expanded mandate for the Fund with regard to financial sector issues ('. . . the operational content of the Fund's mandate has been updated over time by Executive Board decision').[43] The document also acknowledges that the option of amending the Articles of Agreement would be a difficult one.[44]

---

39 IMF, 'The Fund's Mandate – The Legal Framework' (22 February 2010) <www.imf.org/external/np/pp/eng/2010/022210.pdf> accessed 15 January 2015. IMF, 'The Fund's Role and Mandate – An Overview' (22 January 2010) <www.imf.org/external/np/pp/eng/2010/012210a.pdf> accessed 15 January 2015.

40 IMF, 'The Fund's Role' (n 39).

41 The IMF is both at the centre of the international monetary system and at the centre of the international financial system. The phrase 'international monetary system' covers the official arrangements relating to the balance of payments – exchange rates, reserves, and regulation of current payments and capital flows, while the 'international financial system' encompasses the international financial institutions – formal and informal – and the various public and private actors in the so-called 'global financial market'.

42 'And while these powers [conferred upon the Fund] are often expressed in general terms, the degree to which their interpretation can evolve is limited by the plain meaning of the text, as supplemented by the *travaux preparatoires* (legislative history)', see IMF, 'The Fund's Mandate' (n 39).

43 ibid.

44 An amendment to the IMF Articles of Agreement requires the approval by three-fifths of the members, holding 85 per cent of the total voting power (the USA – with close to 17 per cent of the voting power – has an effective veto). The UNCTAD draft principles on promoting responsible sovereign lending and borrowing also constitute a step in the right direction. See <http://unctad.org/en/Docs/gdsddf2011misc1_en.pdf> accessed 15 January 2015.

In my opinion, a creative interpretation of article I and article IV of the IMF Articles of Agreement provides sufficient legal basis for the Fund to exercise the role of 'global sheriff'.[45] [A sheriff does not make rules, but enforces and makes sure individuals comply with the rules. By analogy, a global sheriff is not expected necessarily to make the rules, but to monitor countries' observance with such rules].

In terms of the official interpretation of the Articles of Agreement, the Board of Governors at its first meeting in 1946 made a broad delegation of powers to the Executive Board, in accordance with the possibility foreseen in article XII, Section 2(b). According to the current text of Section 15 of the IMF's By-Laws: 'The Executive Board is authorised by the Board of Governors to exercise all the powers of the Board of Governors, except for those conferred directly by the Articles of Agreement on the Board of Governors'. The Executive Board does indeed have the power of interpretation, though this power has to be exercised consistent with general principles of interpretation, including those set forth in the Vienna Convention on the Law of Treaties.[46]

The BIS could also assume an enhanced role in crisis management, since it acts as a bank for central banks, and could also play a role in the formalization of the standard setting process. According to Peter Cooke:[47]

> My own view, not least because of an involvement with the organisation for over 40 years, is to believe that the BIS is likely to play a critical role in this whole area of work. There are a number of reasons for this. First and foremost, it is there. It also has a measure of independence (despite being subject to the ultimate authority of its central bank shareholders). It has, for many years, been a forum where the macro-economic, macro-prudential issues have been discussed . . . The BIS has widened its membership over the past few years to embrace a much more representative group of countries around the world than its original shareholders. It has also become a little more comfortable in allowing Ministries of Finance to participate in bodies spawned by what has traditionally been a Central Bankers club. It already houses the secretariats of the major international bodies working on banking and insurance regulation. If the securities regulators could be persuaded to establish themselves in Basel [they were not!] sic . . . then the ongoing capacity in and around the BIS to pursue a continuing regulatory and supervisory debate internationally would be unparalleled.

The WTO has 'know-how' with regard to financial services liberalization and dispute settlement. As such its powers in this area could be enhanced. However, WTO lacks expertise when it comes to issues of financial regulation, monetary and financial stability (which have been traditionally the domain of the IMF and the BIS and, of course, of national central banks).

---

45 Lord Eatwell and Lance Taylor proposed the creation of a World Financial Authority in their book *Global Finance at Risk: The Case for International Regulation* (Wiley 2008). See also Kern Alexander, Rahul Dhumale and John Eatwell, *Global Governance of Financial Systems: The International Regulation of Systemic Risk* (OUP 2005); Christoph Ohler, 'International Regulation and Supervision of Financial Markets after the Crisis' in C Herrman and J.P. Terhechte (eds), *European Yearbook of International Law* (Springer-Verlag 2010) 3.

46 See <https://treaties.un.org/doc/Publication/UNTS/Volume%201155/volume-1155-I-18232-English.pdf> accessed 15 January 2015, in particular arts 31 and 32 (S 3, 'Interpretation of Treaties').

47 P Cooke (n 33) xxiv.

As for the FSB, though it is singled out as the pillar of the emerging international financial architecture by many experts, the FSB remains an international standard setter and not a formal international organization.[48] Its role in international financial stability and in the process of setting international standards has been endorsed by the G20. However, it still lacks 'real' powers. In terms of resources, personnel, formal legitimacy and accountability, it has some way to go before it could act as a formal WFO.

Concluding Observations

The crisis has shown that the pursuit of the private interest is at times greatly misaligned with the pursuit of the common good and that, with cross-border banks and financial institutions, national solutions alone or uncoordinated national solutions are not enough to combat systemic risk. International solutions are needed for international problems.

Philip Wood once wrote: 'Financial law is our creature and we tell it what to do.' What should we tell it? First, the future of financial law and regulation should reflect the overlapping jurisdictions that represent the reality of international finance: the national, the European (or regional) and the international dimensions. Secondly, though soft-law rules have filled the vacuum left by the absence of formal international law in this area, greater formalization of the emerging *lex financiera* is needed over time. Thirdly, in the quest for international financial regulation we need a combination of general principles (such as non-discrimination or transparency) – which represent a mix of ethics and efficiency that withstand the passage of time – with more prescriptive technical rules that can be adjusted to new circumstances with flexibility. There are a number of concepts – credibility, confidence, fairness – that should permeate through different layers of regulation and influence the behaviour of bankers and financiers.

Regulation should be designed in good times, when rapid credit expansion and exuberant optimism cloud the sound exercise of judgement in risk management, rather than in bad times, in response to a crisis. The biblical story of Joseph (behind dynamic provisioning) offers instructive lessons in this regard. We must also remember that markets are part of the solution since it is well functioning markets that generate growth.

Capitalism relies on the lure of wealth and the discipline imposed by the fear of bankruptcy. As Lee Buchheit put it in his testimony to the House of Lords on 20 January 2009:[49]

> The fundamental principle of the capitalist system is that within the constraints of the law, and regulation if it is a regulated entity, every enterprise is free to pursue its affairs as it sees fit. No one guarantees that you will not fail, but by the same token, no one places any artificial constraint on your ability to succeed. The sanction that capitalism imposes on imprudence, incompetence, some times bad luck, is failure. It is the brooding presence of that sanction that keeps managers on their toes, that keeps them acting in a prudent way.

---

48 C Brummer (n 35). The FSB became a legal person (an association) under Swiss law in 2013, see <www. financialstabilityboard.org/press/pr_130128.pdf> accessed 15 January 2015. Despite the FSB's new personality, its rule-making powers are still of a soft law nature. See also John Eatwell and Lance Taylor, *Global Finance at Risk* (Polity Press 2000) 81, 83 and 157.

49 <www.publications.parliament.uk/pa/ld200809/ldselect/ldeucom/106/9012002.htm> accessed 15 January 2015.

The financial crisis has triggered a revolution in regulatory thinking. For markets to prosper, markets need rules and international financial markets need international rules. We need an effective system for the cross-border resolution of banks and other financial institutions, and in order to achieve it, we need international law. We also need an effective system for the resolution of sovereign debt crises.

The exercise of supervision (micro and macro) is about gathering information and the IMF, through its surveillance function, is well suited to use the knowledge about Members' financial systems to help map the complex ecosystem of financial intermediaries and infrastructures, of the links and interconnections amongst financial systems worldwide and, on the basis of that information, to provide effective international coordination.

In my opinion, the International Monetary Fund, the institution at the centre of the international monetary and financial system, is best placed to adopt a role as a 'global sheriff' (echoing the words of George Soros in the 2010 Davos meeting) with regard to international financial stability.[50]

---

50 See generally Rosa Lastra, 'The Role of the IMF as a Global Financial Authority', book chapter in Christoph Herrman and Jörg Philipp Terhechte (eds), *European Yearbook of International Economic Law* (Springer 2011) 121–36.

4 Critical Reflections on Bank Bail-Ins[†]

Emilios Avgouleas[*] and Charles Goodhart[**]

Introductory Remarks

The scale of losses flowing from bank failures is initially independent of the identity of those upon whom the burden of meeting that loss falls. But, such losses can also entail critical externalities. These have traditionally justified the use of public bail-outs to avoid the systemic threat that the failure of any bank beyond a certain size carries with it.

Nevertheless, public bail-outs of banks are a source of moral hazard and they undermine market discipline. One of the key principles of a free market economy is that owners and creditors are supposed to bear the losses of a failed venture. Bail-outs can also have a destabilizing impact on public finances and sovereign debt, with UK and Irish finances being held as illustrative examples of the impact of such costs.[1]

These concerns have given rise to reforms to internalize the costs of bank failure of which the foremost is the drawing up of bank creditor bail-ins. Essentially, bail-in constitutes a radical rethinking of who bears the ultimate costs of the operation of fractional reserve banking.

A great momentum has built up for basing resolution on bail-in, which sometimes resembles a 'chorus'.[2] The regulatory authorities in most of the world's developed economies have developed, or are in the process of developing, resolution regimes that allow, in principle, banks to fail without resorting to public funding.

The bail-in approach is intended to counter the dual threat of systemic disruption and sovereign over-indebtedness. It is based on the penalty principle, namely, that the costs of bank failures are shifted to where they best belong: bank shareholders and creditors. Namely,

[†] This chapter was originally published by the same authors as 'Critical Reflections on Bank Bail-ins' (2015) 1 *Journal of Financial Regulation* 3.

[*] Professor (Chair) of International Banking Law and Finance, University of Edinburgh.

[**] Professor Emeritus, London School of Economics. The authors would like to thank for constructive comments Martin Hellwig, Thomas Mayer, Stefano Micossi, Maria Nieto, Huw Pill and the participants of two research workshops at the LSE and EUI. We also thank several present and past officials from regulatory authorities, who have helped to clarify the current situation for us, and have rectified certain errors. All remaining errors, however, are our own responsibility.

1 This argument against bail-outs is not disputed in this chapter. However, bail-out costs cannot be accurately measured unless the costs of the alternative instability is also counted. See M Dewatripont, 'European Banking: Bail-out, Bail-in and State Aid Control' (2014) 34 *International Journal of Industrial Organisation* 37. Moreover, as was the case with the US Troubled Asset Relief Programme the costs of public intervention may be recovered in the long-term making the calculation of the costs of public bail-outs even more complex.

2 Exact wording used in J McAndrews, DP Morgan and others, 'What Makes Large Bank Failures so Messy and What to Do about It?' 20 *Federal Reserve Bank of New York, Economic Policy Review* (Special Issue: Large and Complex Banks, March 2014) 14.

bail-in replaces the public subsidy with a private penalty[3] or with private insurance[4] forcing banks to internalize the cost of the risks they assume.

In these new schemes, apart from the shareholders, the losses of bank failure are to be borne by ex ante (or ex post) funded resolution funds, financed by industry levies, and certain classes of bank creditors whose fixed debt claims on the bank will be converted to equity, thereby restoring the equity buffer needed for ongoing bank operation.

This is an important development, since in the past banks' subordinated debt did not provide any cover when bank liquidation was not an option, which meant that subordinated creditors were bailed out alongside senior creditors by taxpayers.[5] This led to creditor inertia.

Turning unsecured debt into bail-in-able debt should incentivize creditors to resume a monitoring function, thereby helping to restore market discipline. For example, as the potential costs of bank failure would fall on creditors, in addition to shareholders, such creditors should become more alert about the levels of leverage the bank carries,[6] limiting one of the most likely causes of bank failures and the governance costs associated with excessive leverage.[7] Normally, shareholders have every incentive to build leverage to maximize their return on equity.[8]

Such monitoring might, in turn, reduce the scale of loss in the event of a bank failure: creditors could force the bank to behave more cautiously, especially where the bail-in regime allows for earlier intervention and closure than a bail-out mechanism. It should also, in principle, eliminate the 'too-big-to-fail' subsidy enjoyed by bigger banks.

Essentially, bail-in provisions mean that, to a certain extent, a pre-planned contract replaces the bankruptcy process giving greater certainty[9] as regards the sufficiency of funds to cover bank losses and facilitating early recapitalization. Moreover, the bail-in tool can be used to keep the bank as a going concern and avoid disruptive liquidation or dis-membering of the financial institution in distress.

But the idea that the penalty for failure can be shifted onto an institution, such as a bank, is incorrect. Ultimately all penalties, and similarly benefits, have to be absorbed by individuals, not inanimate institutions. When it is said that the bank will pay the penalty of failure, this essentially means that the penalty is paid, in the guise of worsened terms, by bank managers, bank staff, bank creditors, or the borrowers. The real question is which individuals will be asked to absorb the cost.

---

3 TF Huertas, 'The Case for Bail-ins' in PS Kenadjian (ed), *The Bank Recovery and Resolution Directive* (De Gruyter 2013).

4 See, in general, KPMG, 'Bail-in Liabilities: Replacing Public Subsidy with Private Insurance' (July 2012) <www.kpmg.com/Global/en/IssuesAndInsights/ArtsPublications/Documents/bail-in-debt-practical-implications.pdf> accessed 2 December 2014. JN Gordon and W-G Ringe, 'Resolution in the European Banking Union: A Transatlantic Perspective on What It Would Take' Oxford Legal Research Paper Series No 18/2014.

5 S Gleeson, 'Legal Aspects of Bank Bail-Ins' (2012) LSE Financial Markets Group Series Special Paper 205.

6 JC Coffee, 'Systemic Risk after Dodd–Frank: Contingent Capital and the Need for Strategies Beyond Oversight' (2011) 111 *Columbia Law Review* 795.

7 AR Admati, PM DeMarzo, MF Hellwig and P Pfleiderer, 'The Leverage Ratchet Effect' Max Planck Institute for Research on Collective Goods Working Paper Series 2013/13; E Avgouleas and J Cullen, 'Excessive Leverage and Bankers' Pay: Governance and Financial Stability Costs of A Symbiotic Relationship' (2015) 21 *Columbia Journal of European Law* 1.

8 A Admati, PM DeMarzo, MF Hellwig and P Pfleiderer, 'Debt Overhang and Capital Regulation' Rock Center for Corporate Governance at Stanford University Working Paper No 114, 23 March 2012; E Avgouleas and J Cullen, 'Market Discipline and EU Corporate Governance Reform in the Banking Sector: Merits, Fallacies, and Cognitive Boundaries' (2014) 41 *Journal of Law and Society* 28.

9 Coffee (n 6) 806.

The goals of the bail-in process are not the same in every jurisdiction. In the United States the process through which bail-in and subsequent conversion of creditor claims takes place for SIFIs is imbedded in the mechanics and architecture of the resolution process that is applied to systemically important institutions, the so-called Orderly Liquidation Authority (OLA).[10] This means that triggering the bail-in process under Title II of the Dodd–Frank Act (DFA) aims at providing with sufficient capital, following liquidation of the resolved holding company, the entities for which the resolved company acted as parent (see the second section below).

In the European Union (EU), on the other hand, the doom loop between bank instability and sovereign indebtedness has left eurozone governments with a major conundrum. The traditional route of a public bail-out is increasingly ruled out, not only due to a principled adherence to the avoidance of moral hazard, but also due to its potential impact on already heavily indebted countries. The European Stability Mechanism (ESM)[11] acts, amongst other purposes, as a component of the European Banking Union (EBU). Both the new EU Resolution regime, based on the EU Bank Recovery and Resolution Directive (BRRD),[12] and the ESM statute[13] require the prior participation of bank creditors in meeting the costs of bank resolution. This means that either the bank remains a going concern and the bail-in process is triggered to effect bank recapitalization to restore it to health ('open bank' bail-in process) or in conjunction with the exercise of resolution powers treating the bank as a gone concern ('closed bank' bail-in process). This contrasts with DFA's approach to SIFI resolution where only the second approach is used. This bifurcation is likely to prove problematic.[14] Similarly, the intention is that intervention will be sooner (forbearance less), so that losses will be less, but whether that hope will be justified is yet to be seen. We discuss this further in the third section.

The desire to find an effective way to replace the public subsidy and the unpopular bail-out process is entirely understandable and can lead to welfare enhancing outcomes. At the same, time, there is a danger of over-reliance on bail-ins, in part owing to the growing momentum for its introduction. One useful role for an academic is to query contemporary enthusiasm for fear of group-think, which the last crisis has shown may prove a dangerous aspect of policy-making in the financial sector. In placing bail-in at the heart of bank resolution regimes, legislators and regulatory authorities ought not to overlook some important shortcomings attached to this approach. This chapter sets out to discuss these shortcomings and to explain why, arguably, bail-in regimes will not remove, in the case of resolution of a large complex

---

10 Title II of the Dodd – Frank Wall Street Reform and Consumer Protection Act of 2010 (Act (Pub L 111–203, HR 4173).

11 Intergovernmental Treaty Establishing the European Stability Mechanism of 2 February 2012, T/ESM 2012/en 2.

12 Directive 2014/59/EU establishing a framework for the recovery and resolution of credit institutions and investment firms and amending Council Directive 82/891/EEC, and Directives 2001/24/EC, 2002/47/EC, 2004/25/EC, 2005/56/EC, 2007/36/EC, 2011/35/EU, 2012/30/EU and 2013/36/EU, and Regulations (EU) No 1093/2010 and (EU) No 648/2012, OJ L 2014 173/190 [hereinafter BRRD].

13 'European Stability Mechanism By-Laws' 8 October 2012.

14 Notably, although both the US and the European authorities are moving simultaneously towards reliance on bail-in mechanisms, we are struck by how little attention appears to be paid in each to the detail of what the other is doing. It is instructive that in the Special Issue on 'Large and Complex Banks' of the *Federal Reserve Bank of New York, Economic Policy Review*, the papers by McAndrews et al (n 2) and Sommer (n 25) hardly mention Basel III, the BRRD or any European initiative. Equally much of the discussion within Europe on its own resolution mechanisms ignores the DFA, and looks inwards.

cross-border bank, unless the risk is idiosyncratic (for example fraud), or in the event of a systemic crisis, the need for public injection of funds. In our analysis we particularly focus on BRRD's distinction between the resolution of banks that have become bankrupt ('gone concern'),[15] from the recapitalization (also as part of the resolution regime) of banks that have become so fragile as to need intervention and recapitalization, but are not (yet) bankrupt ('going concern').[16] Although this distinction is hallowed in the literature, we argue that it may be less clear-cut in practice than is sometimes suggested.

The chapter is divided in five sections, including the present introduction. The second section discusses the architecture and mechanics of the bail-in process. The third section provides a legal and economic analysis of the challenges facing bail-in centred resolutions. The fourth section examines the obstacles to effective cross-border resolutions using bail-in, utilizing mostly the SPOE approach. The final section provides the conclusions.

The Architecture and Mechanics of the Bail-In Process

Bank Resolution and Bank Bail-In under the Dodd–Frank Act (DFA)

Overview

Under section 204(a) (1) of the DFA, creditors and shareholders bear all the losses of the financial company that has entered OLA. This is in accord with one of the Act's explicit aims, as stated in its preamble: 'to protect the American taxpayer by ending bailouts'. To this effect, Title II of the Dodd–Frank Act provides the Federal Deposit Insurance Corporation (FDIC) with new powers to resolve SIFIs. Under OLA, the FDIC may be appointed receiver for any US financial company that meets specified criteria when resolution under the US Bankruptcy Code (or other relevant insolvency process) would be likely to create systemic instability.

In order to make group resolution effective and to minimize systemic disruption, the FDIC has decided that it will follow the Single Point of Entry approach (SPOE),[17] which is the final step in the implementation of the 'source-of-strength' doctrine (enshrined in section 616(d) of the DFA). In the event of bank failure the top-tier holding company will have to enter into receivership and attendant losses will be borne by the holding company's shareholders and unsecured creditors. Section 210(a)(1)(M) of the Act provides that the FDIC, as the receiver for a covered financial company, succeeds by operation of law to all the rights, titles, powers, and privileges possessed by, inter alia, the creditors of the resolved and all rights and claims that the stockholders and creditors of the resolved institution may have against its assets are terminated, but for their right to receive payment under the provisions of section 210. The FDIC would then form a bridge holding company ('NewCo')[18] and transfer the failed holding company's ownership of healthy operating subsidiaries into it, leaving the holding company shareholders and creditors behind in the estate of the failed holding company. Operating subsidiaries that face no solvency problem will be transferred to the new solvent entity or entities (NewCo).

---

15 Art 43(2)(a) BRRD.

16 Art 43(2)(b) BRRD.

17 Federal Deposit Insurance Corporation (FDIC), 'Resolution of Systemically Important Financial Institutions: The Single Point of Entry Strategy' (18 December 2013) 78 (243) Fed Reg 76614 <www.gpo.gov/fdsys/pkg/FR-2013–12–18/pdf/2013–30057.pdf> accessed 2 December 2014.

18 'The term "bridge financial company" means a new financial company organized by the Corporation in accordance with section 210(h) for the purpose of resolving a covered financial company' (DFA Title II s 201 (3)).

Section 210 of the DFA requires the FDIC to conduct a claims process and establish a claims priority pyramid for the satisfaction of claims against the resolved entity without the use of taxpayer funds. At the conclusion of this process claims against the receivership would be satisfied through a debt-for-securities exchange in accordance with their priority under section 210 through the issuance of debt and equity in the new holding company.

Prior to the exchange of securities for claims, the FDIC would determine the value of the bridge financial company based upon a valuation performed by the consultants selected by the board of the bridge financial company. Yet the FDIC has stated that it expects 'shareholders' equity, subordinated debt and a substantial portion of the unsecured liabilities of the holding company – with the exception of essential vendors' claims – to remain as claims against the receivership.[19]

This is essentially the bail-in process under Title II, which aims at giving the NewCo what is essentially a clean bill of health rather than turning unsecured creditors into NewCo shareholders. OLA's bail-in process will be utilized to resolve the holding company ('closed bank' process), although the operating subsidiaries remain unaffected. In this respect it differs from the BRRD approach that provides an 'open bank' bail-in process[20] in addition to the 'closed bank' process.[21]

By establishing the bridge financial company with significant assets of the parent holding company and substantially fewer liabilities, it is hoped that the bridge financial company would have a strong balance sheet that would put it in a good position to borrow money from customary market sources. The FDIC has indicated that contingent value rights, such as warrants or options allowing the purchase of equity in the new holding company, or other instruments, might be issued to enable funding the transition/resolution. If there are shortfalls or these sources of funding are not readily available, the SPOE approach offers the benefit of FDIC's access to the Orderly Liquidation Fund (OLF), provided that borrowings from the fund can be fully secured and repaid. Any costs incurred by the FDIC as the appointed receiver or other public authority which cannot be covered by the above will be recovered from the industry.

The bail-in approach is not new in US bank resolution practice. For example, in 2008, the FDIC exercised its existing powers and resolved the part of the Washington Mutual group that was not sold to JP Morgan Chase, mainly claims by equity holders and creditors, under the least-cost resolution method. It imposed serious losses on the unsecured creditors and uninsured depositors (deposit amount above USD 100,000).[22] OLA further expands the resolution authority of FDIC, including its power to cherry-pick which assets and liabilities to transfer to a third party (though these will be subject to strict conditions to be further detailed by the FDIC) and to treat similarly situated creditors differently, for example, favouring short-term creditors over long-term creditors or favouring operating creditors over lenders or bondholders. This discretion is curbed by the introduction of a safeguard, under section 210(a)(7)(B), DFA, that creditors are entitled to receive at least what they would have received if liquidation had taken place under Chapter 7 of the Bankruptcy Code (comparable to the 'best interests of creditors' test under the Bankruptcy Code).

---

19 FDIC (n 17) 76618.
20 Art 43(2) (a) BRRD.
21 Art 43(2)(b) BRRD.
22 FDIC Press Release, 'Information for Claimants in Washington Mutual Bank' 29 September 2008 <www.fdic. gov/news/news/press/2008/pr08085b.html> accessed 2 December 2014.

Evaluation

Although the Troubled Asset Relief Program (TARP) and other forms of direct bank capitalization by the US Treasury during the 2008 crisis did not prove to be loss-making, the issue of moral hazard and principled opposition to a private company receiving public assistance in bankruptcy means that one of DFA's key rationales is exclusion of bail-outs. Thus, as mentioned earlier, OLA treats the holding company as a bankrupt (gone) concern. There may, however, be some caveats.

First, the dismemberment of the parent holding company, in order to provide the necessary funding for the recapitalization of the operating banking subsidary(ies) may have reputational impact on the entire group, including the (seemingly unaffected) operating subsidiaries.

For example, Bank XYZ Holding Co. liquidation will inevitably be accompanied by round the clock media coverage. It is hard to imagine what that would mean to the ordinary bank depositor and financial consumer. It is very likely that they will assume that Bank XYZ (operational) is also endangered. One reasonable remedy would be to have the names of the holding company and of the operational subsidiary(ies) separated (ring-fenced), but which part of the group gets which (name) will be an issue with potential consequences for franchise value. Also such name separation may not work. It would not be very hard for the media to explain to ordinary depositors and consumers that it is the parent company of XYZ that has entered into liquidation. A further route would be to conduct OLA in utter secrecy and just announce the parent's liquidation once the process has been concluded. But stock exchange rules, notices to affected bank creditors, potential litigation, and the structure of OLA itself in DFA, which involves so many stakeholders, would make such a 'secrecy' approach impossible.

Could the subsidiary bank, with help from the authorities, really handle the reputational fall-out?[23] Historical evidence of reputational contagion, for example in the case of certain solvent subsidiaries of Bank of Credit and Commerce International (BCCI),[24] would suggest that this could be a real danger. If such depositor flight should then occur, the Central Bank or the Deposit/Resolution Fund (in the USA the Orderly Liquidation Fund (OLF)) might have to pump in large amounts of liquidity. While this would be protected by seniority and collateral, the previous buffer represented by the holding company's capital would, at least initially, no longer be there. So a large portion of the operating company's continuing liabilities might come either from the Central Bank (or OLF) or be backed by the deposit insurance fund, with some potential call on public support.

The second question is about the speed of rebuilding the capital structure of the NewCo after the bankruptcy of the initial holding company. While bail-in is not decided in isolation but is part of a restructuring process under which management is replaced and group business restructured, if NewCo's capital structure is not rapidly rebuilt, authorities would be left with an initially thinly capitalized operating bank[25] plus large public sector liabilities. The government

---

23 No doubt the resolution would have to be accompanied by a careful communication strategy, but the example of Northern Rock shows how this can go wrong.

24 On the contagion triggered by the BCCI failure see A Kanas, 'Pure Contagion Effects in International Banking: The Case of BCCI's Failure' (2005) 8 *Journal of Applied Economics* 101. For details on how fraud complicated the resolution of BCCI subsidiaries see RJ Herring, 'BCCI & Barings: Bank Resolutions Complicated by Fraud and Global Corporate Structure' in Douglas D Evanoff and George G Kaufman (eds), *Systemic Financial Crises: Resolving Large Bank Insolvencies* (World Scientific Publishing 2005) 321. For a depiction of BCCI's complicated structure see fig 1, ibid 6.

25 See for discussion JH Sommer, 'Why Bailin? And How?' (2014) 20 *Federal Reserve Bank of New York, Economic Policy Review* (Special Issue: 'Large and Complex Banks').

cannot force private sector buyers to purchase new equity and (subordinated) debt in NewCo and the prior experience would make private buyers wary. Certainly the authorities could require the operating bank to retain all earnings (for example, no dividends, buy-backs, etc.), but in a generalized financial crisis, it could take a long time to regenerate a new holding company by building up retained earnings. The authorities could massively expedite the process by injecting new capital into NewCo – with the aim of selling off such equity later back to the private sector, but that would just be another form of bail-out. While the HoldCo proposal has been carefully worked out in its initial stage, what is less clear is what might then happen in the convalescent period.

The third question is about costs to the rest of the sector of rolling over maturing bail-inable debt, once it has been announced that losses have been imposed on XYZ Holdings' creditors who hold bail-inable debt in the event of XYZ's failure. The cost of such debt could rise significantly and HoldCos might be tempted to let their own buffers slip below the required level. Of course regulatory authorities could impose sanctions in such cases. But in doing so they will have to consider the impact of rising funding costs to the sector, both in terms of operating costs and in terms of solvency if such intervention takes place, as is likely, in a recessionary economic climate or worse during a generalized bank asset crisis.

The fourth question relates to the interaction between the DFA approach and the Basel III capital requirements, which appear to necessitate an earlier intervention approach than DFA's OLA. Under the Basel rules, relevant authorities should intervene to resolve a bank whenever its core tier 1 equity (CET1) falls below 4½ per cent of Risk Weighted Assets. A bank with CET1 between 0 and 4½ per cent is not formally insolvent, i.e., it is still 'going', rather than 'gone', concern. It is to be hoped that regulators would intervene in a failing bank before the formal insolvency point is reached. But then they would not be able to bail-in senior unsecured debtors under the 'no creditor worse off' (NCWO) principle. Either all the debt in the HoldCo, comprising subordinated debt or contingent capital instruments (Co-Cos), would have to be designated as bail-in-able, which could have a considerable effect on bank funding costs, or the authorities could just not take pre-emptive action, disregarding the Basel III requirement. Either route might prove problematic.

NY Federal Reserve staff express the opinion that US authorities will disregard the Basel III requirement (of earlier intervention/recapitalization),[26] and go on to state that '[t]he resolution authority in our model is "slow" in the sense that it will shut down and resolve a firm only once its (book) equity capital is exhausted'.[27] Perhaps because the costs of such a slow response are recognized, McAndrews et al. express a preference for specially designed bail-inable debt to an equivalent amount of extra equity.[28] Subordinated debt issued ex ante and specially designed by contract to absorb losses by means of conversion or of a write down (called hereinafter *D bail-inable debt*) is essentially a form of pre-paid insurance for bank failure[29] and it has specific advantages and costs. Some of the advantages might remain unproven.

McAndrews, et al. suggest that the existence of sufficient specifically designed debt to absorb the cost of resolution would force earlier intervention by the authorities, before *all* the loss-making buffer had been eaten away.[30] But if the trigger for intervention is to be book value insolvency, it will still be applied far too late to be optimal. If intervention is to be

---

26 McAndrews and others (n 2).
27 ibid 5, 15 and footnote 16 therein.
28 ibid 14–23.
29 Gordon and Ringe (n 4).
30 McAndrews and others (n 2) 14–23.

triggered earlier, prior to book value insolvency, the bank is not legally a 'gone concern', making the satisfaction of NCWO principle problematic. At this stage, it remains unclear how US authorities intend to resolve this conundrum.

The FDIC-BoE Approach to Resolving G-SIFIs and Bail-In

Dodd–Frank explicitly authorizes coordination with foreign authorities to take action to resolve those institutions whose collapse threatens financial stability (Title II, section 210, N). A heat-map exercise conducted by US regulators determined that the operations of US SIFIs are concentrated in a relatively small number of jurisdictions, particularly the United Kingdom (UK).[31] Thus, the USA and UK authorities proceeded to examine potential impediments to efficient resolutions and on a cooperative basis explored methods of resolving them.

This culminated in the joint discussion paper published by the Bank of England (BOE) and the Federal Deposit Insurance Corporation (FDIC) comparing the resolution regime established by DFA Title II to the resolution powers of the UK's Prudent Regulation Authority (PRA).[32] To this effect the two authorities have proposed that they will adopt the single point of entry' (SPOE) approach, when appropriate,[33] in the resolution of G-SIFIs.

The main implication of the SPOE approach to resolution is that G-SIFIs would have to put in place:

- a group structure based on a parent holding company (HoldCo);
- the ring-fencing of (domestic and overseas) subsidiaries that undertake critical economic activities, so that the continuity of these activities can be more easily maintained in a resolution;
- issuance of bail-inable debt by the holding company to enable the group to be recapitalized in a resolution through the conversion of this debt into equity;
- holding company debt will be used to make loans to subsidiaries, so that subsidiaries can be supported in a resolution through writing off these loans.

Although initially a group taken into resolution would be 'owned' by the FDIC (in the US)[34] or, perhaps, under a trustee arrangement (in the UK), the intention is that the group would be returned to private ownership, with the creditors whose debt is converted into equity becoming the new owners of the group. Both the BRRD[35] and UK legislation,[36] implementing government's plans to introduce, with modifications, the Vickers' Report recommendations, include requirements that banks have sufficient capital and debt in issue to make them resolvable using bail-in or other resolution tools.

Under the SPOE approach the continuity of critical economic activities is preserved because – in most cases – the subsidiaries of the holding company should be able to continue

---

31 MJ Gruenberg, speech (Federal Reserve Bank of Chicago Bank Structure Conference, 9 June 2012). Gruenpeng is the Chairman of the Federal Deposit Insurance Corporation.
32 'Resolving Globally Active, Systemically Important, Financial Institutions', a joint paper by the FDIC and the BoE, 10 December 2012.
33 The joint paper recognizes that multiple point of entry (MPE) may be more appropriate in some cases of complex cross-border banks. ibid.
34 S 210(h)(10(2)), Title II, DFA.
35 Art 45(6)(a), (b), BRRD.
36 S 17 and sch 2, Financial Services (Banking Reform) Act 2013, c 33.

in operation, either because they have remained solvent and viable, or because they can be recapitalized through the writing down of intra-group loans made from the holding company to its subsidiaries. A subsidiary would need to be resolved independently only where it had suffered large losses.

Under the FDIC-BoE joint paper, in the UK the equity and debt of a resolved holding company would be held initially by a trustee, though the BRRD now provides alternative methods as well (Articles 47, 48, 50). The trustee would hold these securities during a valuation period. The valuation is undertaken to assess the extent to which the size of the losses already incurred by the firm or expected to be incurred can be ascertained in order to determine the extent of required recapitalization. Namely, valuation of losses determines the extent to which creditor claims should be written down and converted. During this period, listing of the company's equity securities (and potentially debt securities) would be suspended.[37]

Once the amount of required recapitalization requirement has been determined, an announcement of the final terms of the bail-in would be made to the previous security holders. On completion of the exchange the trustee would transfer the equity to the original creditors. Creditors unable to hold equity securities (for example, because they cannot legally hold equity shares) will be able to request the trustee to sell the equity securities on their behalf. The trust would then be dissolved and the equity securities of the firm would resume trading.

We discuss the additional questions raised by cross-border banking, which, however, will be the norm for most SIFIs and by definition for G-SIFIs, in section C(8).

The European Approach

Bail-in is a precondition for bank resolution in the EU and for (ultimately) ESM implemented bank recapitalization within the eurozone. In a nutshell before a Member State is allowed to tap ESM resources for direct recapitalization of a failing bank, a round of bail-in and national contributions must have taken place. National regulators must first impose initial losses representing at least 8 per cent of the bank's liabilities on shareholders and creditors[38] before they can use the national resolution fund to absorb losses or to inject fresh capital into an institution, and then only up to 5 per cent of the bank's liabilities. Historical losses, which have already been absorbed by shareholders through a reduction in own funds prior to bail-in are not included in those percentages.[39] Also nothing in these provisions excludes the possibility that where bank losses exceed 13 per cent of the resolved institution's liabilities, a further bail-in round may take place in order for the residual losses to be absorbed by creditors and non-guaranteed and non-preferred depositors before public money and then ESM funds are used. Injection of public funds (including temporary public ownership under article 58 BRRD) is allowed in any case only in 'the very extraordinary situation of a systemic crisis'[40] subject to approval under the Union State aid framework.[41]

These qualifications make the possibility of injection of ESM funds, borrowed by the Member State in question, an absolute last resort in order both to counter moral hazard and to allay

37 FDIC, BoE (n 32).
38 Arts 44(5) and (7), 37(10)(a), Rec 73, BRRD.
39 Rec 75, BRRD.
40 Art 37(10), BRRD.
41 Art 56, 58, 37(10) BRRD.

any fears of de facto mutualization of liability for bank rescues in the eurozone.[42] It is clear that the EU holds high hopes about the effectiveness of this mechanism, an approximation to which has already been tried in Cyprus in March 2013[43] and for the restructuring of the Spanish banking sector.[44] It is also hoped that bail-in will nullify the need for state aid for the banking sector across the EU and not just within the confines of the eurozone.[45] Nonetheless, as explained earlier, the BRRD does not entirely rule out the possibility of injection of public funds subject to the very strict conditions of articles 37(10), 56, 58 BRRD, and as a last resort, although such injection of public funds would indeed amount to a form of state aid,[46] which must be approved by the EU Commission in accordance with the state aid framework of article 107 TFEU.[47]

Yet the legal entity by legal entity approach raises its own set of difficult issues. In the case of non-EBU groups, resolution colleges might smooth coordination issues but, a bail-in decision has distributional consequences, potentially with clear losers. So in some cases it might even create a crisis of confidence in a Member State's banking system, and strong disagreements are bound to arise as to which subsidiary is bailed-in and which is not. Where there are subsidiaries in non-EBU European countries such disagreements could even go as far as creating serious problems in the relationship of the EBU with non-EBU European countries, especially where losses are bound to fall unevenly. The obvious solution is to follow a group-based resolution approach and aggregate all losses to the group entity for the entire part of the group that is based in the EU. But then any measure of adequacy of bail-in able debt held by the group must be made at the holding company level and for the entire part of the group operating in the EU, otherwise regulators will enforce subsidiarization.

Another significant challenge that the EU approach to bail-in raises is the aforementioned issue of liquidity support from resolution funds and central banks. This could be provided either to each legal entity, against the collateral available to that entity, or channelled through a parent company. In either case, if that happens within the eurozone, all liquidity funding from the central banks would eventually have to be booked on the ECB's balance sheet, at least until the bank is successfully restructured.

---

42 Use of ESM funds when a bank public bail-out proves to be necessary is subject to a number of strict conditions. The ESM may intervene directly only at the request of a Member State stating that it is unable to provide the requisite funds on its own without endangering the sustainability of its public finances or its market access. The relevant institution will also have to be a systemic bank, and the difficulties it faces must threaten the euro zone's financial stability. The ESM takes action only jointly with this Member State, which ensures that countries have an incentive to curb the use of public funds as far as possible. See arts 1–3 of ESM Guideline on Financial Assistance for the Recapitalisation of Financial Institutions.

43 While the authorities would say that the Cypriot case was very different, given the absence of the resolution tools provided by the BRRD, we feel that its implementation gave important further momentum to the adoption of bail-in processes.

44 Under the terms of bankruptcy reorganization of Bankia and of four other Spanish banks, and in accordance with the conditions of the July 2012 Memorandum of Understanding between the Troika (EC, ECB and IMF) and Spain, over 1 million small depositors became Bankia shareholders after they had been sold '*preferentes*' (preferred stock) in exchange for their deposits (FROB, July and December 2012). Following the conversion, the *preferentes* took an initial write-down of 30–70 per cent, which became much wider when the value of Bankia shares eventually collapsed (originally valued at EUR 2 per share, which was further devalued to EUR 0.1 after the March 2013 restructuring of Bankia. 'Bankia Press Release, 'BFA-Bankia expects to culminate recapitalisation in May' March 2013 <www.bankia.com/en/communication/in-the-news/news/bfa-bankia-expects-to-culminate-recapitalisation-in-may.html> accessed 2 December 2014.

45 I Angeloni, N Lenihan, 'Competition and State Aid Rules in the Time of Banking Union' (prepared for the Conference, Financial Regulation: A Transatlantic Perspective, Goethe University Frankfurt, 6–7 June 2014).

46 Art 2(1)(28), BRRD.

47 Rec 57, BRRD. For example, such provision of aid must NOT be 'part of a larger aid package, and the use of the guarantee measures should be strictly limited in time'. Rec 41, BRRD.

Important Challenges of Bail-In Centred Resolution

Is 'Open Bank' Bail-In an Effective Liquidation Substitute?

While OLA provides for the liquidation of the bank holding company, it uses bail-in to leave operating subsidiaries unaffected. The EU, on the other hand, has an 'open' bank resolution process that is reliant on the successful bail-in of the ailing bank. So both jurisdictions view the bail-in process as a substitute to liquidation of either the entire group or of parts of the group, combined of course with the use of other resolution tools. This is not an unreasonable approach, especially in the case of a largely idiosyncratic cause of failure, for example, fraud. But there are four essential conditions that have to be met when using the bail-in process as a resolution substitute: timing, market confidence, the extent of restructuring required, and accurate determination of losses.

The issue of when to trigger the bail-in process, taking also into account the requirements of early intervention regimes (for example, Title III BRRD), is matter of cardinal importance. Identification of the right time and conditions to trigger the bail-in tool in a process that extends conversion beyond specially designed bail-in-able debt will be one of the most important for any bank supervisor. The reasoning leading to supervisors' decision will much resemble first and second order problems in mathematics and logic. If the supervisor triggers bail-in early, then the full measure of losses may not have been fully revealed, risking further rounds of bail-in. But if the supervisor determines to use the bail-in tool at a later stage, when the full scale of losses to be imposed on creditors is revealed, they risk a flight of bank creditors who do not hold *D bail-in-able debt*.

Moreover, speed of resolution/recapitalization (albeit at the expense of flexibility) is one of the reasons for the popularity of bail-in among regulators.[48] Yet, we doubt whether the adoption of bail-in regimes would lead to earlier regulatory intervention than under the bail-out regimes. The aforementioned paper by McAndrews et al. reinforces our view that legal concerns about imposing potentially large losses on private creditors could unduly delay resolution, perhaps until the last possible minute. By then the liabilities needed to be written down could extend beyond HoldCo's specially designated by contract bail-inable debt. Bail-out, being undertaken by the authority of the government, is, we would argue, somewhat less liable to legal suit than bail-in. On the other hand, bail-in of bank liabilities that extends beyond contractually designed bail-able debt affects a wider range of creditors; there are more parties to the negotiation, and hence that may be more protracted. In our view, the more delayed the onset of Resolution, the more essential it will be to put more emphasis on an earlier Recovery phase.

There are also other concerns. In the absence of a fiscal backstop for other parts of the financial system, if bail-in is triggered before measures have been taken to buttress the rest of the financial system, a creditor flight from other banks will be certain, spreading the tremors throughout the financial system, even if those banks retain sufficient amounts of *D bail-in able debt*. Timothy Geithner has eloquently explained this situation:[49]

> The overwhelming temptation [in a crisis] is to let the most egregious firms fail, to put them through a bankruptcy-type process like the FDIC had for community banks and then haircut their bondholders. But unless you have the ability to backstop every other

---

48 See for a critical explanation Sommer (n 25).
49 TF Geithner, *Stress Test: Reflections on Financial Crises* (Random House 2014) 306.

systemic firm that's in a similar position, you'll just intensify fears of additional failures and haircuts.

Secondly, market confidence in the bailed-in institution would have to be quickly restored in order to preserve franchise value and repay official liquidity support.[50] As mentioned in the second section above, this is mostly dependent on how fast the capital structure of the requisite bank (or the new bank in the event of a 'closed' bank process) is rebuilt. If the institution has entered into a death spiral with customers, creditors and depositors fast disappearing and reversing the trend would doubtlessly prove a task of daunting proportions.

Thirdly, triggering the bail-in process will prove unsuccessful if bank losses are not properly identified in some finite form. The determination of bank losses including unrealized future losses must be accurately determined in order to avoid successive rounds of bail-in losses accruing to bank creditors. This might in fact prove a challenging task. For example, bank losses in the recent crisis have consistently been underestimated.

Normally bank failures occur when macro-economic conditions have worsened, and asset values are falling. Bank failures during boom conditions, for example resulting from fraud, such as Barings, are easier to handle with less danger of contagion. In the uncertain conditions of generalized asset value declines, the new (incoming) accountants, employed by the resolution agency, are likely to take a bad scenario (or even a worst case) as their base case for identifying losses, to be borne by the bailed-in creditors, partly also to minimize the above-mentioned danger of underestimation leading to further calls on creditors. Previously the accountants of the failing bank itself will have been encouraged (by management) to take a more positive view of its (going concern) value. Thus the transition to bail-in is likely to lead to a huge discontinuity, a massive drop, in published accounting valuations. This could put into question amongst the general public the existing valuations of other banks, and lead, possibly rapidly, to a contagious crisis, on which we add more below. Finally, restructuring should extend to the underlying business model, which led the bank to bankruptcy in the first place, to avoid several bail-in rounds in the future.

Who Meets the Burden?

Overview

In general, banks have three types of creditors:

- banking creditors, including retail and wholesale depositors, needing to use the provision by the bank of payment and custody services;
- investment business creditors, including swap counterparties, trading counterparties, and those with similar claims from trading activity such as exchanges, clearing systems and other investment business counterparties (including repo counterparties);
- financial creditors, comprising long-term creditors of the bank, including bondholders and other long-term unsecured finance providers.[51]

When banking groups are resolved only the third type of creditors should be affected by bail-in, since banking creditors and investment business creditors will most likely hold claims

---

50 Sommer (n 25).

51 Clifford Chance, 'Legal Aspects of Bank Bail-ins' (2011) <www.cliffordchance.com/publicationviews/ publications/2011/05/legal_aspects_ofbankbail-ins.html> accessed 2 December 2014.

against unaffected operating subsidiaries. This is, however, not the case where, under the EU approach, resolution is undertaken at the legal entity level. Under the BRRD business creditors may be exempted, through pre-designed 'carve-outs'. It is not inconceivable that this exemption may be utilized to shift disproportionately the burden of bail-in onto other classes of creditors such as bondholders and unprotected depositors.

Who Assumes the Burden under the Bail-In Process?

Arguably, in contrast to bail-outs, where all the taxpayers are, in some sense, domestic constituents, an advantage of bail-in is that some creditors may be foreign, but this is an elusive and possibly false advantage. The aim to penalize Russian creditors of Cypriot banks might have played a significant role in the way that 'rescue' was structured. Similarly the treatment of the creditors of Icelandic banks was organized in such a way as to give preference to domestic depositors over foreign bondholders.[52] But the foreign investors would, of course, realize that they were in effect being targeted, so that they would both require a higher risk premium and flee more quickly at the first sign of potential trouble. The result is likely to be that a larger proportion of bank bondholders will be other (non-bank) financial intermediaries of the same country, providing a further small ratchet to the balkanization and nationalization of the banking system. In any case, the BRRD disallows discrimination between creditors on the basis of their nationality or domicile, eradicating this mis-conceived advantage of bail-ins over bail-outs.

With a purely domestic bank, the effect of shifting from bail-out to bail-in will, therefore, primarily transfer the burden of loss from one set of domestic payers, the taxpayers, to another, the pensioners and savers. It is far from clear whether, and why, the latter have broader backs and are better placed to absorb bank rescue losses than the former. One argument, however, is that savers, and/or their financial agents, have made an ex ante choice to purchase the claim on the bank, whereas the taxpayer had no such option, and that, having done so, they could/ should have played a monitoring role. While this is a valid point, the counter-argument is that charities, small or medium-size pension funds, or individual savers, for example, via pension funds, do not really have the expertise to act as effective bank monitors. Thus, forcing them to pay the penalty of bank failure would hardly improve bank governance. On the contrary it would only give rise to claims that they were 'tricked' into buying bail-in-able debt.[53] Arguably, the BRRD makes provision (article 46(3)(c)) for such concerns by giving resolution authorities the power to exempt (in 'exceptional circumstances'), from the application of the bail-in tool, liabilities held by individuals and SMEs beyond the level of insured deposits. The chief rationale for this discretionary exemption is avoidance of contagion (article 46(3) (c), (d), BRRD), a very plausible concern. If it is applied in a wider context, this exemption could provide adequate protection to vulnerable segments of savers' population. These are, in general, weak bank governance monitors and, at the same time, stable sources of cheap funding. Such wider (albeit ad hoc) protection would reinforce the confidence of these parts of society and economy in the banking system.

---

52 See S Goodley, 'Bondholders May Take Legal Action against Iceland over Failed Banks' *The Guardian* (London, 7 November 2010) <www.theguardian.com/business/2010/nov/07/iceland-banks-bondholders-legal-action> accessed 2 December 2014.

53 Would such bail-inable debt be a suitable investment for pension funds, charities, local authorities and individuals? The Pensions Regulator, the Department for Communities and Local Government, the Charities Commission and the FCA may need to consider whether further rules in this area would be necessary. See also for convincing analysis on this matter A Persaud, 'Why Bail-In Securities Are Fool's Gold', Peterson Institute for International Economics, Policy Brief 14–23, November 2014 <www.piie.com/publications/pb/pb14–23.pdf> accessed 2 December 2014.

Governance

The treatment of bailed-in creditors, especially where creditors will be issued new securities rather than having their claims written down, is likely to be complex, time-consuming and litigation intensive. Faced with such costs the original creditors are likely to sell out to those intermediaries that specialize in such situations, for example 'vulture' hedge funds. So, as already seen in the case of the Co-op Bank, ownership may fall into the hands of a group of such hedge funds;[54] the same would probably have happened had there been creditor bail-in in Iceland and Ireland. In Cyprus creditor bail-in has given a large share of ownership to big Russian depositors.[55] In theory, this problem could be resolved by placing caps on how much bail-inable debt different creditors could hold. In practice, however, such caps would encounter legal constraints, at least, under EU law. In addition, if caps are very strict, they would restrict the liquidity of the market for bail-inable debt and could lead to banks having to hold insufficient amounts of bail-inable debt, increasing the need for a public bail-out.

In spite of their many and well documented disadvantages, bail-outs do give governments the power to direct and specify who is to take over the running of the rescued bank. That is not the case with some versions of the bail-in approach. In the USA the role of the FDIC as 'trustee' of the resulting bridge company should, however, deal with this point. But elsewhere the resulting governance structure could become unattractive to the authorities and public. While there is a safeguard that the new managers have to be approved by the regulatory authorities, nevertheless the ethos, incentives and culture of a bank, whose ownership is controlled by a group of hedge funds for example, is likely to differ from that of a bank rescued by a bail-out.

Legal Costs

While there might be a few jurisdictions such as the UK where bail-in regimes can be established by contract, elsewhere this route would lead to a stream of litigation.[56] As a result, in most jurisdictions, including the UK, bail-in regimes are given statutory force (for example, article 50(2) of the BRRD). Yet this does not mean that litigation will be avoided when the bail-in process is triggered. Bail-in regimes that extend beyond *D bail-inable debt* would be seen as encroaching on rights of property, which remain entrenched in countries' constitutions and international treaties. Legal claims will be raised both by shareholders who will see their stakes wiped out and creditors who will see the value of their claims reduced or diminished[57] and it is unlikely that the 'no creditor worse off' (than in liquidation) principle, which both Dodd–Frank[58] and the BRRD[59] have adopted, as a creditor safeguard under the

---

54   Co-op Group, which owned the Cooperative Bank outright, eventually bowed to the demands of a group of bondholders, including US hedge funds Aurelius Capital and Silver Point Capital, and agreed to a restructuring which left them with a 30 per cent stake in the bank. See M Scuffham, 'Co-op to cede control of bank to bondholders', *Reuters* (21 Oct. 2013) <http://uk.reuters.com/article/2013/10/21/uk-coop-bank-bondholders-idUKBRE99K05O20131021> accessed 2 December 2014.

55   A Illmer, 'Russia's rich dominate Cyprus' largest bank' *Deutsche Welle* (18 October 2013) <www.dw.de/russias-rich-dominate-cyprus-largest-bank/a-17146540> accessed 2 December 2014.

56   Gleeson (n 5).

57   For example, see 'Russian Depositors Begin Seizing Property of Cypriot Banks' *Russia Today* (12 April 2013) <http://rt.com/business/laiki-cyprus-banks-arrest-765/> accessed 2 December 2014.

58   S 210(a)(7)(B), Title II, DFA.

59   Art 73(b), BRRD.

bail-in process, will deter the expected stream of litigation. In fact, the principle could make litigation even more likely. Therefore, where the result of government action is that bailed-in creditors receive a demonstrably lower return than they would have done had the bank proceeded to disorderly liquidation, they should be compensated,[60] but by whom and in what form? Would that be in the form of shares in the NewCo or of the recapitalized operating subsidiary? Even so, rapid restoration of public confidence is the only way to make creditors' converted stakes valuable.

Moreover, a significant proportion of the costs of bank resolution could involve settling conflicts of interest among creditors.[61] This is particularly likely to be so in so far as bail in will concentrate ownership amongst 'vulture' hedge funds, whose métier is the use of legal means to extract large rents. Shifting the burden of meeting the costs of recapitalization from a small charge (on average) imposed on the generality of taxpayers to a major impost on a small group of creditors, easily capable of acting in unison, is almost bound to multiply the legal costs of such an exercise manifold, however much the legal basis of this process is established beforehand.

This is easily explainable. In the case of taxpayer-funded bail-outs, everyone's tax liabilities go up a little (and the relative burden has, in a sense, been democratically reviewed and decided); in the case of creditor bail-in, a few will lose a lot, and will, therefore, have stronger incentive to protest and litigate.

Funding Costs

There are two aspects to this, a static and a dynamic one. There have been numerous quantitative studies of the 'subsidy' provided by the implicit government bail-out guarantee to the larger banks which are too-big-to-fail.[62] There is sufficient evidence to show that Too-Big-To-Fail banks are prone to take much riskier assets than other banks.[63]

Such a subsidy is also criticized as undesirable and unfair distortion of competition. Taking advantage of lower funding costs, larger banks cut margins aggressively to edge out smaller competitors.[64] Thus, the subsidy distorts the pattern of intermediation towards larger banks and away from smaller banks and non-bank intermediation, including peer-to-peer channels. But there is a counter-argument. Shifting intermediation to smaller banks or

---

60 Gleeson (n 5).

61 DC Hardy, 'Bank Resolution Costs, Depositor Preference, and Asset Encumbrance' (2013) IMF Working Paper 13/172 <www.imf.org/external/pubs/ft/wp/2013/wp13172.pdf> accessed 2 December 2014.

62 J Santos, 'Evidence from the Bond Market on Banks' "Too-Big-To-Fail" Subsidy' (2014) 20 *Federal Reserve Bank of New York, Economic Policy Review* (Special Issue: 'Large and Complex Banks'); K Ueda and B Weder Di Mauro, 'Quantifying the Value of the Subsidy for systemically Important Financial Institutions' (2011) IMF Working Paper 12/128; Z Li, S Qu and J Zhang, 'Quantifying the Value of Implicit Government Guarantees for Large Financial Institutions' (2011) Moody's Analytics Quantitative Research Group; DP Morgan and KJ Stiroh, 'Too Big To Fail after All These Years' (2005) Federal Reserve Bank of New York Staff Reports, no 220.

63 G Alfonso, J Santos and J Traina, 'Do "Too Big To Fail" Banks Take on More Risk?' (2014) 20 *Federal Reserve Bank of New York, Economic Policy Review* (Special Issue: 'Large and Complex Banks'); M Brandao, LR Correa and H Sapriza, 'International Evidence on Government Support and Risk Taking in the Banking Sector' (2013) IMF Working Paper, 13/94; B Gadanetz, K Tsatsaronis and Y Altunbas, 'Spoilt and Lazy: The Impact of State Support on Bank Behavior in the International Loan Market' (2012) 8 *International Journal of Central Banking* 121.

64 R Gropp, H Hakenes, I Schnabel, 'Competition, Risk-shifting, and Public Bail-Out Policies' (2011) 24 *Review of Financial Studies* 2084.

to other parts of the financial system will take it away from safer, better regulated and more transparent banks (including bigger banks) and towards riskier, less regulated, and less understood channels. In addition, dependent on the state of competition between banks, much of that subsidy will have gone to providing better terms, primarily in the shape of lower interest rates, to bank borrowers. Controversially, perhaps, size improves banks operating costs.[65]

Funding costs may not be a major concern in the case of bail-inable debt but there might be an issue of adverse selection. First, another facet of the same, static question is by how much funding costs of (large) banks have to rise if they have to hold specifically designed by contract bail-inable debt. There is a range of views about the possibility of a rise in bank funding costs. As in the case of equity,[66] if we compare one, otherwise identical equilibrium, with another, when the sole difference is that some categories of bank debt become bail-inable, it is doubtful whether the overall cost of bank funding would rise by much, say 10–30 basis points. Moreover, with a rising proportion of bank creditors at risk from bank failure, there should be a greater benefit, in terms of *lower* funding costs, from a patently safer overall portfolio structure. As explained above, one of the fundamental rationales of bail-in, is that creditors at risk will have an incentive to encourage bank managers to pursue prudent policies, a counter-weight to more risk-seeking shareholders.

Secondly, bail-inable debt may affect banks' choice of assets. If institutions are required to issue a minimum amount of bail-inable liabilities expressed as a percentage of total liabilities (rather than as a percentage of risk weighted assets), critically, this will impose higher costs on institutions carrying large amounts of assets with a low risk weighting (such as mortgages). Such institutions typically hold relatively small amounts of capital as a proportion of their total liabilities. In addition, institutions will face constraints on their funding models and higher costs if they are required to hold bail-inable liabilities in specific locations within a group (for example at group level when their funding is currently undertaken by their subsidiaries).

That bail-in regimes will provide some ex ante incentive to more prudent behaviour seems undisputable. Yet market discipline failed to operate effectively ahead of the current financial crisis and holders of bail-inable liabilities will face the same difficulties as other stakeholders in assessing the health and soundness of bank balance sheets.[67]

In addition, if bank(s) nevertheless run into trouble, then utilization of the bail-in process will give another twist to pro-cyclicality. With bail-in, the weaker that banks become the harder and more expensive it will be for them to get funding. In this respect high trigger Co-Cos would perform better than bail-in-able bonds. While, in principle, increased creditor monitoring could translate into greater focus on prudence and caution for the individual banker, in the face of a generalized shock, a sizeable proportion of the banks in a given country will seem weaker. Thus a shift away from bail-out towards bail-in is likely to

---

65 A Kovner, J Vickery and L Zhou, 'Do Big Banks Have Lower operating Costs?' (2014) 20 *Federal Reserve Bank of New York, Economic Policy Review* (Special Issue: 'Large and Complex Banks').

66 D Miles, J Yang and G Marcheggiano, 'Optimal Bank Capital', Bank of England, External MPC Unit, Discussion Paper 31/2011 <www.econstor.eu/obitstream/10419/50643/1/656641770.pdf> accessed 2 December 2014; A Admati and others, 'Fallacies, Irrelevant Facts, and Myths in the Discussion of Capital Regulation: Why Bank Equity is *Not* Expensive', Working Paper <https://gsbapps.stanford.edu/researchpapers/library/rp2065r1&86.pdf> accessed 2 December 2014.

67 See on complexity as a monitoring barrier Avgouleas and Cullen (n 8).

reinforce procyclicality. The ECB has been cautious about bailing-in bank bondholders for such reasons.[68]

Of course, should the sovereign be in a weak fiscal condition, bail-out costs will give another twist to the 'doom loop' of bank and sovereign indebtedness. But if the costs of recapitalizing the banks in a given country are so large, does it help to shift them from the taxpayer to the pension funds, insurance companies and other large domestic investors, and also on the surviving banks? No doubt the crisis would take a different shape, but would it be any less severe? It could be (politically) worse if people began to fear that their pensions were being put at risk?

Liquidity Concerns

Once the bail-in process has been triggered, it is highly likely that the financial institution would only be able to continue conducting business with the 'lifeline' of emergency liquidity assistance. But the amount of liquidity support that could be provided by central banks and resolution funds (such as the Orderly Liquidation Fund in the US) may be constrained by a lack of sufficient high quality collateral, and by restrictions on any support that might result in losses falling on taxpayers. This would be accentuated if a number of major financial institutions had to be resolved at the same time. Critically, liquidity could be limited to supporting critical economic functions while other parts of the business are resolved.

Naturally, central banks and resolution funds will be reluctant to pre-commit to provide liquidity support in all circumstances. Moreover, cross-border provision of liquidity entails considerable costs and central banks may only provide assistance in their own currencies.[69] Authorities will want to ensure that another ('plan B') option is in place, including the immediate winding down of a failing financial institution through rapid sales and transfers, without liquidity support, which again would depend on a resolution plan drawn up in advance.[70] However, implementation of such plans would negate one of the biggest advantages of ('open bank') bail-in regimes, namely the continuation of the resolved entity or of operating subsidiaries as a going concern.

Bank Creditors' Flight and Contagion

A desideratum for a revenue raising mechanism is that the taxed cannot easily flee. It is difficult to avoid taxation, except by migration, which has many severe transitional costs. In contrast it is easy to avoid being hit with the costs of creditor bail-in; you just withdraw or sell your claim. Consequently, triggering the bail-in process is likely to generate a capital flight and a sharp rise in funding costs whenever the need for large-scale recapitalizations becomes apparent. Creditors who sense in advance the possibility of a bail-in, or creditors of institutions that are similar in terms of nationality or business models will have a strong

---

68 In his 30 July 2013 confidential letter to the then competition commissioner Joaquin Almunia, ECB's president Mario Draghi was reported to have expressed key concerns about the EU's bail-in regime under the draft BRRD. In particular Draghi was reported, by Reuters, who saw the letter, to have said that 'imposing losses on junior creditors in the context of such "precautionary recapitalizations" could hurt subordinated bank bonds' and then adding: '. . . structurally impairing the subordinated debt market . . . could lead to a flight of investors out of the European banking market, which would further hamper banks' funding going forward'. Reuters, 'Draghi asked EU to keep state aid rules for banks flexible' (Milan, 19 October 2013) <www.reuters.com/article/2013/10/19/us-banks-bondholders-draghi-idUSBRE99I03B20131019> accessed 2 December 2014.

69 IMF, Board Paper, 'Cross-Border Bank Resolution: Recent Developments' (2014) 15–17.

70 KPMG (n 4).

incentive to withdraw deposits, sell debt, or hedge their positions through the short-selling of equity or the purchase of credit protection at an ever higher premium disrupting the relevant markets. Such actions could be damaging and disruptive, both to a single institution[71] and potentially to wider market confidence, a point that is also highlighted by proponents of the bail-in tool.[72] In our view, market propensity to resort to herding at times of shock means that it is not realistic to believe that generalized adoption of bail-in mechanisms would not trigger contagious consequences that would have a destabilizing effect.

Where the ceiling of guaranteed deposits is set low a significant number of large depositors might migrate to other schemes such as Money Market Funds or even Investment funds that offer higher interest rates, as in the example of contemporary Chinese shadow banks. It would certainly take a lot of explaining to justify why weakening the liquidity of the regulated banking sector and increasing its funding costs in order to boost liquidity levels and lower the funding costs of the unregulated shadow banking sector is a measure to strengthen financial stability. On the contrary, a lack of Lender of Last Resort type of liquidity support in the unregulated sector could make runs inevitable, increasing the possibility of psychological spill-overs into the regulated sector and generalized panic (as occurred in the USA in 1907).

It is, of course, true that equity holders and bond holders cannot run in the same way that depositors can, but financial counterparties can easily do so and will do so if they do not immediately see a hefty capital cushion in the bailed-in bank.[73] If these flee then equity and bond holders would certainly follow and in their attempt to do so they would drive asset values sharply down to an extent that would make the option of raising new money, or rolling over existing maturing bonds, unattractive or virtually impossible. In such circumstances, bank credit extension would stop, amplifying the downturn, lowering asset values yet further and putting the solvency of other banks at risk. Excluding depositors of all brands from bail-in might reduce the danger of contagion but would not remove it.

Implications of Cross-Border Resolution with Bail-In and the SPOE Approach

The resolution of G-SIFIs with bail-in is extremely challenging. In the absence of a very high level of harmonization of insolvency/resolution rules and coordination structures, a number of obstacles could prove insurmountable, including, differences of creditor hierarchies between jurisdictions,[74] as well as differentiated treatment of creditor classes, including depositors. The paragraphs below explain some of the other challenges that a SPOE resolution of a G-SIFI, with bail-in, will surely encounter.

Cross-Border Coordination

While the SPOE approach in the event of a cross-border resolution involving jurisdictions with long history of cooperation like the US and the UK makes good sense, especially from the resolution effectiveness viewpoint – UK authorities have stated that they are ready to step aside

---

71 C Randell, 'The Great British Banking Experiment – Will the Restructuring of UK Banking Show us How to Resolve G-SIFIs?' (Paper prepared for the LSE Financial Markets Group Conference on 'Banking Structure, Regulation and Competition', November 2011).

72 S Micossi, G Bruzzone and M Casella, 'Bail-in Provisions in State Aid and Resolution Procedures: Are They Consistent with Systemic Stability?' (2014) CEPS Policy Brief, No 318, 9.

73 Sommer (n 25).

74 IMF (n 69) 11, 13–14.

and give the FDIC a free hand in the event of resolution of a G-SIFI with UK subsidiaries[75] – there is little assurance that other overseas authorities will feel the same. The IMF has authoritatively explained how MOUs failed to work in the way it was prescribed and expected during the last crisis.[76]

In order to avoid the possibility of home authorities interfering with transfers to, or from, foreign subsidiaries of the resolved group in the course of resolution, host regulators may force foreign subsidiaries to operate as ring-fenced entities increasing the trend towards disintegration of global banking markets. While this might sound like a reasonable strategy it gives rise to two undesirable consequences. First, capital and other resources within the banking group are not employed efficiently. Worse, during bad times the group is not able to shift resources from a healthy subsidiary to a troubled subsidiary. The latter may be located in a country that is in trouble itself and would greatly welcome an injection of capital and liquidity by the parent to the troubled subsidiary.[77] Secondly, recent data shows that restrictions on intra-group funding might have serious consequences for cross-border capital flows and investment and levels of global growth.[78]

Liquidity Provision as Part of the Resolution Funding Framework

Meeting the liquidity requirements of the operating subsidiaries of the resolved group could be a challenging task, given also that access to market-based liquidity might be severely restricted for the resolved group. In the US, in the event of resolution of a SIFI under OLA, the bridge holding company will downstream liquidity, as necessary, to subsidiaries through intra-company advances. When this is not sufficient the FDIC will act as provider of liquidity through loans to the bridge company or any covered subsidiaries that enjoy super-seniority, or by granting of guarantees (s. 204 of the DFA). Yet the issue is far from resolved as such loans and guarantees might not prove sufficient, especially if the quality of the collateral is not of a very high grade and the FDIC has not concealed that fact.[79] Normally, a G-SIFI is funded mostly through retail, and other short-term, deposits, which in the event of a bail-in could either dry up or even be withdrawn. So, as commonly recognized, a group in resolution may require considerable official liquidity support. This should only be provided on a fully collateralized basis, with appropriate haircuts applied to the collateral, to reduce further the risk of loss, but this depends on the adequacy of the available collateral.

In the UK, the policy for liquidity provision in resolution follows the provisions of the EU Directive (BRRD). The BRRD provides that resolution will primarily be financed by national resolution funds that can also borrow from each other (Art 99 et seq.). The BRRD does not rule out provision of liquidity, in the event of resolution by the central bank.

The BRRD treats the Deposit Guarantee Scheme (DGS) as a creditor that can be bailed-in, with the costs of this falling on other firms, which have to fund the Scheme.[80] Thus, the requisite

---

75 P Tucker, 'Regulatory Reform, Stability and Central Banking' (2014) Hutchins Center on Fiscal and Monetary Policy, Brookings <www.brookings.edu> accessed 2 December 2014.

76 IMF (n 69), 6, Box 1.

77 G Baer, 'Regulation and Resolution: Toward a Unified Theory' (2014) *Banking Perspective: The Clearing House*, 12, 15.

78 'The flow of money through the global financial system is still stuck at the same level as a decade ago, raising fresh concerns about the strength of the economic recovery following six years of financial crisis . . .' These findings were based on research carried by the McKinsey Global Institute for the *Financial Times* and was published by this journal on 7 January 2014.

79 FDIC (n 17).

80 Arts 45(6), 108(b), 109, Recs 71, 110, 111, BRRD.

DGS will have to contribute for the purpose of ensuring continuous access to covered deposits and relevant contributions will be *in cash* for an amount equivalent to the losses that the DGS would have had to bear in normal insolvency proceedings. Namely, the DGS contribution is made in cash in order to absorb the losses from the covered deposits.[81] The DGS is solely liable for the protection of covered depositors.[82] If following a contribution by the DGS, the institution under resolution fails at a later stage and the DGS does not have sufficient funds to repay depositors, the DGS must have arrangements in place in order to raise the corresponding amounts as soon as possible from its members. Otherwise, treating the DGS as an unsecured depositor in the event of a systemic crisis might raise doubt about the sufficiency of funds available to it.

Location of Bail-Inable Debt and of Bank Deposits

Another important issue is where the debt is located, namely, which entity within the group holds the debt. The joint FDIC-BoE paper envisages that, at least for UK groups, bail-in-able debt will be issued by the top operating companies within a group, which, however, may operate in different jurisdictions. This means that the SPOE approach might prove elusive for non-US G-SIFIs. For G-SIFIs with substantial operations in the US, the Federal Reserve has introduced a final rule, implementing its Dodd–Frank mandate, requiring these operations to be held through a US holding company.[83] In the absence of MOUs similar to the one signed between the FDIC and the BoE, it is not clear whether the US authorities would seek to resolve the US operations on a stand-alone basis (by applying the SPOE approach within the US), or would stand back and allow the overseas parent to be resolved without the US authorities taking action. Worse, drawing lessons in a cross-border context from Kupic and Wallison's analysis of SPOE in the domestic US context,[84] we could note that, in the event of failure of major foreign subsidiaries of US Bank Holding Companies (BHC), US authorities might face untenable political dilemmas. Namely, where the US BHC does not hold enough bail-inable debt to recapitalize the failing overseas operation, US authorities would probably have no incentive to intervene, as the US based Holding Company will remain solvent, in spite of the failure of the foreign subsidiary. If they did choose to intervene honouring the SPOE MOU, they would essentially extend coverage of US deposit insurance and of OLF to foreign depositors, probably a politically prohibitive action.

The proportion of foreign creditors can go up dramatically when we move from purely domestic banks to cross-border banks with numerous foreign branches or subsidiaries. Most SIFIs, and all G-SIFIs, are cross-border. Yet, the thrust of many proposals for bank resolution, for example those of the UK Financial Services (Banking Reform) Act 2013 and some earlier Swiss measures, has been to limit taxpayer contingent liability to the local, domestic

---

81 Art 109(3), BRRD.

82 Art 109(1), BRRD.

83 Federal Reserve System, 'Enhanced Prudential Standards for Bank Holding Companies and Foreign Banking', 18 February 2014. In a substantial break with past practice FRB's final rule requires large Foreign Banking Organisations with $50 billion or more of (non-branch) assets in US-chartered subsidiaries and all foreign SIFIs to place all their US operations in a US-based intermediate holding company ('IHC') on which the FRB will impose enhanced capital, liquidity and other prudential requirements on those IHCs, separate from and in addition to the requirements of the parent company's home country supervisor, ibid.

84 Paul Kupiec and Peter Wallison, 'Can the "Single Point of Entry" Strategy be Used to Recapitalize a Failing Bank?' (2014) American Enterprise Institute, Working Paper 2014–08.

part of the bank. But not only will this lead towards further balkanization and localization of banking systems, it also raises the question of how far bail-in of only ring-fenced entities is consistent with a Single Point of Entry (SPOE) resolution mechanisms.

Moreover, legal disputes, and shareholder and creditor objections, will become even more acute where a subsidiary of the holding company is on the verge of failure, while the holding company has other viable and valuable subsidiaries. In such a case it could be perceived as disproportionate to cancel the claims of existing shareholders in the hold-ing company since these retain significant value by virtue of the value of the non-failing group subsidiaries. Even if a value is placed on solvent subsidiaries, so that holding group shareholders are issued new shares of reduced value rather than being wiped out, the bail-in process will be protracted. This development could potentially have a seriously destabiliz-ing impact on the institution that is being resolved, since only speedy resolution can prevent a creditor run on the institution.

Resolving Systemic Subsidiaries

Equally challenging would be the application of SPOE to bail-in when overseas subsidiaries need to be resolved because they are both loss-making and are undertaking critical eco-nomic functions. It may not be possible, or efficient, to resolve them through an injection of capital from the parent holding company. Overseas resolution authorities may choose to exercise their own national resolution powers to intervene in the overseas subsidiaries – or even branches – of US and UK G-SIFIs. This would be consistent with the 'multiple points of entry' (MPE) approach that is the key model under the EU BRRD, and with the growing trend towards 'localization/subsidiarization' under which overseas host authorities seek to protect their national markets through the ring-fencing of operations of foreign firms in their countries.

The EU BRRD makes provision for SPOE group resolution as well as giving the option to operate the bail-in regime on a legal entity basis. The MPE approach in the BRRD reflects the different legal and operating structures across Europe and the fact that each Member State operates, for now, its own Deposit Guarantee Scheme. To minimize friction between resolution authorities the BRRD provides for a consolidated group approach[85] based on close cooperation and coordination through resolution colleges, and on group level resolution plans agreed in advance.[86] Yet, in the event of a group resolution, each national authority would apply bail-in (and other resolution tools) to each entity based in its jurisdiction. Once the new Single Resolution Mechanism comes into force, Euro-wide resolution would be conducted by a single authority and SPOE could become an option, but MPE will still be the adopted route for subsidiaries located in the UK and other EU Member States that are not part of the European Banking Union.

Further Reflections and Concluding Remarks

In our view, the top-down SPOE approach adopted by the US regulators is conceptually superior. Assets and liabilities at the operating subsidiary level are not part of the painful debt restructuring bail-in exercise and may continue operations regardless. Yet there are sceptics

---

85 Arts 13, 69, BRRD.
86 Arts 13, 88, 89, BRRD.

who suggest that FDIC's SPOE, even in a pure domestic context, could lead to amplification of moral hazard and mutualization of group losses among all (ex post) contributors to DFA's OLF.[87] Moreover, there are four clear disadvantages in implementing this approach in the case of G-SIFIs.

First, the (unaffected by resolution) operating subsidiary might, nevertheless, suffer a flight due to reputational contagion, which triggers an irrational but quite likely panic, regardless of parent's ability to sufficiently recapitalize the operating parts of the group through conversion of bail-in-able liabilities. Secondly, apart from closely inter-related banking markets like the UK and the US, where the level of trust between national authorities is high, it is doubtful if any form of non-binding bilateral arrangements, including MOUs, would hold in the event of a cross-border banking crisis, involving a transfer of funds from one jurisdiction to another.[88] The gulf between regulators will become even deeper, if the majority of a certain form of group level funding (for example, tripartite repos) is booked with a specific subsidiary that is not based in the same place as the HoldCo being resolved.[89] Thirdly, it is arguable that when the subsidiary is ring-fenced the regulators may expect the subsidiary creditors, as well as shareholders like the HoldCo, to bear the cost of bail-in. Fourth, the top-down approach could increase scope for arbitrage and regulatory forbearance. In most cases it will be the home country regulator that will have the final word as regards the level of *D bail-inable debt* to be held by the HoldCo. But *D bail-inable debt* could prove more expensive than other subordinated debt. Thus, a home regulator concerned about the health of banks in its domestic market would be much less keen on increasing the cost of funding of its banks, unless legally bound to do so through bilateral or multilateral arrangements with host authorities. Absence of such arrangements could trigger multiple races to the bottom. In addition, there could also be circumstances where home resolution authorities are reluctant to use the bail-in tool because of its adverse impact on specific groups of creditors (for example, article 44(3), Rec. 72 of the BRRD).

A host resolution authority might be tempted to trigger its own resolution and bail-in powers if it was concerned that it might not receive sufficient support from the new bridge holding company to meet losses at, and/or to preserve critical economic functions in, its local subsidiary. The BRRD (article 96, article 1(1)(e), Rec. 102) explicitly extends this power beyond subsidiaries to branches of institutions from outside the EU. By means of this provision, EU Member States can apply resolution tools, including bail-in, to such branches to protect local depositors and to preserve financial stability, independent of any third country resolution procedure, if the third country has failed to act. Similarly, subject to a number of conditions and on the basis EU of financial stability concerns, the BRRD (article 95) gives the right to

---

87 'Unless parent BHCs have substantial loss absorbing capacity, the SPOE strategy will mutualize bank losses through OLF assessments on other large BHCs and designated non-bank financial institutions that are subject to Federal Reserve oversight. The SPOE objective, keeping systemically important subsidiaries open and operating by protecting bank creditors, substantially increases the moral hazard created by deposit insurance. Because depository institution subsidiaries often issue more uninsured liabilities than their parent BHCs, the SPOE strategy protects a far larger group of creditors at the bank level than it puts "at risk" at the BHC level. When this happens, as it often does, SPOE institutionalizes TBTF by providing assurances that all the creditors of large banks will be protected from loss – if necessary, by taxing other large financial firms to reimburse the OLF', Kupiec and Wallison (n 84), 6.

88 Sommer (n 25).

89 DA Skeel, 'Single Point of Entry and the Bankruptcy Alternative' (2014) University of Pennsylvania, Institute for Law & Economic Research Paper No 14–10.

European resolution authorities to refuse to enforce third country resolution proceedings over EU-based subsidiaries.

Accordingly the kind of international cooperation required to allow a top-down approach to operate effectively is unprecedented and it might well form the most challenging aspect of cross-border implementation of bail-in recapitalization in the case of G-SIFIs.

Conclusion

> As the emerging-market crises and the entire history of financial crises made clear, imposing haircuts on bank creditors during a systemic panic is a sure way to accelerate the panic.[90]

In this chapter we have provided an extensive analysis of the legal and economic challenges facing the implementation of bail-in regimes. While we fully understand the revulsion from too-big-to-fail banks and the (political) cost of bail-outs, we are worried that the development of a bandwagon may conceal some of the disadvantages of the new bail-in regimes. While the bail-in approach may, indeed, be much superior to bail-outs in the case of idiosyncratic failure, the resort to bail-in may disappoint unless everyone involved is fully aware of the potential downsides of the new approach.

A bail-in mechanism used for the recapitalization of a bank as going concern has the following advantages, vis-à-vis a bail-out approach:

- lower levels of moral hazard;
- better creditor monitoring;
- protects taxpayers;
- places the burden more fairly;
- should improve ex ante behaviour of bank management;
- mitigates the sovereign/bank debt 'doom-loop';
- fosters competition;
- may facilitate a subsequent private sale.

On the other hand, the bail-in process may also have some important disadvantages over bail-outs, as it could prove to be:

- more contagious and procyclical;
- more litigious;
- slower and more expensive as a process;
- requiring greater subsequent liquidity injections;
- leading to deterioration of governance;
- requiring higher funding costs to banks;
- providing a worse outlook for bank borrowers;
- worsening ex post outcomes.

The equal length of the two lists is happenstance and not indication of which approach should be favoured. This chapter is not intended to claim that the proposed reforms will make the

90 Geithner (n 49), 214.

process of dealing with failing banks necessarily worse. Its purpose is, instead, to warn that the exercise may have costs and disadvantages, which, unless fully appreciated, could make the outcome less successful than hoped. The authorities will no doubt claim that they have already, and fully, appreciated all such points, as and where relevant. But we would contend that many advocates of moving to the latter do not mention such disadvantages at all, or only partially. Perhaps the choice should depend on context.

The bail-in process seems, in principle, a suitable substitute to resolution (whether liquidation of a gone concern, or some other form of resolution in a going concern bank) in the case of smaller domestic financial institutions. It could also be used successfully to recapitalize domestic SIFIs, but only if the institution has failed due to its own actions and omissions and not due to a generalized systemic crisis. Otherwise, a flight of creditors from other institutions, i.e., contagion, may be uncontainable. Even so, successful bail-in recapitalization would require rapid restoration of market confidence,[91] accurate evaluation of losses, and successful restructuring of the bailed-in bank's operations to give it a sound business model to avoid successive rounds of bail-in rescues. It could, of course, prove very hard for regulators to secure all those pre-requisites of a successful bail-in recapitalization in the event of a systemic crisis.

Moreover, generic structural, governance, legal and other risks and costs associated with a cross-border resolution of a G-SIFI (discussed in the fourth section) make the use of the process highly uncertain in its outcome, unless failure was clearly idiosyncratic, for example, as a result of fraud.

In addition, it is erroneous to assume that a preplanned bankruptcy plan will, in reality, work under all conditions to prevent a systemic crisis.[92] This statement by Thomas M. Hoenig – Vice Chairman of the Federal Deposit Insurance Corporation is indicative:[93]

> Unfortunately, based on the material so far submitted, in my view each plan being discussed today is deficient and fails to convincingly demonstrate how, in failure, any one of these firms could overcome obstacles to entering bankruptcy without precipitating a financial crisis. Despite the thousands of pages of material these firms submitted, the plans provide no credible or clear path through bankruptcy that doesn't require unrealistic assumptions and direct or indirect public support.

Given these shortcomings and costs of bail-in bank recapitalization, orderly and timely resolution of a G-SIFI would, arguably, still require fiscal commitments. These could be established by means of ex ante burden sharing agreements, concluded either independently or by means of commitments entrenched in G-SIFI living wills.[94] Moreover, over-reliance on bail-in could deepen the trend towards disintegration of the internal market in the EU,[95]

---

91 Sommer (n 25).

92 See G Karamichailidou and DG Mayes, 'Plausible Recovery and Resolution Plans for Cross-Border Financial Institutions' (paper prepared for the Conference European Banking Union: Prospects and Challenges, University of Buckingham, 21–22 November 2014).

93 Statement of 5 August 2014 <www.fdic.gov/news/news/speeches/spaug0514a.pdf> accessed 2 December 2014.

94 E Avgouleas, C Goodhart and D Schoenmaker, 'Recovery and Resolution Plans as a Catalyst of Global Reform' (2013) 9 *Journal of Financial Stability* 210.

95 Center for European Policy Studies (CEPS), 'Framing Banking Union in the Euro Area: Some Empirical Evidence' (2014) <www.ceps.eu/book/framing-banking-union-euro-area-some-empirical-evidence> accessed 2 December 2014.

while providing uncertain benefits. So, effective recapitalization of ailing banks may still require a credible fiscal backstop. In addition, a fiscal backstop may be essential to avert, in the case of deposits held in the same currency across a common currency area, a flight of deposits from Member States with weaker sovereigns to the Member States with solvent sovereigns.[96] This is more or less a eurozone specific risk, unless the current structures on the use of ESM funds are gradually loosened. EU policy-makers ought to continue their efforts to build one instead of relying on the unproven thesis that the bail-in process can resolve the recapitalization challenges facing the eurozone banking sector.

Finally, achieving the goal of making private institutions responsible for their actions would be the best policy in an ideal world where financial 'polluters' would be held responsible for their actions. But, in practice, it might prove an unattainable goal. If this turns out to be the case then developed societies might have to accept that granting some form of public insurance is an inevitable tax for having a well-functioning banking sector. At the same time, other forms of regulation like structural reform and leverage ratios (plus more emphasis on the prior Recovery stage), if they prove to make banks more stable, should come to the forefront with renewed force.

---

96 D Schoenmaker, 'A Fiscal Backstop to the Banking System' (2014) Duisenberg Business School, DSF Policy Paper No 44.

5 Staying Global and Neoliberal or Going Somewhere Else? Banking Regulation after the Crisis

Mika Viljanen[*]

Local and Global Reactions: Diverging Paths

In 2007, banking regulation all over the world was converging on the second version of the non-binding rule-set drafted by the Basel Committee on Banking Supervision (BCBS), the Basel II.[1] Basel II constituted a global and inherently neoliberal regulatory platform. The basic regulatory strategy built on the balance sheet mediated risk sensitive capital adequacy regulatory paradigm. The technological setup allowed regulators to pursue what was the quintessential neoliberal regulatory strategy: to simultaneously, first, make banks safe and the international banking system stable and, second, refrain from affecting banks' business decisions. The rules promoted stability, but simultaneously set no structural restrictions, banned no instruments and allowed all business models. Risk had to be adequately capitalized, that was all.[2]

The Basel II approach collapsed during the financial crisis. The risk technologies incorporated into the Accord proved unreliable, one after another.[3] Credit ratings were discredited.[4] The value-at-risk measurement approach – the intellectual bedrock of Basel II advanced risk methodologies – disintegrated.[5] Together with the risk technologies, the neoliberal strategy became unhinged. Risk sensitive capital requirements were found insufficient to ensure bank system stability. Consequently, a mad scramble for reforms ensued. Now, years later, the global banking regulation arena has seen a fundamental reshuffle.

Two simultaneous processes took place. On the global level, the newly founded *Financial Stability Board* (FSB) oversaw an overhaul of the Basel Accord. In the reforms, global banking regulators attempted to fix the Basel Accord shortcomings unearthed by the crisis. The

* Collegium Researcher, University of Turku, Finland. This chapter was written while the author was the leader of 'How to rule the economy', a research project funded by the Academy of Finland.

1 Basel Committee on Banking Supervision, International Convergence of Capital Measurement and Capital Standards. A Revised Framework. Comprehensive Version, June 2006 (Bank for International Settlements 2006).
2 Aaron Major, 'Neoliberalism and the New International Financial Architecture' (2012) 19 Review of International Political Economy 536; Bengt 428.Larsson, 'Neo-Liberalism and Polycontextuality: Banking Crisis and Re-Regulation in Sweden' (2003) 32 *Economy and Society*.
3 Jeffrey Atik, 'Basel II: a Post-Crisis Post-Mortem' (2011) 19 *Transnational Law & Contemporary Problems* 731.
4 Efraim Benmelech and Jennifer Dlugosz, 'The Credit Rating Crisis' (2010) 24 NBER Macroeconomics Annual 161.
5 Erik F Gerding, 'Code, Crash, and Open Source: the Outsourcing of Financial Regulation to Risk Models and the Global Financial Crisis' (2009) 84 *Washington Law Review* 127.

Basel II.5[6] and Basel III[7] reforms yanked up capital requirements, improved capital quality, enhanced risk coverage and attempted to mend many of the failed risk technologies.

In a parallel process, a flurry of local regulatory projects was initiated outside the Basel envelope. The United States enacted the Dodd–Frank Wall Street Reform and Consumer Protection Act and the Volcker rule. The United Kingdom put together the Financial Services (Banking Reform) Act in 2013. The EU Commission issued a proposal non-Basel based banking reform package in January 2014,[8] while Germany had already implemented its own set of reforms with Trennbankengesetz. In all these initiatives, the brunt of the impact is carried by rules manipulating the structure of banking groups or permitted activities within them, often both simultaneously. In particular, the initiatives target trading. The US Volcker rule, for example, bans all proprietary trading in banks, while the UK Banking Reform Act requires that all retail banks are ring-fenced, and the EU proposal envisions a proprietary trading ban and potential 'inverse' ring fences.

The contrast between the global and local responses is striking. The core Basel regulatory strategy still pursues a neoliberal agenda of not governing if risks – now, for example liquidity risks included – are captured and adequately capitalized. The local initiatives, instead, apparently entail a return to the paternalist, interventionist – and distinctly non-neoliberal – past of banking regulation by imposing business model restrictions. Under these approaches, banking is regulated and made safe by explicitly constraining the scope of allowed bank business models and corporate structures. The guiding idea is that certain activities are simply too risky to be allowed to continue. As a consequence, the two set of reform initiatives seem to diverge radically from each other.

Objectives and Structure

The objective of this chapter is to inquire into the relationship between these two apparently conflicting regulatory agendas, and ultimately identify the new locus of power where post-crisis banking regulation is made. The key question is: do the local initiatives signify a radical transition in global banking regulation capable of unsettling the neoliberal Basel approach? The answer to the question is complex. A closer inspection of the reform initiatives uncovers an intricate milieu of banking regulation. Any answer to the question could, in fact, only result in crude simplifications.

In the next section, the chapter maps out the Basel landscape. First, I describe the basic Basel II neoliberal regulatory strategy of not governing banks at a distance, but, second, also discusses its tortious, fear-laden nature. Second, I look into the post-crisis Basel reforms and chart the emerging post-crisis Basel regulatory strategies. A perplexing picture of a

---

6 Basel Committee on Banking Supervision, *Revisions to the Basel II Market Risk Framework. July 2009* (Bank for International Settlements 2009); Basel Committee on Banking Supervision, *Enhancements to the Basel II Framework. July 2009* (Bank for International Settlements 2009).
7 Basel Committee on Banking Supervision, Basel III: A Global Regulatory Framework for More Resilient Banks and Banking Systems. December 2010 (Bank for International Settlements 2010); Basel Committee on Banking Supervision, Basel III: International Framework for Liquidity Risk Measurement, Standards and Monitoring, December 2010 (Bank for International Settlements 2010).
8 European Commission, 'Proposal for a Regulation of the European Parliament and of the Council on Structural Measures Improving the Resilience of EU Credit Institutions' COM (2014) 43 final.

frail and fraught neoliberal regulatory project emerges. On the one hand, the fraught Basel II neoliberal edifice is retained but, on the other, the edifice seems to be cracking up. Basel II.5 and Basel III revisions contain initiatives that erode the core Basel II regulatory strategy. The revisions amount to an – admittedly modest and stealthy – structural regulatory project.

In Section 3, the chapter discusses the national and regional regulatory initiatives that the United States, United Kingdom, Germany and European Union have undertaken to supplement the Basel reforms. First, the section maps the basic contours of these structural regulatory reforms. Second, it addresses the regulatory strategy of the initiatives which all impose trading bans of limited scope. My argument is that the structural regulatory initiatives remain at the periphery. They push the riskiest banking activities away from institutions with access to government funding support but fail to fundamentally change the banking landscape. This implies that even the structural regulation projects have not shed their neoliberal roots. The initiatives seem to be primarily there to keep the markets afloat while manipulating their peripheries.

The chapter concludes by a discussion of the interplay of the two regimes. I will argue that the diagnosis stressing the differences between two sets of responses might, in fact, be naive. Both initiatives implement tortious, multifaceted regulatory strategies that do not yield to easy categorizations. The Basel strategy is not exclusively and orthodoxly neoliberal but, rather, contains paternalist and interventionist tendencies which augment its neoliberal agenda with a tacit small-scale structural regulation project. BCBS is manipulating the fringes of the risk sensitive Basel rules to inch out certain bank trading activities. Simultaneously, the structural regulation initiatives also betray their non-neoliberal initial outlook. The structural regulation initiatives prove, upon detailed inspection, underwhelming. The initiatives seem primarily designed to allow neoliberal banking to continue, but in a new institutional setting where some of its most pernicious potential effects and flagrant perverse consequences are contained to ensure that neoliberal global markets are not endangered.

Consequently, a bewildering endgame emerges. The Basel rules and the structural regulation initiatives converge upon a tortious neoliberal strategy which attempts to fix the shortcomings of a neoliberal strategy with somewhat unorthodox tools to keep the neoliberal regulatory framework afloat. Both reforms engage in a form of *damage control neoliberalism* by reregulating banking to allow it to remain as free and unconstrained as possible.

The Basel Strategies

The Basel 2 Strategy

The Dream of Not Governing at a Distance

Basel II[9] went live on 1 January 2007. The day marked a significant transition in banking regulation. The Committee had developed a set of regulatory technologies that made genuinely risk sensitive capital adequacy regulation possible. The new technologies built on value-at-risk (VaR) theory. Under the Internal Models Approach (IMA)[10] advanced banks were tasked to simulate how much money would be lost if a 10-day 1 per cent adverse

---

9 Basel Committee on Banking Supervision (n 1).
10 ibid 176.

market scenario played out, while the Internal Ratings Based Approach (IRB)[11] required banks to calculate the scope of losses in a 0.1 per cent one year scenario and hold an equivalent amount of capital. These loss estimates were, then, imposed on banks as regulatory capital minimum requirements. The less advanced banks had to contend with capital charges determined by borrower credit ratings.

The new set of technologies rendered banking regulation both quantitatively rational and finally genuinely non-interventionist. Remember that the VaR based regulatory capital requirements reflected realistic scenario loss estimates produced by the banks' internal state-of-the-art risk quantification technologies. The technological provenance of Basel II capital charge methodologies was crucial in another respect as well. The assemblage aligned regulatory capital and economic capital methodologies as IMA, IRB and Internal Model Method (IMM)[12] methodologies retrace and enact the same risks as the banks' internal risk control technologies. Consequently, the incentives produced by regulatory and economic capital[13] methodologies were harmonized. Apart from setting an investment hurdle rate, regulators were finally able to refrain from affecting bank investment decisions, while simultaneously capping bank leverage and risk-taking. The perverse incentive effects Basel 1 risk weight scheme had imbued on banks[14] were eliminated. On a theoretical level, these developments signify the fulfilment of a long-standing neoliberal regulatory dream. Basel II allowed BCBS to finally perfect what governmentality scholars[15] would probably characterize as *a non-governing at a distance approach* to regulation. BCBS 'link[ed] calculations at one place with action at another, not through the direct imposition of a form of conduct by force, but through a delicate affiliation of a loose assemblage of agents and agencies into a functioning network'[16] and managed to ensure banking system stability while not affecting the behaviour of the regulated. Bank balance sheets, internal control technologies were all carefully orchestrated to do absolutely nothing but assure adequate capital levels. Or so the regulators hoped.

Living with Bad Models

The description above is, however, an exaggeration. VaR technologies did revolutionize capital regulation, but implementation was an arduous, messy process fraught with problems and dangers. The celebrated risk technologies were, in fact, precarious, fragile, tentative and unreliable.[17] BCBS knew it. As a consequence, technological failures constantly challenged the neoliberal regulatory strategy, rendering it incomplete and experimentalist. BCBS

---

11 ibid 52.

12 ibid Annex 4, 254.

13 Abel Elizalde and Rafael Repullo, 'Economic and Regulatory Capital in Banking: What Is the Difference?' (2007) 3 *International Journal of Central Banking* 87.

14 David Jones, 'Emerging Problems with the Basel Capital Accord: Regulatory Capital Arbitrage and Related Issues' (1999) 24 *Journal of Banking & Finance* 35; Working group led by Patricia Jackson, 'Capital Requirements and Bank Behaviour: the Impact of the Basel Accord' (1999) Basel Committee on Banking Supervision Working Papers, 1/1999; Viral V Acharya, Philipp Schnabl and Gustavo Suarez, 'Securitization Without Risk Transfer' (2013) 107 *Journal of Financial Economics* 515.

15 For example Nikolas Rose, Pat O'Malley and Marianne Valverde, 'Governmentality' (2006) 2 *Annual Review of Law and Social Science* 83.

16 Peter Miller and Nikolas Rose, 'Governing Economic Life' (1990) 19 *Economy and Society* 1, 9–10.

17 Jon Daníelsson, 'The Emperor Has No Clothes: Limits to Risk Modelling' (2002) 26 *Journal of Banking & Finance* 1273.

seemed never able to grasp the elusive prize of full risk sensitivity. The dream was precariously close to turning into a nightmare.

The 1996 Internal Models Approach reform[18] and its subsequent modifications constitute a prime example of how fragile the assemblages were. Despite appearances, IMA was a mess. Computer resources and lacking data handicapped even the most sophisticated actors. Implementation was, in addition, hugely expensive. Even VaR theory struggled to deliver on the promise it held.[19] As a response to the problems, BCBS introduced a complicated system of safety layers and safety arrangements. First, the Committee introduced a brutal multiplication factor treatment of three. All market risk VaR numbers were multiplied by a factor of three to arrive at a suitably conservative capital requirement.[20] In addition, the Committee introduced a back testing procedure to penalise aggressive model construction.[21]

The specific market risk regime added another layer of safety. Most 1996 VaR models failed to account for, e.g., idiosyncratic price shocks and sudden changes in correlation and volatility environments. To mitigate the vulnerability, the Committee first established a 50 per cent Standardized Measurement Method floor for modelled specific market risk capital charges.[22] In 1997, the Committee, however, migrated to a '4×VaR' regime. Until a bank could 'demonstrate that the methodologies it use[d] adequately capture event and default risk', it had to contend with an 'additional prudential surcharge'[23] as the imperfect specific market risk VaR estimates were multiplied by four instead of the normal multiplication factor of three. With these moves, BCBS essentially admitted that most contemporary VaR models were incapable of capturing the full spectrum of market risk. Only in the Basel II reforms the specific risk safety layer was dismantled,[24] but even then the system remained fraught. The Committee acknowledged the fact by conceding that the 10-day 1 per cent VaR framework was fundamentally inadequate and adding the Incremental Default Risk Charge.[25]

The same wary and cautious approach to VaR implementation dominates both the 2004 IRB[26] and 2005 IMM counterparty credit risk rules.[27] For example, before[28] and during the IRBA consultations, the industry strongly pleaded for full authority to model credit risk capital

18 Basel Committee on Banking Supervision, *Amendment to the Capital Accord to Incorporate Market Risks. January 1996* (Bank for International Settlements 1996) 38.
19 Nikolas Nassim Taleb, 'Against VaR' *Derivatives Strategy* (New York City, 15 October 1997) <www.derivativesstrategy.com/magazine/archive/1997/0497fea2.asp> accessed 15 October 2013; Carlo Acerbi and Dirk Tasche, 'Expected Shortfall: a Natural Coherent Alternative to Value at Risk' (2002) 31 Economic Notes 379, 383.
20 Basel Committee on Banking Supervision (n 18) s B.4(i), 45.
21 ibid s B.4(k), 45; Basel Committee on Banking Supervision, Supervisory Framework for the Use of 'Backtesting' in Conjunction with the Internal Models Approach to Market Risk Capital Requirements. January 1996 (Bank for International Settlements 1996); Jon Daníelsson, Philipp Hartmann and Casper G de Vries, 'The Cost of Conservatism: Extreme Returns, Value-at-Risk, and the Basel "Multiplication Factor"' (1998) 11 Risk 101.
22 Basel Committee on Banking Supervision (n 18) s B.4(k), 45.
23 Basel Committee on Banking Supervision, Modifications to the Market Risk Amendment. Textual Changes to the Amendment to the Basel Capital Accord of January 1996 (Bank for International Settlements 1997).
24 Basel Committee on Banking Supervision, The Application of Basel II to Trading Activities and the Treatment of Double Default Effects (Bank for International Settlements 2005) 62.
25 Basel Committee on Banking Supervision (n 1) s 718(xcii).
26 Basel Committee on Banking Supervision, International Convergence of Capital Measurement and Capital Standards. A Revised Framework. June 2004 (Bank for International Settlements 2004).
27 Basel Committee on Banking Supervision (n 24) p 1.III.
28 International Swaps and Derivatives Association, *Credit Risk and Regulatory Capital* (International Swaps and Derivatives Association 1998).

charges. However, the Committee emphatically declined. It did not believe in banks' risk models and risk measurement capabilities.[29] The end-result was a perplexing hybrid credit risk engine that simultaneously constitutes an attempt at implementing a Merton-Vasicek Asymptotic Single Risk Factor credit risk model, but forces banks to build giant, strictly regulated probability of default (PD) generation machineries and constitutes an abashed risk weighting scheme dominated by regulator's discretionary, seat-of-the-pants judgments.[30]

The dream was laden with fear. What emerged was a tortious, halting neoliberal regulatory strategy of regulating the banks as little as the regulators dared.

The Strategy in Crisis

Failure Leads to Reforms

Basel II had, in 2007, put in place a new fear-laden strategy of not governing banks from a distance. In the financial crisis, the fears were confirmed. The technological assemblage underlying the strategy broke down, spectacularly. The Accord was revealed a near-total regulatory failure.[31] First, the rules had failed to force banks to hold adequate capital. To add insult to injury, the capital the banks held was often of questionable quality. Second, unanticipated losses abounded. BCBS had missed a number of important loss drivers. Banks suffered hundreds of billions in losses when securitization assets and other fixed income instrument marks suddenly started to deteriorate. The IMA regime had failed to anticipate the extent of trading book interest instrument losses. Derivative instrument counterparty risk also catered for a nasty surprise. Banks had to make hundreds of billions in credit valuation adjustments.[32]

Reforms promptly followed the failure diagnosis. They came in two waves, pioneered by the *Basel II.5* package[33] published in September 2009 and followed by the *Basel III*[34] a year later.

A Revolution That Never Was

The Basel II.5 and Basel III packages constitute a sweeping overall recalibration of the Accord. Basel III delivered most of the quantitative punch. The package carried out a blunt and brutal recalibration of the minimum capital requirements. Banks were, simply, required to hold significantly more and better quality capital than under Basel II.[35] Simultaneously, the

29 Kevin L Young, 'Transnational Regulatory Capture? An Empirical Examination of the Transnational Lobbying of the Basel Committee on Banking Supervision' (2012) 19 *Review of International Political Economy* 663, 672–74.

30 Basel Committee on Banking Supervision, *An Explanatory Note on the Basel II IRB Risk Weight Functions. July 2005* (Bank for International Settlements 2005).

31 Atik (n 3); Benmelech and Dlugosz (n 4); Gerding (n 5).

32 Financial Services Authority, *The Prudential Regime for Trading Activities: A Fundamental Review* (Financial Services Authority 2010) 42–46.

33 Basel Committee on Banking Supervision, *Revisions* (n 6); Basel Committee on Banking Supervision, *Enhancements* (n 6); Basel Committee on Banking Supervision, *Guidelines for Computing Capital for Incremental Risk in the Trading Book. July 2009* (Bank for International Settlements 2009).

34 Basel Committee on Banking Supervision, *Global Regulatory Framework* (n 7); Basel Committee on Banking Supervision, *International Framework for Liquidity* (n 7).

35 For example Chris Matten, 'Defining Capital' in Richard Barfield (ed) *A Practitioner's Guide to Basel III and beyond* (Sweet & Maxwell 2011).

capital charge structures were revamped to dampen procyclicality and cliff effects and provide a rudimentary macroprudential toolset to regulators.[36] Basel III also added the leverage ratio[37] and the first ever Basel rules on bank liquidity.[38]

The overall recalibration was augmented by measures that addressed specific Basel II risk methodology shortcomings. The Committee both boosted the Accord's risk coverage and repaired many of the risk methodologies it felt had failed during the crisis. These measures are scattered around the Basel II.5 and Basel III packages. Basel II.5 for example implemented sweeping changes to the IMA and the securitization framework, while Basel III fixed many counterparty risk related issues.

From the regulatory strategy point of view the reforms are, nevertheless, relatively subdued. Of course, the Basel III capital requirement recalibration adds new functions to the Accord's list of objectives. The capital conservation and countercyclical buffers have clear macroprudential undertones.[39] The capital conservation buffer also recasts the basic regulatory mechanisms that underlie capital requirements. The rules no more impose a single, inflexible capital standard. Instead, they determine a possible zone for bank capital with a graduated regulatory response to eventual declines in capital levels. The idea is to dampen the procyclicality of regulatory capital.[40] In an ironic twist, the leverage ratio was introduced to backstop the risk sensitive capital requirement regime. The measure's explicit function is to serve as a non-risk based fail-safe measure to mitigate the damage flowing from eventual regulatory failures or banks gaming attempts.[41]

These three changes, however, seem relatively insignificant as regulatory strategy changes. Macroprudential instruments are built on top of the traditional risk sensitive foundations. The buffer structure does make capital regulation more rational but does not affect the core strategy. IMA, IRBA and IMM are retained. Risk weighting still persists as the primary regulatory technology. Leverage ratio, in turn, is a backstop, a last resort measure designed to guard the perimeter of the ordinary rules, at least in theory.[42] Consequently, the core strategy of not governing banks at a distance still remains intact, at least on a superficial level.

Risk Insensitive Risk Measures

This diagnosis seems to concur with BCBS' own understanding of the reforms' effect on the Accord. In the documents, the Committee articulated that it remained committed to pursuing the risk sensitive regulatory approach – albeit the era of one-sided insistence was over.[43] For

36   Stefan Schwerter, 'Basel III's Ability to Mitigate Systemic Risk' (2013) 19 *Journal of Financial Regulation and Compliance* 337; Matthias Drehmann and others, 'Countercyclical Capital Buffers: Exploring Options' (2010) 317 BIS Working Papers.

37   Basel Committee on Banking Supervision, *Global Regulatory Framework* (n 7) 60–63; Kersten Kellermann and Carsten Schlag, 'Occupy Risk Weighting: How the Minimum Leverage Ratio Dominates Capital Requirements' (2013) 21 *Journal of Financial Regulation and Compliance* 353.

38   Basel Committee on Banking Supervision, Basel III: International Framework for Liquidity (n 7).

39   Financial Stability Board, International Monetary Fund, Bank for International Settlements, *Macroprudential Policy Tools and Frameworks* (Financial Stability Board 2011).

40   Rafael Repullo and Javier Suarez, 'The Procyclical Effects of Bank Capital Regulation' (2013) 26 *The Review of Financial Studies* 452.

41   Jürg M Blum, 'Why 'Basel II' May Need a Leverage Ratio Restriction' (2008) 32 *Journal of Banking & Finance* 1699; Katia D'Hulster, 'The Leverage Ratio. A New Binding Limit on Banks' (2009) World Bank. Crisis response. Public Policy for the Private Sector. Note Number 11.

42   Kellermann and Schlag (n 37).

43   Basel Committee on Banking Supervision, The Regulatory Framework: Balancing Risk Sensitivity, Simplicity and Comparability. Discussion Paper. July 2013 (Bank for International Settlements 2013).

example, the Basel II.5 market risk revisions are embedded in a narrative structure that stresses regulatory continuity. The market risk framework had not 'captured some key risks'.[44] The regulatory response was 'strengthening risk capture'[45] and 'enhancing risk coverage'.[46] Thus, the Committee argues that it engages in a number of risk methodology repairs. In Basel II.5, the Committee added the Incremental Risk Charge (IRC), introduced the stressed VaR regime and, in effect, banished most securitizations from the trading book IMA. The pattern repeats in the Basel II.5 securitization framework amendments and Basel III risk methodology reforms. Securitization framework amendments updated the banking book securitization risk weights to, arguably, better reflect the real risks in the assets and later upended the entire methodology. The credit valuation adjustment (CVA) charge was added to capture credit valuation risk, a risk that the Basel II rules had omitted. IMM was, likewise, updated to incorporate the lessons learnt during the crisis.

However, the methodology details diverge from the risk sensitivity narrative. sVaR, IRC and CVA are all quick and dirty fixes, low in theoretical orthodoxy but rich in their quantitative impact.[47] For example the Basel II.5 stressed VaR[48] shares little with theoretically robust market risk estimation, but carries a big stick. The charge forces banks to model expected losses under two distinct scenarios. The first scenario is the 'normal' Basel II 1 per cent 10-day "bad case" future the bank expects to play out within the current expectation window. The second one is the same kind of 1 per cent 10-day future but now with a twist. The banks are required to assume that 'an appropriate stress scenario' – essentially a full blown crisis *à la 2008*—takes place during the ten days. After calculation, the two resultant VaR figures are simply added up to arrive at the IMA capital requirement.[49] The approach seems *prima facie* intuitive and benign.[50] The contrast to the Basel II VaR arrangement is, however, striking. nVaR and sVar combined do not map out the likely extent of losses in any determinate bad case scenario. The arithmetic sum of two risk measures is the arithmetic sum of two risk measures, little else. Thus, the measure has no theoretical backing, even in the limited sense that Basel II measures could claim. Further, sVaR does not build on industry best practice risk estimation practices nor does it constitute a usable input into banks' internal control devices as the measure offers three optimization targets (nVaR, sVaR and the composite). The targets cannot all be attained at the same time.[51] As a consequence, the alignment of regulatory and economic capital methodologies that sustained the non-governing at a distance strategy breaks down.

The same problems plague the IRC and CVA charges. IRC turns the IMA VaR figure into a composite risk measure that layers an IRB equivalent capital requirement on the IMA

44 Basel Committee on Banking Supervision, *Proposed Revisions to the Basel II Market Risk Framework* (Bank for International Settlements 2008) 1.

45 Basel Committee on Banking Supervision, Comprehensive Strategy to Address the Lessons of the Banking Crisis Announced by the Basel Committee. Press Release. 20 November 2008 (Bank for International Settlements 2008).

46 Basel Committee on Banking Supervision, *Revisions to the Basel II Market Risk Framework. July 2009* (Bank for International Settlements 2009) 3.

47 Basel Committee on Banking Supervision, *Analysis of the Trading Book Quantitative Impact Study. October 2009* (Bank for International Settlements 2009).

48 Basel Committee on Banking Supervision, *Revisions to the Basel II* (n 33) s 718(lxxvi)(i).

49 ibid s 718(lxxvi)(k).

50 James M Chen, 'Measuring Market Risk under the Basel Accords: VaR, Stressed VaR, and Expected Shortfall' (2014) 8 *Aestimatio, the IEB International Journal of Finance* 184, 197–98.

51 International Swaps and Derivatives Association and others, Re: 'Revisions to the Basel II Market Risk Framework' (BCBS 148) and 'Guidelines for Computing Capital for Incremental Risk in the Trading Book' (BCBS 149) (ISDA 2009) 8–10.

regime.[52] The resultant risk gauge, again, reflects a non-existent risk with no use in portfolio optimization. The CVA charge,[53] in turn, mangles the credit valuation adjustment risks badly as the charge focuses solely on the counterparty credit risk and misses the market risk vectors of CVA. Again, regulatory and internal incentives diverge.[54]

A Tacit Structural Agenda

The endgame is complicated. Despite insistence on continued risk sensitivity, the Committee has been constructing what essentially seem purposely inauthentic but quantitatively convenient risk measures. The Committee has jettisoned its attempt to pursue theoretical orthodoxy to arrive at quantitatively desirable capital requirements. The strategic move has its costs which after the collapse of risk may be inevitable.[55] The emergence of the "inauthentic" risks, however, transform the BCBS non-governance strategy fundamentally. In Basel II, the risk methodology adjustments could be characterised as temporary adaptations to lacking but improving computational capabilities and risk modelling practices. Now, the manipulations have no such excuses. They articulate direct regulatory and transformational aspirations as BCBS seems to have relinquished its pursuit of incentive alignment. In fact, the Committee is doing the opposite. It consciously allows incentive effects to proliferate if and when they have desirable market structure effects.

In part, the new orientation is simply a function of the limited technical options the Committee was forced to confront. The hope of perfecting risk sensitive capital adequacy technologies was lost during the crisis. No amount of investment in risk measurement technologies will mend the Basel II risk measures as high-fidelity reproduction of real financial risks has been revealed impossible. The new sorry state of risk is acutely visible in the Trading Book Fundamental Review. The Review documents[56] envision a total overhaul of both IMA and Standardized Measurement method. Most importantly, VaR will cease to exist as a regulatory tool. The Committee will replace the 99 per cent 10 day VaR capital charges with a 97.5 per cent variable risk horizon Expected Shortfall (ES) capital measure.[57] Although the measure is technically superior to VaR and mends many of its shortcomings,[58] its status differs drastically from the one VaR enjoyed in 1996. The Committee refuses to peg the fate of market

---

52 Basel Committee on Banking Supervision, *Revisions to the Basel II* (n 33) s 718(xcii).

53 Basel Committee on Banking Supervision, *Basel III: A Global Regulatory Framework* (n 7) Annex 4, s 97–105.

54 Riccardo Rebonato, Mike Sherring and Ronnie Barnes, 'CVA and the Equivalent Bond' (2010) 2010 Risk 118; Global Financial Markets Association, British Bankers' Association and International Swaps and Derivatives Association, Joint Trade Associations' Response to the Basel Committee on Banking Supervision Consultative Proposals to Strengthen Global Capital and Liquidity Regulations, BCBS 164 and 165 Issued on 17 December 2009 (GFMA 2010) 21–22.

55 Basel Committee on Banking Supervision, The Regulatory Framework: Balancing Risk Sensitivity, Simplicity and Comparability n 43.

56 Basel Committee on Banking Supervision, Fundamental Review of the Trading Book. Consultative Document (Bank for International Settlements 2012); Basel Committee on Banking Supervision, Fundamental Review of the Trading Book: A Revised Market Risk Framework. Consultative Document. October 2013 (Bank for International Settlements 2013); Basel Committee on Banking Supervision, Fundamental Review of the Trading Book: Outstanding Issues. Consultative Document. December 2014 (Bank for International Settlements 2014).

57 Basel Committee on Banking Supervision, Fundamental Review of the Trading Book: A Revised Market Risk Framework (n 56) 18.

58 Colin J Thompson and Michael A McCarthy, 'Alternative Measures to Value at Risk' (2008) 9 *The Journal of Risk Finance* 81; Acerbi and Tasche (n 19).

risk regime to the technology. Instead of relying on the ES risk measure, the Committee reverses its basic approach. ES becomes only one tool in the regulators' arsenal, essentially one possible account of what market risk might be. The measure will be embedded into a network of capital floors, stand-alone modelling and piece-meal approval processes that are consciously designed to counteract and limit the impact that ES modelling shortcomings may have on capital requirements.[59] In this assemblage, ES measures will never determine minimum capital requirements on their own. They have to be augmented and contained by a host of other devices that are not and cannot be fully risk sensitive.

Thus, BCBS is trapped in a new regulatory mode. It would like not to govern, but it is technologically incapable of not governing. Simultaneously, the Committee confronts a market that is dysfunctional and contains many actors whose business models now seem undesirable for various reasons. Some actors might expose taxpayers to excessive risks while engaging in activities with little or no perceived social utility. Some of their activities may be politically unpalatable. As a consequence, tensions arise within the set Committee's objectives set. The regulatory strategy of not governing seems to turn into a regulatory strategy where the Commission juggles regulatory tools and risk methodologies to (1) minimize perverse incentives, (2) retain some semblance to risk sensitivity to keep the financial markets afloat, and (3) manage the stability risks which arise as the result of using advanced risk sensitive technologies for regulatory purposes. The complicated strategic game easily conceals the fourth crucial aspect of BCBS's regulatory agenda. If one combines the inauthentic risks with the observation that the quantitative impact of the reforms has fallen squarely on the market risk and counterparty risk frameworks, one has to be wary of the possible existence of a tacit, passive-aggressive structural regulatory agenda. BCBS may be quietly inching out trading operations from banks by manufacturing conveniently high capital charges.

Outside Basel

Local Structural Reforms

Two Agendas

The global response[60] constitutes the baseline for the regulatory reform initiatives triggered by the financial crisis. While all major international financial hubs have committed to implementing the Basel reforms,[61] many have also initiated reforms that go beyond the baseline. The most important subset of these initiatives engages in what is known as structural regulation. Structural regulation is a befitting term to highlight the contrast between the global and local regulatory agendas. In a marked contrast to the official line on Basel reforms, market and bank organizational structures serve as the primary targets in these reforms.

In the following, I will briefly map the local structural regulation initiatives. I will discuss four projects, that is, those undertaken in the United States, United Kingdom, Germany and

---

59 Basel Committee on Banking Supervision, Fundamental Review of the Trading Book: A Revised Market Risk Framework (n 56) 23–30.

60 Financial Stability Board, *A Narrative Progress Report on Financial Reforms. Report of the Financial Stability Board to G20 Leaders. 5 September 2013* (Financial Stability Board 2013); Eric Helleiner, 'What Role for the New Financial Stability Board? The Politics of International Standards after the Crisis' (2010) 1 *Global Policy* 282.

61 Leaders of the Group of Twenty, 'The G20 Seoul Summit, Leaders' Declaration', November 11–12, 2010.

the European Union. The first three have already matured into legislation, while the EU plans still remain on the drawing board with a highly uncertain future.[62] My focus will be on the initiatives' effects on banks' trading activities as trading is the aspect most relevant to the discussion of the relationship between Basel and local reforms. Thus, I will not discuss for example the reforms' recovery or bail-in tool related aspects, which are also partly global projects.[63]

After a brief discussion of each individual initiative, I will sketch out some of the basic tenets in the regulatory strategy of structural regulation. Of course, here no singular strategy will emerge. The different initiatives are situated in highly divergent surroundings with varying banking market structures and political situations. However, one common theme seems to be underpinning all regulatory initiatives. All structural regulation projects walk a fine line between banning trading and keeping it alive, retaining the *status quo* and finetuning the market structures.

United States

The local structural reform initiatives were pioneered by the US Congress in the Dodd–Frank Wall Street Reform and Consumer Protection Act (Pub.L. 111–203, H.R. 4173). The Act contains a number of structural reform initiatives, chief among them the Section 619, the Volcker rule. In the Act, the Volcker rule is a relatively concise provision. It was, however, fleshed out in further detail in a prolonged Agency rule-making process. The process turned the relatively parsimonious four-page legislative text into 300 pages of final rule.[64]

The Volcker rule, now incorporated as § 1851 to Chapter 17 of U.S Code Title 12, introduces a ban on 'proprietary trading'. The underlying idea is simple – and draconian. No 'banking entity' shall 'engage in proprietary trading; or acquire or retain any equity, partnership, or other ownership interest in or sponsor a hedge fund or a private equity fund'. Proprietary trading is defined as 'engaging as principal for the trading account of the banking entity in any transaction to purchase or sell, or otherwise acquire or dispose of, a security, derivative, contract of sale of a commodity for future delivery, or other financial instrument that the Agencies include by rule'.

Despite the apparent harsh blanket ban, the rule allows banking entities to engage in a number of *permitted activities* defined in § 1851(d). The permitted activities are exemptions to the overall ban: if not explicitly allowed in the rule they would have fallen under the ban. The first exemption covers financial instruments issued by US government bodies and agencies. Banking entities may purchase, sell, acquire or dispose of, for example, US government, government sponsored enterprises (GSE) and state and municipal bonds. The second exemption allows banking entities to engage in underwriting and market-making activities,[65] but only 'to the extent that any such activities . . . are designed not to exceed the reasonably expected near term demands of clients, customers, or counterparties'. The third exemption

---

62 Alex Barker, 'Five EU Nations in Talks Over Watering Down Bank Reform' *Financial Times* (London, 30 January 2015) 2.

63 Financial Stability Board, *Resolution of Systemically Important Financial Institutions* (Financial Stability Board 2012).

64 Department of the Treasury and others, 'Prohibitions and Restrictions on Proprietary Trading and Certain Interests in, and Relationships with, Hedge Funds and Private Equity Funds' (2014) 79 *Federal Register* 5535.

65 Committee on the Global Financial System, Market-Making and Proprietary Trading: Industry Trends, Drivers and Policy Implications. CGFS Papers No 52. November 2014 (Bank for International Settlements 2014).

permits 'risk-mitigating hedging activities' which 'reduce the specific risks to the banking entity in connection with and related to such positions, contracts, or other holdings'. This entails that portfolio hedging is no more acceptable. In addition to the three main exemptions, the rule allows for example the purchase of securities on behalf of clients and proprietary trading that occurs solely outside the United States.

United Kingdom

The basic framework of the UK approach to structural reforms was formulated in the Vickers Commission report.[66] The report advocated the strict separation of the deposit-taking banks (known as ring-fenced entities) from other financial institutions and placing severe restrictions on the businesses deposit-taking banks could conduct and assets they could hold.[67] To act as a counterbalance to the strict restrictions, no business model restrictions were to be placed on the non-ring-fenced entities. For them, the regulatory framework would remain largely unchanged, save for the additional loss-absorbency requirements.[68]

The final Financial Services (Banking Reform) Act 2013 implements many of the Vickers Commission proposals. The Act sets up a ring fence around banks' retail operations or 'core activities and services'.[69] If a bank wishes to take deposits from or provide payment or overdraft services to individuals and SMEs – excluding eligible high-wealth non-core depositors – it faces a blanket trading ban. In language similar to the Volcker rule, ring-fenced banks may not 'deal in investments as principal'.[70]

What dealing in investments as principal is, was left to be decided by Treasury secondary rule-making. A Treasury Order[71] was issued in July 2014. The Order establishes a comprehensive ban: ring-fenced entities are barred from engaging in 'all buying, selling, subscribing for or underwriting securities or contractually based investments'. In addition to the trading ban, the UK Act also bans ring-fenced banks from incurring exposures of any kind to financial institutions, save when providing certain payment services. The Order, however, grants a few limited exceptions to the trading ban. Some limited hedging is allowed even if it would entail principal investments. The allowed hedges may, however, only be undertaken if the sole or main purpose of the transaction is to limit the ring-fenced body's exposure to changes in interest rates, exchange rates or commodity prices, the price of residential or commercial property prices indices, share price indices or default risk. The other significant exception allows banks to conclude simple, easily valuable exchange traded derivatives contracts with the entity's account holders.[72]

The UK approach to business model restrictions is strict. Ring-fenced entities are not allowed to do any trading, just engage in plain old vanilla financial intermediation. The stringency of the ring-fence restrictions is, however, offset by their modest reach. Non-ring-fenced banks – or rather the corporate sibling in groups to which the ring-fenced entities belong – enjoy continuous unrestricted freedom to do whatever Basel III or other rules allow.

---

66 Independent Commission on Banking, *Interim Report. Consultation on Reform Options* (Crown 2011) 1; Independent Commission on Banking, *Final Report. Recommendations* (Crown 2011).
67 Independent Commission on Banking, *Final Report* (n 65) 35.
68 ibid 30.
69 Financial Services and Markets Act 2000 Section 142A.
70 Financial Services and Markets Act 2000 Section 142D(2).
71 The Financial Services and Markets Act 2000 (Excluded Activities and Prohibitions) Order 2014 No 2080.
72 Order 2014 No 2080.

They may still engage in market-making and underwriting, proprietary trading and deal in derivatives. The only requirement is that the core services institutions must stand apart from the rest of the group to allow for uninterrupted provision of the core services even in times of crisis. In practice, the independence requirement translates into a list of demands upon banking holding company group structure and inter-group relations. All dealings by the ring-fenced entities with the rest of the group must be on 'arm's length terms'. Further, the ring-fenced body must be able to 'take decisions independently of other members of its group' and not be dependent on the resources which are provided by a member of its group and which would cease to be available to the ring-fenced body in the event of the insolvency of the other member'. All ring-fenced entities also have to be able to function, that is, 'carry on core activities' even if the group becomes insolvent.[73]

Germany

The German Trennbankengesetz is a hybrid of the UK and US initiatives. The Act amended the German Gesetz über das Kreditwesen (10.07.1961, KWG) and imposed a limited ban on speculative trading. As the US Volcker rule, the ban does not cover all trading activities as it contains significant exemptions. In a similar vein to the UK approach, the act also adopts a ring-fencing approach. In contrast to the UK approach, the German solution is inverted: it allows banned activities to be conducted in specific trading entities ring-fenced from the rest of the banking group.

Despite combining aspects from the Volcker rule and UK approach, the German measure is relatively relaxed. The ban prohibits in principle all trading on own account (Eigengeschäfte) and lending to alternative investment managers.[74] The ban is, however, not comprehensive as the Bundestag explicitly excluded market-making, client transaction hedging and interest rate, currency, liquidity and credit risk management transactions from its scope,[75] essentially retracing the Volcker rule. These 'client-serving' transactions were deemed beneficial and allowed to continue in banks, even if other trading on own account is forbidden.

Second, even the remaining narrow proprietary trading prohibitions have a short reach. The prescribed activities can continue within the financial groups, if the activities are consigned to special financial trading institutions (Finanzhandelsinstuten).[76] The trading entities must be separate, ring-fenced organizations, standing economically, legally and organizationally independent from the rest of the group. The independence entails that the entities must have separate capital bases and the group may not provide any funding support to the trading institutions. Still, the groups must supervise the entities' risk-taking and transaction.

The ban does not even affect all German banks. It only extends to a relatively small subset of large German banks as the threshold conditions of the ban are high. To fall under the ban, a bank must be large. It must have either at least 100 billion euros in total assets, or at least 90 billion euros in total assets, if at least 20 per cent of its total balance

---

73 Prudential Regulation Authority, The Implementation of Ring-Fencing: Consultation on Legal Structure, Governance and the Continuity of Services and Facilities. October 2014. Consultation Paper. CP19/14 (Bank of England 2014) 8.
74 KWG § 3(2).
75 KWG § 3(2).
76 KWG § 3(2).

sheet assets are held for trading or as available for sale under International Accounting Standards (IAS) 9.[77]

The German approach, thus, builds on 'ring-fencing' of non-essential bank trading operations. The core banking operations are insulated from risky trading activities not by requiring the core banking entities be stand-alone organizations – as in the UK ring-fencing – but by pushing the trading operations to separate entities with minimal ties to the rest of the banking groups. The philosophy differs from the UK approach. Whereas in UK all trading operations were cut loose from core banking service providers, the Germans allowed useful 'third-party service' trading operations to retain the benefits of funding support flowing from guaranteed deposits. Instead of making sure that the core banking entities survive in any contingency as in the UK approach, the idea is to ensure that entities engaged in speculative trading survive – or rather die – on their own.

European Union

The EU structural reforms are still in the making. The process started in 2012 with the Liikanen report.[78] The Liikanen report advocated the separation of proprietary and other high-risk trading and deposit-taking core banking. The trading ban proposed in the report was comprehensive. The report suggested that all proprietary trading and most assets or derivative positions incurred in the process of market-making should be migrated to specific trading entities. Banks' derivatives activities would be severely restricted to own asset and liability management purposes, as well as liquidity management and provision of hedging services to non-banking clients.

The final proposal by Commissar Michel Barnier was published a year later.[79] The proposal is a watered down version of the Liikanen report. The Commission did not elect to propose a comprehensive EU wide ban on proprietary trading. Instead, the proposal calls for the prohibition of buying and selling and taking positions in financial instruments or commodities 'for the sole purpose of making a profit for own account, and without any connection to actual or anticipated client activity' or client transaction hedging. The already narrow scope is further restricted by a requirement that the activities be conducted by 'desks, units, divisions or individual traders specifically dedicated to such position taking and profit making'.[80]

The proposed ban, however weak, has one strength. Like the Volcker rule, it allows for no ring-fencing. On the other hand, it was not designed to encompass all EU banks. The ban was proposed to only extend to a small selection, maybe 30 in number, of large EU systemically important banks.[81]

The relatively lax trading restrictions are buttressed by rules that would allow for 'potential separation of certain trading activities' subject to national discretion. The Commission proposed to grant national supervisors the discretion to impose trading restrictions which go further than the 'mandatory' trading restrictions affecting the largest banks.[82] The rules on potential separation establish a yearly cycle of assessment of the riskiness of bank trading

---

77 KWG § 3(2).
78 High-level Expert Group on reforming the structure of the EU banking sector, *Final Report* (European Union 2012).
79 European Commission (n 8).
80 ibid 26.
81 ibid 22–23.
82 ibid 26.

operations. If the assessment indicates that the bank's trading operations constitute a threat to the financial stability of the institution or to the Union financial system as a whole, the supervisor would have the right to require the institution not to 'carry out the trading activities', unless the institution demonstrate that 'the reasons leading to the conclusions are not justified'. The trading activities would have to be migrated over to specific trading entities. The trading entities would be independent, separately capitalized entities cut off from support from the rest of the group.

The Strategy of Structural Regulation

Instituting Trading-Free Zones

What is the regulatory strategy of structural reforms discussed above? The first thing to note is that all structural regulation initiatives have trading as their primary target. All projects seek to curb bank trading activities related risk-taking when the activities are not associated with traditional financial intermediation. Second, the ultimate goal in all the projects is not to end all trading but, rather, to contain and limit the collateral damage trading operations may cause to the broader economy and the banking sector in general.[83]

However, within the confines of the loose overall objective, variations are considerable. Even the basic reform makeups differ. The initiatives incorporate two alternative impact channels to attain the objective. First, regulators typically prohibit banks from engaging in certain businesses. The other option is to not forbid trading but to locate the activities deemed too risky to 'safe' locations within the banks' corporate groups.

In the US, the safe non-trading zone has the farthest reach. It encompasses all insured depository institutions, their parent bank holding companies and their subsidiaries. No group structure solution is acceptable. The reach of the safe zone is motivated by a conviction that trading activities cannot be adequately compartmentalized or firewalled within banking groups.[84] To make sure that depositors' funds cannot be used to fund risky gambles, the only option is to make the separation complete and move trading outside banks. No ties to unsafe trading practices may exist, essentially replicating the Glass-Steagal approach. In Europe, the approach is different. In all three initiatives, separation *within* the group structures is deemed sufficient to safeguard core banking activities. However, the methods of achieving separation vary. In the UK, the core banking activities are protected by pushing all safe operations into separate, independent entities and cutting their ties to non-ring-fenced entities by requiring a complete operational and funding separation. In Continental Europe, the risky activities are confined to separate trading entities. The trading entities are insulated from the rest of the group by requiring them to be separately capitalized.

If we want to understand the non-trading safe zones, we must also incorporate the substantive scope of acceptable business models restrictions. The initiatives reflect a trade-off between reach and intensity. The US trading ban is extensive in its organizational reach, but underwhelming in substantive terms. It allows many activities that are hard to discern from speculative trading to continue within the safe zones. In fact, most analysts seem to suggest that the majority of banks' pre-crisis trading operations will fit within the scope of the Volcker rule exemptions.

---

83 For example, Leonardo Gambacorta and Adrian Van Rixtel, 'Structural Bank Regulation Initiatives: Approaches and Implications' (2013) No 412 BIS Working Papers.

84 Paul Volcker, 'Unfinished Business in Financial Reform' (2012) 15 *International Finance* 125, 134.

As a consequence, Volcker rule impact may be, in fact, relatively subdued as market-making and underwriting – allowed activities – already constituted a major share of all bank trading operations and brought in the majority of trading-related profits. For example, according to the 2011 US Government Accountability Office study of six major US banks, the to-be-banned proprietary trading contributed an insignificant portion of the firm's overall profits. The report implies that 'standalone proprietary-trading desks' contributed a combined $5 billion in revenue in 2009, after losses in 2007 and 2008. The numbers pale in comparison to the banks' other revenue sources.[85] Thus, it seems that the extensive reach of the US bans is likely a function of the substantive insignificance of the prohibitions. Blanket separation is possible, because its substantive scope is restricted and, consequently, its effects mild. The initiative simultaneously bans trading, but allows nearly all trading to continue. The approach is the reverse in the UK. The substantive prohibitions are the most far-reaching and draconian of all the four regulatory initiatives, but their reach is very limited. All trading is banned in ring-fenced entities with very narrow and few exemptions, but outside the ring-fenced entities, total freedom reigns with no activities are banned. The rest of the Europe falls somewhere in between.

Once this bifurcated strategy is incorporated into the analytics, the radicalism of the regulatory initiatives starts to dissolve. The initiatives do not aim to radically change the face of banking but, instead, aim at establishing speculation and trading-free 'safe zones' around what are deemed 'essential' banking operations. The idea is to, or at least be perceived as making an effort to, guard these essential activities against the undesirable consequences of unwarranted speculative risk-taking. Trading is pushed out of the banks proper, to somewhere else where it will, supposedly, cause less trouble if things go wrong.

Balancing Costs and Benefits

Why did the regulators choose this avenue? The variations in the reach and scope of the safe zones seem indicative of an important constraint the regulators faced. Instituting the safe zones carries with it significant immediate welfare costs – at least when compared to the retention of the pre-crisis status quo – for uncertain future benefits. Even if the regulators would have wanted to ban trading, they simply could not. Consequently, the reform efforts transformed into a balancing act between the costs and benefits of taking regulatory action against trading.[86]

At the outset, the benefits of curbing trading must have seemed overwhelming.[87] The immediate diagnosis after the financial crisis was that banks' trading operations had driven the international financial system into the ground. The post-crisis loss attribution exercises provide ample evidence that this indeed seemed to be the case. Global banks' trading arms had suffered stupendous losses in 2007 and 2008. Traditional financial intermediation businesses, in turn, seemed to have escaped relatively unscathed.[88] These experiences, alone, suggested that the socially optimal course of action was to force the banks to cut down trading operations significantly to prevent the replay of the crisis in the future.

---

85 US Government Accountability Office, Proprietary Trading: Regulators Will Need More Comprehensive Information to Fully Monitor Compliance with New Restrictions When Implemented. GAO-11–259 (US Government Accountability Office 2011).

86 Donato Masciandaro and Mattia Suardi, 'Delays and Distortions in Reforming Banking Regulation: A Political Economy Tale' (2014) <www.ssrn.com/abstract=2488452> accessed 1 January 2015; Gambacorta and van Rixtel (n 84).

87 For example, UK Government, Impact Assessment Financial Services (Banking Reform) Bill (Crown 2013).

88 For example, Financial Services Authority (n 32) 15.

Simultaneously, the reforms were further advocated by a related concern. When trading was conducted in deposit-taking or systemically important banks, the risky gambles were effectively supported by the funding benefits the banks received from explicit and implicit government guarantees. The issue was politically pressing. In the public perception, the bankers had first reaped the private benefits of reckless risk-taking made possible by the public subsidies and, when the deals had turned sour, left the taxpayers take care of the ensuing mayhem. Perpetuating this allocation of risk was, of course, politically an untenable solution.

The case for curbing bank trading may have been clear-cut and intuitively appealing, but it does have its weaknesses.[89] First, the understanding that trading in general was the main culprit in the crisis may be biased. The detailed accounts of losses contained in the few publicly available detailed post-crisis loss attribution exercises suggest a loss landscape dominated by the collapse of the securitization markets. In the BCBS Trading Book Group exercise, mortgage trading, ABS trading, portfolio credit derivatives and securitization warehouse losses account for well over a half of all trading-related losses, while 'proprietary trading' – whatever that means – amounts to a tiny fraction of the total.[90] The UK's more granular exercise unearthed a similar picture.[91] The securitization blow-up was a *sui generis* event.[92] It had relatively little to do with bank's non-securitization trading operations. This diagnosis, of course, should change the regulatory agenda. If the crisis was chiefly caused by the collapse of the securitization businesses, targeting all bank trading operations indiscriminately would add little value. The global and local securitization related initiatives should have already taken care of the problem.

Second, there are costs to removing trading from the banks' business model inventory. All initiatives, of course, will have significant one-off implementation and operating costs.[93] In addition, they have significant, yet diffuse market structure implications. The main concern US banks raised was that the Volcker rule would negatively impact market liquidity and disrupt price discovery in some markets.[94] In the UK, critics raised the concern that ring fences might cause diversification benefits to be lost and cause some businesses to struggle to find hedging service providers[95]. The elimination of deposit funding support was feared to drive credit ratings down in non-ring-fenced entities making the provision of non-core banking services very expensive.[96] However, these costs are often diffuse and hard to evaluate and even harder to pack into an intuitively convincing story. To get at the costs, one would have to imagine markets where trading would continue unabated.

---

89 For example, Randall D Guynn and Patrick Kenadjian, 'Structural Solutions: Blinded by Volcker, Vickers, Liikanen, Glass Steagall and Narrow Banking' in Andreas Dombret and Patrick S Kenadjian (eds), *Too Big to Fail III: Structural Reform Proposals. Should We Break Up the Banks?* (De Gruyter 2015).

90 Basel Committee on Banking Supervision (2012) (n 56) 57–58.

91 Financial Services Authority (n 32) 38.

92 Neil Fligstein and Adam Goldstein, 'The Anatomy of the Mortgage Securitization Crisis' *Markets on Trial The Economic Sociology of the US Financial Crisis Part A*, vol 30 (Emerald Group Publishing Limited 2010); Larry Cordell, Yilin Huang and Meredith Williams, 'Collateral Damage: Sizing and Assessing the Subprime CDO Crisis'. (2012) Federal Reserve Bank of Philadelphia Working Papers 11–30/R.

93 Office of the Comptroller of the Currency, *Analysis of 12 CFR Part 44* (Office of the Comptroller of the Currency 2011); Prudential Regulation Authority (n 73).

94 Oliver Wyman, The Volcker Rule Restrictions on Proprietary Trading: Implications for Market Liquidity (Oliver Wyman 2012); Anjan V Thakor, The Economic Consequences of the Volcker Rule (United States Chamber of Commerce 2012) 1; Tracy Alloway, Gina Chon and Michael Mackenzie, 'Lew Challenged Over Impact of Volcker Rule on Capital Markets' Financial Times (London, 10 July 2014) 11; PriceWaterhouseCoopers, Impact of Structural Reforms in Europe. Report for AFME (PWC 2014).

95 Standard & Poor's, Europe's Ring-Fencing Proposals Could Make Big Banks Safer to Fail, but also Have Broader Consequences. July 11, 2013 (Standard & Poor's 2013); Sam Fleming, 'Banks Remain in Dark on Unanswered Questions about Ringfence Proposals' *Financial Times* (London, 7 October 2014) 3.

96 Emma Dunkley, 'New Bank Rules "Risk Raising Charges"' *Financial Times* (London, 10 December 2014) 23.

A Tortious Strategy

In the end, the proponents of curbing trading prevailed, at least for the time being, in what may ultimately amount to a Pyrrhic victory. Trading is suppressed, but the bans are far from being comprehensive. Structural initiatives ended up walking a tight rope between, on the one hand, making the financial system safer, preventing future meltdowns and protecting the taxpayers, while, on the other, keeping the economy and the banks rolling.

This trade-off characterizes the regulatory strategy of structural regulation. The initiatives muddle along, manipulate banking structures as little as possible to quell public anger, attempt minimize risks to depositors and taxpayers, while simultaneously trying to minimize the destabilizing effects the measures may have on the established structures of banking and the prerequisites for economic growth. Senators Merkley and Levin, who introduced the Volcker rule into the Dodd–Frank Act, describe the situation aptly. 'The Merkley-Levin provisions were designed to protect the financial system by targeting proprietary trading at banking entities and systemically significant non-bank financial companies, while allowing those firms to continue to engage in client-oriented, risk-reducing, or other traditional banking activities that facilitate the formation and deployment of capital'.[97]

Trading is restricted at some quarters and to a degree, but not entirely suppressed. Risk-taking may continue, if its location and scope is carefully structured to minimize the risks and maximize welfare gains. Some activities are deemed undesirable because they are inherently too risky or simply because the activities are impossible to legitimize in the current opinion climate. These activities are either migrated to safer locations outside the core of the banking system or, if banned, defined narrowly to allow the less threatening operations to continue. Moving the activities outside the banks allows regulators to deflect concerns that the remaining trading might still constitute a risk to financial stability and taxpayer and depositor funds – and of course to argue that risks to financial stability have, in fact, diminished and long-term economic growth prospects will improve. The institutional collapses which may still happen due to trading blow-ups should not threaten the system anymore. Further, taxpayers will be off the hook as the governments have no urgent interest in bailing out the now non-essential trading institutions which, in addition, are now set up to fail safely and have ample bail-in capital. The second option is to argue that the institutions should be small enough to be systemically insignificant reinforcing their safety as components of the financial system.

Of course, the ugly truth is that problems may, in fact, be only shuffled to new locations. Sir John Vickers seems right: the true objective of structural regulation is to facilitate a restructured universal banking model, made safe enough but still left familiar enough not to unhinge the existing market structures.[98]

The Remains of Neoliberalism

What happens when the Basel Accord and the local structural regulation initiatives collide? Do the structural reforms unhinge the balance of power in global banking regulation, move the focus back to local jurisdictions and impose a new distinctly post-neoliberal financial order on the global financial markets? Or will global banking remain dominated by the neoliberal, as-little-as-possible Basel approach?

---

97 Jeff Merkley and Carl Levin, 'The Dodd–Frank Act Restrictions on Proprietary Trading and Conflicts of Interest: New Tools to Address Evolving Threats' (2011) 48 *Harvard Journal on Legislation* 515, 539.

98 John Vickers, 'Banking Reform in Britain and Europe (Paper Presented at the Rethinking Macro Policy II: First Steps and Early Lessons Conference Hosted by the International Monetary Fund Washington, DC, April 16–17, 2013) <www.imf.org/external/np/seminars/eng/2013/macro2/pdf/jv2.pdf> accessed 2 July 2014.

There is no clear-cut answer. First, we should note the commonalities in the post-financial crisis Basel and local regulatory strategies. In both strategies, regulators are keen to cautiously manipulate the perimeters of acceptable banking practices in order to increase the safety and stability of the financial system – or at least be seen making an effort. Neither of the projects constitutes a headlong rush to any direction. Both the Basel and local initiatives are primarily instrumental to retaining the status quo. This is acutely reflected in the scope and ambition of the structural reforms. The reforms have been reactive, small-scale, rearguard actions in which aggressive, disruptive structural regulation has evaded the regulators. Combined with the Basel reforms, what has emerged is a piece-meal regulatory strategy that fixes highly localized deficiencies, while simultaneously holding on to the general market makeup. Regulators are engaged in limited market structure manipulation, but fall short of enacting an overall vision of what the financial markets should be like in the future, apart from the commitment to retaining the status quo as far as possible.

Second, the focus on retaining much of status quo is indicative of the regulatory and ideological logics underlying both projects. In fact, the similarities entail that my working hypothesis of a stark contrast between a neoliberal Basel and the non-neoliberal local initiatives largely vanishes into thin air. Basel is no more a distinctly neoliberal, as-little-as-possible-regulation project. While Basel has admittedly retained much of its basic neoliberal character, the covert structural regulation and the impending simplification reforms the Committee will undertake have modified its ideological orientation.

In large swaths of the Accord, BCBS still works on banks using the neoliberal tools and tactics, by affording the regulated as much freedom as possible. Nevertheless, BCBS has abandoned much of its former commitment to thorough risk sensitivity. It no more seeks to align regulatory and economic capital methodologies at the cost of stability. The fading commitment has been replaced by an increasing but reluctant willingness to use convenient risk measure calibrations to manipulate market structures to ensure the sustainability of financial markets. This entails a reconfiguration in the Basel neoliberalism. The Committee has been forced to migrate to a post-orthodox, *damage control strand of neoliberalism*. In this strand of neoliberalism, faith in self-sustaining markets and self-regulating banks has been lost. The guiding intellectual principle is the exact opposite: financial markets will self-destruct if left to their own devices and the regulators have to manipulate them to keep them aloft and functioning by constant interventions.

In the Basel Accords, this translates to a policy shift. Instead of merely trying to get out of the way, the Committee is focusing on manipulating banks and market structures to contain their destructive tendencies and ensure the continued existence of the markets. Now, it is crucial to note that the same orientation very clearly underlies the local structural regulation initiatives. In this sense, the local structural initiatives fail to be distinctly non-neoliberal despite their explicit interventionism. The primary aim of the local initiatives is the same as in Basel: to keep the banking systems aloft, disrupt their ordinary operations as little as possible, while simultaneously manipulating the structures in order ensure their future viability. However, when a vision of the desirable markets is missing, the reforms become like grappling in the dark. Neoliberal orthodoxy is gone, interventions abound, but no clear alternatives emerge. Banking regulation is on its way to being a zombie, like its neoliberal siblings.[99] Regulation is all about damage control within an as-free-as-possible banking regime.

99 Jamie Peck, 'Zombie Neoliberalism and the Ambidextrous State' (2010) 14 *Theoretical Criminology* 104; Wolfgang Streeck, 'How Will Capitalism End?' (2014) 87 *New Left Review* 35.

6 State of Necessity and Sovereign Insolvency

*Vassilis Paliouras**

Scope of the Necessity Defence under International Law and Sovereign Debt Litigation

Necessity is a rule of international law that allows the invoking State to escape its responsibility for the commission of an internationally wrongful act.[1] In that sense, necessity does not constitute a norm of international law that imposes upon a State an obligation to act in a certain way or to abstain from a particular behaviour (primary rule), but rather a rule that regulates the circumstances under which the abrogation of such an obligation is excused (secondary rule). Therefore, the commission of an international wrong is a *sine qua non* conceptual precondition for the operation of the necessity plea, as codified in the Articles on State Responsibility for Internationally Wrongful Acts (ASRIWA) of the International Law Commission (ILC).

The scope of the necessity defence under general international law was the object of a controversial decision of the German Constitutional Court on the Argentine default of 2001, which held that a State cannot invoke a state of necessity vis-à-vis its private creditors to excuse the non-performance of contractual obligations that are governed by domestic law.[2] The counterargument advanced by a strong dissenting opinion by justice Gertrude Labbe-Wolff in that case was that necessity can operate independently from its customary origin given that it is also a general principle of law recognized in most municipal legal orders. In fact, the view of justice Wolff is closely connected with the proposition of the existence of

---

* PhD Candidate, Queen Mary College, University of London.

1 According to art 25 of the ILC Articles on State Responsibility for Internationally Wrongful Acts (ASRIWA), '(N)ecessity may not be invoked by a State as a ground for precluding the wrongfulness of an act not in conformity with an international obligation of that State unless the act: (a) is the only way for the State to safeguard an essential interest against a grave and imminent peril; and (b) does not seriously impair an essential interest of the State or States towards which the obligation exists, or of the international community as a whole. In any case, necessity may not be invoked by a State as a ground for precluding wrongfulness if: (a) the international obligation in question excludes the possibility of invoking necessity; or (b) the State has contributed to the situation of necessity.' Art 27 ASRIWA reads, 'The invocation of a circumstance precluding wrongfulness in accordance with this chapter is without prejudice to: (a) compliance with the obligation in question, if and to the extent that the circumstance precluding wrongfulness no longer exists; (b) the question of compensation for any material loss caused by the act in question.'

2 Federal Constitutional Court of Germany, Order of the Second Senate of 8 May 2007, Joined Cases 2 BvM 1–5/03, 1, 2/06, 60 *Neue Juristische Wochenschrift* 2610 <www.bundesverfassungsgericht.de/SharedDocs/Entsc heidungen/EN/2007/05/ms20070508_2bvm000103en.html> accessed 15 January 2015.

a primary rule of 'financial necessity' – either as a matter of customary law or as a general principle of law – independent of that codified by article 25 of the ASRIWA.[3]

Leaving aside the question of whether a primary rule of financial necessity constitutes *lex lata* in international law, the decision of the German Constitutional Court could be also criticized because it did not inquire whether the Argentine default engaged the international responsibility of the country, but instead adopted the dogmatic position that a state of necessity could not be accepted under any circumstances to excuse the non-performance of private law obligations of a State towards its foreign creditors.[4] This position, however, corresponds to a parochial dualist perception that does not appreciate the significant overlap between domestic and international law. In the context of sovereign insolvency, this overlap is evidenced in a particularly stark manner; whereas mere non-payment of debt is nothing more than an instance of breach of contract, and as such actionable only under the *lex contractus*, governmental interference that reaches a certain level of intrusiveness with contractual rights may violate the minimum standard of treatment that should be accorded to the property of foreigners. What is more, sovereign insolvency may give rise to claims under Bilateral Investment Treaties (BITs) even for actions that fall short of a violation of the international minimum standard of treatment. Accordingly, even in cases of debt owed to private creditors under domestic law, there is scope for the application of the necessity defence.

These observations, however, doctrinally sound as they arguably are, do suffer from an important paradox. It would thus appear that sovereign debtors that have treated their creditors in the most egregious ways could potentially escape responsibility by invoking a state of necessity, whereas debtor States that interfered with creditors' rights in a less intrusive manner would have to pay their creditors at par and on time, as no international responsibility claim could be sustained in the first place.

It is submitted, nevertheless, that this paradox can be dealt with in two ways. Thus, by adopting a dualist position, one could claim that obligations under domestic and international law function on different levels and as such their non-fulfilment entails different consequences. If international law provides for secondary rules that regulate the performance of primary obligations and recognizes certain grounds for precluding responsibility in case of their violation, this should be in no way determinative of how domestic legal orders deal with the issue of non-performance of municipal law obligations and under which circumstances an excuse can be maintained.

The second way to address the paradox is to accept that there is a primary rule of financial necessity pursuant to which a State that faces severe financial difficulties is free to escape its responsibility – either as a matter of the *lex contractus* or international law – vis-à-vis its

---

3 This view arguably finds support in the Basis of Discussion No 4 submitted by the Preparatory Committee to the Council for the 1930 Hague International Law Codification Conference, according to which: 'A State incurs responsibility if, without repudiating a debt, it suspends or modifies the service, in whole or in part, by a legislative act, unless it is driven to this course by financial necessity' (1930) 24 *AJIL* 51.

4 The approach of the Constitutional Court is also in sharp contrast with the view of the International Law Association (ILA) on this matter, according to which: 'In terms of the basic fabric of international law, it would be surprising if an individual or institution were to receive a higher degree of protection than a State. In general, aliens will enjoy only a minimum standard of protection, whereas the rules on the relationship between States reflect the principle of sovereign equality. Moreover, the rationale underlying the concept of necessity contains nothing to justify providing the debtor State with less protection against an alien than against another State. At least in the absence of an express stipulation to the contrary, it thus should not be assumed that a debtor State has stricter obligations, in a State of necessity, vis-à-vis an alien than against another State' (1988) 63 *International Law Association Conference Report* 418, 431–32.

creditors. This approach offers the advantage of symmetrical treatment of creditors no matter whether a default or a restructuring is sanctioned under international or domestic law and can be therefore justified on equitable grounds. On the other hand, such a rule would be logically distinct from the necessity defence codified in the ASRIWA, something that not only leaves its content obscure and susceptible to speculation but also disunites the concept of necessity under international law. In the remainder of the chapter, necessity will be understood in its well-accepted form, that is, as a secondary rule of international law subject to the conditions of the ASRIWA, leaving open the question regarding the existence of a special rule of financial necessity.

Before proceeding to the more substantive parts of the analysis regarding the operation of the necessity defence in the context of sovereign insolvency, one last issue needs to be briefly touched upon. The preceding discussion has implicitly assumed that claims on the basis of international law will be more or less 'cordially' taken by a domestic court. The reality, however, is that domestic courts engage with international law in much more subtle and less harmonious ways.[5] To further perplex the matter, it needs to be pointed out that while the evaluation of the conduct of foreign States pursuant to the forum State's domestic law is commonplace (as far as *jure gestionis* acts are involved), the equality of States under international law poses limitations to the ability of a municipal court to determine whether another State acted according or contrary to its international obligations.[6] Still, instances may arise where, no matter the gravitas of the ruling at the international plane, domestic courts will sanction another State's actions on the basis of international law.[7] Furthermore, an important trend towards a shift from private law litigation before municipal courts to international arbitration may be *ante portas* for sovereign debt disputes.[8]

Origins of the Necessity Defence

In the sovereign debt context, the possibility of a State successfully invoking necessity could frustrate the attempts of its creditors to enforce their contractual rights before international

---

5 On that point, ILA Study Group on Principles on the Engagement of Domestic Courts with International Law (2012) 75 *International Law Association Conference Report* 971.

6 Andre Nollkaemper 'Internationally Wrongful Acts in Domestic Courts' (2007) 101 *AJIL* 760, 775. According to the writer, 'The court's determination may or may not be shared by a court in a different jurisdiction or an international court but, as a result of the fundamental starting point of sovereign equality, will have no automatic legal consequences for the alleged wrongdoing State'.

7 *Jurisdictional Immunities of the State (Germany v Italy: Greece intervening), Judgment, ICJ Reports 2012*, 99. The background of the dispute were decisions of the Italian courts that had found Germany responsible for the murder of civilians in occupied territory, the deportation of civilian inhabitants to slave labour and the deportation of prisoners of war to slave labour. These acts were sanctioned by the Italian courts not only as torts or delicts under domestic law, but as violations of international humanitarian law as well. Furthermore, the Italian courts found that the customary international law rule of State immunity was not applicable in that instance. The lack of decisiveness as a matter of international law of the Italian courts' decisions is demonstrated by the subsequent ruling of the ICJ which settled the matter authoritatively. For the corrective role of the ICJ in that case see ILA (n 5) para 31.

8 *Ambiente Ufficio S.p.A. and others v Argentine Republic*, ICSID Case No ARB/08/9, Decision on Jurisdiction and Admissibility, 8 February 2013; *Abaclat and others v Argentine Republic*, ICSID Case No ARB/07/5, Decision on Jurisdiction and Admissibility, 4 August 2011. In a recent award however the tribunal declined to exercise jurisdiction over sovereign bonds *see Poštová banka, a.s. and ISTROKAPITAL SE v Hellenic Republic*, ICSID Case No ARB/13/8. The claimants in that case have initiated annulment proceedings. A case regarding the Greek sovereign debt restructuring is still pending *see Cyprus Popular Bank Public Co Ltd v Hellenic Republic*, ICSID Case No ARB/14/16.

and domestic courts or tribunals. Evidently, this fact opens the door of abuse on the part of the sovereign debtor that could seek insulation from its liability in cases of opportunistic defaults. Of course, the possibility of abuse is not unique in the context of financial distress and sovereign debt crises, but has posed similar questions in other fields of international relations. Throughout the nineteenth and early twentieth century States regularly invoked necessity and a threat to their natural law right to 'self-preservation' as a political and moral excuse for open military interventions.[9] These abusive pleadings of the theory created a back-lash in legal doctrine that ranged from an outright denial of its existence to its qualification to particularly stringent preconditions.[10]

Before entering into the main inquiry of the chapter regarding the substantiation of the necessity plea in cases of sovereign insolvency, a presentation of the findings of early inter-national jurisprudence on necessity would be instructive in order to understand its origins and development. Although international courts and tribunals that dealt with the question invariably confirmed the existence of a necessity defence under general international law, the conditions that attached to it were so onerous that as a practical matter preclusion of international responsibility was virtually impossible. Indeed, in a jurisprudence that spans from 1795 to 1939 it was only in one case that a defence of necessity was accepted by an international tribunal.

Perhaps the oldest case cited recognizing the existence of a state of necessity in interna-tional law is the *Neptune* case (1795). In this case the US brought claims on the basis of the Jay Treaty against Great Britain for the capture of US vessel *Neptune* and its cargo in high seas during the British–French war.[11] The mixed commission ruled that although 'extreme necessity may justify the seizure of neutral property', the particular circumstances of the case did not correspond to an 'extreme' or 'irresistible' necessity.[12]

In the case of the *Russian Indemnity*,[13] the Permanent Court of Arbitration declined to accept a state of necessity argument advanced by the Ottoman government for the non-payment of interest on bonds that Russian subjects received as war reparations according to a series of treaties that followed the Ottoman–Russian war of 1877–78. The tribunal accepted the principle of necessity under international law; however, it did not find that 'the payment of the comparatively small amount of about 6 million francs due to the Russian claimants would imperil the existence of the Ottoman Empire or seriously compromised its internal or external situation'.[14]

Socobelge[15] is another case of the era brought before the PCIJ that dealt with the ques-tion of necessity. In that case a Belgian financial firm, *Société Commerciale de Belgique*, had obtained two arbitral awards against Greece that called for repayment of a debt that the Greek State had contracted with the company. Greece argued that the State's budgetary situation and external debt restructuring amounted to a state of necessity that made the execution of the awards impossible, notwithstanding the effect of res judicata. The court did not examine the merits of Greece's necessity invocation, as it found that it did not have jurisdiction in

---

 9 Roberto Ago, Addendum to the Eighth Report on State Responsibility, Doc A/CN4/318/ADD 5–7 (1980) *Yearbook of the International Law Commission*, vol II, pt 1, 13, 37–38.
10 ibid 47.
11 ibid 34.
12 ibid.
13 *Affaire de l'indemnité russe (Russie, Turquie)* (Russian Indemnity Case) [1912] 11 UNRIAA 421.
14 ibid 443.
15 *The Société Commerciale de Belgique*, [1939] PCIJ Series A/B, Fasc no 78, 160–90.

ascertaining the country's financial condition and capacity to pay. Although the court's ruling offers no guidance with regard to the substantiation of the theory of necessity, the parties' pleadings are significant in that vein. Both countries accepted that, in principle, a state of necessity could preclude a State's responsibility for non-payment of its debt obligations.[16] What is more, they did so by making reference to the essential State interest of 'economic existence', which included 'the normal functioning of public services', 'social peace', as well as 'public health and security'.[17] This reasoning is much more liberal compared to natural-law inspired ideas that were prevalent at that time and reduced the notion of 'essential interest' to self-preservation.

In *French Railroads Company of Venezuela*,[18] the Permanent Court of Arbitration found that the ongoing civil war in Venezuela had created such threats to the preservation of the State that the country was required to commit its revenues to that purpose and to subordinate the claims of the French company for damages to its property due to hostilities. Hence, once more in this early jurisprudence, necessity was equated to the self-preservation of the pleading State.

It goes without saying that the precedential value of the case law cited above has been considerably diminished in light of the adoption of the ASRIWA. The ILC has indeed taken a different view on the character of the 'essential interest' under threat in a state of necessity, something that should be accepted as evidence that customary international law has been developed towards a construction of the term that allows States to respond to situations falling short of a threat to their self-preservation. Thus, the importance of this early jurisprudence today lies not in the articulation of precise criteria against which State conduct should be evaluated, but to a spirit of constrain that invariably underlies all the cases and suggests that a state of necessity under general international law will be only accepted under exceptional circumstances. At the same time, however, another important insight of the early jurisprudence on necessity is that courts and tribunals that dealt with the plea in the financial context accepted, even *in abstracto*, that necessity remains a ground for precluding wrongfulness where non-fulfilment of international obligations has taken place due to economic constrains. It follows that the interpretation of the conditions set out in the relevant Articles of the ILC should take place under the light of these observations.

ICSID Jurisprudence and Substantiation of the Necessity Defence in Sovereign Insolvency

Non-Precluded Measures Clauses

A first issue that needs to be addressed before analysing the requirements of a state of necessity pursuant to recent ICSID jurisprudence is the effects of Non-Precluded Measures (NPMs) clauses on the claims of investors seeking to trigger the international responsibility of the debtor State following a debt default or restructuring. NPMs clauses allow parties to a BIT to escape responsibility for actions that would otherwise be in violation of the treaty's substantive terms where these actions were necessary to safeguard the host country's public order and essential security interests or the maintenance or restoration of international peace or security.

---

16 Ago Report (n 9) para 30.
17 ibid paras 28–29.
18 *French* Company *of Venezuela Railroads (France v Venezuela)* [1905] 10 UNRIAA 285.

An important interpretative question with regard to NPMs clauses concerns their relation with the general international law defence of necessity. A number of early ICSID awards that dealt with the matter concluded that the two concepts are essentially identical, thereby inserting the stringent conditions of a state of necessity under general international law into the treaty standard of NPMs clauses.[19] According to the Annulment Committee in *Sempra*, this constituted failure to apply article XI of the US–Argentina BIT and amounted to a manifest excess of powers pursuant to article 52(1)(b) of the ICSID convention.[20] In *LG&E* and *Continental* the tribunals concluded that the satisfaction of the conditions of a state of necessity under general international law and those of article XI of the US–Argentina BIT cannot be reduced to a single test.[21] Still, the two tribunals adopted elements of the general international law plea of necessity into their analysis of article XI of the US–Argentina BIT, as they both assessed whether Argentina contributed to the creation of a state of necessity. By adopting a different rationale, the *LG&E* and *Continental* tribunals concluded that Argentina did not contribute to the creation of the crisis and thus they absolved the country from responsibility on the basis of article XI of the US–Argentina BIT.

In a later award the tribunal in *El Paso*[22] reached the opposite conclusion. The tribunal based the relevance of the 'own contribution' test for the purposes of interpreting article XI of the US–Argentina BIT on an alleged general rule of international law that prohibits a party from invoking necessity when it has contributed to the State of affairs amounting to necessity.[23] Furthermore, the tribunal stated that in ascertaining the meaning of article XI of the US–Argentina BIT was guided by article 31(3) of the Vienna Convention on the Law of Treaties (VCLT).[24] Thus, in sharp contrast to the awards in *LG&E* and *Continental*, the tribunal concluded that Argentina's own contribution to the situation of necessity prevented her from relying on the NPMs clause of the US–Argentina BIT.[25]

The award in El Paso constitutes an unfortunate setback to the early awards in CMS, Sempra and Enron that have read into article XI of the US–Argentina BIT the stringent test of article 25 of the ASRIWA. It is important to keep in mind though that, in the words of the ILC, 'it is not the function of the Articles (that is the secondary rules provided by the ASRWIA) to specify the content of the obligations laid down by particular primary rules, or their interpretation'.[26] Given that NPMs clauses and the general international law defence of necessity operate at different levels, as primary and secondary rules respectively, there is no ground for resorting to article 31(3) of the VCLT to determine the meaning of the former on the basis of the latter.

---

19 *CMS Gas Transmission Company v Argentine Republic*, ICSID Case No ARB/01/8, Award, 12 May 2005, paras 353–78; *Sempra Energy International v Argentine Republic*, ICSID Case No ARB/02/16, Award, 28 September 2007, paras 375–78; *Enron Creditors Recovery Corporation (formerly Enron Corporation) and Ponderosa Assets, L.P. v Argentine Republic*, ICSID Case No ARB/01/3, Award, 22 May 2007, para 333.

20 *Sempra Energy International v Argentine Republic*, ICSID Case No ARB/02/16, Decision on Annulment, 29 June 2010, paras 197–203.

21 *LG&E Energy Corp, LG&E Capital Corp and LG&E International Inc v Argentine Republic*, ICSID Case No ARB/02/1, Decision on Liability, 3 October 2006, para 206; *Continental Casualty Co v Argentine Republic*, ICSID Case No ARB/03/9, Award, 5 September 2008, para 167.

22 *El Paso Energy International Co v The Argentine Republic*, ICSID Case No ARB/03/15, Award, 31 October 2011.

23 ibid paras 617–24.

24 ibid para 624.

25 ibid para 656.

26 International Law Commission, Report of the Commission to the General Assembly on the work of its fifty-third session, Doc A/CN 4/SER A/2001/Add 1 (pt 2) [2001] *Yearbook of the International Law Commission*, vol II, pt 2, 31, para 4.

If recourse to the general international law concept of necessity is not appropriate for ascertaining the meaning of BITs' NPMs clauses, then the question of which interpretative method should be used arises. A first relevant inquiry is whether NPMs clauses' references to 'public order' and 'essential security interests' cover exclusively civil unrests and national security concerns or if situations of economic necessity are also qualified. It appears in that regard that international jurisprudence has generally interpreted the notion of 'security interests' rather liberally. In the *Oil Platforms* case the ICJ noted that both the US and Iran recognized 'some of the interests referred to by the US – the safety of US vessels and crew, and the uninterrupted flow of maritime commerce in the Persian Gulf as being reasonable security interests of the US'.[27] This permissive stance to economic concerns in the interpretation of 'security interests' has been consistently followed by the ICSID tribunals that examined the emergency measures of Argentina in the context of its 2001 financial collapse.[28]

Another issue that may give rise to interpretative perplexity concerns the causal nexus that needs to be established between regulatory measures and protected policy interests under NPMs clauses. In that regard, the language used in each treaty should be the starting point of every interpretative exercise. US practice for instance requires measures to be 'necessary', while the New Zealand–China BIT uses the more open ended phrase 'directed to'.[29]

In interpreting a NPMs clause in the US–Nicaragua Treaty of Friendship, Commerce and Navigation (FCN), the ICJ applied a strict nexus requirement by holding that '[t]he measures taken must not merely be such as tend to protect the essential security interests of the party taking them, but must be "necessary" for that purpose'.[30] The Court later confirmed its view in *Oil Platforms* in the context of the US–Iran FCN Treaty, in a case that involved the use of force in potential violation of article 2(4) of the UN Charter.

As White and Von Staden note, however, the broader context within which these ICJ rulings took place was the use of force and its legality in *jus ad bellum*, and as such, extrapolating the restrictive reading of 'necessary' by the ICJ to the field of investment treaty arbitration is not appropriate. The same authors argue for more lenient standards of interpretation, such as the 'margin of appreciation' analysis or the 'less restrictive means' approach, that would essentially shift the risks of State action in exceptional circumstances from host States to investors.[31] The tribunal in *Continental* in fact expressly adopted the 'least restrictive means' test in ascertaining the content of 'necessary' for the purposes of article XI of the US–Argentina BIT by drawing parallels with WTO jurisprudence on article XX of the GATT.[32] Thus, although Argentina was absolved from responsibility with regard to the corralito (the imposition of the bank freeze), the devaluation of the Peso and the pesification of dollar liabilities,[33] the restructuring of certain government securities did not satisfy the 'less restrictive means' standard.[34] This stresses that sovereign debt defaults and restructurings may not be considered as measures that are necessary to achieve the protected objectives of NPMs clauses even where more permissive to State action interpretations were to be used.

---

27 *Oil Platforms (Islamic Republic of Iran v United States of America)*, Judgment, ICJ Reports 2003, 161, 196.

28 *LG&E* para 238 (n 21); *CMS* paras 331–32; *Enron* para 332; *Sempra* para 374 (n 19).

29 William Burke-White and Andreas Von Staden 'Investment Protection in Extraordinary Times: The Interpretation and Application of Non-Precluded Measures Provisions in Bilateral Investment Treaties' (2007–08) 48 Virginia Journal of International Law 307, 342.

30 *Military and Paramilitary Activities in and against Nicaragua (Nicaragua v United States of America)*. Merits, Judgment. ICJ Reports 1986, 14, 141.

31 WB White and A. Von Staden (n 29) 346.

32 *Continental* (n 21) para 192.

33 ibid 201–14.

34 ibid 220–21.

The interpretation of NPMs clauses' 'necessary' language that White and Von Staden argue for is in fact very similar to the public law standards of review that will be analysed below in the context of article 25 ASRIWA. This, however, does not neglect the independent standings of the treaty and general international law concepts of necessity, neither constitutes inappropriate 'interpretative application' of the ILC standard via article 31(3) of the VCLT. Indeed, the other stringent requirements of article 25 ASRIWA, such as the 'own contribution' test, should remain irrelevant when interpreting a boilerplate NPMs clause.

'Only Way' and 'Own Contribution' Requirements

A successful invocation of the necessity plea under general international law requires the cumulative satisfaction of the stringent conditions stipulated in article 25 of the ASRIWA.[35] The extensive case law of ICSID tribunals on the Argentine crisis clearly demonstrates that the satisfaction of some of these conditions in the context of a sovereign debt crisis pose a particularly high threshold to the pleading State. These conditions relate to the requirements that the invoking State did not have any other way to safeguard its essential interests (only way requirement)[36] and of non-contribution to the situation of necessity (own contribution requirement).[37] Because of the particular difficulty that the two requirements are likely to cause to the substantiation of a necessity plea in cases of sovereign insolvency, the following lines present in some detail the positions taken by ICSID tribunals so far.

With regard to the only way requirement, an overwhelming majority of tribunals held that the emergency measures enacted by Argentina as a consequence of its dramatic economic meltdown were not the only way to deal with the crisis.[38] In all these cases tribunals heard expert opinions by distinguished economists that proposed a number of alternative economic policy measures that would have not affected investors' interests so drastically.

Regarding Argentina's own contribution to the crisis, an equally large number of tribunals ruled that external causes may had been an important factor in the creation of the crisis, but poor domestic economic and fiscal policies were at least equally important.[39] Thus, Argentina's contribution to the state of necessity was deemed substantial, thereby precluding a successful invocation of the plea.

Against this vast and uniform case law, there are three cases, *LG&E*, *Continental* and *Enron Annulment*,[40] suggesting – in one way or the other – that the general international law plea of necessity can be accepted in the context of financial crises.

---

35 *Gabčíkovo-Nagymaros Project (Hungary/Slovakia)*, Judgment, ICJ Reports 1997, 7.

36 According to art 25 1(a) of the ASRIWA, '(N)ecessity may not be invoked . . . unless the act is the only way for the State to safeguard an essential interest against a grave and imminent peril'.

37 According to art 25 2(b) of the ASRIWA, '(I)n any case, necessity may not be invoked by a State as a ground for precluding wrongfulness if the State has contributed to the situation of necessity'.

38 *CMS* paras 323–24; *Sempra* paras 350–51; *Enron* paras 307–309 (n 19); *Suez, Sociedad General de Aguas de Barcelona S.A., and InterAguas Servicios Integrales del Agua S.A. v The Argentine Republic*, ICSID Case No ARB/03/17, Decision on Liability, 30 July 2010, para 238; *Total S.A. v The Argentine Republic*, ICSID Case No ARB/04/01, Decision on Liability, 27 December 2010, paras 223, 345, 483–84; *EDFI et al v Argentina*, ICSID Case No ARB/03/23, Award, 11 June 2012, para 1172.

39 *CMS* para 329; *Sempra* para 354; *Enron* paras 311–13 (n 19); *Suez* para 241; *EDFI* paras 1173–76 (n 38); *Impregilo S.p.A. v Argentine Republic*, ICSID Case No ARB/07/17, Award, 21 June 2011, para 358; *National Grid plc v The Argentine Republic*, UNCITRAL, Award, 3 November 2008, para 260.

40 *Enron Creditors Recovery Corporation (formerly Enron Corporation) and Ponderosa Assets, L.P. v Argentine Republic*, ICSID Case No ARB/01/3, Decision on the Application for Annulment, 30 July 2010.

The award in *LG&E* is often cited as one of the very rare cases in international jurisprudence that a necessity defence under general international law is being accepted. A careful reading of the award reveals, however, that the determining factor in that case was the operation of article XI contained in the US–Argentina BIT. To be sure, the tribunal indeed accepted that the conditions of the necessity plea had been satisfied in the present case, but quite evidently it did so as a matter of *dicta*.[41]

The analysis of the substantive conditions of the necessity plea by the Annulment Committee in *Enron*, on the other hand, is much more detailed and well-reasoned. In relation to the only way requirement, the Annulment Committee criticized the Enron tribunal for adopting a literal interpretation of article 25 ASRIWA without considering its other potential interpretations.[42] The Committee argued that the tribunal's reading of article 25 ASRIWA, pursuant to which the mere existence of alternative economic policies precludes the operation of the necessity plea, led it to substitute its legal judgment regarding the evaluation of the conditions of article 25 ASRIWA with an expert testimony that could merely confirm the availability of alternative economic policies.[43] In essence, the Committee suggested that in interpreting article 25 ASRIWA the tribunal had to adopt a more flexible standard of review instead of embarking into a rigid literal interpretation.

Quite significantly, the Committee proposed an interpretation of article 25 ASRIWA pursuant to public law standards of review of governmental acts, such as the less restrictive means analysis and the margin of appreciation doctrine.[44] As will be shown below, the Committee's rationale can be better understood as proposing a uniform standard of review that combines elements of both the less restrictive means analysis and the margin of appreciation doctrine.

With regard to the issue of a State's own contribution to the situation of necessity, the Annulment Committee in Enron once more argued that the tribunal merely applied an expert testimony on an economic question instead of engaging in a legal analysis of the requirements of article 25(2)(b) ASRIWA.[45] According to the Committee, the fact that the pleading State's actions objectively contributed to the state of affairs amounting to necessity does not negate the operation of the plea. A further subjective element is required, according to which a certain degree of fault on the part of the State should be established.[46]

The tribunal in *Continental* on the other hand examined the question of Argentina's own contribution to the crisis in the context of a non-precluded measures clause and found that the country could not be barred from invoking article XI of the Argentina–USA BIT because of the adoption of presumably unsound economic policies.[47] What is significant in the tribunal's rationale is the suggestion that to the extent that domestic economic policies are supported by the international financial community, as was the case with the official support of Argentina's currency board by the International Monetary Fund (IMF) and the US government

---

41 *LG&E* (n 21) para 245: '(W)hile the Tribunal considers that the protections afforded by art XI have been triggered in this case, and are sufficient to excuse Argentina's liability, the Tribunal recognizes that satisfaction of the state of necessity standard as it exists in international law (reflected in art 25 of the ILC's Draft Articles on State Responsibility) supports the Tribunal's conclusion.'

42 Enron Annulment (n 40) para 369.

43 ibid 376–77.

44 ibid 370, 371, 372.

45 ibid 393.

46 ibid 389.

47 *Continental* (n 21) paras 234–36. The tribunal stated, however, that the evaluation of 'own contribution' in the context of NPM clauses differs from that applied in the general international law standard.

for instance, the pleading State cannot assume ultimate responsibility for their failure and eventual creation of a crisis.[48]

The findings in *Enron Annulment* and *Continental* with regard to Argentina's own contribution to the crisis and the only way requirement introduce elements of flexibility in the general international law doctrine of necessity that are needed in order to make it operable in situations of financial distress. Be that as it may, these findings are isolated instances in an otherwise uniform ICSID jurisprudence that has consistently negated the availability of the defence of necessity in the context of the Argentine crisis. Therefore, as a practical matter, a turn of this trend in ICSID case law should not be expected in the foreseeable future. Still, it is suggested that by turning to the decisions in *Enron Annulment* and *Continental* future tribunals and other adjudicatory bodies dealing with sovereign debt crises will gain valuable insight in balancing creditors' rights with debtor States' essential interests. This issue is further examined below.

Starting with the Enron Annulment Committee's public law approach to the only way requirement of article 25 ASRIWA, one may challenge the appropriateness of introducing flexible standards of review such as the least restrictive alternative or the margin of appreciation analysis in the context of a general international law doctrine that has been purposefully drafted (through the ASRIWA) in a particularly restrictive manner.

Still, there may be cases where judicial authorities owe a certain degree of deference to governmental organs for reasons of improved institutional capacity or even democratic legitimacy.[49] Accordingly, where adjudication touches upon sensitive issues posited at the core of societal and constitutional organization, such as a State's ability to provide for vital public services, deferential standards of review of governmental measures can be seen as an appropriate mechanism to reconcile a State's essential interests with its international obligations. It appears therefore, that there is no compelling reason why economic emergency measures could not be reviewed in a similar way in order to assess whether the conditions of the necessity plea have been satisfied. In fact, it has been supported that article 25 ASRIWA constitutes a type of 'inherently flexible standard-type norm', for which deferential standards of review are appropriate.[50] Indeed, a closer reading of the only way requirement arguably supports this proposition. Article 25 1(a) allows the invocation of necessity if a measure is the only way to safeguard an essential interest. At the same time, the commentary to the Articles notes that the plea is precluded if there are other means to do so, even if they are 'more costly or less convenient'.[51] However, the cost or inconvenience that the alternatives involve are tolerable as long as they do not impede the essential interest under protection itself.[52]

The tribunals that rejected the operation of the necessity defence on the grounds of non-satisfaction of the only way requirement, failed to assess the relative effectiveness of different policies in actually safeguarding Argentina's essential interests. As mentioned above, for these tribunals the mere existence of alternative measures with less significant effects on investors sufficed to negate the defence.

---

48 ibid 235–36.
49 Yuval Shany 'Towards a General Margin of Appreciation Doctrine in International Law?' (2005) 16 *EJIL* 907, 919–20.
50 ibid 914–15 and accompanying note 46.
51 International Law Commission (n 26) 83 para 15.
52 Roman Boed 'State of Necessity as a Justification for Internationally Wrongful Conduct' (2000) 3 *Yale Human Rights & Development Law Journal* 1, 18.

The Annulment Committee indeed criticizes the Enron tribunal exactly on that ground, by stating that 'A second question not addressed by the Tribunal is whether the relative effectiveness of alternative measures is to be taken into account'.[53] While the Committee appears to propose three alternative interpretations to the 'only way requirement' that the tribunal had to consider,[54] the Committee's rationale can be better understood by unifying these apparently different interpretations. It is therefore argued that the best way to approach the only way requirement of article 25 ASRIWA is through a hybrid standard of review that combines elements of the margin of appreciation doctrine and the least restrictive alternative analysis. Accordingly, a first step is the evaluation of the relative effectiveness of different economic policies in safeguarding a particular State interest. This in turn presupposes the determination of a level of protection accorded to an essential interest under threat. At that stage, a margin of appreciation could be given to the pleading State to determine the desired level of protection. Once this level has been established, the State would be able to adopt those policies capable of achieving the desired level of protection, and in case that two or more policies are equally capable of doing so, it would be required to opt for those that involve the minimum violation of international law. Importantly, the State's assessments will always be subject to a residual good faith and reasonableness review,[55] a standard that, although significantly lenient, can insulate against abusive invocations of the plea.

The Annulment Committee in *Enron* also struck down the tribunal's finding that Argentina's contribution to the crisis precluded the invocation of the necessity defence. As already mentioned, the Committee essentially read in article 25 2(b) ASRIWA an element of fault as a prerequisite of a determination that a State contributed to the situation of necessity. To be sure, this approach echoes the view expressed by the International Law Association, according to which 'in a judicial proceeding, this rule (then article 33 2(c) of the ILC Draft Articles, the predecessor of article 25 2(b)) would force a court to determine whether the debtor State had acted in deliberate disregard of generally held views and had foreseen or should have foreseen that it would be unable to repay the loan'.[56] The tribunal in *Continental* adopted a similar line of reasoning in applying the 'own contribution' requirement. According to the tribunal's rationale, Argentina's rigid monetary policy, its loyal application of IMF prescriptions and broader subscription to the 'Washington Consensus' rulebook prior to the adoption of the emergency measures, precluded the suggestion that the country contributed to the crisis.

Such a permissive attitude to the pleading State readings of the own contribution requirement of article 25 2(b) ASRIWA are in congruence with the view that the capacity of ICSID tribunals to substitute their judgment for a country's economic policies is tenuous.[57] Furthermore, it is not difficult to see that a literal interpretation of article 25 2(b) ASRIWA would not only render it inapplicable in cases of sovereign debt distress but would also result in absurd outcomes, as a State could be precluded from invoking necessity merely because it issued debt in the first place. From a doctrinal perspective, this would turn basic interpretative canons on their head. Although the ASRIWA do not constitute treaty obligations, that does not preclude the application of established rules of treaty interpretation in ascertaining the

---

53 *Enron Annulment* (n 40) para 371.
54 ibid 370–72.
55 Yuval Shany (n 49) 910–11.
56 International Law Association (n 4) 430–31.
57 Michael Waibel 'Two Worlds of Necessity in ICSID Arbitration: CMS and LG&E' (2007) 20 *Leiden Journal of International Law* 637, 648.

meaning of the general international law rules they reflect.[58] Accordingly, the customary rule of necessity should be construed on the basis of the cardinal principle of effective interpretation (*ut res magis valeat quam pereat*), that is in a way that incarnates its object and purpose. The very essence of the necessity plea is to inject flexibility into international obligations so to allow for derogation under exceptional circumstances, while safeguarding against abusive invocation. Given that a literal interpretation of article 25 2(b) ASRIWA would devoid the rule of any meaning in cases of financial crises, recourse should be sought to an interpretation that would make necessity operable in situations of serious economic distress. This view is corroborated by the findings of the early jurisprudence on necessity that consistently accepted that, as a matter of principle, the plea should be available in the context of economic crises.[59]

It would then follow, that 'substantial contribution' to the situation of necessity under article 25 2(b) ASRIWA should not be interpreted in a strictly objective manner. States should not be precluded from invoking necessity merely because otherwise reasonable and *bona fide* economic policies eventually miscarried. In an environment where domestic economic policies are continuously monitored by supranational authorities it is perfectly plausible to gauge reasonableness and diligence in economic policy planning: adjudicatory bodies can reach informed decisions in that vein by turning to IMF article IV surveillance reports or to recommendations issued under article 121 of the Treaty of the Functioning of the European Union (TFEU). Where a financial crisis has been preceded by consistent disregard by the national authorities of economic policy advice, this fact would furnish important evidence of unsound economic management and could preclude the invocation of necessity.

Substantiation of the Necessity Plea

This final section addresses the question of which would be the approach of an adjudicatory body to a necessity defence advanced by a country that has defaulted on or restructured its debt contrary to its international obligations under the light of the ASRIWA and relevant jurisprudence. It is argued that the possibility of invoking necessity should remain open to distressed sovereign debtors. Still, it is further suggested that such a conclusion is in no way panacea for the resolution of sovereign debt crises. This is so because even if the defence were to be accepted *in casu*, its built-in limitations would preclude a comprehensive solution of the debtor county's problems.

As a first step, a court assessing the satisfaction of the substantive conditions of the plea in the context of sovereign insolvency should examine whether continuing servicing the debt normally represents a grave and imminent peril to the debtor country's essential interests. According to the ILC, the notion of 'essential interest' cannot be substantiated in the abstract, that is, there is not a *numerus clausus* of interests that are qualified as essential. On the contrary, the evaluation of protected State interests under article 25 ASRIWA should take place on a case by case basis.[60] ICSID tribunals that dealt with the question of whether a sovereign debt crisis puts at risk the State's essential interests in the context of the Argentine crisis connected that issue with an assessment of the severity of the crisis that the State faces.[61] While

---

58 Alexander Orakhelashvili, *The Interpretation of Acts and Rules in Public International Law* (OUP 2008) 497. For a different view, Anastasios Gourgourinis 'The Distinction between Interpretation and Application of Norms in International Adjudication' (2011) 2 Journal of International Dispute Settlement 31, 36.
59 See the heading "Origins of the Necessity Defence" above in this chapter.
60 International Law Commission (n 26) 83 para 15.
61 *CMS* paras 319–22; *Enron* paras 305–307; *Sempra* paras 348–49 (n 19).

a number of tribunals found that the standard would be satisfied only if a 'compromise to the very existence and independence' of the State existed,[62] others adopted a more lenient approach and ruled that Argentina's essential interests were indeed threatened.[63] Still, this dichotomy in ICSID jurisprudence may only be apparent, given that even those tribunals that did not find that an essential interest of Argentina was in peril, in fact went on to examine the other requirements of article 25 ASRIWA. That could be interpreted as an implicit acceptance that an essential interest of the country was actually affected.[64] As it has been aptly put, sovereign insolvency is a 'spoliator', a 'destroyer';[65] it results in the drying up of the whole economy, as trade, investment and credit shrink. After a while, even the most basic functions of a State may be in question. Excluding rare instances of opportunistic debtor behaviour, the State's most essential interests are indeed at stake. As demonstrated in the previous lines, this is also supported by theory and case law.

Next, a court or tribunal would examine whether the default or restructuring was the only way to safeguard a given essential interest. Following the test outlined above, the pleading State would determine a reasonably desired level of protection for the essential interest at stake. Subsequently, it would have to provide evidence that the desired level of protection could not have been achieved by diverting budgetary resources to debt service (without thereby threatening other essential interests) or by imposing smaller losses to creditors. The adjudicator would then decide on the basis of the evidenced provided whether the quantum of losses that creditors suffered is tolerable. Importantly, in making this decision she would be bound by the country's determination of the degree of protection accorded to its essential interests, which would serve as a proxy of the appropriate debt relief that the country will ultimately receive.

The next step would be to weigh the debtor State's interests with those of the State(s) to which the obligation is owed or of the international community as a whole, pursuant to article 25 1(b) ASRIWA. The most intriguing question regarding this provision is whether the interests of non-State actors are to be taken into account in the balance. According to article 33 paragraph 2 of the ASRIWA, non-State actors are not precluded from invoking the protections of the secondary rules, subject to the scope of the primary obligation in question. To be sure, international jurisprudence has allowed the possibility of individuals effectively being the direct holders of rights established under treaties at the interstate level.[66] It appears that this would be indeed the case in the context of investment related disputes where investors are the ultimate beneficiaries of protections under international investment agreements.

The findings of tribunals on the Argentine crisis lack a balancing test between the essential interests of the pleading State, on the one hand, and those of investors on the other. Instead, the tribunals only inquired if damages to investors' interests amounted to a harm to the interests of their home countries and expressly negated such possibility.[67] Although this approach

---

62 ibid.

63 *LG&E* (n 21); para 257 *Impregilo S.p.A.* (n 39) paras 346–50; *Suez* (n 38) para 238.

64 *Enron Annulment* (n 40) para 359.

65 International Law Association (2010) 74 *International Law Association Conference Report* 978, 982.

66 *LaGrand (Germany v United States of America)*, Judgment, ICJ Reports 2001, 466, 494.

67 The tribunals in *Enron* and *Sempra* were apparently more accommodative to investors' interests in that regard in noting that 'in the context of investment treaties there is still the need to take into consideration the interests of the private entities who are the ultimate beneficiaries of those obligations. The essential interest of the Claimants would certainly be seriously impaired by the operation of article XI or State of necessity in this case', *Enron* para 342, *Sempra* para 391 (n 19). Still, it appears (although the relative rationale is somehow blurred) that the tribunals considered the interests of investors not legally significant in the context of art 25 1(b) ASRIWA. The tribunal in *Impreglio* noted that '(T)he interests of a small number of a Contracting State's nationals or legal

neglects the reference made in article 25 1(b) to the interests of the 'international community as a whole', it is rather certain that even if the right test was applied the balance would tilt in favour of the pleading State. Indeed, it is hard to imagine how even the most essential interest of an investor could outweigh a State's interest to its economic survival.

Then, the alleged adjudicatory body would move to examine if the international obligation in question excludes (explicitly or implicitly) the invocation of necessity, as per article 25 2(a) ASRIWA. Explicit exclusion is part of certain humanitarian conventions, whereas implicit exclusion may be inferred from the object and purpose of a rule.[68] An argument could be made in this regard that the protections of international investment agreements establish such rules, given that it is in times of emergency that their protection is more needed to investors. Although this is indeed accurate as far as typical risks associated with general regulatory interests of the host State are concerned,[69] the case would be different in exceptional circumstances of crisis under which the general international law doctrine of necessity would normally operate. Therefore, the object and purpose of investment agreements cannot be interpreted as implicitly precluding a plea of necessity. This is indeed corroborated by the findings of tribunals regarding Argentina that almost invariably support that assumption.

As a final step, the court would be required to assess the last condition of article 25 of the ASRIWA regarding the State's own contribution to the situation of necessity. The ILC in its commentary of the ASRIWA makes clear that contribution should be distinguished from causation and that only the former is required for the purposes of article 25 2(b).[70] Accordingly, even if exogenous factors were effectively the cause for the creation of a sovereign debt crisis – financial contagion from another region or speculative flows of external capital for instance – that would not absolve the State from responsibility, as long as domestic policies had already created important vulnerabilities that became apparent only after an external shock. As the vast majority of the tribunals that examined the Argentine crisis noted, financial crises will almost certainly be the outcome of an interplay between domestic and external factors.

As it was argued above, however, there are both policy and doctrinal objections to a literal and strictly objective interpretation of article 25 2(b) ASRIWA. Accordingly, 'substantial contribution' of the pleading State to the creation of necessity by virtue of internal economic policy failures should not be lightly assumed. *Bona fide* and reasonable economic policies that have the seal of approval of international watchdogs such as the IMF and the European Commission cannot be deemed as 'contributions' to a state of necessity merely because they did not bring about the expected outcomes. Economics is more an art than a science and what seemed as optimal regulatory action *ex ante* may well be proved flawed *ex post*. The view advocated here has also the added advantage of improving the accountability of international institutions charged with supervising national economic policies. Although international agencies will not be held directly responsible for ill advising national authorities, it would be much more difficult to put the blame of financial failure exclusive on debtor States that have acted pursuant to their instructions.

In case there was a conclusion that the State has satisfied all the conditions of article 25, article 27 would come into play. According to article 27 (a), preclusion of wrongfulness is

---

entities are not consistent with or qualify as an 'essential interest' of that State' para 354 (n 39). Similarly, the tribunal in *Suez* (n 38) para 239.

68 International Law Commission (n 26) 84.

69 Given that 'the purpose of investment treaties is to address the typical risks of a long-term investment project', Rudolf Dolzer and Christoph Schreuer, *Principles of International Investment Law* (OUP 2012) 22.

70 International Law Commission (n 26) 78 para 9.

temporary as the international obligation in question is revived when the state of necessity ceases to exist. Thus, necessity can only lead to a postponement of international duties and not to their termination. Therefore, by the time necessity no longer subsists, the State would be required to continue servicing its debt regularly. This means that excessive indebtedness is not addressed per se by necessity, as only temporary moratoria and not write-offs of debts are covered by the plea. Consequently, a successful invocation of necessity can merely offer some breathing space for the State and probably additional leverage in the negotiations with its creditors.[71] Alas, a comprehensive solution of its woes can be only achieved through debt reduction, for which necessity is not a substitute.

Conclusion

The preceding discussion has demonstrated that the general international law defence of necessity poses a very high threshold of satisfaction for debtor States seeking to invoke it in cases of insolvency. This is hardly surprising considering that the doctrine was originally developed in the context of *jus ad bellum* and thus the codification of the customary principles made by the ILC reflects the concern towards abusive recourse to armed force, a recurring event during the nineteenth and early twentieth century. Still, a case law spanning from the *Russian Indemnity* case until the recent Argentine default might have rejected its application *in casu* but has confirmed that necessity may be invoked in circumstances of extreme financial distress. If these jurisprudential findings are of any practical significance, then an effective interpretation of the conditions of article 25 ASRIWA is one that makes the necessity plea operable in the context of financial crises. Hence, it has been suggested that flexible standards of review originating from public law adjudication are pertinent in ascertaining whether the conditions of necessity have been satisfied. This is also consistent with the view that adjudicatory bodies should exercise judicial restraint when called to assess issues of national economic management.

Nevertheless, from a policy perspective, necessity is a rather incomplete tool in dealing with sovereign insolvency. As it has been succinctly noted, necessity could merely function as a rescheduling of the sovereign's obligations,[72] whereas what will be likely needed to restore solvency will be drastic debt reduction. Even if successful, a necessity defence could not possibly perform this task.

As a practical matter, international law remains surprisingly underdeveloped in the field of sovereign insolvency. International investment agreements may offer promising causes of actions to creditors, but up until today liability on that ground remains unchartered territory. As far as there is no significant progress towards the development of primary rules regarding State responsibility in cases of sovereign insolvency, the defence of necessity will remain 'dormant'.[73] In the context of international investment arbitration, NPMs clauses contained in a number of international investment agreements will be able to prevent the host State's responsibility in situations of economic emergency. In these situations the general international law plea of necessity is likely to be redundant, as NPM clauses should be interpreted as presenting a lower threshold of satisfaction. Be that as it may, the necessity plea remains a residual defence that can acquire significance in the realm of sovereign insolvency adjudication. In cases of extreme financial difficulties, States can and should be allowed to seek recourse to it.

---

71 Michael Waibel (n 57) 642.
72 ibid 641–42.
73 This would not be the case if one accepts the existence of a primary rule of financial necessity as described in the first part of the chapter.

Part III
Trade Law

7 The WTO – A Suitable Case for Treatment? Is It 'Reformable'?

*Friedl Weiss**

Through foreign trade, people's satisfaction, merchants' profit and countries' wealth are all increased.

Ibn Kaldun, fourteenth-century Arab philosopher

There should be a code of laws of a much larger extent, for a nation attached to trade and navigation, than for a people who are contented with cultivating the earth.

Montesquieu

Preliminary Remarks

We are accustomed to and expect seeing scientific discoveries in the natural sciences being enacted in prescriptive norms of law – for example health, technical or food standards – but it is probably very rare, if not unique for paradigmatic new thinking in the social sciences to be so implemented by rules of law.

Yet it is David Ricardo's brilliant and as yet in principle unfalsified economic theorem of comparative trade advantage[1] which constitutes the trade policy underpinning of the legal edifice of the World Trade Organization (WTO). Indeed, after the demise of the theory and practice of mercantilism, it would seem to have become an enduring theoretical paradigm, unchallenged even by its most vociferous sceptics and critics. Paradoxically, this is also confirmed by those who lament the return or proclaim the end of neoliberalism.[2]

For some dissenters, however, it is seriously flawed in present day circumstances. Stripped of its underlying assumptions of immobile factors of production such as labour, capital and institutions like the multinational firms, it is 'no longer necessarily valid', as big companies can produce about everything everywhere. This nullification of Ricardo's assumption, it is argued, has deprived the WTO of its guiding theoretical wisdom, making it obtusely dogmatic, its fall seemingly unavoidable.[3] Eminent economists such as Stiglitz see the very nature of WTO disciplines as unsuitable for DCs.[4] On the other hand there is ample evidence that countries are

---

* University of Vienna.
1 Ricardo said that if *relative* costs in two countries differ, there must be opportunities for mutually advantageous trade between them.
2 cf Andrew Lang, *World Trade Law after Neoliberalism: Re-imagining the Global Economic Order* (OUP 2011).
3 Alice H Amsden, 'The WTO: A Sweet or Sour Chinese Banquet?' in Zdenek Drabek (ed), *Is the World Trade Organization Attractive Enough for Emerging Economies?* (Palgrave Macmillan 2010) 72, 73.
4 Zdenek Drabek and Wing Thye Woo, 'Who should join the WTO and Why?: A Cost-benefit Analysis of WTO Membership' in Zdenek Drabek (ed), *Is the World Trade Organization Attractive Enough for Emerging Economies?* (Palgrave Macmillan 2010) 249, 249.

generally keen on joining the WTO. It would appear safe to assume that the WTO has grown into an organization of near universal membership because of the undiminished universal validity of the paradigm as representing best trade policy scientific practice, rather than in spite of it. Some WTO Members though have expressed regrets to have joined it or that their great expectations have been sorely disappointed. Yet no WTO Member has ever abandoned membership nor, as far as can be made out, has anybody advocated the abolition of the WTO.[5] On the contrary, many ponder how to improve its functioning to provide better and more effective service to its Members. Given its mostly uncontested status, it can surely still serve both as dependable fundament and starting point for urgently necessary reforms of a non-discriminatory multilateral trade order. Are perennial, mostly academic and civil society-based debates about reforming the WTO not the best proof that all WTO institutional reforms must ultimately implement it, subject to necessary adjustments reflecting contemporary global concerns?[6]

If so, this should make WTO institutional and dispute settlement reform in principle a simple matter of mustering the requisite political will to pick or elaborate the most suitable proposal for reform. We know, however, it is not so simple since it is part of the 'political economy', 'in the mix' so to speak with a wide range of interests beside trade. Rather than to revisit let alone rehearse the well-known and often highly technical inventory of numerous proposals for WTO reform made by WTO Members and academic commentators or debates between them,[7] this chapter examines, necessarily with a broad brush: first, some conceptual and contextual matters and, secondly, aspects of governance directly or implicitly adumbrated in three quotations from recent WTO practice – Appellate Body Reports and work of the WTO Committee on Trade and Environment, namely on: the status of non-trade-related concerns; the WTO – 'constitution'; and WTO transparency.

Introduction: Concepts and Context

Concepts

Although the title of this chapter refers to 'reform' and 'international' economic governance, it is surely safe to think of 'reforms' and 'global' economic governance through WTO reform,

---

5 See, however, for example James Goldsmith, *The Trap* (Carroll & Graf 1995) 44: 'The GATT must be rejected. It is too profoundly flawed to be a stepping stone to a better system'; also Maurice Allais, Nobel laureate in economics formulating these views for example in arts in *Le Figaro* of 15 and 16 November 1993, entitled respectively 'Une gigantesque mystification' and 'Une erreur fondamentale'.

6 It is tempting – as it must have been for Rudolf von Jhering when distinguishing mechanical from psychological causality – to contrast scientific veracity in the natural and social sciences: the status of Ricardo's paradigm in economics to that of Copernican heliocentrism in astronomy, or to Einstein's theory of relativity in physics. Nobody today would seriously adhere to geo-centrism nor dismiss the theory of relativity; see Jhering's *Der Zweck im Recht*, 1877.

7 See for example, EU Petersmann (ed), *Preparing the Doha Development Round: Improvements and Clarifications of the WTO Dispute Settlement Understanding* (Conference Report, Robert Schumann Centre for Advanced Studies, EUI 2002); Thomas Cottier and Manfred Elsig (eds), *Governing the World Trade Organization: Past, Present and beyond Doha* (CUP 2011); Thomas Cottier, 'Preparing for Structural Reform in the WTO' in William J Davey and John Jackson (eds), *The Future of International Economic Law* (OUP 2008) 59; Debra Steger, 'The Culture of the WTO: Why it Needs to Change' in William J Davey and John Jackson (eds), *The Future of International Economic Law* (OUP 2008) 45.

whether of its institutional, procedural or substantive law.[8] Concepts involved include 'globalization', 'governance' and 'reform'.

Globalization

'Globalization', though not a new phenomenon as Paul Krugman once reminded us,[9] has perhaps become the most pervasive and ubiquitous concept since the 1990s. It appears to have found instant appeal across a range of intellectual interests. Whether fervently embraced, or vilified, it is living reality. We are part of it as much as it is part of our daily professional and personal experience, language and mode or even habit of thinking. Still, many feel threatened by it, target the WTO as emblematic for their concerns and support protectionist measures promised them by politicians of all ilk. Despite, following '9/11', a noticeable slowdown in globalization, its demise, though proclaimed in many obituaries, never occurred. On the contrary, globalization intensified and peaked prior to the onset of the global financial crisis.[10] This, according to some, reflected financial globalization, the last in a cycle of globalizations.[11] The next, it is argued, won't be of the meanwhile widely discredited neoliberal, Washington concensus-based kind which was characteristic for the post-Cold War period of market triumphalism in the roaring nineties.[12] More likely, it will be driven more by the growing prosperity of the emerging economies than the austerity of the G7 economies.[13] In this new 'inter-polar world' of trade governance, already adumbrated in the Doha Round, power will be redistributed more rapidly, not merely between Western and rising powers, but also between states and non-state actors, making the conclusion of multilateral accords even more challenging while deepening the existential interdependence.[14]

While '*interdependence*' was the dominant concept used to characterize international relations in a decentralized system between economically disparate sovereign territorial states (particularly industrialized and developing countries), '*globalization*' is the concept of choice used to denote integration as well as an end of fragmentation. To the extent that *globalization* reflects a certain trend towards increasingly common, harmonized, standards, it may also appear as manifestation of centralization on a global scale, which in turn necessitates global institutional management. However, there are also cautionary tales concerning the asymmetrical distribution of gains from globalization, a matter of pressing contemporary concern.

While the contours of globalization, like those of the universe, remain mysterious, it comprises essentially two components. Sticking with metaphorical images drawn from astrophysics, it has a socio-economic dimension, comparable to dark energy which repels, pushing the universe apart; and a legal-institutional dimension, comparable to dark matter, the gravity of which pulls it together.

---

8 Friedl Weiss, 'Globalization through WTO Integration: Neither Friend nor Foe' (2003) 30 *Legal Issues of Economic Integration* 95.

9 P Krugman, *Pop Internationalism* (The MIT Press 1997) 208, 212.

10 Tony McGrew, 'After Globalisation? WTO Reform and the New Global Political Economy' in Thomas Cottier and Manfred Elsig (eds), *Governing the World Trade Organization: Past, Present and beyond Doha* (CUP 2011) 20, 31.

11 Harold James, *The Creation and Destruction of Value: The Globalization Cycle* (Harvard University Press 2009) 144.

12 David Harvey, *The Enigma of Capital* (Profile Books 2010) 38.

13 IMF, *World Economic Outlook* (2010).

14 Giovanni Grevi, 'The Intepolar World: A New Scenario' (2009) EU Institute for Security Studies, Occasional Paper No79, 23.

The Socio-Economic Dimension

Worldwide trends toward the opening of national markets, combined with innovation and transfer of communications and information technology, have significantly altered modes of production, distribution and exchange of goods and services. Production and trade flows are 'global', and capital moves with unsettling speed, and mostly uncontrollably, across permeable state structures in the 'borderless' world economy. National economies of the major trading nations are increasingly integrated into one global market.

On the other hand, benefits from increased trade and investment flows in recent years manifestly bypassed the majority of developing countries, while their external debts still grow. It has also been observed that while further liberalization particularly in such areas as information technology and telecommunications favours developed countries, liberalization in areas of particular interest to developing countries such as textiles, agriculture and the movement of natural persons, proceeds at a much slower pace, if at all.

The Legal-Institutional Dimension

Whatever else globalization represents, to the international lawyer it is clearly a process of peaceful normative, regulatory and/or adjudicative integration through which certain socio-economic values have come to be enshrined in and accepted as global standards governing the conduct of international and transnational actors, that is of states and other entities including companies.

From a legal perspective, globalization appears to be a process through which 'global market forces' have wrested the initiative if not the power for contextual agenda-setting from states. Most, if not all of international economic – and trade law is market driven.[15] 'Regulation', a resource and public good, is demanded and acquired by economic operators, designed primarily for their benefit, but supplied by the political process.[16] In that sense globalization is localization in disguise: domestic socio-economic claims and issues, transformed into and 'repatriated' as claims and issues of global concern requiring 'regulatory attention' in form of 'dezentraler Kontextsteuerung'.[17] Global markets, as was mentioned, existed already before the First World War. However, it was in response to the massive destruction of economic life in both world wars that multilateral institutions were created – the League of Nations, the International Labour Organization (ILO), the Bretton Woods Institutions, the International Trade Organization (ITO) Havana Charter – to re-establish, rekindle, organize and manage certain aspects of global markets. Contemporary intergovernmental arrangements such as the Organization for Economic Cooperation and Development (OECD) and G7[18] have not yet shown sufficient resolve and vision to provide such balanced macro-economic management of multilateral trade and monetary affairs.[19] Therefore, most of the debates concerning global socio-economic management are being conducted in the WTO from time to time.

15 IBRD/The World Bank, 'Fostering Markets: Liberalization, Regulation and Industrial Policy', (1997) in *The State in a Changing World, The World Development Report*, 61.
16 George J Stigler, 'The process of Economic Regulation' (1972) 17 *The Anti-Trust Bulletin*, 207 ff.
17 G Teubner and H Willke, 'Kontext und Autonomie' (1984) 5 *Zeitschrift für Rechtssoziologie* 4; similarly, G Teubner, ' "Global Bukowina": Legal Pluralism in the World Society' in G Teubner (ed), *Global Law without a State* (Dartmouth 1997) 3.
18 Formerly G8; G7 after suspension of Russia in 2014.
19 The financial and economic crisis has apparently galvanized governments and the Bretton Woods institutions to discuss certain systemic reforms.

Governance

Wherever in the world total or partial governance failure occurs, we witness search for desperately needed new or better governance. Perhaps, however, former US President Clinton's memorable quip 'it's the economy, stupid' should be recast to read: 'It's economic governance, stupid'.

New governance will be required when none existed or existing governance failed, disintegrated or fell into disuse. This may happen after desperately cataclysmic events, such as the world wars of the twentieth century, or should have happened after the Great Financial Crash 2008–2009.

The first contingency, lack of or dysfunctional governance, involves institution – designing and – building, the second, governance failure, most likely root-and-branch reform. Every time, under either contingency, the proverbial lessons of history need relearning and better, more provident governance infrastructures – institutions and procedures – to be put in place to prevent a recurrence of those events, retrospectively.

Better governance will normally be envisaged when underlying interests have changed or to reaffirm constitutional values and to simplify legal systems so as to strengthen implementation and compliance, thereby filling gaps in the system and enhancing legal certainty.[20] Under such conditions less radical reform involving adaptive responses to changed societal circumstances (socio-economic, technical, etc.) will suffice.

Good governance, desirable yet still a largely evocative concept rather than evident in significant let alone uniform international practice, is based on a number of common shared governance values and principles of certain international organizations, including the WTO, the EU,[21] the OECD, the United Nations Development Program (UNDP), the UN Economic and Social Commission for Asia and the Pacific (ESCAP) and the International Monetary Fund (IMF).[22]

The Commission on Global Governance (CGG) defines the governance problem as consisting of overcoming the flaws and inadequacies of existing institutions in order to resolve conflicts in an increasingly interdependent world, resolve them peacefully and democratically, and cooperate in managing finite resources and the redistribution of welfare. It argues that nation states are no longer able to manage international affairs as sovereigns, and identifies a need to 'weave a tighter fabric of international norms, expanding the rule of law worldwide and enabling citizens to exert their democratic influence on global processes.'[23]

Reform

Any reform has both a conservative and a progressive connotation, building on as well as improving the existing system of rules. Clearly, the establishment of the WTO itself was not seen to represent a radically new departure, nor as an attempt to revive the abortive

---

20 See Working Group on EU Administrative Law, 'State of Play and Future Prospects for EU Administrative Law' (2011) Working Document; and ReNEUAL, *Model Rules on EU Administrative Procedure* (2014).

21 See Friedl Weiss, 'Transparency as an Element of Good Governance in the Practice of the EU and the WTO: Overview and Comparison' (2007) 30 *Fordham International Law Journal* 1545; Panagiotis Delimatsis, 'Institutional transparency in the WTO' in Andrea Bianchi and Anna Peters (eds), *Transparency in International Law* (CUP 2013).

22 Cecilia Juliana Flores Elizondo, 'Good Governance in the IMF: An Eclectic Theoretical Appraisal of Decision-Making Processes' (2013) 10 *Manchester Journal of International Economic Law* 271.

23 Commission on Global Governance, *Our Global Neighbourhood* (OUP 1995) xiv.

ITO's Havana Charter with its broad socio-economic scope. On the contrary, it was the final stage of a gradual evolution to strengthen the system originally established under the General Agreement on Trade and Tariffs (GATT) 1947. In fact, the WTO was expressly designed to secure continuity, but also reflected adaptability, by updating its preamble to include the objective of 'sustainable development'.[24]

Still, not only the scope and coverage of WTO rules increased (General Agreement on Trade in Services or GATS, Agreement on Trade-Related Aspects of Intellectual Property Rights or TRIPS, Dispute Settlement Understanding or DSU), their very characteristics also changed significantly.

Whereas the GATT was primarily concerned with 'negative integration' – the progressive reduction of tariffs and the regulatory containment of non-tariff barriers combined with the complimentary goal of non-discriminatory trade – the WTO represents a shift to 'positive integration', requiring Members to legislate and enforce measures relating to technical standards, health and safety standards and intellectual property rights so as to bring about harmonized standards among Members.

Obviously, whenever reform is being contemplated, a clear focus on goals and means for achieving them is called for, both of course presupposing agreement on the problem(s) that need fixing.

However, before briefly sketching out some selected historical antecedents to the contemporary debate about international economic governance, it is necessary to lay out a few contextual considerations.

Abridged Historical Context

Pre-WTO

The explicit trade-employment link in the title of the 1948 UN Conference on Trade and Employment held in Havana, which established the ultimately abortive Havana Charter for the ITO, was no fluke, nor a dictate of victorious Allies, but reflected a shared conviction, the Havana consensus as it were, that liberalizing trade would create jobs, which misguided protectionism of the 1930s had helped destroy. Thus, as for trade, the Havana mantra was both compellingly simple and scientifically uncontested: David Ricardo's paradigm of comparative advantage crafted in 1817[25] was to become enshrined as perennial principle in legally binding disciplines for the conduct of multilateral trade relations, a boost to welfare creation through liberalized trade, metaphorically its object and purpose.[26]

Yet ideological, not trade-related objections to, inter alia, 'Fair Labour Standards' (Article 7 ITO Charter), feared by members of the US Congress as heralding the spread of socialist ideology, prevented ratification of the entire Havana Charter.

---

24 See preamble, arts XVI(1) WTO, 3(1) DSU. See also Nico Schrijver and Friedl Weiss (eds), *International Law and Sustainable Development* (Martinus Nijhoff 2004).

25 David Ricardo, *On the Principles of Political Economy and Taxation*.

26 It is not here suggested, of course, that Ricardo's implicit paradigm could as such ever have become an 'object and purpose' in any of the meanings of that term featured in the Vienna Convention on the Law of Treaties (especially art 31 VCLT), whether in the abortive ITO, the residual GATT or the WTO and its covered agreements. On the concept see generally David S Jones and Thomas N Saunders, 'The Object and Purpose of a Treaty: Three Interpretive Methods' (2010) 43 *Vanderbilt Journal of Transnational Law* 565.

Post-WTO

The global financial crisis has highlighted the problem of how to create effective resolution schemes for systemically important institutions. This 'too big to fail' issue is not a new phenomenon. Exactly the same considerations where at play when the first systemic attempt was made to regulate capital markets in the United States in the aftermath of Roosevelt's election in 1932. Then the contours of the problem where defined by state–federal rather than intergovernmental relations with a focus on the electricity and gas markets rather than the financiers who facilitated their expansion. What becomes clear from an evaluation of the history is the importance of political will.

Just as the IMF, though sidelined by the Asian financial crisis, managed to reinvent itself, though perhaps sub-optimally,[27] so it seemed at first that the global financial crisis spurred WTO Members' on to conclude the Doha Round of multilateral negotiations so as to avert trade protectionist reflexes.

Be that as it may, taking the pulse of the multilateral trading system of the WTO marking its twentieth anniversary this year, few would disagree that despite its still growing membership[28] and global trade coverage – approximately 98 per cent of global trade – it would seem in poor institutional health, though far from terminally ill. Some, however, consider it moribund, mothballed in Doha, because stuck in its own ways of 'free trade imperialism',[29] unable to accomplish significant major negotiating results on the big tough issues of agriculture, services and industrial goods even after lengthy negotiations. On the other hand, and perhaps unsurprisingly, following Pascal Lamy's 'we are in a crisis' comment at the 2005 Hong Kong Ministerial,[30] Roberto Acevedo the current Director General of the WTO appeared upbeat when he hailed the 2003 Doha Declaration on the TRIPS Agreement and Public Health, as well as the 2013 Trade Facilitation Agreement (TFA)[31] and the Trade Facilitation Agreement Facility (TFAF)[32] as proof that the WTO 'can deliver'.[33]

WTO reform involving negotiations between all groups of WTO Members, the major trading powers as well as the DCs and LDCs, can be a frustratingly arduous process, as manifestly shown by the interminable Doha Round. There can be little doubt that such frustration prompted certain WTO Members to resort to second-best, but easier to negotiate and tailor-made Regional Trade Agreements (RTAs) instead, thereby further degrading

---

27 Ngaire Woods, 'Global governance after the Financial Crisis: A New Multilateralism or the Last Gasp of the Great Powers?' (2010) 1 *Global Policy* 51.

28 WTO membership numbered 161 in April 2015.

29 Alice H Amsden, in Zdenek Drabek (ed), *Is the World Trade Organization Attractive Enough for Emerging Economies?* (Palgrave Macmillan 2010) 83.

30 Some even use the hyped up label of 'existential crisis' as crisis of multilateralism, McGrew (n 10) 21.

31 The TFA was concluded at the Bali Ministerial meeting of the Doha Round in December 2013; the Protocol of Amendment inserting the TFA into Annex 1A of the WTO Agreement was adopted by the General Council on 27 November 2014. It contains a range of technical measures to expedite the movement, release and clearance of goods, including goods in transit which impose obligations on WTO Members to increase transparency, to implement streamlined and modernized border procedures and control techniques, and to improve governance through disciplines on rule and decision-making processes.

32 The TFAF was formally launched by WTO Director General Roberto Acevedo and became operational on 27 November 2014.

33 Speech on 'WTO at 20: What Challenges for the Future?' at the Annual Parliamentarian Workshop, Singapore, 25 May 2015.

and undermining the WTO's multilateral non-discriminatory trade system.[34] Even though RTA negotiations can be troublesome too as evidenced, for instance, by the passionately antagonistic public debates and political tussles surrounding the Transatlantic Trade and Investment Partnership (TTIP) agreement, the ongoing even accelerating proliferation of Free Trade Agreements (FTAs), Plurilateral Trade Agreements (PTAs), RTAs and the like, covering all continents[35] and regions, is deemed symptomatic for the WTO's seemingly declining role as the guardian of non-discriminatory global trade. Yet even this latter assessment is ambivalent for two reasons: firstly, how is one to measure decline or just mere disenchantment, considering that the WTO's own dispute settlement system functions reliably well, judged by the WTO Members using it? Secondly, is such proliferation of RTAs the cause for or the consequence of disaffection with the WTO as variously perceived by its Members? And: is it necessarily all bad? After all the CGG has argued that the 'potential of regional cooperation has in many ways been insufficiently exploited in most parts of the world', a view that at least some academic commentators concur with, being critical of the narrow debate largely dominated by economists between 'global level only' and the 'layered governance' – schools, a debate in which efficacy trumps other motives, ideas and factors affecting policy preferences. Yet it is also for reasons of efficacy in controlling free-riding that regional institutions are preferred over global ones.[36] Nonetheless, membership of the WTO is still growing though somewhat more slowly than during the post-Uruguay Round heydays, approaching UN-like near universality of membership, approximately two-thirds of WTO Members being DCs or LDCs.[37]

As with all diagnostics, of course, symptoms must be traced to plausible causes for the prescription of effective remedies. And herein resides the first almost insurmountable difficulty, as opinions differ between trade policy analysts and trade economists and WTO legal experts as to which of the WTO's problems is or has been most directly germane to its current predicament.[38]

Institutional reforms of the WTO[39] have been proposed by many, including on decision-making[40] and dispute settlement.[41]

---

34 Friedl Weiss, 'Coalition of the Willing: The Case for Multilateralism vs. Regional and Bilateral Arrangements in World Trade' in C Calliess, G Nolte and T Stoll (eds), *Coalition of the Willing: Avantgarde or Threat?* (2007) 8 *Göttinger Studien zum Völker-und Europarecht* 51.

35 See the recently announced Tripartite Free Trade Area (TFT&A) pact concluded in Egypt between the Southern African Development Community (SADEC), the East African Community (EAC) and the Common Market for Eastern and Southern Africa (COMESA) bringing together 26 African states in a single new 'continental' African free trade zone from the Cape to Cairo.

36 Helge Hveem, 'Global Governance and the Comparative Political Advantage of Regional Cooperation' in Diana Tussie (ed), *The Environment and International Trade Negotiations: Developing Country Stakes* (Macmillan Press 2000) 133, 147.

37 The original GATT 1947 was signed by 23 contracting parties; in 2007 the WTO had 150 members; cf Zdenek Drabek, Wing Thye Woo, 'Who Should Join the WTO and Why?: A Cost-benefit Analysis of WTO Membership' in Zdenek Drabek (ed), *Is the World Trade Organization Attractive Enough for Emerging Economies?* (Palgrave Macmillan 2010) 249.

38 Some views, in hindsight, appear extreme. Thus a former trade policy economist at the LSE viewed the newly created WTO as an unnecessarily bureaucratic institutional monster in the service of and pandering to the protectionist leanings of its Members.

39 See for example Mary Footer, *An Institutional and Normative Analysis of the World Trade Organization* (Martinus Nijhoff 2006).

40 Manfred Elsig and Thomas Cottier, 'Reforming the WTO: The Decision-making Triangle Revisited' in Thomas Cottier and Manfred Elsig (eds), *Governing the World Trade Organization: Past, Present and beyond Doha* (CUP 2011) 289.

41 Gabrielle Marceau (ed), *A History of Law and Lawyers in the GATT/WTO: The Development of the Rule of Law in the Multilateral Trading System* (CUP 2015); for an early contribution to the debate see Friedl Weiss (ed),

It would, of course, be impossible as well as presumptuous even to attempt to establish a comprehensive *anamnesis* of the GATT and the WTO since their inception. Institutions evolve as do, of course, the interests of their Members, a correlation that cannot easily be disregarded. The fact remains that, generally speaking, International Institutions remain the creatures of their founding Members, a truism particularly apposite to the WTO, which is known to operate as a so-called Member-driven organization.[42]

Still, if the trading system of the twenty-first century is to succeed in 'raising standards of living, ensuring full employment and a large and steadily growing volume of real income and effective demand, and expanding the production and trade in goods and services . . . in accordance with the objective of sustainable development',[43] the WTO must be equipped to achieve these goals. Can it realistically be expected to live up to its own goals without some major overhaul of its governance system?

Trade and 'Non-Trade' Concerns

> we understand the WTO Agreement, as a whole, to reflect the balance struck by WTO Members between trade and non-trade-related concerns . . . (2012 AB Report *China – Measures Related to the Exportation of Various Raw Materials*)

'Non-Trade' Concerns – Introductory Observations

In the eyes of many the WTO has become an embodiment of globalization as well as of the menace it holds for humanity. More recently, however, the latter fears have given way to a positive appraisal of its unique two-tier dispute settlement system. It constitutes a central element in providing security and predictability to the multilateral trading system and is essential to the effective functioning of the WTO and the maintenance of the rule of law and of a proper balance between the rights and obligations of Members. Furthermore, it might also be utilized for the adjudication of issues directly affecting peoples' lives.

These issues reflect a broad range of non-trade concerns including environmental protection and global warming (climate change), biodiversity, food security, development policies, human rights, labour standards,[44] health, medicines, animal welfare, eco-labelling, biotech products, distribution of resources, economic prosperity, social welfare, ethical issues, and even security. A combination of the aggregated expectations with a lack of effective decision-making capacity of the WTO as well as of other major global institutions compounded disenchantment with them.

Improving WTO Dispute Settlement Procedures: Issues and Lessons from the Practice of Other International Courts and Tribunals (Cameron/May International Law and Policy 2000); Dan Sarooshi, 'Reform of the World Trade Organization Dispute Settlement Understanding' in I Mbirimi, B Chilala and R Grynberg (eds), *From Doha to Cancun: Delivering a Development Round* (Common Wealth Secretariat 2003) 105; Dan Sarooshi, 'The Future of the WTO and Its Dispute Settlement System' (2005) 2 *International Organizations Law Review* 129; also 'The WTO, Globalization, and the Future of World Trade' (2000) 24 *Fordham International Law Journal*; EU Petersmann (ed), 'Preparing the Doha Development Round: Improvements and Clarifications of the WTO Dispute Settlement Understanding' (Conference Report, EUI 2002); William Davey, 'The WTO's Dispute Settlement System' (2001) 42 *South Texas Law Review* 1199.

42 See the WTO website <www.wto.org> where the notion is circumscribed as 'decisions taken by consensus among all members'.

43 Preamble to the WTO Agreement, para 1.

44 For a critical view of 'fair trade demands' see for example, Jagdish Bhagwati, 'Trade Liberalisation and "Fair Trade" Demands: Addressing the Environmental and Labour Standards Issues' (1995) 18 *The World Economy* 745.

Governments called upon to address these non-trade concerns may do so by using different types of measures, most prominently measures concerning processes and production methods of products. These may involve either product-related processes and production methods (PR PPMs), that is, measures which prescribe processes and production methods that affect the characteristics of products;[45] or non-product-related processes and production methods (nPR PPMs), that is, measures which prescribe processes and production methods that do not, or only in a negligible manner affect the characteristics of products.[46]

It is the second types of measures, that is the nPR PPMs which are most controversial, particularly two issues. The first concerns the consistency of unilateral nPR PPMs with the obligations under the WTO Agreement; the second the relevance of other international agreements for unilateral nPR PPMs measures addressing non-trade concerns.

Thus, the WTO has lately become the chief battleground for ideas supportive of or opposed to further expansion of its role and of its transformation into an institution for global economic governance discharging comprehensive competences akin to or even exceeding those of the abortive Havana Charter (labour standards, commodity agreements, restrictive business practices, reconstruction and development) and of those attributed to the United Nations' Economic and Social Council (ECOSOC), one of the principal organs established under the Charter of the United Nations.[47]

It is scarcely surprising that pressure is mounting to use the services of the WTO for the governance of globalization. This would involve the negotiation of regulatory standards,[48] as well as their coordination, administration and enforcement – in short, the construction of some kind of 'global public policy' in such areas as the management of trade-related environmental standards, social justice in a globalized economy, investment and competition policy and electronic commerce.

Integrating Law, Practice and Policies on Core Societal Values

One commentator on post-Second World War economies, writing in the late forties, praised the Universal Declaration of Human Rights as a milestone in man's fight for liberty and human dignity and suggested action by states to firstly, outlaw exchange controls, secondly, to safeguard free competition and prohibit monopoly practices by business or labour and thirdly, to devise laws to encourage savings, investments and enterprise.[49]

Whatever the merits of this set of prescriptions, it is clear that they reflect an integrated view of post-war socio-economic life. All trade-related issues together enshrine socio-economic and political values and conditions forming the context of trade.[50] The origin of the linkage between labour rights and standards and multilateral trade rules coincided with the establishment of the ILO, while the cognate link between employment, human rights and

---

45 For example, prohibition of growth hormones in cattle rearing for meat production; prohibition of pesticides in the production of vegetables, etc.

46 For example, measures requiring the use of 'dolphin-friendly nets' in tuna fishing.

47 Friedl Weiss, 'The WTO and the progressive development of international trade' (1998) 39 *Netherlands Yearbook of International Law* 71.

48 Phillip Harter, 'Negotiating Regulations: A Cure for Malaise' (1982) 17 *Georgetown Law Journal* 1 ff.

49 P Cortney, *The Economic Munich, The ITO Charter, Inflation or Liberty, The 1929 Lesson* (Philosophical Library 1949) 132.

50 See F Weiss, 'The GATT 1994: Environmental Sustainability of Trade or Environmental Protection Sustainable by Trade?' in K Ginther et al (eds), *Sustainable Development and Good Governance* (Martinus Nijhoff 1995) 382.

trade was made during the negotiations of the Havana Charter. Central to these issues, as indeed to the link between environmental protection and trade, is the question of the legality of unilateral trade measures as a means of enforcing trade-related standards. While demands for a 'social clause' in the WTO in the sense of binding minimum social standards[51] have subsided for now,[52] this highly complex and controversial issue is unlikely to be resolved anytime soon.

Managing Social Issues: Labour Standards

Some have referred to the trade connection of both environmental and labour standards as 'social issues'. As far as labour standards are concerned, this reflects a perception of a new global struggle between capital and labour and the resulting downward pressure on wages and labour standards. Given the centrality of low labour costs to the workings of comparative advantage, one could argue that labour standards are more relevant to trade than intellectual property rights which the United States had successfully brought into the world trade regime through the TRIPS Agreement. For instance, developing countries might in the future campaign for an accommodation of their comparative advantage in labour services.[53]

Managing Social Issues: Environmental Standards

Regarding environmental protection and, to a lesser extent, consumer protection, governments are expected to assume some kind of scientific-managerial role pursuant to an ostensibly ideologically neutral scientific logic of intervention to protect an emerging new balance between ecological interdependence and political independence, between market and communitarian or collective views, and between environmental concerns and economic development and trade objectives. However, already in the GATT debates on the complex interface between trade and environmental policies exposed profound differences of opinion.[54] These, however, were to some extent patched up rather than reconciled by the insertion into the preamble to the Agreement Establishing the World Trade Organization of the evocative concept of 'sustainable development'.[55] That principle requires the 'rule of trade' to be applied in a manner that respects the principle of sustainable development and protects and preserves the environment, allowing members to pursue valid conservation goals.[56]

The first of three legal issues which preoccupied GATT/WTO Panels concerns the consistency of unilateral nPR PPMs with the central non-discrimination obligations of the

51 See for example Friedl Weiss, 'Internationally Recognised Labour Standards and Trade' in Friedl Weiss, Erik Denters and Paul de Waart (eds), *International Economic Law with a Human Face* (Kluwer Law International 1998) 79 ff.

52 The Final Declaration of the First WTO Ministerial Conference held in Singapore in December 1996 deemed the ILO to be the competent body to set and deal with these standards.

53 Nigel Harris, 'Free International Movement of Labour' *Economic and Political Weekly* (26 January 1991) 163–64. See also the Revised draft of the World Bank's proposed labour safeguard – its Environmental and Social Framework – of August 2015.

54 J Whalley, 'The Interface between Environmental and Trade Policies' (1991) 101 *The Economic Journal* 180 ff; RG Tarasofsky and F Weiss (1997) 8 *Yearbook of International Environmental Law* 582–603.

55 United Nations Conference on Environment and Development (UNCED) held at Rio de Janeiro 1992.

56 See Appellate Body Report *United States – Import Prohibition of Certain Shrimp and Shrimp Products*, 12 October 1998, WT/DS58/AB/R, paras 3.152; 3.168.

GATT, a question which hinges on the 'likeness' of the products involved. The answer at first provided by the *US-Tuna (Mexico) Panel* in 1991 was that nPR PPMs are not relevant to determine whether products are 'like' if that PPM does not affect the physical characteristics of the product.[57] This would be bad news from an animal welfare perspective, as it would mean that 'livestock' products not produced consistently with animal welfare requirements are 'like' 'livestock' products produced consistently with animal welfare requirements. However, case law on the concept of 'likeness' has evolved and in *EC – Asbestos* (2001) the Appellate Body (AB) adopted a more nuanced approach to the determination of 'likeness', holding that it is fundamentally a determination of the nature and extent of a competitive relationship between and among products. For example, carpets made by children, if shunned by consumers, may lead to a situation in which there is in fact no or only weak competition between these carpets and those made by adults. However, as it seems likely that consumers will mostly be guided by the price and other aspects that are not related to the conditions (for example labour, animal welfare, environmental) under which the products were produced, this approach does not serve these non-trade concerns well. This leaves recourse to the general exceptions of article XX GATT, in particular paras (a), (b) and (g), as only option to justify an otherwise GATT inconsistent nPR PPM measure. Since as is evident from WTO panel practice, the case-by-case approach to the reconciliation of the conflicting goals of environmental concerns and trade liberalization has failed, a more systematic approach to their integration is called for. Some litigant parties have invoked principles or rules of non-WTO International Agreements to justify their trade restrictions for environmental purposes or to protect human rights or labour standards. However, in their analysis of article XX GATT panels have merely shown willingness to acknowledge these agreements as relevant factual evidence that the measure taken was legitimate. Yet, in the current state of legal doctrine, their direct application as 'legal norms' by the WTO DS bodies is considered a bridge too far.

Still, panels have repeatedly advocated that WTO Members conclude bilateral, regional, multilateral or global agreements on environmental protection. This points towards an exceedingly arduous process of linking existing and future multilateral environmental agreements (MEAs) to the WTO system as a whole. Alternatively, the WTO itself could become instrumental in appropriate trade-related environmental global standard setting. However, considering the diversity of views and policies of WTO Members on this matter, such positive, harmonizing integration of trade and environmental concerns may prove elusive. In this respect the Doha Ministerial Declaration merely envisages negotiations on the applicability of WTO rules as among parties to the MEA without prejudice to the WTO rights of any Member that is not a party to the MEA.

Refining the WTO – 'Constitution'?

> The authors of the new WTO regime intended to put an end to the fragmentation that had characterized the previous system. This can be seen from the preamble to the WTO Agreement according to which they were 'Resolved . . . to develop an integrated, more viable and durable multilateral trading system encompassing the General Agreement on Tariffs and Trade, the results of past trade liberalization efforts, and all of the results of the Uruguay Round of Multilateral Trade Negotiations.' (*Brazil — Desiccated Coconut, AB Report 1997*)

---

57 See for example Friedl Weiss, 'The Second Tuna GATT Panel Report' (1995) 8 *Leiden Journal of International Law* 135.

WTO – A Constitution for Trade?

The WTO as self-proclaimed 'common institutional framework for the conduct of trade relations among its Members'[58] was hailed as perhaps the most significant result of the Uruguay Round of multilateral trade negotiations, particularly its dispute settlement system. Although the WTO Agreement, the WTO's constitutive Treaty, cannot conceivably be likened to a written constitution implying also judicial review of acts of other government organs,[59] the AB's approach to constitutional interpretation, as is evident from the above citation appears, nonetheless, to rely on some kind of theory of original meaning[60] to the exclusion of the opposite approach, 'living constitutionalism'. In so far as the AB's observation in *China – Raw Materials* contains a claim that all the conceivable non-trade-related concerns have been captured in the WTO Agreement as a whole, Members could arguably be denied all rights to regulate non-trade-related concerns in exercising their right to regulate trade.

Could this *obiter dictum* possibly amount to a freezing of non-trade concerns to the extent contemplated by the historical drafters of the GATT and only updated programmatically by the inclusion of the modern concept of sustainable development in the WTO's preamble? Might this constitute an implicit excuse for Members to probe the limits of trade restrictions pursuant to legitimate contemporary non-trade concerns, even at the risk of condemnation by the AB for breach of WTO rules? This must be doubted, especially in view of other AB *dicta* evidencing an evolutionary approach to the interpretation of the WTO as a 'living instrument', governing 'the real world where people live and work and die'.[61] In any event, as mentioned, the WTO is close to becoming a truly universal organization, comparable to the United Nations. Yet, unlike the UN, it attracts a great deal of hostile comment by different groups of 'civil society'. While some popular disaffection with the workings of the WTO is patently misdirected, the WTO being, as the well-worn mantra has it, a Member-driven organization, certain criticism shared by both defenders and detractors of the WTO is clearly justified.[62]

One such criticism concerns the legitimacy and decision-making of its institutions. It has rightly been observed that the shift of standard setting and regulatory activity from national governments to intergovernmental bodies such as the WTO, a shift from government to governance, entails a certain loss of transparency, and democratic accountability. Put simply, the question is whether the WTO, as currently structured and administered, is equipped for the onward march of globalizing trade and trade-related relations?

---

58 Art II WTO Agreement.

59 See, however, the analytical triad of legislative, executive and judicial powers invoked by Steve Charnovitz, 'A post-Montesquieu Analysis of the WTO' in Thomas Cottier and Manfred Elsig (eds), *Governing the World Trade Organization: Past, Present and beyond Doha* (CUP 2011) 265; on the controversies between constitutional and non-constitutional (nationalist) approaches to reforming the multilateral trading system, see Christian Joerges and Ernst-Ulrich Petersmann, *Constitutionalism, Multilevel Trade Governance and International Economic Law* (2nd edn, Hart 2011).

60 Keith E Whittington, *Constitutional Interpretation: Textual Meaning, Original Intent, and Judicial Review* (University of Kansas 1999).

61 Appellate Body Report *EC – Measures Concerning Meat and Meat Products (Hormones)*, 16 January 1998, WT/DS26/AB/R, WT/DS48/AB/R WT/DS26/AB/R, para 187. See Asif H Qureshi, *Interpreting WTO Agreements: Problems and Perspectives* (2nd edn, CUP 2015).

62 Tony McGrew listed amongst the structural and procedural failings of the WTO, inter alia, the dysfunctional trade negotiations, the rise of PTAs, the incoherence of global trade policy and the erosion of the MFN principle, McGrew (n 10) 26. For a comprehensive assessment of the WTO's institutional flaws as well as for proposals to overcome them, see the Sutherland Report: Sutherland Peter, Bhagwati Jagdish et al, *The Future of the WTO* (WTO 2004).

Three features of the WTO as an international organization need to be underlined; first and most obvious is its centrality to global economic governance; second, it is surprisingly democratic, at least in its formal decision-making procedure (in contrast to for example the IMF); third, there are tensions and contradictions between formal and informal realities, especially in terms of its decision-making procedures. Two areas of reform merit particular attention. One is 'institutional', concerning the WTO's decision-making process; the other related area is 'procedural', involving the WTO's system for the settlement of disputes.

WTO Decision-Making

Decision-making occupies a central place in most discussions of institutional reforms. In the WTO it has been linked with crisis and identified in the literature as an important hindrance to be overcome.[63] Formally each WTO Member has an equal vote. Since there is no equivalent to the Security Council, the WTO might in theory be considered even more democratic than the United Nations. Turning from theory to practice, *oligarchy* comes closer than *democracy* to describing decision-making at the WTO. Nonetheless, *informal oligarchy* remains in tension with *formal democracy* which creates interesting potential for change. It is the traditional, hegemonial or parochial 'Green Room' process, the old 'club model' of multilateralism (including the G8/G7), which needs to be modernized.[64] That process of decision-making involves a relatively small number of self-selected developed and some large developing countries deciding on divisive issues. Decisions so taken are then conveyed to the larger membership for final decision. However, in the WTO we also have a fairly rich and complex 'administrative hinterland', a hidden world of governance which, some authors have suggested,[65] consists of a large administrative infrastructure of committees, working parties and review groups, which potentially play a more dynamic, cooperative and reflexive role in the governance of the international economy than has usually been acknowledged.[66]

Reforming the WTO Dispute Settlement System

The WTO dispute settlement system is arguably the most important innovative element of the WTO as the principal organization of global economic governance.
    While this is not the place for a detailed discussion of the thorny and protracted issue of the reform of the Understanding on Rules and Procedures Governing the Settlement of Disputes

---

63 Friedl Weiss, 'WTO-Decision-making: Is it Reformable?' in Daniel L.M. Kennedy and James D. Southwick (eds), *The Political Economy of International Trade Law, Essays in Honour of Robert E. Hudec* (CUP 2002) 68; for a searching analysis of consensus decision-making see Mary Footer, 'The WTO as a 'living instrument': the contribution of consensus decision-making and informality to institutional norms and practice' in Thomas Cottier and Manfred Elsig (eds), *Governing the World Trade Organization: Past, Present and beyond Doha* (CUP 2011) 217; Robert Kissack, 'Crisis Situations and Consensus Seeking: Adaptive Decision-making in the FAO and Applying its Lessons to the Reform of the WTO' in Thomas Cottier and Manfred Elsig (eds), *Governing the World Trade Organization: Past, Present and beyond Doha* (CUP 2011) 241.
64 Kent Jones, 'Green Room Politics and the WTO Crisis of Representation' (2009) 9 *Progress in Development Studies* 349; McGrew (n 10) 24.
65 Andrew Lang and Joanne Scott, 'The Hidden World of WTO Governance' (2009) 20 *European Journal of International Law* 575, 576.
66 Ernst-Ulrich Petersmann, *International Economic Law in the 21st Century* (Hart 2012).

(DSU),[67] nor of the multitude of scholarly proposals for reform made over the years,[68] suffice it to point out that in order to balance and thereby integrate trade-related values, it would be imperative for the system to be freed from its traditional and self-imposed adjudicative isolation from relevant practice in international law.[69] However, while the AB searches and even seeks to broaden the parameters of its powers, for example with the device of 'completing the legal analysis',[70] it is far too dependent upon the watchful if not vigilant membership of the WTO guarding against the AB usurping judicial power through the exercise of its tools of interpretation.[71]

Transparency – Legitimacy: Treaty Provisions, Panel Practice

> The function of WTO transparency provisions is to 'support the proper functioning of the multilateral trading system, by helping to prevent unnecessary trade restriction and distortion from occurring, by providing information about market opportunities and by helping to avoid trade disputes from arising'.[72]

Transparency: Hallmark of Good Governance

Good governance, as a concept, is scarcely present in the WTO legal framework. However, elements of good governance can be found in Section 2 of Part III of the TRIPS Agreement on Civil and Administrative Procedures and Remedies. Accordingly, WTO Members are obliged to guarantee certain judicial rights, in particular fair and equitable judicial procedures for enforcing intellectual property rights.[73] However, these requirements do not guarantee individual rights but merely require Members to ensure that national IPR proceedings are organized and conducted in accordance with a minimum standard. Thus, this implicit reference to good governance entails obligations for WTO Members.

'Transparency' on the other hand, does play an important role in WTO law, being defined as the 'degree to which trade policies and practices, and the process by which they are established, are open and predictable'.[74] Commonly two types of transparency are distinguished: Internal and external transparency.

---

67 See the Ministerial Decision of 1994 on the Application and Review of the DSU within 4 years of the entry into force of the WTO Agreement pursuant to which another decision was envisaged on whether to continue, modify or terminate the DSU; WTO Members continue to make numerous proposals for reform.

68 See for example, Steve Charnovitz, 'Rethinking WTO Trade Sanctions' (2001) 95 *American Journal of International Law* 792.

69 See the *Bananas* and *Hormones* Cases; Friedl Weiss (ed), *Improving WTO Dispute Settlement Procedures: Issues and Lessons from the Practice of Other International Courts and Tribunals* (Cameron May 2000).

70 See for example AB Report *European Communities – Measures Affecting Asbestos and Asbestos-Containing Products*, 12 March 2001, WT/DS135/AB/R, paras 78–79, stating ' . . . In previous appeals, we have, on occasion, completed the legal analysis with a view to facilitating the prompt settlement of the dispute, pursuant to art 3.3 of the DSU.'

71 Friedl Weiss, 'National and International Courts' in F Ortino and EU Petersmann (eds), *The WTO Dispute Settlement System 1995–2003* (Kluwer Law International 2004) 177.

72 See <www.wto.org/english/thewto_e/minist_e/min96_e/environ.htm> accessed 15 January 2015.

73 Art 42 TRIPS: WTO Members shall provide fair and equitable civil judicial procedures for enforcing intellectual property rights, including timely written notice, representation by independent legal counsel, right to substantiate claims and present all relevant evidence.

74 WTO Glossary, available at: <www.wto.org/english/thewto_e/glossary_e/glossary_e.htm> accessed 15 January 2015.

Internal transparency in the WTO context means equal access to WTO negotiations and decisions by all Members and in particular the transparency of the WTO decision-making process to its Members.[75] External transparency, by contrast, refers to public and citizens access to information about WTO procedures and decisions. Especially since the turbulent Seattle Ministerial Conference, the WTO has made considerable efforts to improve both external and internal transparency.

Article X GATT

Doctrinal Views

According to *Charnovitz*, one of the most positive but least known features of WTO law is the rule laid down in article X GATT requiring national governments to publish laws, regulations, judicial decisions and administrative rulings affecting trade.[76] *Howse* too acknowledges the potentially democracy-enhancing effect of the provisions of article X GATT, while rightly pointing out that it had been given relatively little attention so far.[77]

The origins of the GATT must obviously be seen against the background of the post-Second World War situation, in which the GATT 'provided rules to buffer or interface between the international objective of sustained liberalization and the objectives of domestic policy'.[78] By imposing notification obligations on contracting parties, article X GATT aimed at ensuring transparency of and trust in the new international trade order.

Article X GATT had been adapted from the 1946 US Administrative Procedures Act (APA).[79] When GATT entered into force in 1947, it 'grandfathered' the existing legal systems of GATT Contracting Parties.[80]

However, the notification requirement under article X GATT has never been enforced and its provisions, therefore, long been viewed as weak and ineffective. Although it was frequently cited in dispute settlement proceedings and in complaints, violations of article X GATT have typically been pleaded only as 'add-ons' to other more promising legal claims of violations of WTO rules. WTO and GATT panels have habitually refused to rule on article X claims where a measure has already been found to violate another, more substantive GATT or WTO obligation, most recently in August 2014 in *Argentina – Measures Affecting the Importation of Goods*.[81]

---

75 Steve Charnovitz, 'The WTO and Cosmopolitics' (2004) 7 *Journal of International Economic Law* 675, 678.
76 ibid.
77 Robert Howse, 'How to Begin to Think about the "Democratic Deficit" in the WTO' in Stefan Griller (ed), *International Economic Governance and Non-Economic Concerns* (Springer 2003) 79, 91.
78 Sylvia Ostry, 'External Transparency: The Policy Process at the National Level of the Two Level Game' (2002) WTO Advisory Group, 3 ff.
79 ibid, 21.
80 Paragraph 3(c) of art X provides: 'The provisions of subparagraph (b) of this paragraph shall not require the elimination or substitution of procedures in force in the territory of a contracting party on the date of this Agreement which in fact provide for an objective and impartial review of administrative action even though such procedures are not fully or formally independent of the agencies entrusted with administration enforcement.'
81 Panel Report *Argentina – Measures Affecting the Importation of Goods*, 22 August 201, WT/DS438/R, WT/DS444/R, WT/DS445/R; Warren Maruyama, 'The WTO: Domestic Regulation and the Challenge of Shaping Trade' (2003) 37 *The International Lawyer* 677 ff.

Panel Practice

In *Japanese Measures on Imports of Leather*, the United States argued, as a subsidiary matter, that Japan had also nullified or impaired benefits under articles II, X(1), X(3) and XIII(3) GATT. Typically, however, in view of the findings that the import quotas violated Article XI GATT, the Panel found it unnecessary to make a finding on these matters.[82]

In *Indonesia – Autos*, the Panel had to examine whether a series of measures taken by Indonesia to develop its domestic automobile industry was inconsistent with article X as well as with articles I and III GATT. The Panel found that the Indonesian National Car Programme violated 'the provisions of article I and/or article III of GATT' and did not, therefore, consider it necessary to examine Japan's claims under article X GATT.[83]

Similarly, in *Argentina – Hides and Leather*,[84] the EC invoked article X GATT, amongst claims of violations of other provisions, but this time the Panel made some essential clarifications of the interpretation of article X(3)(a) GATT. It emphasized the concept of 'uniformity' relating to the requirement in article X(3)(a) GATT that laws and regulations shall be administered 'in a uniform, impartial and reasonable manner'. It also ruled that the provision of article X(3)(a) should 'not be read as a broad anti-discrimination provision' but that it required 'uniform administration of Customs laws and procedures between individual shippers and even with respect to the same person at different times and different places'.[85]

The first case in which article X GATT played a central role is that of *EC-Selected Customs Matters*,[86] in which the United States complained of various deficiencies in the European Communities' (EC) administration of customs laws and regulations, particularly in the area of the classification and valuation of products for customs purposes, as well as of the EC's failure to institute tribunals or procedures for the prompt review and correction of administrative action in customs matters. The United States considered this practice to be inconsistent with the EC's obligations under articles X(1), X(3)(a) and (b) of GATT 1994. The Panel found that the EC had partially violated article X(3)(a) GATT, in only 3 out of 19 cases involving tariff classification and customs valuation.

The Panel found that the EC had not acted inconsistently with the requirements of article X(3)(b) of the GATT 1994. Article X(3)(b) of the GATT 1994 would not necessarily mean that the decisions of the judicial, arbitral or administrative tribunals or review procedures 'must govern the practice of *all* the agencies entrusted with administrative enforcement *throughout the territory* of a particular [WTO] Member'.[87]

On appeal by the United States the AB partially reversed the Panel's findings.[88] Regarding the requirement of uniform administration in article X(3)(a) GATT, the AB reversed the Panel's finding that article X(3)(a) of the GATT 1994 only relates to the *application* of laws

---

82 Panel Report *Japanese Measures on Imports of Leather*, 15/16 May 1984, GATT 31 BISD 94, 114. See also *Republic of Korea – Restrictions on Imports of Beef* — Complaint by Australia, 7 Nov. 1989, GATT 36 BISD 230, para 108; *Canada – Import Restrictions on Ice Cream and Yogurt*, 5 December 1989, 36 BISD 68, 92.

83 Panel Report *Indonesia – Certain Measures Affecting the Automobile Industry Autos*, 2 July 1998, WT/DS54/R,WT/DS55/R,WT/DS59/R,WT/DS64/R, para 14.152.

84 The provisions invoked were GATT art III(2), X, XI and XX.

85 Panel Report *Argentina – Measures Affecting the Export of Bovine Hides and the Import of Finished Leather*, 19 December 2000, WT/DS155/R, paras 11.81–11.84.

86 Panel Report *European Communities – Selected Customs Matters*, 16 June 2006, WT/DS315/R.

87 Paras 7.539, 7.556 and 8.1(e).

88 AB Report *European Communities – Selected Customs Matters*, 11 December 2006, WT/DS315/AB/R.

and regulations, but not to laws and regulations as such. Instead, the AB found that legal instruments that regulate the application or implementation of laws, regulations, decisions and administrative rulings of the kind described in article X(1) of the GATT 1994 can be challenged under article X(3)(a).

With respect to the review mechanisms for administrative action relating to customs matters, the AB upheld the Panel's finding that article X(3)(b) of the GATT 1994 does not require that first instance review decisions must govern the practice of *all* the agencies entrusted with administrative enforcement *throughout the territory* of a particular WTO Member. The AB reversed the Panel's finding that the United States was precluded from challenging certain instruments of the EC's customs legislation listed in the request for the establishment of a panel as a whole or overall, but upheld the Panel's conclusion that the EC did not breach article X(3)(b) of the GATT 1994.

Article X GATT is not, of course, the only GATT (see also article XVII(4) GATT stipulating notification requirements with respect to state trading enterprises) or WTO provision in the entire institutional framework of the WTO which contains notification obligations, as do numerous other agreements, underlining the central importance of notification obligations for the world trade system.[89]

Transparency Provisions in WTO Agreements

References to transparency are ubiquitous within the legal framework of the WTO. Provisions explicitly referring to the term 'transparency' and provisions on notification obligations are closely linked to each other and cannot, therefore, always be separated from one another. This can be seen for example in article 12 Anti-Dumping Agreement (AD), which is referred to as a 'transparency' provision in the GATT Analytical Index, but which under the title 'Public Notice and Explanation of Determinations' contains a notification obligation.[90] However, the fact that public notice should also be given to other interested parties is at the same time an important contribution to transparency.

Under the heading 'Transparency', article III GATS obliges the Members to publish promptly and at the latest by the time of their entry into force, 'all relevant measures of general application which pertain to or affect the operation of this Agreement'. International agreements pertaining to or affecting trade in services to which a Member is a signatory shall also be published. Moreover, each Member has to inform the Council of Trade in Services at least once a year of the introduction of 'any new, or any changes to existing, laws, regulations or administrative guidelines which significantly affect trade in services covered by its specific commitments under this Agreement' (article III(3) GATS). Furthermore, article IV(4) GATS sets out some notification requirements and envisages the establishment

---

89 See further examples in: arts III(4), VI ('Domestic Regulation') of the GATS; art 7 SPS Agreement; arts 5, 6 Antidumping Agreement; arts 8, 25 Subsidies Agreement, and the Background Note by the Secretariat on 'Notification Requirements under the Agreement on Subsidies and Countervailing Measures' of 14 April 2015 G/SCM/W/546/Rev 6; arts 3, 4, 62 TRIPS; art 12 Safeguards Agreement (SG); art 5 TRIMS; art XXIV(5) GPA; a Working Group was established by the Council for Trade in Goods on 20 February 1995, pursuant to pt III of the Ministerial Decision on Notification Procedures in Marrakesh.

90 Art 12(1): 'When the authorities are satisfied that there is sufficient evidence to justify the initiation of an antidumping investigation pursuant to art 5, the Member or Members the products of which are subject to such investigation and other interested parties known to the investigating authorities to have an interest therein shall be notified and a public notice shall be given.'

of contact and enquiry points, a clear illustration of the linkage between transparency and notification obligations.

The Government Procurement Agreement (GPA) seeks to open up government contracts for goods and services through 'transparency of laws, regulations, procedures and practices regarding government procurement'[91] and, to that end, incorporates a number of specific obligations.[92]

Transparency in Dispute Settlement

Transparency plays also an important role in the WTO Dispute Settlement Mechanism. Amongst several provisions that aim at ensuring a transparent procedure, article 18(2) DSU requires that a summary of confidentially submitted submissions of a party to a dispute be disclosed to the public upon request of a Member.[93] However, there is an exception to the rule of article 18(2) – the classification of an information as business confidential information (BCI). This exception has been invoked quite frequently by WTO Members, prompting Panels and the AB to clarify the exact scope and the limits of the exception of business confidential information.

In *Canada – Aircraft*, the Panel adopted special 'Procedures Governing Business Confidential Information' that went beyond the protection afforded by article 18.2 of the DSU, but Canada declined to submit BCI under the revised Procedures because they did not provide the requisite level of protection. The Panel stated that in its view, the final Procedures would 'strike a reasonable balance between (1) the need for "reasonable access" to BCI by the Panel and the other disputing parties, and (2) the need to provide private business interests with adequate protection for their proprietary business information'.[94]

In *Canada – Aircraft* and *Brazil – Aircraft*, the AB made a preliminary ruling that it was not necessary to adopt additional procedures to protect business confidential information in the appellate proceeding but that the existing provisions concerning confidentiality of dispute settlement proceedings were sufficient.[95]

In its final ruling in *Canada – Aircraft*, the AB stated that the provisions of articles 17(10) and 18(2) DSU apply to all Members of the WTO, and that they furthermore oblige them

---

91 Agreement Establishing the World Trade Organization, Annex 4(b), Agreement on Government Procurement.

92 These comprise obligations regarding: (1) tendering procedures; (2) qualification of suppliers; (3) timely publication of any conditions for participation; (4) publication of invitations for participation in proposed procurements; (5) 'fair and non-discriminatory' selection procedures; (6) adequate time limits and deadlines; (7) submission, receipt, and opening of tenders 'under procedures and conditions guaranteeing the regularity of the openings'; (8) contracts must be awarded to the entity determined to be 'fully capable of undertaking the contract' and which is either the lowest bidder or offers the 'most advantageous' tender; and (9) transparency of terms and conditions; see Warren Maruyama (n 81) 687.

93 Art 18(2) DSU: 'Written submissions to the panel or the Appellate Body shall be treated as confidential, but shall be made available to the parties to the dispute. Nothing in this Understanding shall preclude a party to a dispute from disclosing statements of its own positions to the public. Members shall treat as confidential information submitted by another Member to the panel or the Appellate Body which that Member has designated as confidential. A party to a dispute shall also, upon request of a Member, provide a non-confidential summary of the information contained in its written submissions that could be disclosed to the public.' Appendix 3: 'Where a party to a dispute submits a confidential version of its written submissions to the panel, it shall also, upon request of a Member, provide a non-confidential summary of the information contained in its submissions that could be disclosed to the public.'

94 Panel Report *Canada – Measures Affecting the Export of Civilian Aircraft*, 14 April 1999, WT/DS70/R, para 9.68.

95 AB Preliminary Ruling on *Canada-Aircraft* and *Brazil-Aircraft*, adopted on 11 June 1999.

to maintain the confidentiality of any submissions or information they have submitted or received in AB proceedings. Finally, the AB concluded that it did not consider it necessary to adopt *additional* procedures for the protection of business confidential information in these appellate proceedings.[96]

In *EC – Bananas III (US) (Article 22.6 — EC)*, the United States requested the Arbitrators to establish procedures for the handling of business confidential information. The United States proposed to establish a system of BCI: regular BCI and super BCI,[97] to which the EC objected arguing that working procedures on confidentiality should not be adopted on a case-by-case basis. The Arbitrators agreed with the United States that special rules were justified in light of the type of information involved, but did not in the end accept the need for special treatment of super BCI.[98]

Besides Article 18(2) DSU, transparency also features in other DSU provisions. Thus, Article 4(4) DSU requires notification of the WTO Secretariat that Members have entered into consultations under the DSU.[99] Moreover, increased transparency can essentially contribute to a more efficient enforcement mechanism as detailed and early information about the merits of a particular case and about policies applied is a precondition for effective enforcement.[100]

Does the WTO Grant Transparency to Individuals?

Although the WTO Agreement imposes many reporting, notification and transparency requirements upon its Members, it does not impose similar requirements upon the WTO itself. The legal framework of the WTO does not determine openness and transparency as fundamental principles of trade law, and no right to information is granted to individuals. However, there is one exception that can be found in Article 18(2) and in Annex 3 of the DSU, which states that a summary of confidentially submitted submissions of a party to a dispute has to be disclosed to the public upon request of a Member. However, practice has not been impressive so far.[101] Basically, WTO external transparency 'begins at home', stemming from rights and responsibilities of governments, not of those of individual traders. However, some exceptions to this rule can be found, for example in the Subsidies and Countervailing Measures (SCM) Agreement which includes the rights of 'interested parties' other than those of Member governments. Consumer groups are specifically named in the Anti Dumping

---

96 AB Report on *Canada-Aircraft*, 2 August 1999, WT/DS70/AB/R, paras 145 and 147, and AB Report *Brazil-Aircraft*, 2 August 1999, WT/DS46/AB/R, paras 123 and 125.

97 Regular BCI was described as company-specific information that was non-public and sensitive, but that could be extrapolated from other public and non-public information available to governments and the company's competitors. Super BCI was described as non-public, sensitive company-specific information that could not be so extrapolated.

98 Decision by the Arbitrators *European Communities – Regime for the Importation, Sale and Distribution of Bananas – Recourse to Arbitration by the European Communities under* art *22.6 of the DSU*, 9 April 1999, WT/DS27/ARB, paras 2.2.–2.5.

99 Art 4(4) DSU provides that 'All such requests for consultations shall be notified to the DSB and the relevant Councils and Committees by the Member which requests consultations. Any request for consultations shall be submitted in writing and shall give the reasons for the request, including identification of the measures at issue and an indication of the legal basis for the complaint.'

100 Bernard M Hoekman and Petros C Mavroidis, 'WTO Dispute Settlement, Transparency and Surveillance' (2000) 23 *The World Economy* 527, 540.

101 See Charnovitz, who terms it a semi-exception (n 75) 679. Charnovitz also characterizes art X as a 'good governance' provision whose value has become 'better understood as a driver of development and equity'.

Agreement. The Agreement on Safeguards includes an obligation for the importing country to carry out an investigation including 'public interest hearings', which could also include interest groups. Similar provisions are laid down in article 22 TRIPS on the protection of geographical indications and article VI GATS on domestic regulation. Although these examples do provide some procedural participatory rights, for the most part the WTO rules situate the determination of the policy process in the domestic arena of the Member governments. One major exception is the Trade Policy Review Mechanism (TPRM).[102]

The TPRM is an important tool aiming at the enhancement of transparency, which puts trade and related policies under review on a periodic basis in order to ensure significantly greater transparency of national policies. Through informed public understanding, the effectiveness of the domestic policy-making process should be enhanced. However, *Howse* has taken the view that its democratic potential has not been realized because of the narrow policy perspective adopted in examining Members' policies and the non-appropriate realization of the potential of broad civil society input. On the other hand, an appropriately reformed TPRM could contribute to a greater extent to the enhancement of domestic democratic accountability for trade and related policies.[103]

In general, the GATT/WTO framework can be seen as an arena where information asymmetries have been severe and the understanding of trade rules quite poorly developed.[104] *Charnovitz* has suggested, therefore, that the WTO should take legislative action to open up to civic legitimacy because openness would contribute to the enhancement of legitimacy as well as to greater public support for the WTO's mission.[105]

Some progress has, however, been made since the establishment of the WTO in 1995. Indeed, the WTO attaches particular importance to a transparent relationship with NGOs and has adopted Guidelines for Arrangements on Relations with NGOs in 1996.[106] These guidelines were intended to serve as the principal foundation upon which the increasing interaction between the WTO and civil society should be built. Moreover, the WTO Secretariat hosts regular information briefings for NGOs and regularly transmits to the WTO Members lists of documents submitted by NGOs.

Recent Developments

Among the most significant improvements in the area of external transparency is the WTO website which provides access to a great variety of informative documents, including those of Trade Policy Reviews.

Transparency was also an integral part of the Doha Ministerial Declaration including a commitment to transparency:

> Recognizing the challenges posed by an expanding WTO membership, we confirm our collective responsibility to ensure internal transparency and the effective participation of all Members. While emphasizing the intergovernmental character of the organization,

---

102 Ostry (n 78) 21 ff.
103 Howse (n 77) 92; Hoekman and Mavroidis (n 100) 527; Ostry (n 78) 22.
104 Howse (n 77) 83.
105 Charnovitz (n 75) 679.
106 Guidelines for Arrangements on Relations with Non-Governmental Organizations – Decision adopted by the General Council on 18 July 1996, WT/L/162.

we are committed to making the WTO's operations more transparent, including through more effective and prompt dissemination of information, and to improve dialogue with the public. We shall therefore at the national and multilateral levels continue to promote a better public understanding of the WTO and to communicate the benefits of a liberal, rules-based multilateral trading system.[107]

Transparency in government procurement was also one of the four so-called 'Singapore issues', alongside investment, competition policy and trade facilitation. It should be mentioned, lastly, that in December 2006 the General Council decided to establish a Transparency Mechanism for Regional Trade Agreements, in view of the ever increasing numbers of RTAs notified to the WTO.[108]

Final Assessment and Outlook

WTO transparency has become much more than just a vogue word. As a particular aspect of good governance it is not only incumbent upon states but can and should also be guaranteed by international organizations.

While good governance as such is only of minor importance in the WTO legal framework, transparency has a particular role to play in the international trade order, as is amply illustrated, *inter alia*, by numerous notification obligations contained in various WTO agreements, as well as by its regular promotion since the establishment of the WTO, including the recent decision on a transparency mechanism for RTAs.

Clearly, transparency potentially averts misconceptions, distrust and suspicion and thus enhances legitimacy. There is room for improvements in the WTO. Whether these can be implemented will depend on general developments, in particular the eventual outcome of the Doha Development Round, if any.

Concluding Remarks

After almost all is said, the question whether the WTO is 'reformable' can be answered affirmatively, if based on a broad understanding of 'reform', including evolutionary reform, encompassing institutional, procedural and adjudicative adjustments to practice. In fact, after the demise of the Havana Charter, the GATT contracting parties, lacking the support of a purposefully designed treaty-based institutional infrastructure, became accustomed to operating pragmatically, seeking and frequently failing to reach consensus on incremental improvements to their practice, let alone on creating a fully-fledged International Organization. Even the Ministerial Declaration of Punta del Este which launched the Uruguay Round of multilateral negotiations did not envisage the establishment of the WTO. Instead, the 'Functioning of the GATT System' was to be enhanced through 'understandings and arrangements'. And it was, of course, also this pattern of flexibility inherent in GATT/WTO negotiations which the European Court of Justice consistently invokes so as to deny provisions of the GATT, the WTO and of its covered agreements direct effect in the EU.[109] Perhaps, in view of

---

107   Doha Ministerial Declaration, adopted on 14 November 2001, WT/MIN(01)/DEC/1, para 10.
108   WTO General Council, Transparency Mechanism of for Regional Trade Agreements, Decision of 14 December 2006, WT/L/671, to be implemented on a provisional basis in accordance with para 47 of the Doha Ministerial Declaration.
109   Joined Cases 21–24/72 *International Fruit Co* [1996] ECR I — 06177, paras 20–21.

that antecedent history of evolutionary reform practice, ambitious blueprints for institutional and procedural reform are not even called for as long as incremental systemic improvements, however patchy, remain rooted in the fundamentally unchanged commitment to the shared common value of a liberal non-discriminatory multilateral trading system. After all, procedure, by definition, and one might add institutions, are no more than ways of getting somewhere.[110]

---

110 HWA Thirlway, 'Procedural Law and the International Court of Justice' in Vaughan Low and Malgosia Fitzmaurice (eds), *Fifty Years of the International Court of Justice: Essays in Honour of Sir Robert Jennings* (CUP 1996) 389.

8 Interdependence and WTO Law

*Chios Carmody**

Introduction

A volcano erupts in Iceland and flights across Europe are grounded, causing damage to sup-ply and value chains.[1] A tsunami hits the coast of Japan and production lines across Asia and much of the rest of the world grind to a halt.[2]

These two episodes – both very real and very devastating – illustrate the degree to which the modern global economy, and by extension, the international community, have become a function of interdependence. As a matter of economics interdependence sustains current liv-ing standards. Life cannot continue without it. One former British prime minister has gone so far as to describe interdependence as 'the defining characteristic of the modern world'.[3]

In the midst of this ceaseless inter-relating and productivity has come the WTO Secre-tariat's 'Made in the World Initiative' (MIWI). The Initiative, which was kicked-off in 2010, highlights the way in which the global economy has become so interconnected that politi-cians' traditional preoccupation with trade deficits may be irrelevant. The Initiative's debut study, conducted by Japan's Institute of Developing Economies (IDE), reveals that global economic activity seriously overstates the 'problem' of trade balances because most advanced goods are composed of components from multiple sources, cross national boundaries several times in the course of their production, and integrate additional elements like services, design and intellectual property, so that it is no longer appropriate to refer to them as the product of any one country. Instead, they should be designated as 'Made in the World'.[4] The IDE study

* Associate Professor & Canadian National Director, Canada–United States Law Institute, Faculty of Law, Uni-versity of Western Ontario, London, Ontario, Canada N6A 3K7. Email: ccarmody@uwo.ca. The author would like to thank members of the Research Project 'International Law and the New Governance after the Economic Crisis' and the Department of Public International Law, Faculty of Law, Universidad de Granada, for their invi-tation to present this contribution at the conference 'The Reform of International Economic Governance', 10 October 2014.

1 For a discussion of the eruption of the Eyjafjallajökull volcano in Iceland in April 2010 and its disruptive effect on European supply chains see Urs Uhlmann, 'Eruption Disruption' *Canadian Underwriter* (Toronto, August 2010) 18.
2 The March 2011 Great Tohoku Earthquake and Tsunami devastated the north-east coast of Japan with the most powerful natural disaster in Japan's modern history. Over 4 million units of vehicle production were lost because of the disasters in Japan, with 90 per cent of them from Japanese automakers. Manufacturing in several sectors in China, Southeast Asia and the US was affected for several months thereafter because of north-eastern Japan's linchpin status in global supply chain networks, Bill Canis, 'The Motor Vehicle Supply Chain: Effects of the Japanese Earthquake and Tsunami' (*Congressional Research Service* R41831, 23 May 2011) <www.fas.org/sgp/crs/misc/R41831.pdf> accessed 15 January 2015.
3 Tony Blair, 'What I've Learned' *The Economist* (London, 31 May 2007).
4 See IDE-JETRO, *Trade Patterns and Global Value Chains in East Asia* (2011) <www.wto.org/english/res_e/booksp_e/stat_tradepat_globvalchains_e.pdf> accessed 15 January 2015.

infers that, at least for the moment, the phenomenon of interdependence is really an issue of statistical measurement, of numbers and empiricism, rather than anything more.

At the same time, the WTO is not simply an organization devoted to the exchange of trade concessions and the measurement of their interaction in quantitative terms. Over the last two decades it has developed an impressive, and occasionally controversial, dispute settlement system that highlights the WTO Agreement as a system of law. Examining this development it is possible to wonder what the role of law is in the interdependence that MIWI emphasizes? Is interdependence purely a quantitative issue, or does it have *qualitative* consequences?

What I suggest in this contribution is that law, including WTO law, traditionally has difficulty dealing with interdependence due to the atomized way in which law is arranged. At the risk of some simplification, the architecture of law can be understood as the assembly of rights and obligations. The phrase 'rights and obligations' is in fact well-known in WTO law.[5] What I maintain in this chapter, however, is that a legal system's stress upon 'rights' and 'obligations' obscures the natural way in which these two basic legal elements interact and are, in their operation, themselves a manifestation of interdependence. Bearers of individual rights and obligations need them to regulate their relationship, and a single 'right' or 'obligation' will be sustained by many other supporting rights and obligations.[6] These can be thought of coordinately as the basic elements of a legal system.

So far, many analyses of WTO law have neglected this aspect of the law – interdependence – because the law itself does not appear outwardly to conform to a model of interrelation. Much of the early experience with WTO law has, in fact, been seen through the filter of WTO dispute settlement which appears, superficially at least, to be concerned with singular, or clusters of, obligations, as in the *EC – Bananas* case, where the issue revolved around the EC's obligation to apply an MFN tariff, or more rarely, with the vindication of

---

5   See GATT Art XXIV: 1, 'the provisions of this para shall not be construed to create any *rights or obligations* as between two or more customs territories; SPS Art 2, 'Basic *Rights and Obligations*'; DSU Art 3.2, '(T)he dispute settlement system of the WTO is a central element in providing security and predictability to the multilateral trading system. The Members recognize that it serves to preserve the *rights and obligations* of Members under the covered agreements, and to clarify the existing provisions of those agreements in accordance with customary rules of interpretation of public international law. Recommendations and rulings of the DSB cannot add to or diminish the *rights and obligations* provided in the covered agreements'. In the Panel Report *Argentina – Footwear Safeguards*, 25 June 1999, WT/DS121/R, the panel stated that the WTO Safeguards Agreement represented 'a re-establishment of multilateral control' over safeguard action, something which 'implies a new balance of *rights and obligations* that in some cases modifies the *whole package of rights and obligations* resulting from the Uruguay Round negotiations', ibid para 8.58. Similarly, in discussing the scope of the 'safe haven' to WTO subsidies disciplines in Panel Report *Brazil – Aircraft*, 26 July 2001, WT/DS46/RW/2, the panel observed that existing arrangements 'reflects a negotiated balance of *rights and obligations*, which is not for a panel to upset', ibid note 86. The panel went on to observe that '(I)f the Participants were to abuse their power to modify the scope of the safe haven, the recourse of other Members would be to renegotiate the second paragraph of item (k)'. It added, 'it should be pointed out that the various exceptions provided for in the WTO Agreement are an integral and important part of the carefully negotiated balance of *rights and obligations* of Members'. And in discussing entitlement to invoke countermeasures in Decision of the Arbitrator *US – FSC*, 30 August 2002, WT/DS108/ARB, the arbitrator observed that 'the entitlement to countermeasures is to be assessed in light of the legal status of the wrongful act and the manner in which the breach of that obligation has upset the balance of *rights and obligations* as between Members', ibid para 5.24.

6   The matrix of a legal system may be said to approximate what Philip Allott has described as 'a network of infinite density and complexity in which everything, without exception, is subject to countless legal relations', Philip Allott, *The Health of Nations* (CUP 2002) 85. Thus, '. . . the relationship between two legal persons can be analysed in many different ways and . . . an analysis in terms of one particular legal relation always implies the existence of *many other supporting legal relations* . . .'. Philip Allott, *Eunomia* (OUP 1990), 162, para 10.50 (emphasis added).

rights, as in the *EC – Tariff Preferences* case, where the issue was the EC's right to apply differential conditionality as a test for a country's access to certain trade-related benefits.[7] Because of this artificial segregation, the fact that legal rules are about interdependence may be easy to miss. Thus, WTO law may have more in common with MIWI than is at first evident or is commonly supposed.

These points are important to understand and appreciate because the global economy is becoming characterized by webs of cooperation that involve ever more proximate and intensive interdependence. Evolutionary psychology suggests that this interdependence is becoming more pervasive so that we may not be able to live without it. It is, in fact, so pervasive, that we take it for granted, from the orange juice on our tables every morning to the music we listen to made from synthesized sound tracks involving hundreds of artists around the world. Yet it is also changing the way we *think* – and that we *must think* – in an era of globalization. This has implications for the shape of international law generally.

In 1964 Wolfgang Friedmann posited the view of international law as a 'law of cooperation'.[8] The ideas put forward in this article regard the actual state of international law, at least in the realm of WTO law, as now surpassing Friedmann's conception. They infer that WTO law is developing along a much steeper trajectory of collaboration and driven by a much more intensive degree of interaction than Friedmann foresaw, one that I term a 'law of interdependence'. In contrast with Friedmann's conception, the law of interdependence goes beyond a *voluntary* desire to cooperate and evidences an *obligatory* impulse to collaborate. Simply put, countries can no longer isolate themselves from the global trading system without putting themselves at a significant disadvantage. In important ways they have become the subjects of interdependence.

From Interface to Interdependence

Interdependence arises in the mutual reliance of actors upon each other. It originates in our biology, something that has been intuited by other theorists and commentators of international law. Thus, Emmerich de Vattel observed in *The Law of Nations* (1758):

> Such is man's nature that he is not sufficient unto himself and necessarily stands in need of the assistance and intercourse of his fellows, whether to preserve his life or to perfect himself and live as befits a rational animal . . . From this source we deduce a natural society existing among all men. The general law of the society is that each member should assist the others in all their needs, as far as he can do so without neglecting his duties to himself – a law which all men must obey if they are to live conformably to their nature and to the designs of their common Creator; a law which our own welfare, our happiness, and our best interests should render sacred to each of us. Such is the general obligation we are under of performing our duties; let us fulfil them with care if we would work wisely for our greatest good.[9]

---

7   *EC – Bananas*, WT/DS27; *EC – Tariff Preferences*, WT/DS246.

8   Wolfgang Friedmann, *The Changing Structure of International Law* (Columbia University Press 1964) 61–62. At that time Friedmann characterized the change as follows: '(T)his move of international society, from an essentially negative code of rules of abstention to positive rules of cooperation, however fragmentary in the present state of world politics, is an evolution of immense significance for the principles and structure of international law', ibid 62.

9   Emmerich de Vattel, *The Law of Nations, or the Principles of Natural Law, Applied to the Conduct and to the Affairs of Nations and Sovereigns* (1758) (tr CG Fenwick) (1916) 5, quoted in Philip Allott, *The Health of Nations* (n 6) 414.

However, interdependence is a difficult subject to address, both because it is so pervasive and so fleeting. Interdependence exists as an independent phenomenon, and yet at the same time, it is woven into the fabric of everything else. We have to think long and hard before accepting its primacy as an explanation for the shape of the law.

Developments in communication, manufacturing, logistics and retailing over the last two decades have led to the globalization of production.[10] For the most part, production now takes place in immense, highly sophisticated supply chains that span the globe and ensure the smooth flow of product from input suppliers to the ultimate consumer. Participants must be nimble and broad-minded. The conceptual modifications required are profound. Alan Waller has observed:

> The difference in skill requirements in today's highly competitive fast-changing world is that we need to have visibility and control of our supply chain in order to compete. Manufacturers need to think upstream about supply and *be driven by the end customer*. Retailers need to satisfy their customers but need to think supply chain to achieve this. Wal-Mart sees their core skill as being 'A procurement agent for the consumer', hence their focus on supply chain management in all that they do.[11]

Other supply chain experts have pointed out that supply chain manufacturing requires participants to shift from mere 'interfacing' to integrating their production. Supplier selection becomes supplier collaboration. Arm's length relationships are replaced by total commitment. Confrontational behaviour makes way for integrated forms of cooperation. Short-term planning is exchanged for longer term thinking.[12] In sum, a transactional perspective is replaced by a relational one that emphasizes the linkage of the parties across time.[13] Individual components become part of a greater whole.

Inevitably, this configuration requires the removal of barriers so that the entirety of production, which can involve many stages among a number of independent contractors, become a common enterprise. Stuart Emmett and Barry Crocker have observed:

> In a world-class supply chain . . . barriers cannot remain. It cannot be that the flow of product, information and finances between the links in the chain are allowed to be compromised by the perception of company boundaries. Despite the fact that supply chains are made up of different companies and that there may be both legal restriction and

---

10 Stephen Poloz, former Chief Economist of Export Development Canada (EDC), points out that 'globalization' has three separate dimensions: globalization of sales, production and distribution, Stephen Poloz, *The New Global Trade Game: Will Canada be a Player, or just a Spectator?* <www.cagt.ca/05dinner02.pdf> accessed 15 January 2015.

11 Alan Waller, Foreword in Stuart Emmett and Barry Crocker, *The Relationship-Driven Supply Chain* (Ashgate 2006) 2 [emphasis added].

12 Emmett and Crocker, *The Relationship-Driven Supply Chain* (Ashgate 2006) 32.

13 Interdependence has also been recognized at a political level by leading statespersons. See for instance Kofi Annan, 'The Meaning of the International Community' UN Press Release, 15 Sept. 1999, SG/SM/7133, PI/1176, '(O)urs is a world in which no individual, and no country, exists in isolation. All of us live simultaneously in our own communities and in the world at large . . . We are connected, wired, interdependent'; Tony Blair (n 3), referring to interdependence as 'the defining characteristic of the modern world'; The White House, 'Remarks on a New Beginning' made to students at Cairo University, 4 June 2009, Barack Obama observing that '(G)iven our interdependence, any world order that elevates one nation or group of people over another will inevitably fail. So whatever we think of the past, we must not be prisoners to it. Our problems must be dealt with through partnership; our progress must be shared'.

operational difficulties, these must be overcome so that the supply chain is treated as a whole and is optimised as a whole.[14]

In some cases, the degree of unity and integration creates something new that one dominant participant is interested in holding on to because it aligns with a company's core functions. The supply chain is something of value that an enterprise is interested in preserving and exploiting over time. In other cases, the supply chain may represent an expense or a threat for a participant and so the pattern of relationships is ended.[15] In still others, corporate reorganizations may spin off part or all of the chain as one participant transitions to new operations under different conditions. The supply chain, now reconfigured, will draw on pre-existing patterns of relationships and behavioural memory to fulfil some new function.

Each of these possible supply chain outcomes depends upon the product in question, the actors involved, and a host of other factors that impact upon a supply chain's resilience and integrity. Like living organisms, supply chains exhibit distinct identities. They evolve and are adaptive. Very few are completely alike.

They are also sensitive. The need for smooth interaction of many parts exposes supply chains to disruptions and makes then vulnerable to external shocks and opportunistic behaviour, as the incidents canvassed at the outset of this chapter demonstrated. Thus, the requirement for a 'unity' of operation can be both beneficial and detrimental.

The independent persona of the supply chain is, in addition, something that can have consequences in law. For legal purposes the supply chain can assume certain attributes of personality, which is especially important to those who are interested in differentiating their product from competitors. In environmental products, 'fair' trade and organic certification, for instance, the chain itself becomes the source of intellectual property, such as in a designation of 'traditional speciality guaranteed', or trademark.[16] Potential participants have to commit to meeting certain requirements in order to become involved.

Experts have also noticed a recurrent feature of supply chains. This is the fact that as supply chains mature and their outputs become subject to greater competition, power shifts to the 'end' of the supply chain.[17] Consumers and purchasers become more important, leading to a culture of 'Just Say Yes'.[18] Walmart, like many other large retailers, routinely uses its enormous marketing clout to wrest continuous discounts from suppliers, a tactic that promotes a 'race to the bottom' as upstream suppliers perennially scout for the most cost-effective source. In certain industries, this movement is offset to a degree by the desire to ensure quality control and preserve supplier ties.

Legal analysis may be tempted to reduce the various interacting elements of a legal system to 'rights' and 'obligations', and indeed for the purposes of manageability, often must do so. Nevertheless, the law's natural reductivism should not obscure the fact that what is being

---

14 Emmett and Crocker (n 12) 8.

15 For instance, a particular type of customer with special needs may be one that the principal supplier decides not to cater to due to capacity constraints or shift in focus it would require of the business model. This dilemma is often encapsulated in the business adage 'Do Not Serve Customers You Cannot Satisfy', see John Mentzer, *Fundamentals of Supply Chain Management* (SAGE 2004) 100.

16 'Traditional Speciality Guaranteed' (TSG) is a designation under EU legislation that refers to foods that either by virtue of raw materials, production method or processing features are distinctive and therefore protected. It has been in place since 1992. For discussion see Andrea Tosato, 'The Protection of Traditional Food in the EU: Traditional Specialities Guaranteed' (2013) 19 *European Law Journal* 545.

17 William Copacino, *Supply Chain Management* (CRC Press 1997) 42.

18 'Most manufacturing companies today are being pressed by their customers to provide more for less – that is, lower prices, greater value, higher levels of customer service, and additional value-added services', ibid 39.

contemplated in *any* legal analysis is, in some sense, the reflection a series of relationships embodying interdependence. Interdependence is characteristic of virtually all human endeavour and is why individuals who come together in the form of communities must agree on the assignment of rights and obligations. They must be responsible and there must be reciprocity, even if that reciprocity is not always equal.

Interdependence in WTO Law

In this chapter I take the view that all law can, in one form or another, be understood as being about interdependence. We often say that for there to be a right, there must be a corresponding obligation (i.e. right = obligation).[19] Yet the manifestation of this basic relationship is not immediately apparent. To maintain that law – or international law – is ultimately about interdependence seems far-fetched, especially when looked at through the frame of individual legal rules and disputes. How is it possible, for instance, to assert that a rule concerning maritime delimitation or immunity or *jus cogens* are really about interdependence? At this level of scrutiny the link with interdependence is hard to see.

Interdependence is likewise a difficult subject to identify in WTO law. The WTO Agreement never expressly mentions the term 'interdependence' and WTO panels and the Appellate Body have only rarely referred to it. Still, considered carefully, one can see that interdependence is a pervasive theme throughout the treaty. Several descriptions offered by panels and the Appellate Body illustrate the material way in which interdependence generated by trade concessions is transforming the global economy. For example, the panel in *US – Underwear* described the overseas extension of the US textile and clothing industry during the early 1990s as follows:

> In the course of the last six years, there has been a significant change in the US cotton and manmade fibre underwear manufacturing industry which has significantly switched from producing and assembling underwear domestically to producing components in the United States for assembly in other countries and subsequent return to the same enterprises in the United States for marketing. This pattern of co-production has enabled the companies in this industry to maintain their share of the US market by making use of the labour force available outside the country while at the same time controlling the source of raw materials, the production timetable, the types and amounts of underwear to be produced and the marketing of the final product. Moreover, these co-production operations were consistent with the policies of the United States, which was encouraging investment and production in Mexico and the Caribbean Basin.[20]

Similarly, in *Mexico – Telecoms* the panel observed that:

> . . . basic telecommunications services supplied between Members do require, during the delivery of the service, *a high degree of interaction* between each other's networks, since

---

19 Wesley Hohfeld pointed out that the terms 'rights' and 'obligations' encompass a much wider array of legal relationships than their normal appellation might suggest. One of Hohfeld's most important contributions to the study of jurisprudence was to maintain that there are at least four correlative relationships in law: rights and obligations, privileges and no rights, powers and liabilities, immunities and disabilities. For an outline of these ideas see Wesley Hohfeld, 'Fundamental Legal Conceptions as Applied in Judicial Reasoning' (1917) *Yale Faculty Scholarship Series*, Paper 4378.

20 Panel Report *US – Restrictions on Imports of Cotton and Man-Made Fibre Underwear*, 8 November 1996, WT/DS24/R, para 2.1.

the service typically involves a continuous, rapid and often two-way flow of intangible customer and operator data. The interaction results in a seamless service between the originating and terminating segments, which suggests that the service be considered as a single, cross-border service.[21]

And in *US – Aircraft* WTO decision-makers detailed the multinational list of suppliers involved in manufacturing the Boeing 787 Dreamliner:

> Completion of sub-assemblies and integration of systems takes place in Everett, Washington, with many components being pre-installed before delivery to Everett. The 787 composite wings are being manufactured by Mitsubishi Heavy Industries. The horizontal stabilizers are being manufactured by Alenia Aeronautica in Italy, and various parts of the fuselage sections are being built by Alenia in Italy, Vought in Charleston, South Carolina, Kawasaki Heavy Industries and Fuji Heavy Industries in Japan, Alenia in Italy and Spirit Aerosystems in Wichita, Kansas. The main landing gear and nose landing gear are being supplied by the French company Messier-Dowty, while passenger doors are being made by Latécoère in France, and the cargo, access and crew escape doors by Saab in Sweden.[22]

WTO decision-makers in *US – Aircraft* noted that as a result of globalized manufacturing Boeing has 'shifted responsibility for detailed component design to suppliers, and focuses on systems integration, managing overall requirements, as well as the assembly process. The 787 is essentially assembled from large substructures designed and produced by suppliers.'[23]

This description implies that what has arisen between Boeing and its suppliers is an elaborate network of relationships that is responsible for creating a sophisticated final product made out of components from many sources. Much modern manufacturing is in fact often characterized by these relationships. They value coordination and integration so that manufacturing and delivery of the product becomes, in some sense, unified.

Unification places its own demands on participants in the supply chain. Participants need to consider matters differently. They must develop shared understandings about individual and common goods and must agree on the allocation of rights and obligations between participants, often at great levels of detail. This is because increased interdependence requires increased coordination.

The experience of Boeing and many other companies in the global economy demonstrates the way that interdependence modifies *thinking*, a modification ultimately reflected in the

---

21 Panel Report *Mexico – Telecommunications Services*, 2 April 2004, WT/DS204/R, para 7.38 [emphasis added].
22 Panel Report *United States – Civil Aircraft (Second Complaint)*, 31 March 2011, WT/DS353/R, Appendix VII F 1, para 25.
23 ibid para 24. Former WTO Director-General Pascal Lamy described a similar phenomenon in the global textiles value chain. The chain spans countries involved in the 'mere assembly' of imported fabric for export (such as China, Romania and Vietnam); to 'original equipment manufacture' where apparel products are manufactured in full, going beyond mere assembly (such as in Turkey); to 'original design manufacture' where in addition to full product manufacture a country can create ready-made collections at different levels of sophistication (such as in Turkey and Hong Kong); and all the way to 'original brand manufacture' where a country becomes the buyer in the value chain and starts to manage the supply network (such as in the US and Italy). See Pascal Lamy, 'What Cannot Be Counted Does Not Count' (speech by the WTO Director-General to the Economic Development Foundation (IKV) and the Economic Policy Research Foundation of Turkey (TEPAV), Istanbul, 14 March 2013).

shape of the law. Philip Allott has explained how the transformation generated by international law is chiefly a *mental*, as opposed to a *material*, process:

> To change our idea of the world, to speak of the world in a new way, is to change what our world will become. The road from the ideal to the actual lies, not merely in institutional novelties, or programmes and blueprints for social change, but also, and primarily, in a change of mind.[24]

Perhaps the most graphic manifestation of this demand for a change in thinking is panel and Appellate Body criticism in situations where governments have failed to consider the interests of other member countries. For example, in *US – Gasoline*, the Appellate Body observed that while the introduction of baseline emission requirements for 'clean' gasoline was considered unfeasible in the domestic context, there was 'nothing in the record to indicate that [the US] did other than disregard that kind of consideration when it came to foreign refiners'. It concluded that '[t]he resulting discrimination must have been foreseen, and was not merely inadvertent or unavoidable'.[25] Similarly in *US – Clove Cigarettes*, the panel noted that '[i]t seems to us that the effect of banning cigarettes with characterizing flavours other than menthol is to impose costs on producers in other Members, notably producers in Indonesia, while at the same time imposing no costs on any U.S. entity'.[26] This criticism can be understood as evidence of the gradual emergence of the idea of a 'common good' under WTO law, itself reflective of a developing sense of community. The criticisms can be understood as an exhortation upon governments to consider more than their own narrow interests.[27]

At the same time, with the specialization of function that interdependence allows, governments and countries are also much more careful to define their allocation of rights and obligations. Each participant is more likely to fulfil specific tasks and the degree of refinement must be reflected in legal arrangements, including the definition of WTO law.[28]

So descriptions of interdependence are abundant in WTO case law, yet direct recognition of economic interdependence and the way that it shapes legal rules are rare.[29] The Preamble

---

24 Philip Allott, *Eunomia* (n 6) xxxiii.

25 Appellate Body Report *United States – Standards for Reformulated and Conventional Gasoline*, 29 April 1996, WT/DS2/AB/R, 28.

26 Panel Report *United States – Measures Affecting the Production and Sale of Clove Cigarettes*, 2 September 2011, WT/DS406/R, para 7.289.

27 Indeed, as part of WTO arrangements they are now in many instances required to do so. For instance, TBT Art 2.9 includes obligations inviting notification and comment in national standard-setting whenever a relevant international standard does not exist or the technical content of a proposed technical regulation is not in accordance with the technical content of relevant international standards. Likewise, SPS Art 3.4 provides that 'Members shall play a full part, within the limits of their resources, in the relevant international organizations and their subsidiary bodies, in particular the Codex Alimentarius Commission, the International Office of Epizootics, and the international and regional organizations operating within the framework of the International Plant Protection Convention, to promote within these organizations the development and periodic review of standards, guidelines and recommendations with respect to all aspects of sanitary and phytosanitary measures'.

28 This is also evident, for instance, in instruments of international commercial law such as the International Chamber of Commerce's International Commercial Terms (INCOTERMS). INCOTERMS were first introduced in 1936 but in their latest revision, introduced in 2010, foresees a much higher degree of specificity among parties in relation to such issues as place of delivery.

29 For additional recognition of supply chain relationships in WTO case law see Panel Report *Canada – Certain Measures Affecting the Automotive Industry*, 11 February 2000, WT/DS139/R, WT/DS142/R, para 10.254, referring to 'vertical integration and exclusive distribution arrangements between manufacturers and wholesalers in the motor

of the WTO Agreement mentions, for instance, 'expanding the production of and trade in goods and services' and 'entering into reciprocal and mutually advantageous arrangements' as basic aims of the treaty, but again, these references are generalized and appear not to contemplate the multidimensional, tentacular way that modern manufacturing and service supply has evolved since the WTO Agreement was concluded in 1994. Thus, the multinational nature of many supply and value chains coexists uneasily with a state-based system of international trade governance.

For instance, there are a number of WTO provisions that presuppose the interdependence of producers and consumers in supply chains. Article 3.1 of the WTO Safeguards Agreement provides, for instance, that:

> A Member may apply a safeguard measure only following an investigation by the competent authorities . . . This investigation shall include reasonable public notice to all interested parties and public hearings or other appropriate means in which importers, exporters and other interested parties could present evidence and their views, including the opportunity to respond to the presentations of other parties and to submit their views, inter alia, as to whether or not the application of a safeguard measure would be in the public interest.

The safeguard provision thus requires an 'investigation', with notice to 'importers, exporters and other interested parties' and an assessment of whether the proposed safeguard would be in the broad 'public interest'. What the provision foresees is an assessment of competing needs for the import, including the needs of competitors, consumers and downstream users of the product as an input. Likewise, in articles 6.11–12 of the WTO Antidumping Agreement and article 19.2 of the WTO Subsidies and Countervailing Measures Agreement national authorities contemplating trade action are encouraged to give consideration to up- and downstream interests that might be affected by anti-dumping or countervailing measures. In this sense WTO law is not purely *product*-oriented. In the realm of trade restrictions, in particular, it aims to take account of the wider interests potentially in issue due to economic linkage.

---

vehicle industry'; Decision by the Arbitrator *European Communities – Regime for the Importation, Sale and Distribution of Bananas*, 9 April 1999, WT/DS27/ARB, para 6.12, refusing to acknowledge 'losses of US exports in goods or services *between the US and third countries* . . . [as] constitute[ing] nullification or impairment of even *indirect* benefits accruing to the United States under the GATT or the GATS for which the European Communities could face suspension of concessions. To the extent the US assessment of nullification or impairment includes *lost US exports* defined as *US content incorporated in Latin American bananas* (eg US fertilizer, pesticides and machinery shipped to Latin America and US capital or management services used in banana cultivation), we do not consider such lost US exports . . .' [emphasis in original]; Appellate Body Report, *European Communities – Export Subsidies on Sugar*, 28 April 2005, WT/DS265/AB/R, para 279, observing that 'economic effects of WTO-consistent domestic support may "spill over" to benefit export production. Such spill-over effects may arise, in particular, in circumstances where agricultural products result from a single line of production that does not distinguish between production destined for the domestic market and production destined for the export market'; Panel Report *Mexico – Definitive Countervailing Measures on Olive Oil from the European Communities*, 4 September 2008, WT/DS341/R, para 7.202; Panel Report *Mexico – Measures Affecting Telecommunications Services*, 2 April 2004, WT/DS204/R, para 7.40; Decision by the Arbitrator, *United States – Subsidies on Upland Cotton*, 31 August 2009, WT/DS267/ARB/2, para 5.149, noting that 'it may be especially difficult to have recourse to alternative suppliers [for the purposes of retaliation] without significantly upsetting the supply chain'.

Interdependence is also a noticeable feature of WTO dispute settlement where, despite a superficially 'bilateral' aspect to disputes, rules have evolved to accommodate relatively liberal rights of participation for third parties. For instance, DSU Article 10.1 provides:

> The interests of the parties to a dispute and *those of other Members under a covered agreement at issue* in the dispute shall be fully taken into account during the panel process.[30]

Commenting on these rules the panel in *Australia – Apples* noted that 'not only have third parties the *right* to make submissions in a dispute, but panels have the *legal obligation* to consider them'.[31] Again, this is different from other international legal systems like the International Court of Justice, international investment arbitration or international criminal law, where bilateral emphasis in litigation is much more pronounced.[32] This characteristic speaks to the multipolarity of many WTO disputes and the way that the definition of WTO law is part of a broader common endeavour.[33]

Still, references recognizing the express connection between legal and substantive interdependence are comparatively rare. One reference occurred in *EC – Bananas III*, a dispute involving a large number of Latin American, Caribbean, African and Asian suppliers of bananas to the EC market. Complainants included the United States, a negligible exporter of bananas. Arbitrators therefore had to contend with the EC assertion that the US lacked an

---

30 Emphasis added.
31 Panel Report *Australia – Measures Affecting the Importation of Applies from New Zealand*, 9 August 2010, WT/DS367/R, para 7.76 [emphasis added]. See also Appellate Body Report *United States – Import Prohibition of Certain Shrimp and Shrimp Products*, 12 October 1998, WT/DS58/AB/R, para 101. For the difficulties of doing so see Panel Report *Canada – Measures Relating to Exports of Wheat and Treatment of Imported Grain*, 6 April 2004, WT/DS276/R, para 6.6ff. For instances where panels have actively considered third party submissions, see Appellate Body Report *European Communities – Anti-Dumping Duties on Imports of Cotton-Type Bed Linen from India*, 8 April 2003, WT/DS141/AB/R para 142–44; Panel Report United States – Subsidies on Upland Cotton, 8 September 2004, WT/DS267/R, para 7.443; Appellate Body Report *United States – Final Countervailing Duty Determination with Respect to Certain Softwood Lumber from Canada*, 15 August 2006, WT/DS264/AB/RW, para 98, 112; Panel Report *United States – Measures Affecting Trade in Large Civil Aircraft (Second Complaint)*, 31 March 2011, WT/DS353/R para 7.767. Panels have often noted that WTO dispute settlement has consequences for third parties. Third parties also play an important role in surveillance, monitoring and general 'fine-tuning' of rights and obligations raised in dispute settlement. See, for instance, submissions by the EC in Appellate Body Report, *Canada – Measures Affecting the Export of Civilian Aircraft*, 21 July 2000, WT/DS70/AB/RW, para 19. At the same time, the potential number of third parties in any dispute appears to have resulted in a slight tightening of requirements for third party standing as compared with dispute settlement under GATT, particularly in cases where 'enhanced' standing is requested: see Panel Report *United States – Anti-Dumping Act of 1916*, 29 March 2000, WT/DS162/R, para 6.33; Panel Report *European Communities and Certain Member States – Measures Affecting Trade in Large Civil Aircraft*, 30 June 2010, WT/DS316/R, para 7.166; Panel Report United States – *Measures Affecting Trade in Large Civil Aircraft (Second Complaint)*, 31 March 2011, WT/DS353/R, para 7.16; Decision by the Arbitrators, *European Communities – Regime for the Importation, Sale and Distribution of Bananas — Recourse to Arbitration by the European Communities under Art 22.6 of the DSU*, 9 April 1999, WT/DS27/ARB, para 2.8, re third parties in compliance proceedings.
32 See Christine Chinkin, *Third Parties in International Law* (1994). More recently some commentators have detected a slight relaxation in the ICJ's traditionally restrictive interpretation of requests to intervene under ICJ Statute Arts 62–63, see Paolo Palchetti, 'Opening the International Court of Justice to Third States' (2002) 6 *Max Planck UNYB* 139.
33 Cases involving large numbers of third parties are numerous, including *EC – Sugar* (WT/DS267, 25 third parties), *EC – Bananas* (WT/DS27, 20 third parties), *US – Zeroing* (WT/DS294–11 third parties), *US – Cotton* (13 third parties), *US – Section 301* (WT/DS152, 17 third parties), *China – Raw Materials* (WT/DS394–16 third parties).

exporter interest and could not seek to retaliate. In dismissing the EC's objection the arbitrators observed:

> Indeed, with the increased *interdependence* of the global economy, which means that actions taken in one country are likely to have significant effects on trade and foreign direct investment flows in others, Members have a greater stake in enforcing WTO rules than in the past since any deviation from the negotiated balance of rights and obligations is more likely than ever to affect them, directly or indirectly. Since the United States is likely to be affected by the EC regime, it would have an interest in a determination of whether the EC regime is inconsistent with the requirements of WTO rules. Thus, in our view a Member's potential interest in trade in goods or services and its interest in a determination of rights and obligations under the WTO Agreement are each sufficient to establish a right to pursue a WTO dispute settlement proceeding.[34]

The reluctance to refer more directly to interdependence may stem from a pragmatic appraisal that the concept of interconnection can only be taken so far. Taken to extremes, anything can be linked to anything, emptying the concept of meaningful content.

Thus, whereas interdependence is evident in certain aspects of WTO law, there are limits to its recognition. As a result, WTO law can appear curiously double-aspected. For instance, while WTO law contains a relatively expansive definition of who can participate in a safeguard hearing, as outlined above, the *initiation* of a safeguard complaint is restricted to members of a defined 'industry'. Several GATT and WTO decisions have also made clear that, despite the integrated nature of many production processes, the term 'industry' is to be interpreted restrictively, consistent with the character of safeguards as an exceptional countermeasure to 'fair' trade. The right of initiation is limited to producers of the *product*, not those involved in the *process* by which a product is made.[35]

A second area where interdependence is problematic is with respect to 'pass-through' analysis in countervailing action. Here, the issue that arises is whether or not subsidies received by an input producer or product may be assessed for the purposes of countervailing action against downstream products. Several GATT and WTO panels have considered a variety of circumstances involving the potential for pass-through determinations.[36] To date, the GATT/WTO jurisprudence has established that for an indirect input subsidy to be countervailed, the investigating authority needs to conduct a pass-through test.[37] The main principle is that a national authority is not allowed to base its findings on a mere presumption of subsidy

---

34 Panel Report *European Communities – Regime for the Importation, Sale and Distribution of Bananas*, 22 May 1997, WT/DS27/R/USA, para 7.50 [emphasis added].

35 Thus, in *US – Lamb* for instance, the panel noted that 'the factor of economic interdependence between producers of raw, intermediate and final products is not relevant for the industry definition'. The panel also observed the difficulty of quantifying interdependence for the purposes of defining which economic operators could be part of an 'industry', see Panel Report *United States – Safeguard Measures on Imports of Fresh, Chilled or Frozen Lamb Meat from New Zealand and Australia*, 21 December 2000, WT/DS177/R, para 7.83; see also Appellate Body Report *United States – Safeguard Measures on Imports of Fresh, Chilled or Frozen Lamb Meat from New Zealand and Australia*, 1 May 2001, WT/DS177/AB/R, para 94. For GATT decisions see *United States – Definition of Industry Concerning Wine and Grape Products* (adopted by the SCM Committee on 28 April 1992), SCM/71, BISD 39S/436; *Canada – Imposition of Countervailing Duties on Imports of Manufacturing Beef from the EEC*, 13 October 1987, not adopted, SCM/85.

36 See for instance *US – Lead and Bismuth II*, WT/DS138; *US – Certain EC Products*, WT/DS212.

37 Sherzod Shadikhodjaev, 'How to Pass a Pass-Through Test: The Case of Input Subsidies' (2012) 15 *JIEL* 621.

transmission from an input producer to a producer of the processed product if they operate at arm's length from each other. Proposals made in the Doha Development Round generally reflect and develop this principle further. Codification of the pass-through principle would bring more clarity and consistency to this area given the potential distortion that a subsidy introduces down the production chain.

Still another area where interdependence is problematic is in the retaliation phase of WTO dispute settlement. Arbitrators and commentators have voiced concern about the difficulties that retaliation poses for secondary or downstream users of products which may be targeted as part of selective market closure. Their inclusion within supply chains makes the authorization to retaliate of questionable value. In *EC – Bananas III (Ecuador) (Art 22.6 – EC)*, for instance, the arbitrator examining Ecuador's request to retaliate in a non-correspondent sector against EC restrictions on Ecuadorian banana exports observed that Ecuador was a developing country with little industrial infrastructure and, consequently, the suspension of concessions in relation to capital, intermediate or other input goods, which constitute direct inputs into domestic production, had the potential to be damaging to Ecuadorian economic operators. As a result, the arbitrator referred to the possibility of retaliation in the field of services and intellectual property.[38]

Likewise, in *US – Cotton*, a dispute involving claims by Brazil that the US continued to subsidize US agricultural producers beyond limits permitted under the WTO Agreement on Agriculture, the arbitrator assessing Brazil's proposal to retaliate in non-correspondent sectors had to determine whether the proposal was 'practicable or effective' as required under DSU Article 23:3. The prevalence of vertical integration meant that one consideration the arbitrators had to take into account was whether it would be especially difficult for Brazilian importers of consumer products to have recourse to alternative suppliers without significantly upsetting the supply chain. The arbitrators concluded that:

> While there is no exact mathematical precision to this determination, we consider that, for the purposes of our assessment in these proceedings, a US share of imports of 20 per cent constitutes a reasonable threshold by which to estimate the extent to which Brazil may be able to find alternative sources of supply for these three remaining categories of consumer goods imports.[39]

These determinations mean that the multidimensional quality of interdependence as a concept makes it hard to accommodate within the framework of WTO law. Everything cannot be related to everything else, and yet, in some sense, it is.

Made in the World

The many references above suggest that no clear picture of interdependence has emerged in WTO law yet. It is a polarizing subject, one which tugs in different directions, although more recently there are some indications that it is being accorded attention in WTO thinking. In 2010 the WTO Secretariat launched a 'Made in the World Initiative' to provide a better

---

38 Decision by the Arbitrators *European Communities – Regime for the Importation, Sale and Distribution of Bananas – Recourse to Arbitration by the European Communities under Art 22.6 of the DSU*, 24 March 2000, WT/DS27/ARB/ECU, para 173.

39 *US – Cotton* (n 29) para 5.181.

evaluation of international trade to an economy and to highlight economic interdependence, the contribution of services to trade and improved assessments of 'value added'. MIWI's kick-off crystallized in the form of a report, *Trade Patterns and Global Value Chains in East Asia*, issued in 2010 and co-sponsored by Institute of Developing Economies, an arm of the Japan External Trade Organization (JETRO), and the WTO Secretariat.[40]

The central premise of MIWI and the *Trade Patterns* report is that national borders do not matter as much as they once did. The report observed 'that much of [international] trade these days comprises components or intermediate goods and services that pass from economy to economy before becoming part of a final traded product'. The report noted that:

> The distinction between 'them' and 'us' that has traditionally defined our way of thinking about imports and exports is increasingly outmoded. Products are no longer 'made in Japan', or 'made in France'; they are truly 'made in the world'.[41]

According to the report this reformulation 'redefines the nature of trade relations that are now characterized by a much closer inter-relationship'. Consequently, the report maintains that 'we need to promote a conceptual and statistical shift in the way trade is most commonly perceived in policy debates'.

Using the experience of the 'Asian success story', *Trade Patterns* highlights the way that 'increasing fragmentation of value chains has led to an increase in trade flows in intermediate goods'.[42] Consequently, '[s]pecialization is no longer based on the overall balance of comparative advantage of countries in producing a final good, but on the comparative advantage of "tasks" that these countries complete at a specific step along the global value chain'. *Trade Patterns* notes the profile of countries that have achieved success by integrating into supply and value-chain manufacturing. It includes low tariffs on semi-processed goods, good logistics, upgraded infrastructure, and foreign direct investment as an essential part of the offshoring strategies of multinational companies.

The report reveals 'a dialectical relationship characterized by significant structural diversity on the one hand and a high degree of complementarity on the other one'.[43] This complementarity of production 'is both a cause and an outcome of deepening economic interdependency among countries'. The report outlines the following consequence:

> Global value chains translate into 'trade in tasks', with partners specializing in specific skills according to their comparative advantage. This creates new trade and job opportunities, the net balance of which depends on the labour intensity of the products and the overall trade balance of each economy.[44]

Trade Patterns does a good job of providing an introduction to the phenomenon of interdependence, but the report also emphasizes how interdependence challenges the WTO's existing regulatory structure. Since the report's release the organization has struggled to accommodate this phenomenon and appears to be unsure of its place in a state-centric system.

---

40 See IDE-JETRO (n 4).
41 ibid 3.
42 ibid 4.
43 ibid 5.
44 ibid.

The MIWI agenda is an uncertain one of symposia and studies, but as yet, little in the way of specific policy prescriptions for the organization itself. At the moment most of its focus is statistical and empiric rather than normative. If interdependence is now so pervasive and if it challenges the state-centred model of 'rights and obligations', what is the solution? The Secretariat provides no immediate answer to this question, and indeed, there may be none. Instead, in introducing the IDE-JETRO report the then-WTO Director-General Pascal Lamy called upon the global public to 'pursue the dialogue virtually' through a website.

It is also easy to be a little suspicious of MIWI. It rose to prominence after a keynote speech by one of the WTO deputy director generals, Alejandro Jara, in May 2010. MIWI can be seen to fulfil an ambition of developing countries, some of which want to promote more of a development dimension in the WTO and hence stress the idea of 'trade in tasks'.[45] As such, it may be regarded as a sop. Since the accession of the new WTO Director-General, Roberto Azevedo, in May 2013, institutional attention to MIWI has fallen off, at least if indications on the WTO website are to be taken at face value. The section of the site devoted specifically to MIWI has only been minimally updated.

Conclusion

A comprehensive idea of WTO law suggests that the ultimate product of WTO concessions and commitments is greater interdependence. However, the sheer inability to grapple with and 'de-construct' interdependence, to fix and put a number to it, may be an indication of its 'oneness', its centrality and fundamentality. The behaviour of countries in the resolution of several WTO-related matters suggests that they intuit this point, something that may presage a greater role for *qualitative* as opposed to *quantitative* measures of trade benefit in future.[46]

All of the above, however, does not obscure the fact that interdependence is not a neutral value, not unreservedly positive. The reference to 'chains' in supply and value chains can be understood as a contemporary form of bondage.[47] Feminism, in particular, has done much

---

45 Behind the re-characterization is the more general idea that there should be a focus on 'equitable and efficient dispersal' of the three factors of production – capital, knowledge and labour. Existing trade statistics are therefore, at most, incidental. This opinion is part of a broader set of convictions that past trade talks have consistently delivered unbalanced trade deals favouring the richer industrial states over their poorer, less able developing counterparts as well as a fear that ongoing negotiations over a 'Trans-Pacific Partnership' are a US-led attempt to divide the Asia region and contain the rise of China.

46 A number of commentators have written of the difficulty of deepening transnational integration when quantification is problematic. For an overview see Geza Feketekuty, 'Appendix: A Guide to Services Negotiations' in Aaditya Mattoo et al, *A Handbook of International Trade in Services* (OUP 2007) 553, '(T)he shortcomings of the trade data are compounded by the difficulty of making a quantitative assessment of the degree of protection provided by regulatory measures. It is much easier to calculate the protection provided by a tariff or a quota than the protection provided by a regulatory measure. Negotiators in services thus lack the kind of detailed data that would enable them to estimate the impact of negotiated reductions in particular barriers . . .'.

47 Stewart Macaulay has written about the negative effects of interdependence: 'Even discrete transactions take place within a setting of continuing relationships and interdependence. The value of these relationships means that all involved must work to satisfy each other. Potential disputes are suppressed, ignored, or compromised in the service of keeping the relationship alive . . . Power, exploitation, and dependence are also significant. Continuing relationships are not necessarily nice. The value of arrangements locks some people into interdependent positions. They can only take orders', Stewart Macaulay, 'An Empirical View of Contract' (1985) *Wisconsin Law Review* 465.

in the past century to unmask the matrices of power in traditional relationships that result in subordination. Critical legal scholars such as Martti Koskenniemi have also condemned interdependence as simply another justification for communitarian thinking – thinking that is but one part of a flawed 'international legal project'.[48] These reservations suggest that interdependence needs to be constantly questioned and re-evaluated going forward.

48 Martti Koskenniemi, *From Apology to Utopia* (CUP 2005) 477.Koskenniemi describes communitarian thinking as emerging in three standard forms: a Grotian tradition, interdependence, or the appeal to a *conscience universelle*. He criticizes interdependence as a trope, or form of argument, based on the premise that '(H)umanity today, taking into consideration the whole world, knows that "one world" has become the imperative of survival.' In Koskenniemi's view these sorts of arguments 'start . . . from a negative experience of autonomy as egoism and proceeds so as to compel normative order by referring to norms "naturally" given by the needs of interdependence'. With respect to interdependence, I maintain that interdependence needs to be understood not simply as an argument, but as a *fact*. For examination of interdependence as less than it might be see the *DHL Global Connectedness Index* <www.dhl.com/content/dam/flash/g0/gci_2012/download/dhl_gci_2012_complete_study.pdf> accessed 15 January 2013, and 'Going Backwards' *The Economist* (London, 22 December 2012) 105.

9 Reforming the Law and Institutions of the WTO

The Dangers of Unexpected Consequences

Gregory Messenger[*]

Introduction

In the face of a global economic uncertainty the World Trade Organization (WTO) is presented with two interconnected and pressing needs. The first is to encourage further liberalization at the multilateral level and remedy the increasingly uneven and fragmented economic prospects offered by ever larger 'super' regional trade agreements such as the Transpacific Partnership or the Transatlantic Trade and Investment Partnership.[1] The proliferation of such agreements can cause not only trade diversion but also fragment the regulatory landscape for trade, further increasing legal uncertainty and adding costs for traders.[2]

The second challenge is to elaborate and clarifying the existing legal disciplines applicable to the Membership. A number of WTO agreements require further clarification, while others need amendment or alteration.[3] Though this was an understandable position to have taken given the extraordinarily complicated negotiations during the Uruguay Round, what was not foreseen was the widespread deadlock in the negotiating branch of the WTO.[4] Add to this the increasing size of the Membership (now close to universal), changing circumstances relating to technological and regulatory changes, and the need for legal reform becomes acute. While multilateral negotiations have made modest progress, there are still considerable challenges ahead.[5]

Though difficult, reform nonetheless presents opportunities for Members not only to improve WTO law but also to do so in a manner that serves their interests. Indeed, an institution such as the WTO, with its comparatively detailed set of disciplines and effective compliance mechanisms, is especially attractive to Members for this purpose. This chapter seeks to identify the risks involved in expecting reform to produce results coincident with Members' interests or objectives, drawing attention to the dangers of unexpected consequences for Members who may find that their reforms do not lead to the results they originally intended.

---

[*] Lecturer in Law, University of Liverpool.

1 Former includes Australia, Brunei, Canada, Chile, Japan, Malaysia, Mexico, New Zealand, Peru, Singapore, the US and Vietnam while the latter still under negotiation is between the EU and US.
2 See generally, Lorand Bartels and Federico Ortino (eds), *Regional Trade Agreements and the WTO Legal System* (OUP 2006).
3 For example, art X.1 General Agreement on Trade in Services, 15 April 1994, LT/UR/A-1B/S/1 <http://docson line.wto.org> accessed 15 January 2015. 'There shall be multilateral negotiations on the question of emergency safeguard measures based on the principle of non-discrimination. The results of such negotiations shall enter into effect on a date not later than three years from the date of entry into force of the WTO Agreement.'
4 Richard Steinberg, 'Judicial Lawmaking at the WTO: Discursive, Constitutional, and Political Constraints' (2004) 98 *American Journal of International Law* 247.
5 The Bali package representing the culmination of the Doha Round thus far.

It further suggests that the relationship between expectations and outcomes can offer insights into the nature of WTO law more widely.

By way of demonstration, the chapter identifies two interrelated areas of WTO law, one institutional and one substantive, where the expectations of the Members in question were not borne out. The first is in the creation of the new dispute settlement system at the WTO through the conclusion of the Dispute Settlement Understanding (DSU).[6] In particular, the role that the Appellate Body has developed for itself. In spite of the expectations of the negotiating parties and the 'constitutional' checks put in place, the Appellate Body has positioned itself at the heart of WTO law, drawing strong criticism for judicial activism and expansion of its remit.[7] The second example, related though distinct, is the interpretation of Article 17.6 Anti-Dumping Agreement (ADA) and its role in the 'zeroing' debate.[8] This provision, which provides a different standard of review for panels in assessing the compliance of anti-dumping determinations than in other areas of WTO law, has been interpreted in a surprising way, contrary to the US administrative law principle upon which it was based (that of '*Chevron* deference').

The objective here is not to criticize the Appellate Body's institutional development or interpretative method, but rather to identify the disjoint between expectations and outcomes. These failures demonstrate the difficulty in designing an institution or rule-set to serve one's own interests. Nonetheless, we can draw lessons from these experiences, paying heed to the key role of institutional identities and interests in shaping how rules are subsequently applied, though with the caveat that identities are fluid, ever more so in an increasingly multi-polar global economy.

Institutional Reform: Expectations of a Dispute Settlement System

Dispute settlement at the WTO is often contrasted with its earlier incarnation during the GATT years (1947–1995).[9] WTO dispute settlement, we say, is 'rule based' unlike the 'power based' system of the GATT years, now conducted by lawyers rather than diplomats.[10] Clearly this is a caricature, as the system developed over the 1947–1995 period, most notably after the introduction of the Tokyo Round Understanding in 1979 which marked a considerable shift.[11] Though progressive formalization of dispute settlement took a step forward in the Tokyo Round Understanding, it was still hampered by a number of institutional defects. Most notable of these was the practical inability of panel reports to be adopted, thus undermining their legal weight. Desiring a more formal and efficient system which would ensure

---

6 Understanding on Rules and Procedures Governing the Settlement of Disputes (15 April 1994) LT/UR/A-2/ DS/U/1 <http://docsonline.wto.org> accessed 15 January 2015.

7 For example, John Greenwald, 'WTO Dispute Settlement: An Exercise in Trade Legislation?' (2003) *Journal of International Economic Law* 113; Claude E Barfield, *Free Trade, Sovereignty, Democracy: The Future of the World Trade Organization* (American Enterprise Institute 2001); and from a Resolution of the US House of Representatives, 'the WTO dispute settlement process is not working and has been guided by politics rather than by legal principles' (H Res 441, 17 November 2003) in response to the *US – Steel* dispute (DS252).

8 Agreement on Implementation of art VI of the General Agreement on Tariffs and Trade 1994, 15 April 1994, LT/ UR/A-1A/3 <http://docsonline.wto.org> accessed 15 January 2015.

9 On the influences at play in the reform of dispute settlement: Gregory Messenger, 'The Development of International Law and the Role of Causal Language' (2016) 2 *Oxford Journal of Legal Studies*.

10 John H Jackson, *The World Trading System: Law and Policy of International Economic Relations* (2nd edn, MIT Press 1997) 109; Joseph HH Weiler, 'The Rule of Lawyers and the Ethos of Diplomats: Reflections on the Internal and External Legitimacy of WTO Dispute Settlement' (2001) 35 *Journal of World Trade* 206.

11 Understanding on Notification, Consultation, Dispute Settlement and Surveillance, 28 November 1979, BISD 26S/210.

that compliance with the new agreements concluded during the Uruguay Round could be ensured, negotiations over an effective dispute settlement system at the WTO began.

The negotiating history indicates that (especially during the first half of the round) the GATT Contracting Parties expected dispute settlement under the WTO to be an entirely different creature to that found in other areas of international law. Unlike disputes at the International Court of Justice or the European Court of Human rights, trade disputes were to be resolved in a *sui generis* manner. The EEC (as it was then) expressed the mood succinctly stating: 'The GATT dispute settlement machinery is original and specific; there is *no equivalent* in other areas of international relations.'[12]

Not only was the nature of dispute settlement to be different, but also the process whereby decisions were reached. Note, rather than focusing on specific forms of legal reasoning which would be expected in other situations, here the EEC warned:

> The [dispute settlement] machinery cannot and must not be used to create, through a process of *deductive interpretation*, new obligations for contracting parties, or to replace the negotiating process. One of the objectives of the Uruguay Round is to eliminate certain ambiguities and diverging interpretations of the General Agreement and Codes, and this will make a fundamental contribution to dispute settlement.[13]

Instead, the role of the dispute settlement system was to provide negotiated settlements, conciliation, and where the final resolution 'should not be of a judicial nature'.[14] The proposed introduction of appellate review was debated, not out of a concern over the creation of a new autonomous institution but rather that the speed and efficacy of the dispute settlement system would be affected were parties to automatically appeal in all disputes.[15]

During the Uruguay Round (at least until the final stages) it would seem that the negotiating parties did not expect to create an institution which is now lauded for its formal and highly legalized nature.[16] Given the complex and wide-ranging negotiations taking place with numerous groups, it may well be that the parties did not see the wider consequences of what was agreed in each specific area.[17] In any case, the development of the Appellate Body's role since the creation of the WTO was not a certainty.[18]

Indeed, if we look to the text of Article 17 DSU, which grants competences to the Appellate Body, it is startlingly lacking in legal descriptors.[19] Note Article 17.1 DSU:

> A standing Appellate Body shall be established by the DSB. The Appellate Body shall hear appeals from panel cases. It shall be composed of seven persons, three of whom

---

12 Communication from the European Economic Community (EEC), 24 September 1987, GATT Doc MTN GNG/NG13/W/12, para 1 (emphasis added).

13 ibid (emphasis added).

14 Communication from Brazil, 7 March 1988, GATT Doc MTN GNG/NG13/W/24.

15 See Note by the Secretariat, 13 November 1989, GATT Doc MTN GNG/NG13/16, para 21; Note by the Secretariat, 15 December 1989, GATT Doc MTN GNG/NG13/17, para 9; Note by the Secretariat, 28 May 1990, GATT Doc MTN GNG/NG13/19, para 8.

16 James Crawford, 'Continuity and Discontinuity in International Dispute Settlement: An Inaugural Lecture' (2014) 1 *Journal of International Dispute Settlement* 1, 4.

17 I am grateful to Chris Parlin for raising this point.

18 Richard Steinberg (n 4) 250.

19 Though nonetheless using the term 'appellate' which does conjure legal images. I am grateful to David Zaring for raising this point.

shall serve on any one case. Persons serving on the Appellate Body shall serve in rotation. Such rotation shall be determined in the working procedures of the Appellate Body.

There is no mention of a court, no tribunal, and no judges. The number of members is lower than judges at other international courts,[20] and they are part-time.[21] Neither panels nor the Appellate Body issue judgments but rather reports, which must be adopted to have legal effect.[22] The Dispute Settlement Body, a political organ of all Members of the WTO, must adopt reports which though, in practice a formality due to the negative consensus rule, nonetheless creates an open space wherein the Membership can voice concerns over the interpretation offered by the Appellate Body.[23] The furore arising from the acceptance of *amicus curiae* briefs by the Appellate Body is one such example, with the representative of Hong Kong, China going so far as to claim:

> the acceptance of *amicus curiae* briefs by the Appellate Body was not explicitly provided for in the DSU nor had it been envisaged during the negotiations of the DSU. The unilateral expansion by the Appellate Body of its legal authority, which went beyond the DSU, was not only an act of judicial activism but also a violation of the amendment provisions under article X:8 of the WTO Agreement.[24]

Such a public forum for criticism can function as a strict control on the Appellate Body's autonomy. Note how the statement of Hong Kong, China focused its criticism by reference to the DSU and the WTO Agreement.[25] This prioritization of the text encourages both panels and the Appellate Body to establish and maintain their own legitimacy through terms set by the DSU. Thus the 'textual' fixation of the WTO dispute settlement institutions which has become a hallmark of legal reasoning in world trade.[26]

The way in which panels and the Appellate Body have responded to the guidance laid out for them is an interesting one. Unlike the expectations outlined so far, they have created different identities, though in each instance using the DSU as a lodestar. What is of particular interest is the way in which their interpretation of the DSU and other agreements has caused consternation amongst some Members who view a more appropriate alternative as the obvious choice to hand. As we shall see below, it is not necessarily that the Appellate Body or panels have interpreted the DSU or ADA *incorrectly* but rather that the expectation of how they would interpret the text has not been borne out by practice.

---

20 Peter Van Den Bossche, 'The Making of the "World Trade Court": The Origins and Development of the Appellate Body of the World Trade Organization' in Rufus Yerxa and Bruce Wilson, *Key Issues in WTO Dispute Settlement: The First Ten Years* (CUP 2005) 65–66 citing the numbers of other permanent judges on international tribunals: 15 on the International Court of Justice, 18 on the International Criminal Court and 21 on the International Tribunal for the Law of the Sea.

21 Establishment of the Appellate Body: Recommendations by the Preparatory Committee for the WTO approved by the Dispute Settlement Body on 10 February 1995, 19 June 1995, WT/DSB/1, paras 10–12.

22 Art 16.4 DSU in the case of panel reports and art 17.14 DSU in the case of Appellate Body reports.

23 Dan Sarooshi, *International Organizations and Their Exercise of Sovereign Powers* (OUP 2005) 79; Petros Mavroidis, 'Amicus Curiae Briefs before the WTO: Much Ado about Nothing', *Jean Monnet Working Paper* 2/01, 8.

24 Minutes of Meeting, Dispute Settlement Body, 7 July 2000, WT/DSB/M/83, para 15.

25 Marrakesh Agreement Establishing the World Trade Organization, 15 April 1994, LT/UR/A/2 <http://docsonline.wto.org> accessed 15 January 2015.

26 Claus-Dieter Ehlermann, 'Six Years on the Bench of the "World Trade Court"' (2002) 36 *Journal World Trade* 605, 616.

Panels and the Appropriate Standard of Review

For panels, Article 11 DSU sets out their responsibilities as well as the appropriate standard to apply in cases of review. The Appellate Body has stressed what it considers the principal role of panels in this context, confirming in its now famous dictum in *EC – Hormones*:

> The function of Panels is to assist the DSB in discharging its responsibilities under this Understanding and the covered agreements. Accordingly, a Panel should make an *objective assessment of the matter* before it, including *an objective assessment of the facts* of the case and the *applicability of and conformity with the relevant covered agreements*, and make such other findings as will assist the DSB in making the recommendations or in giving the rulings provided for in the covered agreements. Panels should consult regularly with the parties to the dispute and give them adequate opportunity to develop a mutually satisfactory solution.[27]

The appropriate standard of review for panels is thus neither a full revision of the decision before it (i.e. *de novo* review) nor total deference to the Members' administrative agency. Instead, the requirement is for an 'objective assessment' which involves considering evidence and making factual findings.[28] The exact content of the 'objective assessment' is unclear and there has been considerable debate over its limits.[29]

The negotiating history of Article 11 DSU shows serious concerns of the US over the level of deference that panels were to give national agency determinations.[30] Increasingly concerned over the potential of intrusive involvement in domestic determinations the US was keen to incorporate a form of '*Chevron* deference' into the DSU.[31]

US administrative law is particularly sensitive to the relationship between separate branches of government and the appropriate scope of involvement of one in the affairs of another. Under the *Chevron* doctrine, in instances of delegated authority, both agency and courts are to abide by Congress' intent where it is clear.[32] Where Congress' intent under the delegating legislation is not clear the agency's interpretation of the legislation (and thus its duties and how it carries them out) is to be deferred to so long as it is not unreasonable.[33] In practice this creates a hierarchy of authority: Congress' wishes are to be given priority where clear; failing that, where its instructions are unclear (intentionally or inadvertently) the agency's judgment is to be given priority.[34] Only where the agency acts unreasonably is the judiciary to review its acts. The reasons given for such deference are debated although four bases have been suggested:

> The Court suggested that the judiciary should defer to agencies because (1) Congress intends the courts to do so, (2) agencies exercise delegated legislative power when they

---

27 Appellate Body Report *European Communities – Measures Concerning Meat and Meat Products*, 16 January 1998, WT/DS26/AB/R and WT/DS48/AB/R para 116 *(emphasis in original)*.

28 ibid para 133.

29 Ross Becroft, *The Standard of Review in WTO Dispute Settlement: Critique and Development* (Edward Elgar 2012) 50–52.

30 Indicated in interviews conducted by John H Jackson: Steven P Croley and John H Jackson, 'WTO Dispute Procedures, Standard of Review, and Deference to National Governments' (1996) 90 *American Journal of International Law* 193, 194–95.

31 ibid 194–95.

32 *Chevron USA Inc v Natural Resources Defense Council, Inc*, 467 US 837 (1984).

33 ibid 842–44.

34 ibid 865–66.

issue interpretations, (3) agencies are more politically accountable than courts, and (4) agencies have the necessary technical expertise that courts often lack.[35]

This approach is designed to 'foster democratic values by ensuring that policy decisions are being made by politically responsible bodies'.[36] It is thus a form of 'counter-*Marbury* for the administrative state'[37] concerned with protecting the decisions of agencies from intrusive judicial involvement. *Chevron* is one of the most cited cases in US law, more than three foundational US Supreme Court decisions combined:[38] *Marbury v Madison*, *Brown v Board of Education*, and *Roe v Wade*.[39] At its heart, *Chevron* deference aims to ensure the legitimacy of decision-making via horizontal balances (i.e. between the branches of government and the exercise of their powers through delegation). At the WTO it would ensure that national agency determinations (which are politically accountable, at least within some systems) could not be unduly intruded upon by a supranational body which does not have equivalent accountability structures in place.

Understandably, the other participants in the Uruguay Round who did not share the same constitutional settlement and culture of the US were concerned that such an approach would limit the potential effect of panels, restricting their ability to examine national measures. The result was deadlock.[40] A resolution was found by accepting Art 11 DSU in its current form but incorporating a more restrictive standard of review under Article 17.6 ADA. The more restrictive standard under Article 17.6 ADA was then to be reappraised for potential wider application (this did not happen).[41]

Article 17.6 ADA sets out instruction for the standard of review for both facts and law. On the appropriate standard of review for facts it states:

> in its assessment of the facts of the matter, the Panel shall determine whether the authorities' establishment of the facts was proper and whether their evaluation of those facts was unbiased and objective. If the establishment of the facts was proper and the evaluation was unbiased and objective, *even though the Panel might have reached a different conclusion, the evaluation shall not be overturned*;[42]

On the standard of review of law, panels are directed that:

> the Panel shall interpret the relevant provisions of the Agreement in accordance with customary rules of interpretation of public international law. *Where the Panel finds that a*

---

35 Editorial, 'Justifying the Chevron Doctrine: Insights from the Rule of Lenity' (2010) 123 *Harvard Law Review* 2043, 2043–44.

36 ibid 2063. This has been strengthened by the Supreme Court's decision in *Coeur Alaska, Inc v Southeast Alaska Conservation Council*, 557 US 1 (2009) in which the Court retreated from previous decisions that had served to undermine *Chevron* deference, notably *United States v Mead Corp*, 533 US 218 (2001).

37 Stephen G Breyer and others, *Administrative Law and Regulatory Policy: Problems, Text, and Cases* (6th edn, Aspen 2006) 246.

38 ibid.

39 5 US 137 (1803), 347 US 483 (1954) and 410 US 113 (1973) respectively.

40 On the negotiating history of art 11 DSU, Matthias Oesch, *Standards of Review in WTO Dispute Resolution* (OUP 2003) 72–80.

41 Decision on Review of art 17.6 of the Agreement on Implementation of art VI of the General Agreement on Tariffs and Trade 1994, adopted by the Trade Negotiations Committee, 15 December 1993 (1994) 33 *ILM* 1140.

42 Emphasis added.

relevant provision of the Agreement admits of more than one permissible interpretation, the Panel shall find the authorities' measure to be in conformity with the Agreement if it rests upon one of those permissible interpretations.[43]

The clear nature of the bargain struck, and the well-known nature of *Chevron* deference, created an expectation that Article 17.6 ADA would produce results in accordance with (particularly the US') expectations. However, as will be seen below, the outcome has been quite distinct. Meanwhile, Article 11 DSU has been understood by panels as focusing on their fact-finding role in the dispute settlement system.[44]

The Judicialization of the Appellate Body

Contrary to the expectations of negotiators identified earlier, the Appellate Body has taken on the mantle of an international judicial body, a 'World Trade Court'.[45] This development, by no means inevitable, has had a profound influence on the way that the Appellate Body examines cases before it.[46]

The first seven members of the Appellate Body were instrumental in defining its role as it stands today. In the words of one current Appellate Body member, they 'shared a nearly missionary belief in the importance of the task entrusted to them'.[47] The Appellate Body has subsequently sought to maintain its legitimacy, acting as a 'strategic quasi-judicial actor'[48] through decisions of particular 'constitutional' importance.[49] We might identify *US – Gasoline*[50] (confirming the position of the WTO within the wider firmament of international law) and *US – Shrimp Turtle*[51] (setting out the scope of non-WTO obligations in the interpretative process of the Appellate Body) amongst others of particular interest.[52] Aside from these decisions, the Appellate Body has also developed its own Working Procedures to help clarify and develop the limited guidance left by the DSU.[53]

---

43 Emphasis added.
44 See generally, Michelle Grando, *Evidence, Proof, and Fact-Finding in WTO Dispute Settlement* (OUP 2009) ch 5. This tension is heightened due to the Appellate Body's inability to complete incomplete factual records.
45 Claus-Dieter Ehlermann (n 26). See also: Gregory Messenger, *The Development of World Trade Organization Law: Examining Change in International Law* (OUP 2016), chapter 2.
46 Peter Van Den Bossche (n 20) 63–64. Also, Peter Van Den Bossche, 'From Afterthought to Centerpiece: The WTO Appellate Body and its Rise to Prominence in the World Trading System' *Maastricht Faculty of Law Working Paper* 2005/1.
47 Peter Van Den Bossche (n 20) 69, 'most, if not all, members appointed in November 1995 shared a nearly missionary belief in the importance of the task entrusted to them'.
48 James McCall Smith, 'WTO Dispute Settlement: The Politics of Appellate Body Rulings' (2003) 2 *World Trade Review* 65, 79. See also Ingo Venzke, *How Interpretation Makes International Law: On Semantic Change and Normative Twists* (OUP 2014) 188–95.
49 Deborah Z Cass, 'The "Constitutionalization" of International Trade Law: Judicial Norm Generation as the Engine of Constitutional Development in International Trade' (2001) 12 *European Journal of International Law* 39.
50 Appellate Body Report *United States – Standards for Reformulated and Conventional Gasoline*, 29 April 1996, WT/DS2/AB/R, para 17.
51 Appellate Body Report *United States – Import Prohibition of Certain Shrimp and Shrimp Products*, 12 October 1998, WT/DS58/AB/R.
52 John H Jackson, 'The Varied Policies of International Juridical Bodies – Reflections on Theory and Practice' (2004) 25 *Michigan Journal of International Law* 869.
53 Currently: *Working Procedures for Appellate Review*, 16 August 2010, WT/AB/WP/6.

Among the notable innovations, Van den Bossche has identified Rule 4 of the Working Procedures, which sets out a mechanism for the 'exchange of views' between all members before finalizing a report, as a key way to resolve the dangers of inconsistency and reduced authority that the three member divisions may otherwise have caused.[54] More generally the Working Procedures have served to ensure the judicial character of the procedures at the Appellate Body as opposed to the more informal pre-WTO dispute settlement practices.[55]

Taking the embedded textual focus stemming from the DSU[56] and the Appellate Body's desire to establish a mandate as a global trade court, the result is a balance between a textual focus in interpreting the covered agreements and, insofar as this textual approach allows, deference to Members' own determinations.[57] The key point to note here is how the legal instruments constituting the Appellate Body as an institution influence its identity, though not necessarily as expected: the individual actions and priorities of the actors involved have played an important part in its development.

Reappraising Article 17.6 ADA: The Zeroing 'Saga'

The development of an independent judicial identity on the part of the Appellate Body has had a lasting impact on the way in which it interprets the covered agreements, as has the US' expectation of how it was to perform. For our purposes, the specific provision made for the standard of review in the area of anti-dumping investigations is of interest.

Anti-Dumping and the Practice of Zeroing

Anti-dumping duties are a form of contingent protection in that they allow Members to impose duties on goods sold at below normal value (dumped) which cause or threaten to cause injury to a domestic industry.[58] Dumping is not (in most cases) a governmental act, rather it is private and thus not regulated directly by the WTO which concerns itself primarily with public (i.e. governmental) action (though Article VI GATT does 'condemn' dumping where it causes injury). While dumping itself is not regulated, the response by Members to it (the introduction of anti-dumping duties) is. The introduction of anti-dumping duties requires an investigation into the circumstances and value of the goods in question. Dumping occurs where the normal value of the good is greater than its export price, with the difference constituting the margin of dumping. The margin of dumping determines the level of duties that may be introduced.[59]

The calculation of anti-dumping duties is a technical exercise that raises a number of challenges for the investigating authority. How should normal value be calculated, for example? One might take average prices, or calculate costs including labour and raw materials. Under

---

54 Peter Van Den Bossche (n 20), 69–71.
55 Robert E Hudec, 'The New Dispute Settlement System of the WTO: An Overview of the First Three Years' (1999) 8 *Minnesota Journal of Global Trade* 1.
56 Strengthened by the inclusion of the 'cannot add to or diminish the rights and obligations . . .' provision in the 29 November 1982 Ministerial Declaration, Geneva.
57 This is most notably the case in sanitary and phytosanitary investigations.
58 For an economic analysis, see the relevant sections: Kyle W Bagwell and others, *Law and Economics of Contingent Protection in International Trade* (CUP 2009).
59 Art 9.3 ADA.

Article 2.1 ADA, normal value is the 'comparable price, in the ordinary course of trade, for the like product when destines for consumption in the exporting country'.[60]

Similar challenges arise in calculating the export price. It can be the transaction price (i.e. what is actually paid for the good) or alternatively can be constructed 'on the basis of the price at which the imported products are first resold to an independent buyer, or if the products are not resold to an independent buyer, or not resold in the condition as imported, on such reasonable basis as the authorities may determine'.[61]

When calculating the margin of dumping (that is, the difference between the normal value and export price) the ADA gives some guidance: 'margins of dumping . . . shall normally be established on the basis of a comparison of a weighted average normal value with a weighted average of prices of all comparable export transactions or by a comparison of normal value and export prices on a transaction-to-transaction basis'.[62] While the ADA gives guidance, one area on which it is silent is the practice of 'zeroing'.

When calculating the margin of dumping we could take, broadly speaking, one of two approaches. Where the export value is higher than the normal value, we can identify the difference and attribute it a negative value. Alternatively we can attribute it a zero (hence the term). By calculating the margin in this second way, the value of the anti-dumping duties is higher than it would be otherwise. In essence, zeroing disregards negative contributions to the calculation of the dumping margin and instead only takes into account the positive values.

There are different forms of zeroing. The two most common are 'model zeroing' and 'simple zeroing'. In the case of model zeroing, the practice involves separating products into different types or categories (models) and then calculating dumping margins by comparing the weighted average normal value and the weighted average export price for each model. Where the margin is negative for that model (i.e. export price is higher than normal value) the number is set to zero. Where positive, it is added to the general calculation. In the case of simple zeroing, the comparison is between the prices of individual export transactions against monthly weighted average normal values. Where the export price is higher than the weighted average normal value, the negative figure is set to zero. Thus in both cases, the dumping margin is greater than it would be if the 'zeroed' values where calculated without having been set to zero.[63]

This has been the most contentious area in anti-dumping case law: numerous disputes, conflicts between panels and the Appellate Body, heated criticisms in the Dispute Settlement Body, and political ramifications in national arenas.[64] The question of whether zeroing itself is compliant with WTO law is not of itself a particularly problematic one: it is the relationship

---

60 Note that the use of 'like products' under the ADA is not the same as under art I GATT or art III GATT. Note under art 2.6 ADA: 'Throughout this Agreement the term "like product" ("produit similaire") shall be interpreted to mean a product which is identical, ie alike in all respects to the product under consideration, or in the absence of such a product, another product which, although not alike in all respects, has characteristics closely resembling those of the product under consideration'.

61 Art 2.3 ADA.

62 Art 2.4.2 ADA.

63 For a more detailed account of the different forms of zeroing: Tania Voon, 'The End of Zeroing? Reflections Following the WTO Appellate Body's Latest Missive' (2007) 34 *Legal Issues of Economic Integration* 211; Bernard Hoekman and Jasper Wauters, 'US Compliance with WTO Rulings on Zeroing in Anti-Dumping' (2011) 10 *World Trade Review* 5.

64 For a table of zeroing disputes: Dukguen Ahn and Patrick A Messerlin, '*United States – Anti-Dumping Measures on Certain Shrimp and Diamond Sawblades from China*: never ending zeroing in the WTO?' (2014) 13 *World Trade Review* 267, 274.

between the practice as reviewed by panels and the Appellate Body and the expectations of the Membership (and in particular the US) that has made it a flashpoint.

Litigious Ping-Pong: The Treatment of Zeroing at the WTO

The ADA is superficially silent on zeroing: it neither prohibits nor permits the practice. *EC – Bed Linen* was the first WTO case to examine this issue at the WTO. The panel found against the EC on its use of zeroing, a finding upheld by the Appellate Body.[65]

In the wake of this decision, the EU came into compliance with commendable alacrity. Though Article 21.5 DSU proceedings continued, they were largely supportive of the EC's legal reform in the wake of the Appellate Body report.[66] In hindsight it is not particularly surprising: while zeroing was arguably within the legitimate scope of interpretations of calculation methods permitted by the ADA, a specific finding against it left little room for discussion.

Though *EC – Bed Linen* ruled out the use of zeroing, technically this was only with regard to 'model zeroing'. Over the following years the US found a number of its anti-dumping investigations or anti-dumping legislations challenged at the WTO.[67] In each instance, zeroing was prohibited, narrowing the scope of the possible use of the methodology until at last there was no scope for zeroing in any instance. With the exception of a 'rogue' panel rejecting the reasoning of prior Appellate Body reasoning in *US – Final Anti-dumping Measures on Stainless Steel from Mexico*, the WTO view (and that of the Membership) was that the US was intransigent in its instance on using zeroing in anti-dumping investigations.[68] The US' continued use of zeroing was a non-compliance event, roundly criticized by the Membership. It is worth noting here the nature of DSB meetings and their process: in essence, Members take turns in identifying and questioning continued non-compliance by other Members. In the face of such criticism, the US' position on zeroing seemed wilful.

The *US – Continued Existence and Application of Zeroing Methodology* dispute formalized these concerns, challenging the US' position and gaining a definitive statement on the illegality of zeroing as a method for calculating anti-dumping duties. In the Appellate Body report, a concurring opinion directly clarified the situation. Acknowledging that the dispute over zeroing had been reasonable given the ambiguity of the text, and the underlying rationale of the measures, nonetheless the final statement was clear:

> There are arguments of substance made on both sides; but one issue is unavoidable. In matters of adjudication, there must be an end to every great debate. The Appellate Body exists to clarify the meaning of the covered agreements. On the question of zeroing it has spoken definitively. Its decisions have been adopted by the DSB. The membership

---

65 Panel Report *EC – Anti-dumping Duties on Imports of Cotton Type Bed Linen from India*, 30 October 2000, WT/DS141/R, para 6.119; Appellate Body Report *EC – Anti-dumping Duties on Imports of Cotton Type Bed Linen from India*, 1 March 2001, WT/DS141/AB/R, para 66.

66 The art 21.5 panel found in favour of the EC, while the Appellate Body reversed only one finding: Appellate Body Report *EC – Anti-dumping Duties on Imports of Cotton Type Bed Linen from India (art 21.5)*, 8 April 2003, WT/DS141/AB/RW, para 146.

67 For instance: *US – Final Dumping Determination on Softwood Lumber from Canada* (DS261); *US – Laws, Regulations and Methodology for Calculating Dumping Margins* (DS 294); *US – Final Dumping Determination on Softwood Lumber from Canada (art 21.5)* (DS 264/RW); *US – Measures Relating to Zeroing and Sunset Reviews* (DS 322).

68 'Systemic non-compliance': Dukguen Ahn and Patrick A Messerlin (n 64) 275.

of the WTO is entitled to rely upon these outcomes. Whatever the difficulty of interpreting the meaning of 'dumping', it cannot bear a meaning that is both exporter-specific and transaction-specific. We have sought to elucidate the notion of permissibility in the second sentence of article 17(6)(ii). The range of meanings that may constitute a permissible interpretation does not encompass meanings of such wide variability, and even contradiction, so as to accommodate the two rival interpretations. One must prevail. The Appellate Body has decided the matter. At a point in every debate, there comes a time when it is more important for the system of dispute resolution to have a definitive outcome, than further to pick over the entrails of battles past. With respect to zeroing, that time has come.[69]

Indeed, the Appellate Body affirmed its authority over the WTO through a number of interpretative moves.[70] It stated that Appellate Body reports are binding under the DSU, a largely uncontested claim.[71] It continued that the precedential value of reports aids in the fulfilment of the aims of the DSU (specifically finding expression in Art 3.2 DSU), and that the continuity of reports, forming the WTO *acquis*, is thus essential in creating legitimate expectations and ensuring security and predictability to the WTO system.[72] While the basis for such claims may be contentious, the WTO has largely followed this approach, hence the surprise when the panel in *US – Stainless Steel (Mexico)* refused to follow prior Appellate Body reasoning. Most importantly and most strongly, it repeated its statement from *US – Stainless Steel (Mexico)* that:

> [the] creation of the Appellate Body by WTO Members to review legal interpretations developed by panels shows that Members recognized the importance of consistency and stability in the interpretation of their rights and obligations under the covered agreements.[73]

Whatever the role of the Appellate Body may play in its current form, it is questionable that this was the original intention of the Membership, especially in light of the evidence above. Zeroing was neither prohibited nor permitted, thus, from a *Chevron* inspired perspective, one would expect a respectful distancing on the part of the WTO dispute settlement institutions. These institutions, however, have their own priorities, quite distinct from those the US would expect them to have. It is a complex picture, with reasonable positions on both sides.

Irrespective, the narrative relating to zeroing was framed in terms of compliance and systemic integrity of the WTO legal system. The behaviour of the US, however, was not based on bull-headedness but rather a specific expression of frustration with the inability to reconcile expectations with outcomes.

---

69 Appellate Body Report *US – Continued Existence and Application of Zeroing Methodology*, 4 February 2009, WT/DS350/AB/R, para 312.

70 ibid para 362.

71 Though, Judith H Bello, 'The WTO Dispute Settlement Understanding: Less is More' (1996) 90 *American Journal of International Law* 416; Judith H Bello, 'Review: *The Jurisprudence of the GATT and the WTO: Insights on Treaty Law and Economic Relations* by John H Jackson' (2001) 95 *American Journal of International Law* 984.

72 Thus constituting 'established practice' of the institution: art2(1)(j) Vienna Convention on the Law of Treaties between States and International Organizations or between International Organizations, 21 March 1986, UN Doc A/CONF 129/15.

73 Appellate Body Report *US – Final Anti-Dumping Measures on Stainless Steel from Mexico*, 30 April 2008, WT/DS344/AB/R, para 161.

Interpreting the US Response to the Zeroing Cases

The reticence of the US to comply with its obligations under the Anti-Dumping Agreement has stimulated questions over the specific problems relating to anti-dumping law and its questionable underlying economic coherence.[74] It has also raised concerns over compliance procedures and effectiveness of the WTO dispute settlement system, one that has thus far been viewed positively. The refusal of the Panel in *US – Stainless Steel (Mexico)* to follow the Appellate Body's previous findings likewise raised eyebrows.[75] Underlying all of these debates is a common presumption: notably, that the US (for better or worse) has lost the argument on zeroing and as the lone recalcitrant Member, insisted on its own approach to anti-dumping calculations and ignored the practice and pleas of the Membership.[76]

Instead of engaging with the question of whether the Appellate Body was correct in this decisions, or whether the US is regressing to a 'GATT-era' approach to compliance, here the focus is somewhat different. Why is it that the US insisted on pursuing zeroing as a legitimate form of calculation for anti-dumping margins for so long? Note, for example, the desire to reform the rules on anti-dumping following the Doha Declaration,[77] where amongst the contentious issues has been the question of zeroing. Positions on this topic ranged from a 'total prohibition of zeroing irrespective of the comparison methodology used and in respect of all proceedings to a demand that zeroing be specifically authorized in all contexts'.[78]

It cannot simply be that the US prefers to introduce greater anti-dumping duties than it otherwise would be able to: the same is true of the EU which nonetheless came into compliance following the *EC – Bed Linen* dispute.[79] Nor is it the case with other Members who not only do not use the zeroing methodology but have explicitly prohibited it under more recently concluded free trade agreements.[80] There is, of course, considerable political pressure within the US, especially within Congress. However, rather than viewing such hostility through a lens of self-interest, here it is suggested that such a response is symptomatic of a deeper conflict.

The argument here is that the US' recalcitrance is directly related to its frustrated expectations. The specific wording of Article 17.6 ADA, already a compromise from a US perspective, was to ensure that a deferential standard of review be applied, at the least in anti-dumping disputes. The aim of Article 17.6 was clear, and the context from which it came, the US' own *Chevron* doctrine, well known. Instead, the Appellate Body repeatedly rejected the use of zeroing, in a wide range of different situations from original investigations to reviews.

It is the nature of WTO law to encroach upon any number of highly contentious areas: the protection of human health, biodiversity, moral standards, national security, and environmental protection. The subject matter of the zeroing disputes does not display the same level of emotive resonance, and yet, the response to these cases has been impassioned. Though

---

74 This has been a long-standing concern: Joseph Stiglitz, 'Dumping on Free Trade: The US Import Trade Laws' (1997) 64 *Southern Economic Journal* 402.

75 Sungjoon Cho, 'A WTO Panel Openly Rejects the Appellate Body's "Zeroing" Case Law', 12 *ASIL Insight* 3 (11 March 2008); Petros Mavroidis, *Trade in Goods* (2nd edn, OUP 2012) 439.

76 Bernard Hoekman and Jasper Wauters (n 63) 38ff.

77 Doha Ministerial Declaration, 20 November 2001, WT/MIN(01)/DEC/1, para 28.

78 Negotiating Group on Rules, 'New Draft Consolidated Chair Texts of the AD and SCM Agreements', 19 December 2008, TN/RL/W/236, 6.

79 The EU was, with the US, the principal user of anti-dumping duties during the GATT years, hence their unity in negotiations on the ADA, Petros Mavroidis (n 75) 424.

80 For example, art 2.8(1)(h) Singapore-Jordan Free Trade Agreement, 29 April 2004 <www.fta.gov.sg/fta_sjfta. asp?hl=5> accessed 15 January 2015.

the content of the dispute may be technical, the way in which it is examined is not: it is a direct incursion into the highly developed constitutional tradition of the US. The peculiarity here is that the Appellate Body's interpretative approach is largely aimed toward ensuring its legitimacy and protecting it from exactly this sort of criticism. Hence, the difference to NAFTA panels where the directions given are considerably more detailed.[81]

Note, the US response to the Appellate Body report in *United States – Anti-dumping measures on certain hot rolled steel products from Japan*:[82]

> The specific and unique provisions in article 17.6 had been deliberately included to provide a special standard of review in anti-dumping investigations, intended to prevent panels from second-guessing the factual and legal determinations made by national authorities, and were an important part of the balance of rights and obligations assumed by the Members in agreeing to the Anti-Dumping Agreement. They could not be minimized or eliminated by dispute settlement reports. In this connection, the Appellate Body had aptly observed in its report in the case on 'Hormones' that to adopt a standard of review that was not clearly rooted in the text of a specific Agreement may well amount to changing the finely drawn balance in the competencies conceded by Members and those jurisdictional competencies retained by Members for themselves. As stated by the Appellate Body, neither a panel or the Appellate Body was authorized to do that.[83]

The US statement is both a call to the past deal on Article 11 DSU and the compromise relating to Article 17.6 ADA, and a plea to return to the proper reading of the text of the DSU as the US understands it.

What is of particular interest is that the Appellate Body has pursued the line on zeroing in a less deferential mode exactly because that is how it understands its direction from the DSU and its place in the WTO. Note, for example, how Article 3.2 DSU is both the motivation for criticism of the Appellate Body's position in failing to appreciate the role of Article 17.6 ADA and thus 'add[ing] to or diminish[ing] the rights and obligations provided in the covered agreements', and at the same time is the basis for the Appellate Body's own position in 'providing security and predictability to the multilateral trading system'.[84]

Concluding Remarks: Insights from Expectations

The purpose of this chapter has not been to draw a negative image of the potential of reform for international economic law at either a substantive or institutional level (if indeed we can truly draw such a distinction). Rather, the aim has been, first, to identify the limitations of legal reform as the cure for systemic problems and second, to draw attention to the relationship between the frustrated expectations of legal reform and the conception of how law functions from the point of view of the reformer.

By creating a more effective mechanism for the settlement of disputes, and a more developed set of rules for the conduct of anti-dumping investigations, Members might have

---

81 The contrast is especially notable in the softwood lumber dispute: Chios Carmody, 'Softwood Lumber Dispute (2001–2006)' (2006) 100 *American Journal of International Law* 664, 673.

82 Appellate Body Report *United States – Anti-dumping Measures on Certain Hot-rolled Steel Products from Japan*, 24 July 2001, WT/DS184/AB/R.

83 Minutes of Meeting, Dispute Settlement Body, 2 October 2001, WT/DSB/M/108, para 70 (footnote omitted).

84 Art 3.2 DSU. See (n 69) ff and corresponding text.

expected greater clarity and certainty rather than less. In the context of such widespread legal reform and institution building, a few gaps in the text might have seemed entirely reasonable. Yet it is these gaps that have become the battleground for disputes, disputes that are necessarily resolved by the dispute settlement (i.e. quasi-judicial) branch of the WTO in the face of the paralyzed rule-making (i.e. quasi-legislative) branch. We have seen how the identity of the Appellate Body has made this process both easier (in its willingness to engage in rule-elaboration) but also harder, in that it challenges the fundamental national assumptions of some of the Membership (here notably the US).

Thus instances of reform or legal change that do not produce expected outcomes can help us to find explanations for how the legal framework at the WTO has developed in the way that it has. The clearest of these has been that expecting successful outcomes in one's own interests based on using domestic models of law, or holding assumptions of how institutions will behave as law-appliers, belies the deeply complicated and complex nature of law generally, and legal institutions specifically. In particular it indicates a restricted view of how law focuses in different ways, not only through processes of interpretation and application but also through actors, including newly created institutions. For reform to produce desired outcomes, a greater appreciation of the complexities and multifaceted nature of law is required. We cannot expect institutions to behave as instructed at a fixed point in time, nor the law to be applied in the way in which it has been in other legal systems. Instead, reform must be tempered by sensitivity to law's multifaceted nature, working not only in mechanistic terms but also as a powerful constraint, an empowerer and constitutor of identities both internationally and domestically.[85]

---

85 See further Gregory Messenger (n 45).

10 A History of Success?

Proportionality in International Economic Law

*Valentina Vadi**

> Undoubtedly, philosophers are in the right when they tell us that nothing is great or little otherwise than by comparison.
>
> *Jonathan Swift*, Gulliver's Travels

Introduction

The migration of the proportionality analysis from constitutional law to a number of other areas of law is deemed to be a paradigm of successful legal transplant. While some aspects of proportionality analysis are deeply ingrained in international trade law and European Union (EU) law, proportionality analysis has gradually found its way to international investment law and arbitration. Proportionality is often depicted as an ideal mechanism for balancing opposing interests and thus creating equilibrium between different public goods – namely economic growth spurred by foreign direct investment and trade on the one hand, and other public interests on the other.

Can proportionality analysis be a useful tool of judicial governance in international economic law to promote the perceived legitimacy of the latter? Can it facilitate the consideration of the commonweal in investment economic law and/or contribute to the humanization of the same? If so, can one size of proportionality analysis fit all needs in international trade, international investment law and EU law? Or should a more nuanced and varied understanding of proportionality – as adopted by the Court of Justice of the European Union (CJEU) – be adopted to cope with different needs in various institutional settings? What are, if any, the possible shortcomings of proportionality analysis? How can these shortcomings be addressed?

The chapter shows that while the concept of proportionality has analytical merits, it also presents a number of pitfalls when applied to the context of economic disputes. While proportionality is a general principle of EU law,[1] and is deeply ingrained in international trade law, no consensus seems to have arisen with regard to its legal status in international law. If proportionality was a general principle of law, or was deemed to reflect state practice (and thus constitute an element of customary law) it could be eventually used in international investment law and arbitration as part of the applicable law or as a matter of treaty interpretation. In the uncertainty as to the legal status of proportionality in international law, the legal grounds for considering proportionality in investor-state arbitration can be problematic. Certainly, if the applicable law is the law of the host state and this law includes the

---

* Professor of international economic law, Lancaster University, United Kingdom.
1 See generally Evelyn Ellis (ed), *The Principle of Proportionality in the Laws of Europe* (Hart Publishing 1999).

proportionality principle, such principle becomes relevant in the context of investment treaty arbitration. This chapter concludes that more comparative and international law studies are needed to ascertain the legal status of proportionality in international law.

The chapter proceeds as follows. *First*, after a brief introduction, it highlights the promises and pitfalls of the proportionality analysis. *Second*, it focuses on the specific migration of the notion of proportionality from its constitutional matrix to the regional sphere, focusing on EU law as a case study of successful legal migration. *Third*, it investigates the use of the proportionality analysis in international investment law and arbitration. *Fourth*, it examines the use of the proportionality analysis in international trade law. *Fifth*, it addresses some critical methodological questions concerning the migration of constitutional ideas and the identification of general principles of law. The conclusions will then sum up the key arguments of the study.

Proportionality: A Cosmopolitan Destiny?

Proportionality has moved across a wide range of national, regional and international legal systems.[2] As a legal concept, proportionality expresses the idea that there should be a balance between competing objectives or values. In a number of constitutional traditions, the concept of proportionality is understood as a methodological framework for balancing conflicting values and aiming at delimiting the legitimate exercise of state authority.[3]

Conceived as a tool for reviewing state conduct (and thus closely connected with the aim of ensuring good governance), the proportionality test is usually articulated in three main phases; suitability, necessity and proportionality.[4] The suitability test requires that the adopted measure be appropriate to achieve the stated aims. There must be a rational, logical and causal relationship between the measure and its objectives. The necessity test aims at verifying that the measure was the least restrictive available alternative or that no less drastic means were available. The proportionality test in the narrow sense requires adjudicators to ascertain that the benefit obtained from realizing the objective exceeds the harm caused by the adopted measure.

The main reason for proportionality's success in the marketplace of ideas is its ability to: (1) restrain the exercise of public authority; (2) shape judicial review; and (3) manage private actors' expectations. This section examines these three functions of the proportionality analysis.

First, proportionality is based on 'a culture of justification' which 'requires that governments should provide substantive justification for all their actions . . .'.[5] In order to be legitimate, a governmental action must be 'justified in terms of its "cogency" and its capacity for "persuasion," that is, in terms of its rationality, reasonableness',[6] and efficiency.[7]

---

2 Moshe Cohen-Elya and Iddo Porat, *Proportionality and Constitutional Culture* (CUP 2012) 2, noting that in the past decades proportionality has become 'one of the most prominent instances of the successful migration of constitutional ideas'.

3 Jacco Bomhoff, 'Balancing, the Global and the Local: Judicial Balancing as a Problematic Topic in Comparative (Constitutional) Law' (2008) 31 *Hastings International and Comparative Law Review* 555.

4 Jan H Jans, 'Proportionality Revisited' (2000) 27 *Legal Issues of Economic Integration* 239, 240–41.

5 Moshe Cohen-Eliya and Iddo Porat, 'Proportionality and the Culture of Justification' (2011) 59 *American Journal of Comparative Law* 463, 467.

6 ibid 475.

7 ibid 467.

Proportionality is a 'deliberative methodology',[8] which requires that all of the relevant factors be considered and can insert 'Socratic contestation' in the deliberative process of governmental action.[9] It then requires that a balance be struck according to the importance of the relevant interests depending on the contextual circumstances.

Second, proportionality limits the subjectivity of the adjudicator, empowering courts and tribunals to review state conduct in a significant fashion, and providing a structured, formalized and seemingly objective test. All awards and decisions must state the reasons on which they are based;[10] failure to state such reasons is a ground for annulment of the award.[11] Proportionality also allows adjudicators to adopt nuanced decisions rather than 'all-or-nothing' approaches[12] and to structure their analysis in a framework which 'may produce better and more convincing reasoning, and enable clearer assessment . . . of tribunals', thus enhancing predictability.[13] In addition, proportionality can provide 'a common language that transcends national borders and that allows for dialogue and exchange of information' between courts and tribunals.[14] Proportionality analysis can constitute an entry for non-economic interests as expressed in general principles of law into the argumentative framework of adjudication and thereby help to overcome the fragmentation of international law.[15]

Finally, proportionality can also delimit – and thus indirectly define – the legitimate expectations of private actors vis-à-vis regulatory or other types of governmental interference with their vested rights. Proportionality analysis can 'reduc[e] the sense of defeat for the losing party. As such, it is consensus-oriented because it acknowledges explicitly that there are valid constitutional arguments on both sides and that the arguments outweighed by the opposing ones do not lose thereby their constitutional weight'.[16]

Despite the success of proportionality analysis in a number of fields,[17] its legal status remain unsettled. Some authors contend that proportionality is an emerging general principle of international law,[18] or even an already established one.[19] If one admits that such proposition is true, then such a contention would constitute a formidable entry point for proportionality analysis in supranational adjudication, as adjudicators could refer to

8 Iddo Porat, 'Some Critical Thoughts on Proportionality' in Giorgio Bongiovanni, Giovanni Sartor and Chiara Valentini (eds), *Reasonableness and Law* (Springer 2009) 243, 244.

9 Mattias Kumm, 'The Idea of Socratic Contestation and the Right to Justification: The Point of Rights Based Proportionality Review' (2010) 4 *Law & Ethics Human Rights* 141.

10 See generally Pierre Lalive, 'On the Reasoning of International Arbitral Awards' (2010) 1 *Journal of International Dispute Settlement* 55, 55.

11 Convention on the Settlement of Investment Disputes between States and Nationals of Other States (ICSID Convention or Washington Convention), Washington, 18 March 1965, in force 14 October 1966, 575 UNTS 159, art 52(1).

12 Benedict Kingsbury and Stephan Schill, 'Public Law Concepts to Balance Investors' Rights with State Regulatory Actions in the Public Interest – The Concept of Proportionality' in Stephan Schill (ed), *International Investment Law and Comparative Public Law* (OUP 2010) 75, 79.

13 ibid 103.

14 Cohen-Eliya and Porat, 'Proportionality and the Culture of Justification' (n 5), 472.

15 Stephan Schill, 'Cross-Regime Harmonization through Proportionality Analysis: The Case of International Investment law, the Law of State Immunity and Human Rights' (2012) 27 *ICSID Review FILJ* 87.

16 Wojciech Sadurski, 'Reasonableness and Value Pluralism in Law and Politics' in Giorgio Bongiovanni, Giovanni Sartor and Chiara Valentini (eds), *Reasonableness and Law* (Springer 2009) 129, 145.

17 See generally Alec Stone Sweet and Joseph Mathews, 'Proportionality Balancing and Global Constitutionalism' (2008) 47 *Columbia Journal of Transnational Law* 73, 98–111.

18 Andreas Kulick, *Global Public Interest in International Investment Law* (CUP 2012), 169.

19 See generally Enzo Cannizzaro, *Il principio della proporzionalità nell'ordinamento internazionale* (Giuffré 2000).

proportionality in their awards as either part of the applicable law, under article 42 of the Convention on the Settlement of Investment Disputes between States and Nationals of Other States (ICSID Convention),[20] or as a rule of international law applicable in the relations between the parties under article 31(3)(c) of the Vienna Convention on the Law of Treaties (VCLT).[21] If proportionality is a general principle of law, it can help the interpreter address the high level of indeterminacy of treaty provisions. Others contend that also good faith interpretation, as restated by article 31(1) of the VCLT may require some balancing between the public and the private interest.[22]

Proportionality: The Perils of Success

The migration of the concept of proportionality from constitutional law to the supranational sphere poses a range of challenges. In particular, its viability as the main tool for balancing different interests and values has been challenged on five grounds: (1) institutional competences; (2) scale of values; (3) cultural arguments; (4) incommensurability and (5) overprotection of property rights.

First, proportionality can be perceived as running against the traditional allocation of institutional competences among the executive, the judiciary and the administrative organs. Democratic arguments run against using balancing to review the host state's decisions, because adjudicators would second-guess the decisions of the host state by repeating the original decision-making process.[23] By considering different alternatives to given measures under the necessity test, and by balancing competing interests under the proportionality test the adjudicator interferes with the regulatory autonomy of states, supplanting the role of legitimately deputed decision-makers.[24] The rise of the proportionality analysis 'as a juristic method, rather than a method restricted to legislation, threatens the sharp distinction between legislation and legal interpretation . . .'.[25] As Stone Sweet and Mathews put it, 'balancing can never be dissociated from lawmaking: it requires judges to behave as legislators'.[26] In particular, the necessity test would – almost without exception – invalidate the given measure since the adjudicator can always envisage alternatives *ex post* with the benefit of hindsight.

Second, proportionality does not clarify the scale of values to be used in order to evaluate competing objectives. Even if the given measure passes the suitability and necessity tests, it may be considered to be disproportionate under the third prong of the test, when it is assessed in the light of competing norms and objectives. In this context, as Jans put it 'The central question [i]s what must be proportionate to what'.[27] Proportionality analysis tells us nothing about the scale of values that will determine the final outcome. The fact that proportionality concerns

20 ICSID Convention, art 42.
21 Vienna Convention on the Law of Treaties of 23 May 1969, in force 27 January 1980, UN Treaty Series vol 1155, 331.
22 Benedict Kingsbury and Stephan Schill, 'Investor–State Arbitration as Governance: Fair and Equitable Treatment, Proportionality and the Emerging Global Administrative Law' (2009) *New York University School of Law, Public Law & Legal Research Theory Research Paper Series*, Working Paper No 09–46, 23.
23 Iddo Porat, 'Why All Attempts to Make Judicial Review Balancing Principled Fail?' (Paper presented at the VII World Congress of the International Association of Constitutional Law, Athens, 11–15 June 2007) 7.
24 Kulick, *Global Public Interest in International Investment Law* (n 18) 172.
25 David Kennedy, 'Political Ideology and Comparative Law' in Mauro Bussani and Ugo Mattei (eds) *The Cambridge Companion to Comparative Law* (CUP 2012) 35, 36.
26 Stone Sweet and Mathews, 'Proportionality Balancing and Global Constitutionalism' (n 17) 88.
27 Jans, 'Proportionality Revisited' (n 4) 239.

quantity rather than quality leaves the adjudicator free to select his or her own value system, and the relevant criteria to explain why one value is considered more important than another.[28]

Third, not only can proportionality analysis not take into account the cultural context of a given measure but it also risks importing its specific cultural baggage into the adjudicative process. On the one hand, supranational adjudicators may not be familiar with the background of a given policy measure. As Burke White and von Staden point out, 'prioritization of the values chosen by the polity requires both familiarity with those values and a degree of embeddedness within that polity'.[29] However, supranational adjudicators are far removed from the polities over which they exercise control.

On the other hand, proportionality comes from a certain historical setting,[30] reflecting distrust towards the public administration in the aftermath of WWII.[31] In a number of European countries, constitutional law has gained an increasing primacy since the end of the war and the democratic transitions that followed.[32] Constitutional courts have played a key role in making constitutional law effective,[33] aiming to be an 'impenetrable bulwark against any infringement of the rights of the people'.[34] At the same time, lawyers elaborated the respective constitutions on the basis of 'their understanding of state and society' with 'distinct starting points and trajectories'.[35]

Fourth, some values can be incommensurable.[36] While proportionality assumes measurability (i.e., to be balanced, two competing principles should be based on a common denominator),[37] arguments are made that cost-benefit analysis is flawed with respect to public sector decisions due to the incommensurability of certain values.[38]

Fifth, critical legal theorists contend that 'hegemonic elites' might use proportionality to entrench their values and shift power from the democratic process to the courts[39] and that proportionality might have an 'imperialistic effect', in that it might set aside local constitutional values.[40] In the EU law context, the concept of proportionality has fostered the goal of European integration.[41] With regard to investment law, scholars question whether the application of proportionality in investment arbitration could lead to the overprotection of

---

28 Stone Sweet and Mathews, 'Proportionality Balancing and Global Constitutionalism' (n 17) 89.

29 Wiliam W Burke White and Andreas von Staden, 'Private Litigation in a Public Private Sphere: The Standard of Review in Investor–State Arbitrations' (2010) 35 *Yale Journal of International Law* 283, 336.

30 Cohen-Elya and Porat, *Proportionality and Constitutional Culture* (n 2) 8.

31 Michal Bobek, 'Reasonableness in Administrative Law: A Comparative Reflection on Functional Equivalence' in Giorgio Bongiovanni, Giovanni Sartor and Chiara Valentini (eds) *Reasonableness and Law* (Springer 2009) 311, 323.

32 Miguel Schor, 'Mapping Comparative Judicial Review' (2008) 7 *Washington University Global Studies Law Review* 257, 271.

33 Mauro Cappelletti, 'Repudiating Montesquieu? The Expansion and Legitimacy of "Constitutional Justice"' (1985) 35 *Catholic University Law Review* 191.

34 ibid 191 (quoting Piero Calamandrei).

35 Peer Zumbansen, 'Transnational Comparisons: Theory and Practice of Comparative Law as a Critique of Global Governance' *Osgoode Hall Law School Research Paper No 1/2012*, 19.

36 Cass Sunstein, 'Incommensurability and Valuation in Law' (1994) 92 *Michigan Law Review* 779.

37 Aharon Barak, *Proportionality, Constitutional Rights and Their Limitations* (CUP 2012) 482–84, arguing that a common denominator exists in the form of the marginal social importance of each value.

38 Franck Ackerman and Lisa Heinzerling, *Priceless: On Knowing the Price of Everything and the Value of Nothing* (The New Press 2004).

39 Ran Hirschl, *Towards Juristocracy: The Origins and Consequences of the New Constitutionalism* (Harvard University Press 2004).

40 Cohen-Elya and Porat, *Proportionality and Constitutional Culture* (n 2) 8–9.

41 Paul Craig and Gráinne De Búrca, *EU Law – Text, Cases, and Materials* (5th edn, OUP 2011) 532.

foreign investments.[42] The use of proportionality analysis can lead to the overprotection of investors' rights if it is used in a very exacting fashion. In fact the proportionality analysis can restrict the regulatory power of the state to a large extent if arbitral tribunals do not adopt deferential standards of review.

In conclusion, proportionality – like any conceptual framework – is not a neutral process; rather it is based on the primacy and priority of individual entitlements over the exercise of public powers.[43] The spread of the proportionality analysis highlights 'a shift from a culture of authority to a culture of justification,' which is connected, inter alia, to the rise of the human rights movement which developed after WWII. Whether this entails a neglect of a polity's choices towards a judicial dictatorship or the achievement of a higher rule of law – the ultimate rule of law[44] – is open to debate.

Proportionality in European Union Law

The migration of the proportionality analysis from constitutional law to EU law is a paradigm of successful legal transplant. Proportionality is a general principle of EU law and can be used for reviewing EU action and Member State action that falls within the sphere of EU law.[45] Largely fashioned by the Union Courts, proportionality has subsequently assumed treaty status[46] since the inception of the Maastricht Treaty.[47] The criteria for its application are set out in the Protocol No. 2 on the application of the principles of subsidiarity and proportionality annexed to the treaties.[48]

The numerous reasons for the success of proportionality in EU law address the criticisms moved to proportionality in a seemingly effective fashion. Let us consider how the EU courts have transformed the various challenges posed by the proportionality concept in opportunities. *First*, with regard to institutional competences, the courts have interpreted the concept of proportionality in a flexible manner,[49] conferring it a relative character and showing varying degrees of deference. In some cases, the CJEU has adopted 'a very deferential approach', in others it has conducted 'a quite rigorous and searching examination of the justification for a measure which has been challenged'.[50] In a seminal article, De Búrca noted that 'in reaching decisions, the Court of Justice is influenced not only by what it considers to be the nature and the importance of the interest or right claimed by the applicant, and the nature and importance

---

42 Han Xiuli, 'The Application of the Principle of Proportionality in *Tecmed v Mexico*' (2007) 6 *Chinese Journal of International Law* 635.

43 Maria Sakellaridou, 'La Généalogie de la proportionalité' (Paper presented at the VII World Congress of the International Association of Constitutional Law, Athens, 11–15 June 2007) 20.

44 See generally David M Beatty, *The Ultimate Rule of Law* (OUP 2005).

45 Craig and De Búrca, *EU Law* (n 41) 526. See generally Ellis (ed), *The Principle of Proportionality in the Laws of Europe* (n 1); Nicholas Emiliou, *The Principle of Proportionality in European Law: A Comparative Study* (Kluwer 1996).

46 Art 5 TEU, stating that stating that 'any action by the Community shall not go beyond what is necessary to achieve the objectives of this Treaty'.

47 The Treaty on European Union (TEU), signed on 7 February 1992, in force on 1 November 1993.

48 Protocol (No 2) on the application of the principles of subsidiarity and proportionality, annexed to the Treaty on European Union and the Treaty on the Functioning of the European Union by the Treaty of Lisbon of 13 December 2007.

49 Tor Inge Harbo, 'The Function of the Proportionality Principle in EU Law' (2010) 16 *European Law Journal* 158.

50 Gráinne De Búrca, 'The Principle of Proportionality and its Application in EC Law' (1993) 13 *Yearbook of European Law* 105, 111–12.

of the objective alleged to be served by the measure, but by the relative expertise, position and overall competence of the Court as against the decision-making authority in assessing those factors'.[51]

Some authors contend that the Court has adopted a stricter proportionality test when assessing national regulation (vertical dimension) and a more lenient approach when assessing Union regulation (horizontal dimension).[52] Therefore, according to these authors, the court will adopt more demanding proportionality test in the former case, requiring the national legislation to choose the less trade restrictive alternative.[53] In such cases, the Court tends to undertake a strict test of proportionality and only the less restrictive measures will be considered as proportionate.[54] Instead, when reviewing Union action, the court will deem the regulatory measure to be disproportionate only if it finds it manifestly inappropriate to achieve the stated objective.[55]

An alternative viewpoint suggests that the proportionality analysis has been interpreted differently according to the various areas it is applied to.[56] For instance, the Court has showed a more deferential approach in the adjudication of public health-related disputes. By contrast, the Court has adopted a strict proportionality test even for Community measures for instance 'where an individual argues that her rights have been unduly restricted by Union action'.[57] There are a number of examples where such measures were deemed to be disproportionate.[58]

Certainly the varied intensity of the proportionality test is not neutral; rather, it is value-laden, expressing the Court's function, that of adjudicating disputes and promoting European integration.[59]

Second, with regard to the scale of values, the case of the CJEU is rather unique, as the Court has recently acquired a mandate to adjudicate on human rights violations, since the Lisbon Treaty[60] conferred binding nature to the Charter of Fundamental Human Rights.[61]

51 ibid.
52 See generally Takis Tridimas, *The General Principles of EU Law* (2nd edn, OUP 2006) chs 3 and 5.
53 Harbo, 'The Function of the Proportionality Principle in EU Law' (n 49) 172.
54 See eg Case 104/75, *de Peijper* [1976] ECR 613, deeming a national measure conditioning the importation of medical products to the obtainment of certain documents to be disproportionate as a means to protect public health; Case 120/78 *Rewe-Zentral AG v Bundesmonopolverwaltung für Branntwein* [1979] ECR 649, deeming that the measure requiring a minimum alcohol content for a beverage was not necessary to protect consumers as less restrictive ways for protecting them could be envisaged, such as labelling.
55 Harbo, 'The Function of Proportionality Principle in EU Law' (n 49) 172. For instance, in *Hauer*, the Court found that the Community regulatory measure was proportionate and thus not infringing the right to property. The claimant claimed that a Community regulation prohibiting the planting of new vines on certain lands for three years violated her rights to property and to pursue a trade. The claim was dismissed as the Court emphasized that the regulation pursued objectives of general interest and did not constitute a disproportionate and intolerable interference with the property rights of the owner. The prohibition of the new planting of vines for a limited period of time was justified by the objectives of general interest pursued by the Community, namely the reduction of production surpluses and the restructuring of the European wine industry. Case 44/79, *Liselotte Hauer v Land Rheinland-Phalz* [1979] ECR 3727.
56 Harbo, 'The Function of the Proportionality Principle in EU Law' (n 49) 172.
57 Craig and De Búrca, *EU Law* (n 41), 529.
58 See eg Case 114/76 *Bela-Muhle v Grows Farm* (the *Skimmed Milk* Case) [1977] ECR 1211, holding that a regulation requiring animal foodstuff producers to buy skimmed milk powder at a price three times more expensive than its current value was disproportionate.
59 ibid.
60 Treaty of Lisbon Amending the Treaty on European Union and the Treaty Establishing the European Community, 13 December 2007, 2007 OJ (C306) 1.
61 Charter of Fundamental Rights of the European Union, OJ C 364/1 (2000).

Not only has the European Union integrated the consideration of human rights in its treaty texts, but it is also negotiating its accession to the European Convention on Human Rights (ECHR).[62] Even before these notable institutional developments, since the early 1970s, the Court has considered fundamental rights to be general principles of European law, and has referred to the European Convention on Human Rights as 'a source of inspiration'.[63] Therefore, favouring the objective of European integration does not necessarily entail a predominance of economic interests vis-à-vis other non-economic values as the latter also constitute part of the European project. This is particularly evident in a number of cases.[64]

Third, with regard to the cultural arguments, while the Court has derived the proportionality concept from the legal orders of some Member States,[65] its application of the concept has at times converged[66] and at times diverged from that of national courts.[67] More interestingly, when reviewing state measures the CJEU has acknowledged the possibility of different approaches by Member States to similar issues,[68] and has interpreted proportionality 'in the light of the Member State's particular values, notwithstanding that those values differ from those of other Member States'.[69] In a few cases, the invocation of a norm as reflecting constitutional history and identity has been accepted as a ground for relaxing the proportionality test.[70]

Fourth, with regard to incommensurability, the Court has found a common denominator of the various interests at stake in their social function. Finally, with regard to the eventual overprotection of property rights, relying on the jurisprudence of the European Court of Human Rights, the ECJ has pointed out that such rights are not absolute and there may be cases in which private interests may be limited for the commonweal.[71] While this does not mean that all of the cases adjudicated by the CJEU have reached an optimal balance between

---

62 Convention for the Protection of Human Rights and Fundamental Freedoms, 4 November 1950, in force 3 September 1953, 213 UNTS 222.

63 Gráinne De Búrca, 'After the EU Charter of Fundamental Rights: The Court of Justice as a Human Rights Adjudicator?' (2013) 14 *Maastricht Journal of European and Comparative Law* 168, 170.

64 Cases C-402/05 P and 415/05 P *Kadi and Al Barakaat International Foundation* [2008] ECR I-6351, annulling the regulation that froze the funds of Mr Kadi and finding that such measure infringed the right of effective judicial review, and the right to property. The regulation had given effect to resolutions of the United Nations Security Council (UNSC) adopted against the Al-Qaeda; Case C-36/2002, *Omega Spielhallen und Automatenaufstellungs GmbH v Oberbürgermeisterin der Bundesstadt Bonn* [2004] ECR I-9609, upholding a German ban on the commercialization of violent games for protecting public policy and human dignity.

65 Harbo, 'The Function of the Proportionality Principle in EU Law' (n 49) 172.

66 See eg Case 44/79, *Liselotte Hauer v Land Rheinland-Phalz* [1979] ECR 3727 in which both the national court and the ECJ held that the relevant Community regulation was proportionate to the stated objective.

67 See eg Case 11/70, *Internationale Handelsgesellschaft v Einfuhr und Vorratstelle für Getreide und Futtermittel* [1970] ECR 1125 in which the national court had found that Community measure was disproportionate, while the Court deemed it proportionate to the stated objective.

68 Case C-108/96 *Criminal Proceedings against Dennis Mac Quen et al* [2001] ECR I-837 para 34, stating that 'the mere fact that a Member State has chosen a system of protection different from that adopted by another Member State cannot affect the appraisal of the need for and the proportionality of the provisions adopted'.

69 Craig and De Búrca, *EU Law* (n 41) 532.

70 Case C-208/09, *Sayn Wittgenstein* [2010] ECR I-13693 paras 83 and 92.

71 See eg C-331/88 *R v Minister for Agriculture, Fisheries and Food, ex p Fedesa* [1990] ECR I-4023, upholding a Community regulation prohibiting the use of hormones in meat production; and Case C-210/03 *Swedish Match AB and Swedish Match UK Ltd* [2004] ECR I-11893, paras 56–58, upholding the ban on tobacco for oral use deeming it to be proportionate the stated objective, namely the protection of public health, and acknowledging that other measures such as labelling could not achieve the same preventive effect.

the competing interests,[72] at least there is an indication that this concern has been considered if not addressed by the CJEU.

In conclusion, proportionality has migrated successfully from the national legal systems of the EU Member States to the EU legal system. On the one hand, the EU courts have relied on the legal heritage of the Member States to establish proportionality as a general principle of EU law. On the other, they have interpreted the concept of proportionality in a flexible manner – so flexible as to transcend the classical understanding of proportionality – shaping and adapting it to the various needs of European integration and the parallel protection of human rights and fundamental freedoms.

Ultimately, the migration of proportionality from the national realm to the regional level may constitute a case of 'overfitting legal transplant', i.e. a legal transplant which 'work[s] even "better" in the transplant than in the origin country',[73] fitting particularly well in the peculiar structure of the European Union. In fact, the flexible interpretation of the concept which is at times expanded and at times restricted as if it was an accordion allows the courts of the Union to accommodate the converging divergences of the Member States promoting the European integration while respecting state sovereignty.

Proportionality in Investment Treaty Arbitration

Now the question is: can proportionality be considered part of international investment law and arbitration? Some authors contend that arbitral tribunals should adopt proportionality analysis,[74] stating that 'proportionality analysis offers the best available doctrinal framework with which to meet the present challenges' to the investment treaty system.[75] To the contrary, a few investment law scholars have pointed out that 'there does not seem to be a strong legal basis for the application [of the proportionality analysis] in the cases where it has been applied' and that the conceptual foundations for using proportionality analysis in investment arbitration are shaky.[76]

Most investment treaties do not refer to proportionality.[77] As the European experience shows, however, this does not necessarily mean that proportionality is not part of the investment law system. In fact, this could be the case if arbitral tribunals used such concept. Therefore, an examination of the arbitral practice is of critical relevance for ascertaining whether and, if so how, proportionality has migrated to investment treaty arbitration.

In the past decade arbitral tribunals have increasingly relied on some form of proportionality analysis.[78] This section explores how they have used the concept of proportionality to

---

72 See, for instance, Case C-438/05 International Transport Workers' Federation and Finnish Seamen's Union v Viking Line [2007] ECR I-10779. For commentary, see ACL Davies, 'One Step Forward, Two Steps Back? The *Viking* and *Laval* Cases in the ECJ' (2008) 37 *Industrial Law Journal* 126.

73 Mathias M Siems, 'The Curious Case of Overfitting Legal Transplants' in Maurice Adams and Dirk Heirbaut (eds), *The Method and Culture of Comparative Law: Essays in Honour of Mark Van Hoecke* (Hart Publishing, 2014) 133, 134.

74 See Alec Stone Sweet, 'Investor–State Arbitration: Proportionality's New Frontier' (2010) 4 *Law and Ethics of Human Rights* 46.

75 ibid 48.

76 Benedikt Pirker, *Proportionality Analysis and Models of Judicial Review* (Europa Law Publishing 2013).

77 See, however, Annex 11-B(3)b of the Free Trade Agreement between the Republic of Korea and the United States of America and Annex 2 of the 2009 ASEAN Comprehensive Investment Agreement.

78 This section does not purport to be exhaustive, as some arbitral tribunals may not be disclosed to the public, and other awards may have referred to proportionality only implicitly. This section acknowledges only awards

define substantive standards of protection, including the protection against unlawful expropriation, fair and equitable treatment, and non-discrimination. It also discusses some cases in which the applicable national law required the use of proportionality and other cases in which proportionality defined the ambit of application of given exceptions. Finally, the section concludes discussing how proportionality has been used also with regard to procedural matters.

With regard to the notion of expropriation, in *Tecnicas Medioambientales Tecmed S.A. v the United Mexican States*, which concerned the replacement of an unlimited licence by a licence of limited duration for the operation of a landfill, the Arbitral Tribunal used the concept of proportionality to ascertain whether given measures could be characterized as expropriatory. The Tribunal considered whether such actions or measures were 'proportional to the public interest presumably protected thereby and to the protection legally granted to investments, taking into account that the significance of such impact has a key role upon deciding the proportionality'.[79]

In *Azurix*, which involved a water concession contract, Argentina had enacted measures for the protection of public health after an algae outbreak contaminated water supply after privatization.[80] Warnings not to drink water were enacted and customers were dissuaded from paying their water bills.[81] In order to ascertain whether there was a (compensable) expropriation or a (non-compensable) legitimate exercise of police powers, the Tribunal relied on *Tecmed*, stating that an expropriatory measure must pursue a 'legitimate aim in the public interest' and the means employed must be (reasonably) proportional to the stated objective.[82] The Tribunal dismissed the claim of expropriation.

In *Burlington Resources Inc. v Ecuador*, which concerned an investment in the hydrocarbon industry, Ecuador contended that '[its] intervention in Blocks 7 and 21 did not constitute an expropriation of Burlington's investment; rather, it 'aimed at preventing significant harm to the Blocks' and in Ecuador's view it 'was necessary, adequate, proportionate under the circumstances'.[83] The Arbitral Tribunal confirmed that Ecuador's intervention in the Blocks 'was necessary to avoid significant economic loss and the risk of permanent damage to the Blocks. It was also appropriate because Ecuador entered the Blocks without using force. It was equally proportionate as the means employed were suited to the ends of protecting the Blocks.'[84]

With regard to the fair and equitable treatment standard, in *MTD Equity SDN BHD and MTD Chile S.A. v Republic of Chile*, which concerned the failure of a construction project deemed to be inconsistent with zoning regulations, the Arbitral Tribunal held that fair and equitable treatment is 'a broad and widely-accepted standard encompassing such fundamental standards

---

which have used the concept of proportionality *expressis verbis*. The argument is that the use of some elements of proportionality, like suitability, is a common judicial endeavor and therefore should not be reconnected to proportionality as such; while the implicit use of all of the various elements of proportionality without naming it would give rise to a number of distinct hermeneutical and legitimacy concerns.

79 *Tecnicas Medioambientales Tecmed S.A. v the United Mexican States*, ICSID Case No ARB (AF)/00/, Award, 29 May 2003, para 122.
80 *Azurix v Argentine Republic*, ICSID Case No ARB/01/12, Award, 23 June 2006.
81 ibid para 283.
82 ibid para 311.
83 *Burlington Resources Inc v Ecuador*, ICSID Case No ARB/08/5, Decision on Liability, 14 December 2012, para 164.
84 ibid para 504.

as good faith, due process, nondiscrimination and proportionality'.[85] In *Occidental Petroleum Corporation and Occidental Exploration and Production Company v Republic of Ecuador*, which concerned an investment in the oil sector, the Arbitral Tribunal stated that 'numerous investment treaty tribunals have found that the principle of proportionality is part and parcel of the overarching duty to accord fair and equitable treatment to investors'.[86] The claimant contended that a given sanction imposed by Ecuador was disproportionate and therefore violated legitimate expectations under the relevant BIT.[87] The Tribunal concluded that the measure 'was not a proportionate response by Ecuador in the particular circumstances of this case'.[88]

Yet, in *Glamis Gold v United States of America*, concerning a gold mining project in California, the claimant's attempt to impose upon respondent the burden of justifying the appropriateness of the regulatory measures and proving that they are 'the least restrictive measures available' and 'necessary, suitable and proportionate' failed.[89] The Tribunal noted that 'it is not for an international tribunal to delve into the details of and justifications of domestic law'.[90] It also stated that '[i]t is not the role of this Tribunal, or any international tribunal, to supplant its own judgment of underlying factual material and support for that of a qualified domestic agency'.[91]

With regard to non-discrimination, in *Parkerings v Lithuania*, which concerned the planned construction of a parking area, the Tribunal stated that 'to violate international law, discrimination must be unreasonable or lacking proportionality, for instance, it must be inapposite or excessive to achieve an otherwise legitimate objective of the State'.[92] Yet, in *Pope & Talbot*, which concerned exports of Canadian softwood lumber, the Tribunal dismissed Canada's argument that the foreign investor should prove that it was 'disproportionately disadvantaged' by the measure.[93] The Tribunal considered that the disproportionate advantage test would weaken NAFTA's ability to protect foreign investors.[94]

Other cases referred to proportionality as it was a requirement under the applicable national law. In *Aucoven v Venezuela*, relating to a highway concession, Venezuela argued that Aucoven's claims did not meet the criteria of definiteness and proportionality required by Venezuelan law.[95] In *Spyridon Roussalis v Romania*, the Tribunal considered that '[the] Respondent's conduct did not infringe the principles of legal certainty and proportionality in violation of the full protection and safety clause contained in article 2(2) of the BIT'.[96] The claimant contended that the host state measures were 'in breach of the principles of due

---

85 *MTD Equity SDN BHD and MTD Chile S.A. v Republic of Chile*, ICSID Case No ARB/01/7, Award, 25 May 2004, para 109.

86 *Occidental Petroleum Corporation and Occidental Exploration and Production Co v Republic of Ecuador*, ICSID Case ARB/06/11, Award, 5 October 2012, footnote 7.

87 ibid para 277.

88 ibid para 338.

89 *Glamis Gold, Ltd v United States of America*, Award, 8 June 2009, para 590.

90 ibid para 762.

91 ibid para 779.

92 *Parkerings v Lithuania*, ICSID Case ARB/05/8, Award, 11 September 2007, para 368.

93 *Pope & Talbot v Canada*, Phase 2, NAFTA Ch11, Award, 10 April 2001, paras 43–45.

94 ibid para 79.

95 *Autopista Concesionada de Venezuela, C.A. ('Aucoven') v Bolivarian Republic of Venezuela*, ICSID Case No ARB/00/5, Award, 23 September 2003, para 338.

96 *Spyridon Roussalis v Romania*, ICSID Case ARB/06/1, Award, 7 December 2011, para 358.

process, proportionality and reasonableness.'[97] However, the Tribunal held that the measures adopted by the host state were 'discriminatory, disproportionate or otherwise improper under Romanian law'.[98] In *Occidental Petroleum Corporation and Occidental Exploration and Production Company v Republic of Ecuador*, the claimant contended that 'both international and Ecuadorian law proscribe the unilateral termination of a government contract where . . . the alleged breach was always known and never objected to by the State, and such termination was manifestly unfair, arbitrary, discriminatory and disproportionate'.[99] The claimant alleged that a given decree was 'in breach of the Respondent's obligations under the Treaty and Ecuadorian law because it was unfair, arbitrary, discriminatory and disproportionate'.[100] The Tribunal noted that the proportionality review of the decree 'pervaded the submissions of both parties' as 'the Ecuadorian Constitution firmly establishes as a matter of Ecuadorian law the principle of proportionality'.[101]

In other cases, proportionality was used to define the ambit of application of given exceptions. For instance, in *Continental Casualty v Argentine Republic*, concerning an insurance business, the Tribunal imported the 'weighting and balancing' formula from international trade law.[102] Both parties had referred to the concept of proportionality. The claimant pointed out to Argentina's Supreme Court decisions that declared a given decree 'to be unconstitutional on the grounds that it was an unreasonable measure, lacking in proportionality between the deprivation of property rights and the objective of averting the crisis . . .'.[103] The Tribunal considered that 'the Government's efforts struck an appropriate balance between that aim and the responsibility of any government towards the country's population: it is self-evident that not every sacrifice can properly be imposed on a country's people in order to safeguard a certain policy that would ensure full respect towards international obligations in the financial sphere, before a breach of those obligations can be considered justified as being necessary under this BIT. The standard of reasonableness and proportionality do not require as much.'[104]

Finally, proportionality has been used also with regard to matters of procedure. In *Libananco Holdings Co. Limited v Republic of Turkey*, concerning the seizure of two electric utility companies, the Tribunal stated that 'there needs to be some proportionality in the award (as opposed to the expenditure) of legal costs and expenses.[105] A party with a deep pocket may have its own justification for heavy spending, but it cannot expect to be reimbursed for all its expenditure as a matter of course simply because it is ultimately the prevailing party'.[106] In *Liman Caspian Oil BV and NCL Dutch Investment BV v Republic of Kazakhstan*, concerning a licence to explore and extract hydrocarbons, the Tribunal acknowledged that 'on [the] one hand, ordering the production of documents can be helpful for a party to present its case and in the Tribunal's task of establishing the facts of the case relevant for the issues to be decided, but, on the other hand, (1) the process of discovery and disclosure may be time

---

97 ibid para 394.

98 ibid para 515.

99 *Occidental Petroleum Corporation and Occidental Exploration and Production Co v Republic of Ecuador* (n 86) para 203.

100 ibid para 206.

101 ibid paras 396–401 (on the principle of proportionality in Ecuadorian law).

102 *Continental Casualty Co v Argentine Republic*, ICSID case No ARB/03/9, Award, 5 September 2008, para 192.

103 ibid para 67.

104 ibid para 227.

105 *Libananco Holdings Co Limited v Republic of Turkey*, ICSID Case No ARB/06/8, Award 2 September 2011.

106 ibid para 565(c).

consuming, excessively burdensome and even oppressive and that unless carefully limited, the burden may be disproportionate to the value of the result, and (2) Parties may have a legitimate interest of confidentiality'.[107]

These arbitrations took place in a variety of different locations, were conducted by different arbitral tribunals under different bilateral treaties and concerned different subject matters and causes of action. One may legitimately wonder whether there is any commonality between these awards. One may also legitimately wonder the relevance of discussing previous awards, given the fact that there is no binding precedent in international (investment) law.

Nonetheless, these awards show an increasingly frequent use of some form of proportionality analysis in investor-state arbitration. Proportionality analysis is used in a varying of contexts; for delimiting substantive standards of protection, clarifying procedural matters and even quantifying damages and legal fees. Moreover, awards can and do influence subsequent awards.

Yet, the proportionality analysis is not used consistently in investment treaty arbitration. As mentioned, arbitral tribunals have used the proportionality concept in different contexts. Proportionality is often mentioned in passing together with other concepts such as reasonableness and rationality. Most tribunals have not used it at all. More importantly, no single unified notion of proportionality has been used; rather arbitral tribunals seem to have elaborated ad hoc notions of proportionality depending on circumstances. In the context of investment arbitration, the proportionality analysis lacks the clear and consistent structure it has in other fields of national, regional and international law.[108]

In conclusion, while generic reference to proportionality has increased in the awards rendered in the past decade, a critical mass of awards relying on this test is missing. In addition, at an analytical level, one may legitimately wonder whether proportionality can contribute to better awards given the specific features of international investment law.

Proportionality in International Trade Law

The question as to whether proportionality is a pillar of international trade law remains debated. On the one hand, some scholars point out that the text of the WTO Agreements do not refer to proportionality in explicit terms and that only some elements of the proportionality analysis are used in the jurisprudence of the WTO panels and the Appellate Body.[109] On the other hand, other scholars contend that 'the principle of proportionality is one of the more basic principles underlying the multilateral trading system'.[110]

As this section shows, while the WTO Agreements do not expressly refer to proportionality, the WTO adjudicative bodies have used some elements of the proportionality analysis. This is not to say that there exists a principle of proportionality embedded in WTO law; rather, some elements of proportionality are ingrained in the system for reconciling trade and non-trade

---

107 *Liman Caspian Oil BV and NCL Dutch Investment BV v Republic of Kazakhstan*, ICSID Case No ARB/07/14, Award, 22 June 2010, para 26.

108 Nicholas Di Mascio and Joost Pauwelyn, 'Nondiscrimination in Trade and Investment Treaties: Worlds Apart or Two Sides of the Same Coin?' (2008) 102 *American Journal of International Law* 48, 76, noting that '(T)he majority of the Tribunals have . . . taken a considerably softer approach than the "necessity test" under many GATT article XX exceptions, looking only for a "reasonable" or "rational" nexus between the measure and the policy pursued'.

109 Axel Desmedt, 'Proportionality in WTO Law' (2001) 4 *JIEL* 441.

110 Meinhard Hilf, 'Power, Rules and Principles – Which Orientation for WTO/GATT Law?' (2001) 4 *JIEL* 111, 120.

issues. WTO provisions that reflect elements of the proportionality analysis 'include words such as "necessary", "proportionate", "less trade restrictive", and "commensurate"'.[111] In particular, elements of proportionality analysis play a role in three major areas of international trade law: (1) the General Agreement on Tariffs and Trade (GATT);[112] (2) the Agreement on Technical Barriers to Trade (TBT Agreement)[113] and the Agreement on the Application of Sanitary and Phytosanitary Measures (SPS Agreement);[114] as well as (3) in the determination of countermeasures.[115]

With regard to the first area,[116] GATT article XX provides a list of general exceptions. WTO Members can adopt measures that would prima facie be in breach of the relevant GATT obligations provided that they comply with the conditions laid down in this provision. GATT article XX is divided into two parts. The first part of the provision – generally known as the *chapeau* – relates to the way a given policy is implemented. The second part of the provision includes a detailed list of policy objectives. Some paragraphs require that a measure be necessary to protect a specific public policy objective (e.g. public morals; human, animal or plant life or health). Other paragraphs require that a given measure be related to other objectives such as the conservation of exhaustible natural resources.

The assessment of the necessity of a given measure to reach the particular objectives mentioned in paragraphs (a), (b), (d) and (i) of article XX – including the protection of public morals and of human, animal or plant life or health – requires some elements of the proportionality analysis, namely the suitability and necessity tests. As Shoenbaum points out, there has been a semantic change in the interpretation of necessary, as 'necessary no longer relates to the protection of living things, but to whether or not the measure is a "necessary" departure from the trade agreement.'[117] In the *Thai – Cigarettes* case, the panel stated that trade restrictions were necessary 'only if there were no alternative measures consistent with the GATT or less inconsistent with it, which Thailand could reasonably be expected to employ to achieve its health policy objectives'.[118] In *Korea – Beef*, the AB stated that the necessity of a measure should be ascertained taking into account, first, 'the extent to which the measure contribute to the realization of the end pursued', and, second, 'the extent to which the compliance measure produces restrictive effects on international commerce'.[119] The AB added that 'determination of whether a measure . . . may . . . be "necessary" . . . involves in every case a process of weighting and balancing a series of factors which . . . include the importance of the . . . interests or values protected by that law or regulation at issue, and the accompanying impact of the law

---

111 Andrew D Mitchell, 'Proportionality and Remedies in WTO Disputes' (2007) 17 *EJIL* 985, 987.
112 General Agreement on Tariffs and Trade 1994, 15 April 1994, Marrakesh Agreement Establishing the World Trade Organization, Annex 1A, 1867 UNTS 187, 33 *ILM* 1153 (1994).
113 Agreement on Technical Barriers to Trade, 15 April 1994, Marrakesh Agreement Establishing the World Trade Organization, Annex 1A, 1868 UNTS 120.
114 Agreement on the Application of Sanitary and Phytosanitary Measures, 15 April 1994, Marrakesh Agreement Establishing the World Trade Organization, Annex 1A, 1867 UNTS 493.
115 AD Mitchell, 'Proportionality and Remedies in WTO Disputes' (n 111).
116 Mads Andenas and Stefan Zleptnig, 'Proportionality: WTO Law: in Comparative Perspective' (2007) 42 *Texas International Law Journal* 371.
117 Thomas J Shoenbaum, 'International Trade and Protection of the Environment: The Continuing Search for Reconciliation' (1997) 91 *AJIL* 269, 276, mentioned in Gisele Kapterian, 'A Critique of the WTO Jurisprudence on Necessity' (2010) 59 *ICLQ* 89.
118 Panel Report, *Thailand – Restrictions on Importation of and Internal Taxes on Cigarettes*, 7 November 1990, DS10/R – 37 S/200, para 75.
119 Appellate Body Report, *Korea – Measures Affecting Imports of Fresh, Chilled and Frozen Beef*, 11 December 2000, WT/DS161/AB/R, para 163.

or regulation on imports or exports'.[120] The jurisprudence of panels and AB has treated certain values more deferentially than others. For instance, in the *EC – Asbestos* case, the AB noted that health is 'vital and important to the highest degree',[121] and held that the adopted measures were indispensable. Once the adjudicative body reaches a preliminary conclusion that the measure is necessary, 'this result must be confirmed by comparing the measure with its possible alternatives, which may be less trade restrictive while providing an equivalent contribution to the achievement of the objective pursued'.[122] The necessity test helps identifying 'whether a less WTO-inconsistent measure is reasonably available'.[123] This judicial development marked an evolution 'from the least trade restrictive approach to the less trade restrictive one'.[124]

The necessity test has been criticized as 'overbroad and under-inclusive' at the same time.[125] On the one hand, 'it seems to elevate trade values to a pre-eminent status'.[126] On the other hand, as noted by Trachtman, 'by keeping the regulatory benefit constant and working on the trade detriment side', the necessity test, as it is used at the WTO 'evaluates a much more limited range of options, ignoring other groups of options that may be superior'.[127] However, the fact that the necessity test does not address the chosen level of protection that a member wants to achieve but the design of the instrument it has chosen to use restricts the discretion of the adjudicators and indicates that a fully-fledged proportionality analysis or balancing is still missing from this sector of WTO adjudication.

The assessment of the relation between a given measure and one of the particular objectives mentioned in the specific paragraphs of GATT article XX includes some elements of the proportionality analysis, namely the suitability and proportionality (in the strict sense) tests. For instance, in *US – Shrimp*, the AB clarified that the requirement 'relating to' is about a 'close and genuine relationship of ends and means'.[128] It added that the design of the measure was 'not disproportionately wide in its scope and reach in relation to the policy objective of protection and conservation of sea turtle species'.[129]

After a measure is found to be provisionally justified under any of the specific paragraphs of article XX, the adjudicators turn to the *chapeau* of the same provision to assess whether the application of the measure does not constitute an 'arbitrary or unjustifiable discrimination between countries where the same conditions prevail' or 'a disguised restriction on trade'.[130] Although the *chapeau* does not in itself contain a proportionality requirement, some scholars consider that it is an expression of, or at least 'resembles, a proportionality analysis'.[131] First, lack of proportionality can help ascertaining the arbitrariness or discriminatory nature of given regulatory measures.[132] Second, the AB held that it 'embodies the recognition on the part of

---

120 ibid para 164.
121 Appellate Body Report, *European Communities – Measures Affecting Asbestos and Asbestos Containing Products*, 12 March 2001, WT/DS135/AB/R, para 172.
122 Appellate Body Report, *Brazil – Measures Affecting Imports of Retreaded Tyres*, 17 December 2007, WT/DS332/AB/R, para 156.
123 *Korea – Beef* (n 120) para 166.
124 Andenas and Zleptnig, 'Proportionality: WTO Law: in Comparative Perspective' (n 116) 408.
125 Joel P Trachtman, 'Trade and . . . Problems, Cost-Benefit Analysis and Subsidiarity' (1998) 9 *EJIL* 32, 72.
126 ibid.
127 ibid.
128 Appellate Body Report, *United States – Import Prohibition of Certain Shrimp and Shrimp Products*, 12 October 1998, WT/DS58/AB/R, para 136.
129 ibid para 141.
130 GATT, art XX.
131 Andenas and Zleptnig, 'Proportionality: WTO Law: in Comparative Perspective' (n 116) 411.
132 Desmedt, 'Proportionality in WTO Law' (n 109) 478.

the WTO Members of the need to maintain a balance of rights and obligations between the right of a member to invoke one or another of the exceptions of article XX . . . on the one hand, and the substantive rights of the other Members under the GATT 1994, on the other hand'.[133]

Other elements of the proportionality analysis surface in the interpretation of certain provisions of the SPS and TBT Agreement. For instance, article 2.2 of the SPS Agreement requires that 'Members shall ensure that any sanitary or phytosanitary measure is applied only to the extent necessary to protect human, animal or plant life or health, is based on scientific principles and is not maintained without sufficient scientific evidence . . .'. On the one hand, 'sufficient scientific evidence' has been deemed to embody elements of the suitability test. In *Japan – Apples*, the AB held that the sufficient scientific evidence criterion required 'a rational and objective relationship' between the measure and the relevant scientific evidence.[134] On the other hand, article 5.6 of the SPS Agreement clarifies that measures necessary to protect human, animal or plant life and health should not be 'more trade restrictive than required to achieve their appropriate level of . . . protection, taking into account technical and economic feasibility'.[135]

Finally, elements of the proportionality analysis appear in the determination of countermeasures and in enforcement provisions. For instance, article 46 of the Agreement on Trade-Related Aspects of Intellectual Property Rights (TRIPS Agreement)[136] refers to the 'need of proportionality' in the context of enforcement provisions.[137] In parallel, footnote 9 of article 4.10 of the Agreement on Subsidies and Countervailing Measures (SCM Agreement)[138] clarifies that 'appropriate countermeasures' do not include 'countermeasures that are disproportionate'.[139] In *EC – Bananas*, the arbitrators refused to 'double-count' nullification of benefits, as this would be contrary to 'the general international law principle of proportionality of countermeasures'.[140] In *US – Line Pipe*, the AB held that the idea that 'countermeasures in response to breaches by States of their international obligations' should 'be proportionate to such breaches' is 'a recognized principle of customary international law', which is fully applicable in the WTO system.[141] An arbitral tribunal has similarly acknowledged the 'customary international law' nature of the proportionality requirement for the validity of countermeasures.[142]

In conclusion, while there is no explicit reference to proportionality in the WTO Agreement, and there is uncertainty as to whether proportionality is a general principle of international law, some elements of the proportionality analysis appear in the interpretation and application of certain provisions of the WTO Agreements.

---

133   *US – Shrimp* (n 128) para 156.
134   Appellate Body Report, *Japan – Affecting the Importation of Apples*, 26 November 2003, WT/DS245/AB/R, para 147.
135   SPS Agreement, art 5.6.
136   Agreement on Trade-Related Aspects of Intellectual Property Rights (TRIPS Agreement), 15 April 1994, Marrakesh Agreement Establishing the World Trade Organization, Annex 1C, 1869 UNTS 299, 33 *ILM* 1197 (1994).
137   TRIPS Agreement, art 46.
138   Agreement on Subsidies and Countervailing Measures (SCM Agreement), 15 April 1994, Marrakesh Agreement Establishing the World Trade Organization, Annex 1A, 1869 UNTS 14.
139   SCM Agreement, footnote 9 of art 4.10.
140   Decision by the Arbitrators, *European Communities – Regime for the Importation, Sale and Distribution of Bananas – Recourse to Arbitration by the European Communities Under Art 22.6 of the DSU*, 9 April 1999, WT/DS27/ARB, para 6.16.
141   Appellate Body Report, *United States – Definitive Safeguard Measures on Imports of Circular Welded Carbon Quality Line Pipe from Korea*, 15 February 2002, WT/DS202/AB/R, para 259.
142   *Archer Daniel Midland Co and Tate & Lyle Ingredients Americas, Inc v the United Mexican States*, ICSID Case No ARB(AF)/04/05, Award, 21 November 2007, para 160.

A History of Success?

While the migration of constitutional ideas can be particularly successful in certain contexts, this may not be the case in others. Why is proportionality so successful in EU adjudication and, albeit to a lesser extent, in WTO dispute settlement, while investment treaty tribunals have shown a more fragmented if not recalcitrant approach? The answer is multifold.

First, EU law, WTO law and investment law present very different institutional settings. EU law builds upon and has fostered legal cohesion in the Union, constituting a *sui generis* system lying between a fully-fledged constitutional order and an international organization.[143] Joseph Weiler has argued that 'one of the great perceived truism, or myths, of the EU legal order is its alleged rupture with, or mutation from, public international law and its transformation into a constitutional legal order.'[144] Certainly, the Union is not a federal system, and the failure to ratify an explicit EU Constitution in 2005 signals some reticence in that regard at least in some Member States.[145] Yet, EU law has a 'constitutional dimension'.[146] Over time, the EU treaties have been perceived as having assumed some constitutional features.[147] Although the Treaty of Rome was concluded in the form of an international treaty, it has become the constitutional charter of the Union.[148] In fact, the European Court of Justice played a pivotal role in creating a material constitution in its judgments,[149] holding that the treaties founding the European Communities (now the European Union) established a new legal order whose subjects do not comprise Member States only but also their nationals.[150] Commentators have pointed out that the court 'constru[ed] the European Communities Treaties in a constitutional mode rather than employing the traditional international law methodology'.[151] More fundamentally, the integration project relies on the common constitutional principles of the EU member states.[152]

143 See generally Miguel Poiares Maduro, 'How Constitutional Can the EU Be? The Tension between Intergovernamentalism and Constitutionalism in the EU' in Joseph HH Weiler and Christopher L Eisgruber (eds), *Altneuland: The EU Constitution in a Contextual Perspective*, Jean Monnet Working Paper 5/04.

144 Joseph HH Weiler, *The Constitution of Europe* (CUP 1999) 295.

145 See generally Giuseppe Martinico, 'From the Constitution for Europe to the Reform Treaty: A Literature Survey on European Constitutional Law' (2009) 1 *Perspectives on Federalism*.

146 Wolf Sauter, 'Proportionality in EU Law: A Balancing Act?' (2013) *TILEC Discussion Paper* 4–5, referring to the existence of an 'implicit constitution'.

147 See eg Advocate General Poiares Maduro's Opinion holding that 'obligations imposed by an international agreement cannot have the effect of prejudicing the constitutional principles of the EC Treaty', Case C–402/05 P and C–415/05 P *Kadi and Al Barakaat International Foundation v Council and Commission* [2008] ECR I–6351, para 285.

148 Case 249/83 Parti écologiste *'Les Verts' v EP* [1986] ECR 1357, para 23, stating that '(T)he European Economic Community is a Community based on the rule of law, inasmuch as neither its MS nor its institutions can avoid a review of whether the measures adopted by them are in conformity with the basic constitutional charter, the Treaty'.

149 See Case 26/62 *NV Algemene Transport-en Expeditie Onderneming van Gend en Loos v Nederlandse Administratie der Belastingen* [1963] ECR 13; Case 6/64, *Flaminio Costa v Enel*, [1964] ECR 585; Case 106/77 *Amministrazione delle Finanze dello Stato v Simmenthal SpA* [1978] ECR 629.

150 Opinion 1/91 of the Court pursuant to art 228 of the EEC Treaty on the Draft Treaty on the Establishment of the European Union Economic Area [1991] ECR I-6079.

151 Eric Stein, 'Lawyers, Judges and the Making of a Transnational Constitution' (1981) 75 *American Journal of International Law* 1, 27.

152 Monica Claes and Maartje De Visser, 'Reflections on Comparative Method in European Constitutional Law' in Maurice Adams and Jacco Bomhoff (eds), *Practice and Theory in Comparative Law* (CUP 2012) 143, 168–69, noting that 'by carrying out comparative constitutional research', 'there will be evidence of commonality in constitutional principles . . .' and suggesting that comparative law can contribute to 'constitutional dialogue in Europe'.

In parallel, since the inception of the World Trade Organization in 1995, international trade law has gone through a process of juridification, to an extent unknown before.[153] Some authors have argued that the WTO presents some constitutional features already, albeit this remains contested.[154]

By contrast, international investment law is a relatively fragmented system, where different arbitral tribunals interpret different treaties. Because of the lack of binding precedent in investment arbitration, it may be difficult to elaborate a consistent proportionality test. Furthermore, EU law, WTO law and international investment law are at a different stage of development[155] and this makes their comparison necessarily approximate and perhaps premature.

Second, despite some commonalities, EU law, WTO law and international investment law have very different aims and objectives. All of these systems presuppose a triangular relationship between: (1) the individual (the EU citizen, the trader and the investor respectively); (2) the state (the Member State, the trading nations or host state respectively); and (3) the supranational court (the CJEU or the WTO 'courts' or the relevant arbitral tribunal respectively).[156] Despite this common tripartite framework, very different assumptions underlie the three systems. On the one hand, the once European Economic Community (EEC) 'market citizen' (*Marktbürger*) entitled to market freedoms under the EEC Treaty[157] has become a European Union citizen entitled to human rights, not only of an economic nature. Therefore, the balancing process takes place in a system where economic interests are part of a broader picture. By contrast, both international trade law and international investment law aim at fostering free trade and foreign direct investments respectively thus promoting economic development.[158] Neither the WTO dispute settlement mechanism nor arbitral tribunals have the comprehensive jurisdiction of the CJEU; rather they have a more limited mandate.

Third, while the CJEU has borrowed the proportionality principles from the legal systems of its Member States, and WTO law includes some elements of proportionality analysis, the role of proportionality analysis in international investment law and arbitration is far from settled. Unless the concept of proportionality is a principle of international law, or is part of the applicable law its application might seem shaky in the context of investment treaty arbitration. Moreover, arbitral tribunals have used proportionality in conjunction with other criteria such as reasonableness and rationality.

153   Joseph HH Weiler, 'The Rule of Lawyers and the Ethos of Diplomats: Reflections on the Internal and External Legitimacy of WTO Dispute Settlement', *Harvard Jean Monnet Working Paper 9/00*, 2; Arie Reich, 'From Diplomacy to Law: The Juridicization of International Trade Relations' (1996–97) 17 *Northwestern Journal of International Law & Business* 775, 776.

154   Joel P Trachtman, 'The Constitutions of the WTO' (2006) 17 *EJIL*, 623.

155   While there are thousands of publicly available cases adjudicated by the CJEU, the available investment awards are much more limited.

156   For analogous reasoning with regard to EU law, see Norbert Reich, 'How Proportionate is the Proportionality Principle? Some Critical Remarks on the Use and Methodology of the Proportionality Principle in the Internal Market Case Law of the ECJ' (paper presented at the Oslo conference on 'The Reach of Free Movement', 2011).

157   ibid 11.

158   Jagdish Bhagwati, 'Why Multinationals Help Reduce Poverty' (2007) 30 *World Economy* 211; VN Balasubramanyam, M Salisu and D Sapsford, 'Foreign Direct Investment and Growth: New Hypotheses and Evidence' (1999) 8 *Journal of International Trade and Economic Development* 27.

On the other hand, further reflection on methodological issues is of key importance. Methodological concerns have long been a common feature of comparative constitutional law.[159] Although there is no single methodological model in comparative law, two fundamental approaches to the field have emerged: the functional approach and the cultural approach.[160]

The functional approach relies on the assumption that law addresses social problems and that all societies confront essentially the same challenges.[161] The functional approach thus presupposes similarity among legal systems (*praesumptio similitudinis*),[162] potentially reflecting 'epistemological optimism', i.e., the belief that legal systems are comparable.[163] For instance, Alan Watson contended that there is no inherent relationship between law and society – being autonomous from any social structure, law develops by transplanting.[164] Inevitably, the concept will adapt to the new context. According to Watson, the adaptation does not imply the failure of the transplant; rather it is a natural process.[165]

By contrast, cultural approaches contend that law expresses and develops the cultural features of a society. Therefore, not only do comparativists need to consider the functions of legal concepts, but they also have to contextualize such concepts in their legal matrix and culture of origin.[166] Meaningful comparisons require understanding the cultural context of legal rules.[167] For instance, Otto Kahn-Freund believed that law cannot be separated from its context.[168] According to Kahn-Freund, not only should one verify whether the item that would be borrowed has proven satisfactory in its system of origin, but she should consider whether it would be suitable to the potentially recipient system.[169] Each legal system is unique, reflecting a particular worldview[170] and constituting a 'cultural expression'.[171]

Despite their differences, comparative law methodologies share a number of caveats and a common denominator. For instance, borrowing based on inadequately verified information should be avoided (e.g. when adjudicators rely on sources provided by the parties without further research). Analogously, reference to certain legal systems as examples should

159 See Günther Frankenberg, 'Comparing Constitutions: Ideas, Ideals, and Ideology – Toward a Layered Narrative' (2006) *International Journal of Constitutional Law* 439; Mark Tushnet, 'Some Reflections on Method in Comparative Constitutional Law' in Sujit Choudry (ed), *The Migration of Constitutional Ideas* (CUP 2006) 67; Peer Zumbansen, 'Comparative Law's Coming of Age?' (2005) 6 *German Law Journal* 1073.

160 On the functional approach, see generally Ralf Michaels, 'The Functional Method of Comparative Law' in Matthias Reimann and Reinhard Zimmermann (eds) *The Oxford Handbook of Comparative Law* (OUP 2006) 339. On the cultural approach, see Pierre Lagrand, 'How to Compare Now' (1996) 16 *Legal Studies* 232.

161 See eg Konrad Zweigert, 'Méthodologie du droit comparé' in *Mélanges J Maury* (Dalloz-Sirey 1960) 579.

162 Jaakko Husa, 'Methodology of Comparative Law Today: From Paradoxes to Flexibility?' (2006) 4 *Revue Internationale de droit comparé* 1095, 1107.

163 Mark Van Hoecke, 'Deep Level Comparative Law' in Mark Van Hoecke (ed) *Epistemology and Methodology of Comparative Law* (Hart Publishing 2004) 172–74.

164 See generally Alan Watson, *Legal Transplants: An Approach to Comparative Law* (University of Georgia Press 1974); see also Alan Watson, 'Comparative Law and Legal Change' (1978) 37 *Cambridge Law Journal* 313, 314–15.

165 Watson, *Legal Transplants* (n 164) 19–20.

166 John C Reitz, 'How to do Comparative Law' (1998) 46 *American Journal of Comparative Law* 617, 626.

167 Pierre Legrand, 'How to Compare Now?' (1996) 16 *Legal Studies* 232.

168 Otto Kahn-Freund, 'On Uses and Misuses of Comparative Law' (1974) 37 *Modern Law Review* 1.

169 ibid 6, questioning: 'Are there any principles which may assist us in measuring the degree to which a foreign institution can be "naturalized"?'

170 Pierre Legrand, 'On the Singularity of Law' (2006) 47 *Harvard International Law Journal* 517, 517.

171 Reza Banakar, 'Power, Culture and Method in Comparative Law' (2009) 5 *International Journal of Law in Context* 69, 78 and 93, stressing the dialectical nature of the relationship between law and society.

be justified. If comparisons are made, these should be explicit rather than implicit. The understanding of the borrowed items should be proper, accurate and contextual. More fundamentally, one should consider whether the migration of constitutional ideas to transnational systems fits the culture of such systems.

Finally judicial borrowing cannot be a mechanical process also in consideration of the fact that until recently both comparative law and international law used to have a Westphalian[172] – if not Eurocentric – character.[173] For a long time, comparative law (has) focused on European legal systems; the law of former colonies – with the exception of US law – was largely overlooked. In other words, by limiting its focus to Western legal traditions, comparative law contributed to the legitimization of an order in which peripheral countries were recognized very limited if any creative contribution to the market of legal ideas.[174] Comparative law scholars (have) assumed that law is almost completely of European making, unfolded through nearly the entire world via colonialism, imperialism and trade.

In parallel, the making of international law used to have a predominantly Western character.[175] Some authors have even questioned whether and how international is international law,[176] highlighting 'the idea of international law as an ordering mechanism that draws its categories from an essential culture and yet stands apart from its cultural context'.[177] The origins of international law are imbued of civil law ideas; the fathers of international law – such as Grotius, Gentili and others – borrowed concepts from their traditions which in turn regarded Roman law as the standard by which justice should be measured.[178] Furthermore, international law mainly governed relations among states, despite some treaties which also regulated the interaction between states and indigenous peoples.[179]

In the post-colonial era, however, there is an emergent awareness that diffusion of law does not necessarily lead to convergence, harmonization, or unification of laws. On the one hand, scholars have pointed out the multicultural genealogy of the Western legal tradition.[180] On the other hand, the imported law did not remain the same; legal transplants are 'transformed by the new context'.[181] Furthermore, in a number of countries – the so-called mixed jurisdictions –

---

172 Treaty of Westphalia: Peace Treaty between the Holy Roman Empire and the King of France and their respective Allies, 24 October 1648, available at <www.yale.edu/lawweb/avalon/westphal.htm> accessed 15 January 2015.

173 William Twining, 'Globalization and Comparative Law' (1999) 6 *Maastricht Journal of European and Comparative Law* 217, 233.

174 Jorge González Jácome, 'El uso del derecho comparado como forma de escape de la subordinación colonial' (2006) 7 *International Law: Revista Colombiana de Derecho Internacional*, 295, 301, affirming that 'se está contribuyendo a la legitimación de un orden geopolítico en donde a los países periféricos se les atribuye poca posibilidad creativa en el mercado de las ideas jurídicas'.

175 See generally Anthony Anghie, *Imperialism, Sovereignty and the Making of International Law* (CUP 2005).

176 Kurt T Gaubatz and Matthew MacArthur, 'How International is International Law?' (2001) 22 *Michigan Journal of International Law* 239, 239.

177 Note, 'Aspiration and Control: International Legal Rhetoric and the Essentialization of Culture' (1993) 106 *Harvard Law Review* 723, 738.

178 See generally Benedict Kingsbury and Benjamin Straumann (eds) *The Roman Foundations of the Law of Nations* (OUP 2010).

179 A notable example is the Treaty of Waitangi, signed on 6 February 1840 by representatives of the British Crown and various Māori chiefs from New Zealand.

180 Pier Giuseppe Monateri, 'Black Gaius – A Quest for the Multicultural Origins of the "Western Legal Tradition"' (1999–2000) 51 *Hastings Law Journal* 479, 484, highlighting that Roman law is a multicultural product due to the interaction of different civilizations.

181 Banakar, 'Power, Culture and Method in Comparative Law' (n 171) 82.

the Romano-Germanic tradition and the common law have met and mingled for historical reasons with variegated outcomes.[182] More recently economic globalization has spurred the constant contact and communication among legal cultures facilitating processes of mutual borrowing, cross-fertilization and learning.[183] Therefore many characteristics which define and shape legal families 'are fading or spreading into other systems'.[184]

In conclusion, the migration of proportionality from constitutional law to EU law has been a relatively straightforward process due to the fact that such principles already belonged to the legal heritage of a few Member States. European courts have borrowed the concept of proportionality and adapted it to their own needs. In some areas, the CJEU interprets proportionality in a way that is closer to the reasonableness test than the classical proportionality analysis.[185] While proportionality may have become an *enfant terrible* of the Court due to its unpredictability,[186] the migration has been successful exactly because the European courts have adapted it to the needs of European integration. In parallel, some elements of proportionality analysis appear in the treaty text of some WTO covered agreements. One may wonder whether the same preconditions for success also exist in investment arbitration. Arbitrators should be aware of the methodological risks and opportunities offered by comparative reasoning: more fundamentally, they should be aware of their mandate to adjudicate the relevant disputes 'in conformity with the principles of justice and international law'.[187]

Conclusions

The migration of legal concepts has become an increasingly common phenomenon, highlighting a cosmopolitan character of law.[188] Conceived as an analytical tool to assist adjudicators in determining the interaction between public and private interests, the concept of proportionality has attracted increasing attention by scholars and policymakers and has migrated from constitutional law to a number of other fields of national, regional and international law. Proportionality can restrain the exercise of public authority, shape judicial review and manage private actors' expectations.

This study investigated the question as to whether and if so, to what extent, proportionality has migrated from constitutional law to EU law, international trade law and international investment law. The migration of proportionality to EU law is a paradigmatic case of successful legal transplant. The migration of proportionality to WTO law seems relatively settled. The migration of proportionality to international investment law and arbitration remains a work in progress. Eminent authors forcefully suggest a broader use of proportionality in international investment law and arbitration. Others consider proportionality analysis to be inappropriate for arbitral tribunals. Rather, they consider that a degree of deference should

---

182 Nicholas Kasirer, 'Legal Education as Métissage' (2003–04) 78 *Tulane Law Review* 481.

183 Jaye Ellis, 'General Principles and Comparative Law' (2011) 22 *European Journal of International Law* 949, 966.

184 Colin B Picker, 'International Law's Mixed Heritage: A Common/Civil Law Jurisdiction' (2008) 41 *Vanderbilt Journal of Transnational Law* 1083, 1094. But see Vivian Grosswald Curran, 'Romantic Common Law, Enlightened Civil Law: Legal Uniformity and the Homogenization of the European Union' (2001) 7 *Columbia Journal of European Law* 63, 63 stressing the enduring difference between civil law and common law systems.

185 Harbo, 'The Function of the Proportionality Principle in EU Law' (n 49) 185.

186 Takis T Tridimas, *The General Principles of EC Law* (OUP 1998) 4, stating that general principles of EU law were 'children of national law, but as brought in front of the Court, they became enfants terribles'.

187 VCLT, preamble.

188 Watson, *Legal Transplants* (n 164) 108.

be paid to the sovereign choices of the host state. Against this background, this chapter has examined the relevant jurisprudence and proposed an alternative viewpoint, highlighting the pros and cons, and the methodological issues raised by the migration of proportionality from one field to another. If international economic 'courts' are to use proportionality to form their interpretation of particular provisions, they must ensure that they master the relevant methodological risks and opportunities. In conclusion, the adoption of proportionality is not a neutral process as it may have important consequences. Certainly, more comparative constitutional law studies are needed to address the question as to whether proportionality is a general principle of international law.

11 The International Trading Regime and the Regulation of Trade in Energy Resources

Is Reform Necessary and is a New Energy Agreement within the WTO Framework the Way to Go?

Jenya Grigorova[*]

Introduction

Trade in energy is unique in many regards. Energy resources are unevenly distributed, and this makes for a clear division between net importing and net exporting countries. Traditional energy resources (oil and gas) are exhaustible, and the peak in their production, although impossible to predict with certainty, may have already been reached, or not be very far along the way. This makes it all the more relevant for public policies to promote ways of limiting production and consumption. In this vein, environmental considerations are also of utmost importance in the sector, and State involvement is crucial, both for internalizing environmental externalities[1] and for promoting more environmentally friendly energy sources. Representing a business worth $6 trillion a year,[2] the market of energy is extremely politicized. All of these specificity features are inevitably reflected into different energy policies replicating a will to reduce energy dependence and either ensure autosufficiency, when energy resources are imported, or maximize the economic rent, when they are exported.

The singularity of the energy sector has been used to uphold arguments as to the inapplicability of WTO rules to trade in energy resources. Legally, these arguments consist in finding a kind of tacit gentlemen's agreement among the trading nations, excluding the energy sector from the framework of the multilateral trading system.[3] The argument of the existence of

* PhD Research Fellow, Sorbonne Law School (University Paris 1 Pantheon Sorbonne). I am especially grateful to Professor Helene Ruiz Fabri for the helpful remarks, and to Emanuel Castellarin, Peter Petrov, Lily Martinet, Cecilia Dominguez, Hélène de Pooter and Edoardo Stoppioni for numerous comments on earlier drafts and fruitful discussions. I am also thankful to Professor Antonio Segura Serrano and Professor Luis M Hinojosa-Martínez for organizing, and inviting me to, the conference 'The Reform of International Economic Governance', University of Granada, 9–10 October 2014. The author may be reached at jenya.grigorova@gmail.com.

1 See on this issue David Pearce, 'Energy Policy and Externalities: An Overview' (2001) Nuclear Energy Agency and OECD Workshop Proceedings, Externalities and Energy Policy: The Life Cycle Analysis Approach <www. oecd-nea.org/ndd/reports/2002/nea3676-externalities.pdf> accessed 14 April 2015, and William J Baumol, 'On Taxation and the Control of Externalities' (1972) *American Economic Review*.

2 'The Power and the Glory – A Special Report on Energy' (2008) *The Economist* <www.economist.com/node/ 11565685> accessed 14 April 2015.

3 Wen-chen Shih, 'Energy Security, GATT/WTO, and Regional Agreements' (2009) 49 *Natural Resources Journal*, 433, 439; Enno Harks, 'The International Energy Forum and the Mitigation of Oil Market Risks' in Andreas Goldthau and Jan Martin Witte (eds), *Global Energy Governance: The New Rules of the Game* (Brookings Institution Press 2010) 248; Frank Schorkopf, 'Energie als Thema des Welthandelsrechts' in Stefan Leible, Michael

such a gentlemen's agreement is rather difficult to sustain and seems to only be supported by a very limited number of WTO Members. It is largely contested in legal scholarship[4] and recent cases brought before the Dispute Settlement Body (DSB)[5] prove that the energy sector falls undoubtedly within the scope of application of WTO disciplines.

This much seems to be as far as consensus goes today. But the issue of applicability differs from questions related to actual application. While it may be true that WTO law applies to trade in energy resources, the way in which the specificities of the sector should be reflected in its application is to be debated. It has been suggested that WTO rules, such as they exist now, are not fit to properly tackle issues related to the liberalization of trade in energy resources, and that it may be advisable to adopt a separate agreement on energy trade.

This contribution has the modest objective of examining these proposals and of evaluating their practical viability. It argues that a new Energy Agreement (EA) within the WTO framework would raise more problems than it would give solutions, and that there are alternative options to be considered, if consensus were to develop as to the inadequacy of currently existing rules.[6] In order to evaluate the adequacy of the 'sectoral approach' when it comes to trade in the energy sector, it first provides a brief overview of the experience so far, focusing on the possibility to use existing models for designing a new Energy Agreement. It then proceeds to examine whether this approach could be adequately transposed to the energy sector, given all of its above-mentioned specificities.

The 'Sectoral Approach'

The multilateral trading system has always been fragmented. This fragmentation was the reason for its survival, as much as for its allure. Behind the rhetoric of the single undertaking one can find nowadays a host of different agreements.[7] Some of them, such as the WTO Agreement on Implementation of article VI of the GATT 1994 (Anti-dumping agreement), the Agreement on Subsidies and Countervailing Measures (SCM Agreement) or the Agreement on Preshipment Inspection, expand and further develop existing rules in order to clarify their application. Others use the flexibilities of the legal framework and adjust the rules to the singularities of certain fields. This second group of agreements is namely the result of what we will call 'the sectoral approach'. The expression reflects a process of designing specific rules

---

Lippert and Christian Walter (eds), *Die Sicherung der Energieversorgung auf globalisierten Märkten, Tübingen* (Mohr Siebeck 2007) 93.

4 See among others Gabrielle Marceau, 'The WTO in the Emerging Energy Governance Debate' (2010) 5 *Global Trade and Customs Journal* 83; Yulia Selivanova, 'The WTO and Energy: WTO Rules and Agreements of Relevance to the Energy Sector' (2007) *ICTSD Trade and Sustainable Energy Series*, 1/2007.

5 The recent Appellate Body Report in the case *Canada: Certain Measures Affecting the Renewable Energy Generation Sector* (*Canada: Certain Measures Affecting the Renewable Energy Generation Sector*, 6 May 2003, WT/DS412/AB/R and WT/DS426/AB/R) is certainly the first of many. Several other disputes have been filed contesting the WTO law consistency of measures in the energy sector – cf. the request for consultations recently filed by the Russian federation concerning the EU 'Third energy package' (*European Union and its Member States: Certain Measures Relating to the Energy Sector*, WT/DS476/1) or the on-again-off-again biodiesel dispute between the EU and Argentina (cases DS459 and DS473).

6 This premise is taken here merely as a basis for comparison and is not to be considered a settled matter. On the contrary, the author considers that most WTO rules are flexible enough to address all these issues and that potential *lacunae* can be filled via cooperation with other *fora*.

7 For a systemic approach, see WTO Negotiating group on market access, 'Sector specific discussions and negotiations on goods in the GATT and the WTO', 24 January 2005, TN/MA/S/13.

regulating trade in a predefined set of goods (sector), regardless of whether these disciplines apply alternatively or cumulatively with the general rules. It is suggested that this 'sectoral approach' is not new *per se*, as it has already been used on several occasions throughout the history of the multilateral trading system.

Brief Historical Background of the Sectoral Approach within the Multilateral Trading System

At the outset, the goal of the GATT was to establish rules of general application for trade in all goods. The text, in its initial form stemming from the Havana Charter, contained very few references to particular products or sectors.[8] From the very first cycles of negotiations, however, reductions of tariffs were negotiated on a product-by-product basis.[9] Once the first massive tariff cuts were made, this method was no longer satisfactory and, during the Kennedy Round, Contracting Parties began discussing the possibility of applying tariff cuts across the board on all tariff lines.[10] Nonetheless, several sectors remained too specific and the need was felt to treat them apart: (1) either by means of exceptions, or (2) *via* the establishment of specific negotiation groups (Committee on Agriculture, Groups on Cereals, Meat, and Tropical Products, and Pilot Group on Dairy Products), or (3) finally, in the form of special plurilateral agreements (Memorandum of Agreement on Basic Elements for the Negotiation of a World Grains Arrangement and Agreement relating principally to chemicals).

With the paradigm shift towards further liberalization during the Tokyo Round, sectoral negotiations were seen as a way of addressing all types of barriers (tariff and non-tariff) in specific sectors. A Negotiating Group called 'Sectoral Approach' was established pursuant to a Background Note by the Secretariat, suggesting that 'the main general aim of the sector approach should be to go beyond the standards of liberalization prescribed in the agreed general liberalization formulae'.[11] The Group's work was rather problematic. The sectoral approach fell victim to its prenatal deficiencies: the Contracting parties could agree neither on the sectors to be discussed, nor on the product coverage within the sectors. The risk that the sectoral approach 'might also be used to justify a level of liberalization below the norm set by the general formulae'[12] did indeed materialize. The Group did not manage to push the negotiations forward and was later dismantled. This failure should be attributed to a fall-back in the negotiations conjuncture, rather than to flaws inherent to the technique itself. The sectoral approach did indeed prove to be effective during the Tokyo Round – it resulted in the adoption of several sectoral agreements (the International Bovine Meat Agreement, the Agreement on Trade in Civil Aircraft and the International Dairy Agreement).

In the beginning of the Uruguay Round, proposals were made to adopt a sectoral approach for certain issues, such as bargaining processes for tariff reductions.[13] However, the reigning spirit of unity, which resulted in the 'single undertaking approach', and the rejection of the 'GATT *à la carte*', made it impossible to adopt or even negotiate many sectoral agreements.

---

8 ibid 3.

9 Anwarul Hoda, *Tariff Negotiations and Renegotiations under the GATT and the WTO: Procedures and Practices* (Cambridge 2001) 37, 38, 44 to 52.

10 WTO, 'Sector specific discussions' (n 7) 5.

11 GATT, 'Group 3 (c) – The sector approach' (1975) MTN/3C/1, para 36.

12 ibid para 37.

13 The so-called 'zero-for-zero' agreements.

As a result, most sectoral bargains were embodied in the Members' schedules. Nonetheless, some fields, that were already considered excluded from the general framework, still remained 'special', as no consensus could be reached on their normalization. This led to the conclusion of the Agreement on Agriculture and the Agreement on Textiles.

In the post-Uruguay era only one sectoral initiative resulted in the adoption of a special agreement: the Information Technology Agreement, entered into force on 1 July 1997. Several other proposals were put forward during the preparation of the Seattle Ministerial, in particular one on the initiative of ASEAN countries which included, among others, the energy sector.[14] Its failure could certainly be attributed to the misadventures of Seattle but the absence of subsequent proposals in the same direction shows that the trading nations were not convinced in the first place about the need for such a sectoral agreement. In sum, the energy sector has so far never been discussed within the sectoral approach.

Cursory Systematization of the Sectoral Experience

This brief chronological summary clearly demonstrates the diversity of the models that can be found within the broader concept of the sectoral approach. In some cases, the results of sectoral negotiations are included in the Members' schedules. Although it substantiates the specificities of certain sectors, this technique is merely 'an instrument for modifying the Schedules of concessions or for eliminating a specific non-tariff barrier',[15] and it should not be mistaken for a sectorization process, as the sectors remain solely within the framework of the general disciplines.

If the adoption of special rules is what defines the 'sectoral approach', this broad idea can in turn refer to different techniques. First, some sectoral agreements are designed in order to organize cooperation between exporting and importing nations, mainly by fixing sale and purchase obligations within maximum and minimum price ranges. For instance, the Kennedy Round saw the adoption of such agreements in the cereals sector (plurilateral Memorandum of Agreement on Basic Elements for the Negotiations of a World Grains Arrangement)[16]. This type of arrangement, as suggestive of the sectoral specificities as it may be, is scarcely integrated into the general framework of the multilateral trading system. At the time the approach successfully maintained some issues within the GATT, but the model is now obsolete.

A further degree of sectorization within the general system can be found in the case of agreements that organize the monitoring and the regulation of markets, such as the International Bovine Meat Agreement and the International Dairy Agreement. These two plurilateral agreements, legacy of the Tokyo Round, put into place monitoring bodies that were to evaluate the world offer and supply, and provide for a forum for periodical consultations on all issues concerning trade in these sectors. The two agreements were scrapped in 1997,[17]

---

14 'APEC's 'Accelerated Tariff Liberalization' (ATL) Initiative: Communication from New Zealand (Addendum): Accelerated Tariff Liberalization Initiative: An Outline of the Proposals Developed in the Eight ATL Product Areas', 1999, WT/GC/W/138/Add.1, 5.

15 WTO, 'Sector specific discussions' (n 8) 13.

16 For further developments see Pierre-Michel Eisemann, *L'organisation internationale du commerce de produits de base*, (Bruylant 1982) 196 and John Rehm, 'The Kennedy Round of Trade Negotiations' (1968) 62 *AJIL* 420.

17 The end of these agreements *'s'est effectuée dans l'anonymat le plus total par simple notification de leur retrait par chacune des parties en application de l'art 67 de la convention de Vienne sur les traités'*, Helene Ruiz Fabri and Pierre Monnier, 'L'Organisation mondiale du commerce — droit institutionnel' (2009) 130–10 *Jurisclasseur de droit international* para 94.

mainly because 'countries that had signed the agreements decided that the sectors were better handled under the Agriculture and Sanitary and Phytosanitary agreements'.[18] The short lifespan of these agreements should not be attributed solely to a conviction of the inadequacy of the technique chosen for managing all particular issues related to the sectors. It is rather due to circumstantial factors and to the obvious doubling in *ratione materiae* coverage with the Agricultural Agreement and the SPS Agreement.

The sectoral approach is more palpable in the case of certain agreements aiming at a further liberalization in sectors already covered by the general rules. The first agreement that followed this rationale concerned the chemical sector. The Agreement Relating Principally to Chemicals is 'usually referred to as a 'harmonization' agreement, because participants included in their schedules the same levels for different groups of products'.[19] An analogous logic is found in the design of the Civil Aircraft Agreement and the Sectoral on Pharmaceuticals. More recently the Information Technology Agreement (ITA) had a similar objective[20] although it remains mainly a tariff reduction mechanism. We will examine the adequacy of these models to address the particular issues of trade in energy below.

The highest degree of sectorization identifiable is embodied in two agreements which aim at bringing two sectors, that had come to be *de facto* excluded from the GATT disciplines, back into the multilateral trading system. First, the agricultural sector, although initially regulated by the GATT,[21] was progressively excluded and remained essentially outside the general framework until the end of the Uruguay Round. The reasons for this exclusion are quite complex, but they are essentially related to the political importance of the sector and to the unwillingness of influential contracting parties to subject farm trade to rules that may have appeared too stringent. They chose, instead, 'to take exemptions from or to outright disregard free trade'[22] in the sector. This choice was, at the time, a political one.[23] The GATT did in fact provide for sector-specific rules for farm trade.[24] However, the USA requested and obtained a waiver in 1955. The example was followed by other Contracting parties. When we add to

18 <www.wto.org/english/thewto_e/whatis_e/tif_e/agrm10_e.htm#dairyandbeef> accessed 14 April 2015.

19 WTO, 'Sector specific discussions' (n 7) 9.

20 For further developments see Sacha Wunsch-Vincent, *WTO, E-Commerce and Information Technologies: From Uruguay Round through the Doha Development Agenda: A Report to the UN ICT Task Force* (United Nations ICT Task Force 2005) 39; Sacha Wunsch-Vincent, *The WTO, the Internet and Trade in Digital Products: EC-US Perspectives* (2006 Hart) 81; and WTO, '15 Years of the Information Technology Agreement Trade, Innovation and Global Production Networks' (2012) <www.wto.org/english/res_e/publications_e/ita15years_2012full_e.pdf> accessed 14 April 2015.

21 Stefan Tangermann, 'Agriculture on the Way to Firm International Trading Rules' in Daniel Kennedy and James Southwick (eds), *The Political Economy of International Trade Law: Essays in Honor of Robert E. Hudec* (CUP 2002) 257. See also William Davey, 'The Rules for Agricultural Trade in GATT' in Masayoshi Honma, Akio Shimizu and Hideki Funatsu (eds), *GATT and Trade Liberalization in Agriculture* (1993 Otaru Hokkaido) 59: 'the GATT rules on international trade were always intended to apply to agriculture. As drafted, they had the inherent capacity to regulate trade in agricultural products effectively'.

22 Petros Mavroidis, *Trade in Goods: The GATT and the Other WTO Agreements Regulating Trade in Goods* (2nd edn, OUP 2013) 744.

23 As Robert Hudec put it, 'it would seem difficult to make a case that the GATT's problems with agricultural trade are attributable to weaknesses in the general rules of GATT', Robert Hudec, 'Does the Agreement on Agriculture Work? Agricultural Disputes after the Uruguay Round' (1998) *International Agricultural Trade Research Consortium*, Working Paper 98–92, 8.

24 Art XI(2) provides for an exception to the general rule of prohibition of quantitative restrictions (art XI(1)). Art XVI(3) regulates export subsidies for farm products, allowing subsidization in some cases. However, these texts 'changed faces over the years and turned, through a combination of factors, into a green light for agricultural protectionism', Mavroidis (n 22) 203.

the equation the creation of the European Common Agricultural Policy (CAP), the agricultural sector was *de facto* excluded from the multilateral trading system.[25] It was not until the Uruguay Round that arguments of normalization finally made it to the negotiations agenda and resulted in the adoption of the Agreement on Agriculture (AoA).[26] In a nutshell, this Agreement aims at creating a more competitive environment in the sector before ultimately bringing it back to the general framework.

Similarly, the textiles sector was initially subject to the general GATT rules but trade in textiles took place outside the GATT disciplines. Following a proposal by the USA, a separate textile-specific agreement was put into place. The Multi-Fiber Agreement (MFA) entered into force in 1974, covering a GATT-incompatible situation of discriminatory restrictions that had been developing since 1961.[27] This agreement was a sort of 'mini-GATT' with its own different principles, logic, rules and institutions. So when the Uruguay Round was launched, 'the textiles and clothing sector was barely touched by GATT'.[28] The sectoral negotiations led to the adoption of an Agreement on Textiles and Clothing (ATC), a transitional text providing for an integration agenda and progressive elimination of existing quotas. The agreement was clearly aimed at breaking with the past[29] and the integration process was indeed successful: at the end of the initial 10-year transition period, the ATC ceased to exist (1 January 2005) and trade in the sector is now governed only by general disciplines. The aim of the present contribution is not to study in detail the AoA and the ATC. We will only focus on investigating whether the pattern they follow could be appropriately used for addressing trade in energy.

The Sectoral Approach and Trade in Energy Resources: A New Energy Agreement?

Recently, proposals have been proliferating, essentially in legal scholarship, suggesting the adoption of a sectoral agreement dealing with energy issues. Some of these proposals mark a preference for an integrated approach: J. Pauwelyn mentions, for instance, a sort of 'General Agreement on Trade in Energy';[30] T. Cottier and his collaborators also opt for a similar 'Framework Agreement on Energy within WTO law'.[31] Others are limited to the linkages

---

25 Davey (n 21) 6: 'the GATT rules that were in fact applicable to agricultural imports were not enforced; the GATT rules applicable to export subsidies were interpreted so as to make them largely meaningless'. See also Dominique Carreau and Patrick Juillard, *Droit international économique* (4th edn, Dalloz 2010) para 373.

26 For comments see Melaku Desta, *The Law of International Trade in Agricultural Products: From GATT 1947 to the WTO Agreement on Agriculture* (2002 Kluwer); Joseph McMahon, *The WTO Agreement on Agriculture: A Commentary* (OUP 2006); Hudec (n 24) and Kym Anderson 'Bringing Discipline to Agricultural Policy via the WTO' in Bernard Hoekman and Will Martin (eds), *Developing Countries and the WTO: A Proactive Agenda* (2001 Blackwell) 25–57.

27 For an analysis see Mavroidis (n 22) 784.

28 Marcelo Raffaelli and Tripti Jenkins, *The Drafting History of the Agreement on Textiles and clothing* (International Textiles and Clothing Bureau 1995) 2.

29 As the Panel stated in *US – Underwear*: 'the overall purpose of the ATC is to integrate the textiles and clothing sector into GATT 1994', *United States: Restrictions on Imports of Cotton and Man-Made Fibre Underwear*, 8 November 1996, WT/DS24/R para 7.19.

30 Joost Pauwelyn, 'Global Challenges at the Intersection of Trade, Energy and the Environment: An Introduction' in Joost Pauwelyn (ed), *Global Challenges at the Intersection of Trade, Energy and the Environment* (Centre for Trade and Economic Integration 2010) 7.

31 Thomas Cottier, Garba Malumfashi and others, 'Energy in WTO Law and Policy' in Thomas Cottier and Panagiotis Delimatsis (eds), *The Prospects of International Trade Regulation* (CUP 2011) 211.

between energy trade and environmental issues – J. Bacchus suggests, for example, a 'Sustainable Energy Trade Agreement'.[32] The modalities and the names vary with the angle of attack, but these proposals are all based on the general idea that such a sectoral agreement would be the solution to the archetypal problem in the area: the inadequacy of the general framework of the multilateral trading system to address the specificities of the trade in energy resources.

The ideas argue that an EA would offer a sort of a comprehensive framework for trade in energy, both for goods and services, thus avoiding the classic division of the Marrakech Agreement. Such a new framework would also suggest alternative ways of taking into account environmental concerns avoiding the negative approach of the exceptions mechanism of GATT article XX. A separate EA would also address sector-specific problems, such as transit and third-party access, price fixation, double pricing, production restrictions, etc., in a specific manner. These issues are now left to the general rules 'which were not negotiated with the specificities of the energy sector in mind'.[33]

Surprisingly, very few of these proposals have been sufficiently laid out. This makes it hard to argue with the general intellectual constructions. But it is this absence of details that makes us wonder, what would the terms of a new Energy Agreement be?

The Actors

The projects for the adoption of an EA are rarely effusive concerning its *ratione personnae* coverage. Naturally, preference goes to multilateralism, the only formula that would take into account all different interests and maintain all discussions on energy trade within the WTO framework. However, in the intellectual allure of the formula resides its fundamental weakness – a multilateral agreement needs the acceptance of all Members.[34] The energy sector, though, seems to be one of those issues '*sur lesquels un accord global est manifestement impossible*'.[35]

It seems more realistic to opt for the plurilateral technique: the EA would thus only take legal effect for those Members that accept it pursuant to article II(3) of the WTO Agreement. Naturally, there will always be the possibility of multilateralizing at a later stage.[36] The plurilateral model would ensure that certain initially suspicious Members don't block further liberalization and / or regulation in the energy sector.[37] Discussions will thus remain within the general framework of the multilateral trading system and although the new EA will be *à la carte*, this would still be preferable to complete vacuum.

---

32 James Bacchus, 'A Way Forward for the WTO' in Ricardo Meléndez-Ortiz, Chrisophe Bellmann and Miguel Rodríguez Mendoza (eds), *The Future and the WTO: Confronting the Challenges (A collection of short essays)* (ICTSD 2012) 9.

33 Marceau (n 4) 91.

34 As Matthew Kennedy puts it, 'additions are amendments', Matthew Kennedy, 'Two Single Undertakings – Can the WTO Implement the Results of a round?'(2011) 14 *JIEL* 92.

35 Helene Ruiz Fabri, 'Qui gouverne l'OMC et que gouverne l'OMC?' (2010) 44 *En temps réel* 17.

36 According to Albane Geslin plurilateral agreements are never conceived to remain plurilateral, Albane Geslin, 'Les traités plurilatéraux: quelle(s) utilité(s) dans le système commercial multilatéral?' in Vincent Tomkiewicz (ed), *Les sources et les normes dans le droit de l'OMC* (Pedone 2012) 61.

37 As J Bacchus put it, 'Would the consensus required for adding plurilateral trade agreements to Annex 4 of the WTO treaty prove to be a political obstacle? No, it should not be. Why should some WTO Members object if other WTO Members wish to negotiate WTO-plus obligations that will not bind them unless they choose to be bound by them? Should not all WTO Members, who share a common stake in the ongoing success of the WTO-based world trading system prefer that new trade agreements among WTO Members be made part of that overall system? Would that not be one good way to ensure the security and predictability of the system and otherwise to enhance it?', Bacchus (n 32) 8.

The option of adopting a plurilateral agreement is not univocal: the formula has indeed several varieties. First, parties to the new agreement can agree that only Members who have accepted the agreement will benefit from the liberalization, in a sort of a closed club. This option makes a new EA much more acceptable and attractive as it eradicates the problem of free riders. On the other hand, the initiative will be much harder to accept for other Members. Second, the agreement can also contain a general MFN clause extending its benefits to all Members, parties or not, while the obligations would only bind those who have accepted the EA. Such a 'plurilateral plus' agreement[38] will definitely have a more mitigated altering effect on the global system since '(t)he basic superstructure of the WTO could thus remain the same – one common roof to lodge all agreements – but part of the rulebook would be different, involving deeper and wider commitments for those willing to subscribe to them'.[39] However, it should not be assumed that this would make such an EA easier to agree upon: it will still need cooperation between States with converging interests, willing to extend their obligations with no counterpart.

Although further discussions are definitely needed, it seems that the plurilateral approach might prove to be an innovation laboratory.[40] The initiative will, however, need to surmount numerous hurdles, even if we leave aside the general institutional critique towards all plurilateral agreements, as their nature itself contradicts the *mantra* of the single undertaking. A plurilateral EA will only make sense if the main importing and exporting nations in the energy sector take part. This means that these Members have to be willing '(i) to accept a level of obligations higher than that accepted by other Members; (ii) to apply those obligations to the trade of the other Members to the extent required by the most-favoured-nation rules; and (iii) to enforce those obligations through DSU procedures'.[41] In the current state of affairs, such a will is hard to find – a plurilateral initiative in the energy sector will most probably attract only Members with convergent interests. The new EA will become a forum either for net exporters, or for net importers. Such agreements already exist outside the framework of the WTO[42] and their duplication will be of little use.

Yet another institutional hurdle is related to the integration of the new plurilateral EA within the WTO framework. This integration would need to respect arts. II: 3 and X: 9 of the WTO Agreement. Pursuant to the latter of these texts,[43] the procedures for the addition of a plurilateral trade agreement to Annex 4 of the WTO Agreement requires a consensus decision of the Ministerial Conference, that is of all Members, even if the plurilateral agreement is only binding on some of them. This requirement makes it hard enough to add

---

38　Miguel Rodríguez Mendoza, 'Toward Plurilateral plus Agreements' in Ricardo Meléndez-Ortiz, Chrisophe Bellmann and Miguel Rodríguez Mendoza (eds), *The Future and the WTO: Confronting the Challenges (A collection of short essays)* (ICTSD 2012) 30.

39　Craig Van Grasstek and Pierre Sauvé, 'The Consistency of WTO Rules: Can the Single Undertaking be Squared with Variable Geometry?' (2006) 9 *JIEL* 851.

40　As Professor Jackson put it, 'certain innovations could occur with smaller groupings rather than the whole', John Jackson, 'The WTO "Constitution" and Proposed Reforms: The Seven "Mantras" Revisited', 2001 *JIEL* 75. Petros Mavroidis and Bernard Hoekman have also recently suggested supporting the greater use of plurilateral agreements – Petros Mavroidis and Bernad Hoekman, 'WTO "à la carte" or "menu du jour"? Assessing the case for more plurilateral agreements' (2015) 26 *EJIL* 319.

41　Hunter Nottage and Thomas Sebastian, 'Giving Legal Effect to the Results of WTO Trade Negotiations: An Analysis of the Methods of Changing WTO Law' (2006) 9 *JIEL* 1012.

42　The OPEC and the IEA.

43　For a critical approach to this text see Joost Pauwelyn, 'The Transformation of World Trade' (2005) *Michigan Law Review* 65.

new agreements, even in fields that are less politically charged than that of energy.[44] Finally, even if an EA manages to obtain the necessary accord, the compromises leading thereto will undoubtedly have substantially reduced the level of obligations.[45]

If neither the plurilateraln nor the multilateral formulae work, one could envisage other options, such as a critical-mass agreement 'where Members agree to refrain from blocking consensus where a critical mass of them support a proposed change'.[46] This option, used in the information technology sector, is not less problematic, though: the definition of the 'critical mass' in the energy sector will be extremely difficult,[47] and the attractiveness of the formula will yet again be contingent upon important compromise in the substance. Even if balance were found, it would be extremely fragile and would make it impossible to follow quickly changing trends in energy trade (for instance, any modification of the list of covered products would need the same accord as the initial agreement).

It follows that with the crisis of the multilateral approach, almost sacrificed on the road to universalism, the inherent insufficiency of the plurilateral approach, which seems to be inadequate for issues in the energy sector, and the uncertainties of intermediary regimes, the adoption of an EA will face major institutional hurdles.

The Script: Is 'Copy/Paste' an Option?

The terms of each provision of a potential future EA can be subject to long discussions. None of the proposals develop a comprehensive project as to the provisions of the new agreement, most of them preferring to remain rather vague and general. That is why any effort in this contribution to speculate on all possible provisions of a new EA may prove to be completely useless in the long term. Instead, we suggest adopting a somewhat limited, but less speculative approach, by examining whether the new EA could use the model of existing sectoral agreements, notably the AoA and the ATC, as they are the ones that reflect the most comprehensive efforts of sectorization.

Such a transposition is conditional upon a double convergence: first, a symmetry between the rationale of the existing sectoral agreements and the underlying motivation for a new EA is the necessary premise for any transposition effort;[48] second, only some basic similarity between the issues that need to be addressed would justify such a transposition.

---

44 The experience of the EU proposal for a plurilateral agreement on investments is a perfect example of the difficulties of this procedure: 'The insistence of the European Communities' delegation on commencing negotiations for a plurilateral agreement relating to trade and investment, despite the lack of an explicit consensus from the membership to do so, is largely blamed for the failure of the Cancún Ministerial Conference', Mary Footer, *An Institutional and Normative Analysis of the World Trade Organization* (Martinus Nijhoff 2006) 141–42; see also Faizel Ismail, 'A Development Perspective on the WTO July 2004 General Council Decision' (2005) 8 *JIEL* 396–98.

45 As Helene Ruiz Fabri and Pierre Monnier put it, the only reason why plurilateral initiatives were so successful during the Tokyo Round is because *'le fait que ces accords ne visent en réalité qu'un petit nombre de pays industrialisés, ensuite par le fait qu'on reste à leur propos dans l'esprit qui avait prévalu lors du cycle de Tokyo, à savoir des accords essentiellement incitatifs, faiblement contraignants'*, Ruiz Fabri and Monnier (n 17) para 34.

46 Footer (n 44) 161.

47 See Carlos Pérez Del Castillo and others, 'The Doha Round and alternative options for creating a fair and market-oriented agricultural trade system' (*IPC Position Paper* 2009) 7, '(T)he decision of how to define "critical mass" for any product will inevitably leave some countries dissatisfied. So the question arises as to whether the critical mass defines participation in the negotiations or the share of trade needed to reach an agreement'.

48 The ITA would need to be excluded from the first stage of this analysis as it clearly obeys a logic of further liberalization and cooperation in a sector where the respect of the general rules is considered no longer sufficient by some countries. This logic supposes a prerequisite of complete consensus on the applicability of the general framework that clearly lacks in the energy sector.

The Rationale of the Sectoral Model

The AoA and the ATC were negotiated in situations that appear *a priori* similar: both the farm sector and the textiles sector were initially included, but subsequently excluded, first *de facto* and then *de jure*, from the general legal framework of the GATT. Both agreements are the result of an effort to bring the sectors back to the general disciplines. The *leitmotif* of the AoA and the ATC is therefore analogous and can be resumed in the neologism of 'normalization', a process that indirectly legitimizes or, at least, recognizes the pre-existing exclusion.

The farm sector seems less prone to such normalization. Therefore, the AoA does not provide for a complete reintegration but creates a somewhat peculiar regime combining the application of the general ideas of WTO law with some sector-specific adjustments. Its usefulness is contested by some, appreciated by others.[49] Even today, trade in agriculture is a category in itself: it still is the only area where export subsidies are explicitly permitted, three-digit tariff are still common and 'a number of trade-distortive agricultural domestic support measures are still shielded from the remedies of the exemplary dispute settlement system of the WTO'.[50] The AoA is simply a break with the *de facto* exclusion and an effort to organize it *de jure*. If we see it from this perspective (instead of the traditional approach of regarding it solely as a reintegration agreement), its model may be transposable to the energy sector. This transposition will, however, have to leave aside the need of legitimizing a pre-existing exclusion: although suggestions have been made as to such an exclusion of the energy sector, a detailed study of the negotiations proves that energy was always on the table.

The ATC obeys a logic that may initially seem similar but is in fact entirely different. The textiles sector was completely reintegrated into the general framework, although it may be argued that the success of the ATC is detectable more in theory than in practice.[51] The agreements concluded in 1969 and 1995 were the legal cover for the GATT-inconsistency of practices in the sector, but the ATC fervently condemns the idea of sectorization. Its article 9 prohibits reopening the issue in the future without a consensual decision of the WTO, 'which seems to be a remote possibility'.[52] Transposing this rationale to an EA would be absurd: it would consist in a sectorization with the sole objective of ultimately returning to normality.

The Issues to be Addressed

As mentioned *supra*, only some basic similarity between the issues that need to be addressed will justify using the model of the AoA or the ATC for a new EA. Naturally, the provisions of any sectoral agreement are the reflection of problems of particular concern in the sector. For example, the AoA is adjusted to regulate three main issues: access to import markets (tariff

---

49 Tangermann (n 21) 261 states: '(W)as it necessary to agree on a separate text for agriculture, in order to bring agricultural trade on the main GATT track in this area? It probably was in order to make it crystal clear that everybody . . . had to move to bound tariffs in agriculture, irrespective where countries were coming from'.

50 Hudec (n 23) 7.

51 As Sanjoy Bagchi puts it, 'the end of derogations . . . does not mean that protectionism in the textile sector will be dead. The legacy of fifty years demonstrates that protectionism in the textile sector has always been combined with discrimination', Sanjoy Bagchi, 'The integration of the textile trade into GATT' (1994) 28 *JWT* 41. See also Niels Blokker, *International Regulation of World Trade in Textiles: Lessons for Practice, a Contribution to Theory* (Martinus Nijhoff 1989) 249; Reinhard Quick, *Exportselbstbeschränkungen und Artikel XIX GATT* (Heymann 1983) 235–45; Ivan Bernier, 'Les ententes de restriction volontaire à l'exportation en droit international économique' (1973) *Annuaire Canadien de droit international* 81–82.

52 Bagchi (n 51) 33.

and non-tariff barriers), export subsidies and domestic support. The first of these issues is of minimal importance for the energy sector, as most restrictions to trade in the field are export barriers. The regulation of export subsidies might be of some relevance, especially if the concept of export subsidies is interpreted in a broad enough manner to encompass the much debated practice of double pricing.[53] Export subsidies are, however, already prohibited under the SCM Agreement, the AoA providing only for exceptions.[54] The general rules seem in this case better adapted than the transitional solution of the sectoral agreement. Finally, as far as domestic support goes, this issue is arguably of utmost importance in the energy sector,[55] especially when it comes to relating these policies to environmental objectives. However, the SCM Agreement seems to offer flexible enough solutions, while the rules in the AoA have an extremely limited legal effect. It follows that in this particular case, although a symmetry may be found between the two sectors, the sectoral approach does not suggest any specific rules that would be better adapted for the energy sector.

As for the ATC, the issues it tackles are very different from those that need to be addressed in the energy sector. The main barriers in trade in textiles are related to protectionism by importing countries reflected in import quotas and discriminatory safeguard measures.[56] Protectionism in this traditional sense is not present in the energy sector: countries are on the constant search for diversification of their imports and import restrictions are extremely rare.

---

53 For developments on this issue see Yulia Selivanova, *Energy Dual Pricing in the WTO: Analysis and Prospects in the Context of Russia's Accession to the World Trade Organization* (Cameron May 2008); Vitalyi Pogoretskyy, 'Energy Dual Pricing in International Trade: Subsidies and Anti-dumping Perspectives' in Yulia Selivanova (ed), *Regulation of Energy in International Trade Law* (Kluwer 2011) 181; Yulia Selivanova 'World Trade Organization Rules and Energy Pricing: Russia's Case' (2004) 38 *JWT* 559; Vitalyi Pogoretskyy and Daniel Behn, 'The Tension between Trade Liberalization and Resource Sovereignty: Russia – EU Energy Relations and the Problem of Natural Gas Dual Pricing' (*2010 Conference Political Economy of Energy in Europe and Russia*, Warwick University); Vitalyi Pogoretskyy, 'The System of Energy Dual Pricing in Russia and Ukraine: The Consistency of the Energy Dual Pricing System with the WTO Agreement on Anti-dumping' (2009) 10 *Global Trade and Customs Journal* 313; Sergey Ripinsky, 'The System of Gas Dual Pricing in Russia: Compatibility with WTO Rules' (2004) 3 *WTR* 463; Daniel Behn, 'The Effect of Dual Pricing Practices on Trade, the Environment and Economic Development: Identifying the Winners and the Losers under the Current WTO Disciplines' (*Centre for Energy, Petroleum, and Mineral Law and Policy* 2007); David Tarr and Peter Thomon, 'The Merits of Dual Pricing of Russian Natural Gas' (2004) 27 *The World Economy* 1173; Reinhard Quick, 'Export Taxes and Dual Pricing: How Can Trade Distortive Government Practices be Tackled?' in J Pauwelyn, *Global Challenges* (n 30) 193–96.

54 As Melaku Desta puts it, 'some even feel that, by doing so, the Agriculture Agreement has set a bad example', Desta (n 26) 213.

55 See among others Sadeq Bigdeli, 'Incentive Schemes to Promote Renewables and the WTO Law of Subsidies' in Thomas Cottier (ed), *International Trade Regulation and the Mitigation of Climate Change* (CUP 2009) 155; Sadeq Bigdeli, 'Resurrecting the Dead? The Expired Non-Actionable Subsidies and the Lingering Question of "Green Space"' (2011) 27 *Manchester Journal of International Economic Law* 2; Aaron Cosbey, 'Renewable Energy Subsidies and the WTO: The Wrong Law and the Wrong Venue' (2011) 44 *Subsidy Watch*; Toni Harmer, *Biofuels Subsidies and the Law of the WTO* (2009) ICTSD Issue Paper no 20; Kerryn Lang, *Increasing the Momentum of Fossil-fuel Subsidy Reform: Developments and Opportunities* (2010 UNEP Conference Report); Magnus Lodefalk and Mark Storey, 'Climate Measures and WTO Rules on Subsidies' (2005) 39 *JWT* 11; Luca Rubini, 'The Subsidization of Renewable Energy in the WTO: Issues and Perspectives' (2011) *NCCR Trade Regulation*, Working Paper no 2011/32; Luca Rubini, 'Ain't Waistin' Time no more: Subsidies for Renewable Energy, the SCM Agreement, Policy Space and Law Reform' (2013) 15 *JIEL* 525; Ronald Steenblick, 'Subsidies in the Traditional Energy Sector' in Joost Pauwelyn (ed), *Global Challenges at the Intersection of Trade, Energy and the Environment* (Centre for Trade and Economic Integration 2010) 183; Marie Wilke, *Feed-in Tariffs for Renewable Energy and WTO Subsidy Rules* (2011) ICTSD Issue Paper no 4.

56 Bagchi (n 51) 31.

The ITA seems also practically impossible to transpose, as issues are completely different: the IT sector knows mainly import barriers and problems related to intellectual property. What is more, the ITA is the result of a huge compromise and its provisions are weakly ambitious as the attractiveness of the text needed to be compensated by a reduction of obligations.[57]

The Setting: Organizing the Legal Relationship between a New EA and the General Rules

If some, most, or, ideally, all Members were to agree upon the idea of adopting a separate agreement and even on its actual provisions, this new EA would need to clarify the terms of its integration into the general framework of the multilateral trading system. In other words, the relationship between this new agreement and already existing rules will need to be defined, sooner or later. In this vein, the question will be whether the EA could and should anticipate its unavoidable conflicts, or at least its risk of problematic coexistence with the pre-existing texts.[58]

Any further steps in the analysis will need to be based on the assumption that the new EA will be made part of WTO law *via* its integration in either one of the two lists of separate agreements: those of Annex 1A (if multilateralism is preferred), or those of Annex 4 (if the agreement is plurilateral).[59] Only thus will the EA be a covered agreement under article 1 of the DSU, falling under the *ratione materiae* jurisdiction of the panels and Appellate Body.[60]

Including the EA in the list of annexed agreements is just a premise, it does not provide for an actual solution to the problem of its relationship with the other agreements. Given the complexities of this issue,[61] the acceptability of any new agreement would nowadays be contingent upon designing a precise and clear way of organizing its relationship with the other texts in order to avoid most of these problems which have already occurred in one form or another.

Two options are available to the adventurous designers of a new EA for dealing with this elephant in the room. First, there is a somewhat 'passive' way: it can be left up to the judges to construct the solution. Some of the above-mentioned agreements follow this rationale.[62]

---

57 Wunsch -Vincent, *WTO, E-Commerce and Information Technologies* (n 20) 45.

58 For a presentation of the unavoidability of this sort of conflicts see Joost Pauwelyn, *Conflict of Norms in Public International Law: How WTO Law Relates to Other Rules of International Law* (CUP 2003) 23–24: 'Obviously, the more legal instruments one is faced with, especially when these instruments were negotiated at different points in time, the greater the risk of conflict . . . As autonomous legal instruments, created subsequently to the original GATT 1947, these Uruguay Round agreements sometimes derogated from, and often repeated, partly or fully, their parent GATT provisions. Only at a very late stage of the negotiations was it decided to bring all the results of the Uruguay Round together under one umbrella agreement, to be binding equally on all WTO members. This had the unintended result of creating repetitions, omissions and possible conflicts. No time was left to work out the complex interrelationship between the different legal texts. To reopen the negotiations for that purpose would have jeopardised the delicate consensus reached under each of these legal instruments. This separate consensus was, moreover, not always reached by the same negotiators'.

59 These categories are paradoxically alternative even though it may be possible for a plurilateral agreement to become de facto multilateral, see Geslin (n 36) 62.

60 It should be noted that if the EA is plurilateral, the applicability of the DSU 'shall be subject to the adoption of a decision by the parties to each agreement setting out the terms for the application of the Understanding to the individual agreement, including any special or additional rules or procedures for inclusion in Appendix 2, as notified to the DSB' (Appendix 1, *in fine*, DSU).

61 See for instance Appellate Body Report, *Brazil: Measures Affecting Desiccated Coconut*, 21 February 1997, WT/DS22/AB/R, 15.

62 This choice was not necessarily a conscious one at the time, see Elisabetta Montaguti and Maurits Lugard, 'The GATT 1994 and Other Annex 1A Agreements: Four Different Relationships?' (2000) 3 *JIEL* 474.

Second, the new EA could anticipate the potential incoherences and provide for a clear solution to the problem, much as article 21(1) of the AoA seeks to do.[63]

In more conceptual terms, the relationship between a new EA and the other agreements could adhere to one of two paradigms – it could either be one of accumulation or one of exclusion.

The Relationship of Accumulation

The relationship of accumulation is the general principle, as the Panel noted in *Turkey – Textiles*[64] on the grounds of the doctrine of the *effet utile* (*ut res magis valeat quam pereat*).[65] There is a general presumption against conflict.[66] However, this presumption is not irrefutable.[67] All it does is give some directions as to the interpretation of different provisions in order to avoid conflict where such avoidance is possible.

If the entire rationale behind a new EA is for it to have a strictly cumulative relationship with the other agreements, having no articulation provisions whatsoever would not be a problem. Nonetheless, even in these cases interpretation is what determines whether there is conflict or not. And the solutions provided by the case law are so far quite ambiguous and incomplete, as it would always be the case: the adjudicating process is in its essence supposed to give case-by-case solutions and avoid general observations.

The cumulative model is in itself ambivalent, as it covers two different patterns of non-conflictual coexistence: overlap and complementarity.[68]

Overlap occurs when two provisions have the same coverage and usually one of them deals more specifically with an issue. This would be the dialectic of those provisions of the EA that aim at clarifying the way general rules should be applied in the energy sector: for instance, the extent to which carbon emissions should be taken into consideration when evaluating the similarity of products under GATT articles I and III or what would 'transit' mean in the case of fixed infrastructures under GATT article V. In such cases, the Appellate Body insists on examining the two provisions separately 'to give meaning and effect to the distinct legal obligations arising under these two different legal provisions'.[69] The judge may appear at first glance to adopt a sort of a two-tier test,[70] although in reality the approach clearly gives prevalence to the special provision. Any additional text in the sectoral agreement, which would most probably envisage its prevalence over the general rules, would change nothing to this reasoning.

The other aspect of the cumulative relationship, complementarity, covers situations where provisions cover the same broad matter without there being any overlap (much like GATT article

63 Art 21(1): 'The provisions of GATT 1994 and of other Multilateral Trade Agreements in Annex 1A to the WTO Agreement shall apply subject to the provisions of this Agreement.'

64 Panel Report, *Turkey: Restrictions on Imports of Textile and Clothing Products*, 31 May 1999, WT/DS34/R, para 9.92.

65 Appellate Body Report, *Canada: Measures Affecting the Importation of Milk and the Exportation of Dairy Products*, 13 October 1999, WT/DS113/AB/R, 133.

66 Panel Report, *Indonesia: Certain Measures Affecting the Automobile Industry*, 2 July 1998, WT/DS59/R, para 14.28.

67 See Veronique Guevremont, 'Traités multilatéraux: nouvelles perspectives relatives à l'articulation' in Vincent Tomkiewicz (ed), *Les sources et les normes dans le droit de l'OMC* (Pedone 2012) 31.

68 ibid 31.

69 Appellate Body Report, *Chile: Price Band System and Safeguard Measures Relating to Certain Agricultural Products*, 23 September 2002, WT/DS207/AB/R, para 188.

70 Appellate Body Report, *European Communities: Regime for the Importation, Sale and Distribution of Bananas*, 9 September 1997, WT/DS27/AB/R, para 203.

XIX and the Safeguards Agreement). This situation is not problematic at all, but unfortunately it is extremely rare and would only be of relevance for the energy sector if the new EA is quite limited in its approach. Adding a special provision to the sectoral agreement to manage such a situation is of little use.

Whether the cumulative relationship is one of overlap or one of complementarity, another particular issue will still be in need of further clarification, preferably by means of a special provision in that sense. It concerns to the much-discussed possibility of using the general exceptions of GATT article XX to cover non-compliance with other legal instruments. The AB has had to deal with this issue twice, both in relation with China's Accession protocol.[71] The judges admit that it would, in principle, be possible for a general exception to cover a violation of a special provision, even contained elsewhere than the general agreement, but this possibility is contingent upon the existence of a 'gateway' in the special text. Since the AB is clearly reluctant to make any broad statements on this issue, it seems preferable to add special provisions to any new agreement, either providing for such a gateway or excluding any deduction of its existence.

The Relationship of Exclusion

The relationship of exclusion is exceptional. It stems from a clear intention in that sense, expressly provided for in the sectoral agreement. The model is found either when new rules are clearly incompatible with the old ones (discrepancy *a posteriori*), or when there is an express derogation clause in a special agreement (discrepancy regulated *a priori*). In both cases what defines the relationship of exclusion is the fact that adherence to rule A makes it impossible to comply with rule B.

A new EA might contain rules that are so specific that complying with them would entail a violation of the general rules: for instance, it may prohibit export tariffs, much as the NAFTA does, while GATT article II clearly does not provide for such a prohibition. In this case, the underlying conflict will not be prevented simply by choosing not to add a special provision addressing the situation. On the contrary, such an omission would only allow for the issue to be dealt with pursuant to a general rule that institutes a '*sorte de hiérarchie de crise*'.[72] This rule is contained in the General Interpretative note to Annex 1: A.

The special rules of an EA will prevail over the general ones if conflict is indeed found, but the key concept of conflict is extremely complex. In a nutshell, it covers two situations: '(i) clashes between obligations contained in GATT 1994 and obligations contained in agreements listed in Annex 1A, where those obligations are mutually exclusive in the sense that a Member cannot comply with both obligations at the same time, and (ii) the situation where a rule in one agreement prohibits what a rule in another agreement explicitly permits'.[73]

This narrow interpretation of the concept of conflict avoids finding contradictions where such do not exist or are only deceptively apparent. Choosing to hand over all articulation to

---

71 Appellate Body Report, *China: Measures Affecting Trading Rights and Distribution Services for Certain Publications and Audiovisual Entertainment Products*, 21 December 2009, WT/DS363/AB/R and Appellate Body Report, *China: Measures Related to the Exportation of Various Raw Materials*, 30 January 2012, WT/DS394/AB/R, WT/DS395/AB/R and WT/DS398/AB/R.

72 Yves Nouvel, 'L'unité du système commercial multilatéral' (2000) 46 *Annuaire français de droit international* 669.

73 Panel Report, *European Communities: Regime for the Importation, Sale and Distribution of Bananas – Complaint by the United States*, 22 May 1997, WT/DS27/R/USA, para 7.159. For further developments see Panel Report, *Indonesia: Certain Measures Affecting the Automobile Industry* (n 66) footnote 649, and Pauwelyn, *Conflict of Norms* (n 60).

this Interpretative Note may be a sensible solution. However, this choice will most probably fall victim to the *lacunae* of the Note. It is indeed extremely limited as it only refers to conflicts between a special text and the GATT and does not address the question of the relationship between different special agreements. This conflict is, however, lurking in the background in the energy sector, especially considering suggestions that a new EA contain detailed disciplines on energy subsidies that may be in conflict with the more general rules of the SCM Agreement. One cannot but admit that if the EA does not contain an articulation provision, solutions will need to be found on a case-by-case basis and on the grounds of a conflict rule that is clearly insufficient.

If the EA were to manage a priori this conflictual relationship, it would fall into the category of the derogations. A derogation specifically permits Members to act inconsistently with the GATT in order to adhere to the sectoral agreement. The result is not very different from what would happen if things were left to the Interpretative Note concerning the GATT, but the sectoral agreement will have prevailed on the grounds of its own provisions. However, the situation would differ substantially concerning the other agreements.

Such a derogation provision can use the model of article 21(1) of the AoA. The ambiguity of this text has been haunting panels and the AB for years,[74] but the judges seem to have found and followed an interpretation method that shows a clear effort to maintain coherence especially where conflict is not inevitable. This logic is, however, related to the particular place of the AoA and to its rationale of reintegration. If a new EA were to contain a similar clause, this logic would not be transposable to its interpretation, as its rationale will most probably not be one of reintegration. Most certainly, the formula used will not change the general idea that 'whenever it is possible for a WTO Member to simultaneously comply with both (agreements), it should do so'.[75] However, the interpretation of the concept of 'conflict' may be broader, in the search of a more appropriate regulation given the specificities of the sector. All of these possibilities (and dangers) need to be taken into consideration when designing the new articulation clause.

Conclusion

Trade in the energy sector is nowadays making, quite abruptly, its entrance (or, for some, its comeback) into the general framework of the multilateral trading system. Nonetheless, WTO law may in some cases appear not flexible enough to take into consideration the specificities of this sector. If a sectoral Energy Agreement is to be designed its provisions will need to be carefully drafted in order to avoid as many interpretation predicaments as possible. However, the need of consensus on all of these issues will undoubtedly result in somewhat reduced obligations and there is still no guarantee that all possible complications will be resolved in advance. Arguably, such a modification of the existing general framework will be insufficient. If we change the angle of attack, and instead suggest that the flexibilities of the general rules, combined with some daring interpretations by panels and the Appellate Body, allow for sufficient consideration of the specificities of energy trade, this will not only prove to be a less conflictual way of dealing with the problem, but also reinforce the system instead of fragmenting it.

---

74   See for instance Appellate Body Report, *European Communities: Regime for the Importation, Sale and Distribution of Bananas*, 9 September 1997, WT/DS27/AB/R and Appellate Body Report, *United States: Subsidies on Upland Cotton*, 3 March 2005, WT/DS267/AB/R, para 530.
75   Mavroidis (n 22) 753.

12 Multilevel Governance in Food Security Regulation

With the Example of Costa Rican Rice

Carolina Palma[*]

Food Security Approaches and Tools to Tackle Food Insecurity

Achieving food security,[1] that is, meeting the challenge of feeding 9 billion people by the year 2020, is taking a predominant role in both national and international agendas. It is a challenge to ensure food supply for a growing population, but especially when people are still suffering from hunger and malnutrition. Despite the fact that a sufficient amount of food is being produced globally, it is alarming that malnutrition is estimated to be the cause of 30 per cent of infant deaths and that approximately 850 million people are undernourished.[2] However, undernourishment and malnourishment are not the only concerns when it comes to food security. Obesity and bad nutrition are also problems since globally there are more people that are overweight than underweight. Undernourishment is a challenge not only in Asia, which was home to 65 per cent of the world's undernourished people in 2010–2012 (Asia having the largest population), but also in Africa, where the prevalence of undernourishment is 23 per cent, compared to 8 per cent in Latin America and the Caribbean.[3] Even though the proportion of the population in developing countries that is undernourished has fallen over the past two decades, statistics show that the pace of decline has slowed. This situation presents a challenge for the growing middle classes in developing countries that are faced with increasing urbanization, larger nutritional needs, and greater meat consumption[4] on less land,[5] while also suffering the effect of climate change.[6]

---

[*] PhD Candidate at the World Trade Institute, Bern University and Professor for International Law and Multilateral Trade, University of Costa Rica. Carolina.palma@wti.org.

1 Food security exists when all people, at all times, have physical, social and economic access to sufficient safe and nutritious food that meets their dietary needs and food preferences for an active and healthy life. In: FAO World Food Summit, 'Rome Declaration on World Food Security' (United Nations 1996).

2 OECD, *Global Food Security* (Organization for Economic Co-operation and Development 2013) 22.

3 OECD (n 2) 23.

4 Feeding animals takes up to 1,700 calories per person out of the chain, whereas livestock adds only 500 calories, Craig Pearson, 'A Fresh Look at the Roots of Food Insecurity' in Rosemary Gail Rayfuse (ed) *The Challenge of Food Security: International Policy and Regulatory Frameworks* (Edward Elgar Publishing 2012) 23.

5 However, it is important to note that it is debatable whether there will be a shortage of food and whether these factors really have an influence on food security. According to FAO, the amount of food should increase 70 per cent by 2050, but studies from the IIASA show that there could be 1.3 billion hectares of grassland and open woodland suitable for agriculture if needed, which amounts to 80 per cent of the area of current crop fields. Even so, most authors coincide that the best approach is agricultural intensification and not extensification, Paul McMahon, *Feeding Frenzy: The New Politics of Food* (Profile Books 2013) 79–81.

6 Whether climate change will have such an impact on food security is debatable and is subject to further discussion.

In a world where famines and undernourishment are causes of poverty, crucial questions arise as to how to address food security. The discussion on food security is anchored in three dimensions: food production, food trade and investment in food. The interplay of these dimensions in the battle against food insecurity, from a regulatory standpoint, is complex. First, the definition of food security has a political dimension, and different approaches have made it difficult to reach a consensus in regulation. For some, food security needs small farmer protection[7] and therefore trade should not interfere with national policies for small farmer protection. For others, farmers cannot feed themselves alone, they also need trade and trade liberalization rules that allow food access, whereas market-distorting policies potentially impede the achievement of long-term food security.[8] Thus, internal policies that are consistent with trade rules are not always coherent and integrative in their approach to food security.[9] This chapter looks at some of the policies found in precepts with special emphasis on WTO regulations from the Agreement on Agriculture (AoA) that have an impact on food security and provides an example on how multilevel governance operates in practice.

To ensure food security, policies have been targeted across all the relevant areas, namely food availability, accessibility, utilization and stability. Some of the discussion examines how food production policies increase yield[10] by optimizing productivity per area, reducing waste,[11] and having governmental support for farming policies and technologies. However, there is some evidence that over the last two decades food supplies have grown faster than the population in developing regions, resulting in rising food availability per person. Average dietary energy supply adequacy – dietary energy supply as a percentage of the average dietary energy requirement – has risen by almost 10 per cent over the last two decades in developing regions as a whole.[12] In addition, global food availability is considered a reachable goal.[13] Although the world's population will increase to 9.3 billion by 2050, which will require an agricultural growth of 60 per cent (meaning an additional 1.1 per cent per year), the world can still produce enough food to feed the population given the current portions of arable land and its potential.[14]

---

7   Olivier De Schutter, *International Trade in Agriculture and the Right to Food* (Friedrich-Ebert-Stiftung 2009); Olivier De Schutter, 'The World Trade Organization and the Post Global Agenda Putting Food Security First in the International Trade System' (2011) Briefing Note 04 <www.srfood.org/images/stories/pdf/otherdocuments/20111116_briefing_note_05_en.pdf> accessed 15 January 2015. De Schutter contends that existing WTO rules do include certain flexibilities for States to pursue food security-related measures. However, he also affirms that in no circumstances should trade commitments be allowed to restrict a country's ability to adopt measures guaranteeing national food security. The criticism by some relates to the wrong solutions, for instance Christian Häberli, 'The WTO and Food Security: What's Wrong with the Rules?' in Rosemary Gail Rayfuse (ed) *The Challenge of Food Security: International Policy and Regulatory Frameworks* (Edward Elgar Publishing, 2012) 150.

8   Häberli (n 7) 149.

9   ibid 161–67. Those who call for a food security impact assessment for each negotiating proposal, also later propose reforms in stockpiles, tariff rate quota (TRQ) fills, and export restrictions, Christian Häberli, 'Three "Bali Deliverables" for More Food Security' (2013) NCCR Trade Regulation Working Paper No 2013/44 <www.wti.org/fileadmin/user_upload/nccr-trade.ch/wp4/Working_Paper_No_2013_44.pdf> accessed 15 January 2015.

10   Pearson (n 4) 25.

11   ibid 27.

12   FAO, *The State of Food Insecurity in the World* (United Nations 2013).

13   McMahon (n 5) 2. Also evidence supporting the literature: OECD-FAO, 'Agricultural Outlook' (OECD 2012).

14   Much has been written in terms of food availability. Starting with Malthus, who predicted a gloomy future where food would not have been available for this generation. However, according to FAO, over the past 50 years the

Concerning food accessibility, part of the literature points out that the challenge lies in raising the incomes of the poor[15] with household entitlements[16] and proper distribution.[17] As proof that raising incomes is crucial, statistics show that there were as many hungry people in the world when international food prices were at an all-time low as there are today with higher food prices.[18] Addressing the vulnerable population's access to food, the literature finds that some of the solutions to improve food access are higher incomes,[19] better trade rules,[20] and increased investment in food.[21] Some of the regulatory difficulties lie in the fact that institutions dealing with food security issues have different approaches to it, and therefore come up with several regulatory alternatives. In the next section, some of these instruments are analysed by pointing out diverging regulatory views.

Regulatory Instruments Contributing to Food Security

Background

The history of the concept of food security can be traced back to the twentieth century after the Second World War when processes of reconstruction and decolonization were taking place.[22] There was a need for a food regime and some institutions took over the task of defining it such as the International Monetary Fund (IMF) and the World Bank (WB). Other organizations followed and procured the duty of developing a transversal conceptualization through institutions like the Food and Agriculture Organization (FAO), the Organization for Economic Co-operation and Development (OECD) and the World Trade Organization (WTO). However, the term food security was first incorporated into international policies in the early 1970s after a shortage of wheat. As a result, States started to secure their own food supplies.[23] This shortage revealed how volatile and unreliable food supply could be and led to initiatives of international instruments to eradicate hunger such as the World Food Conference from the FAO and the International Fund for Agricultural Development (IFAD). Finally, after a series of attempts to address food security, the 1996 World Food Summit produced the current definition: 'Food security exists when all people, at all times, have physical, social

---

amount of food per person has actually increased, OECD (n 14) 32. This does not mean that crucial challenges such as climate change, energy and land erosion should not be addressed, since these variables can completely change food availability.

15 OECD (n 14) 11.

16 See Sen (n 18).

17 Amartya Sen, *Development as Freedom* (OUP 1999) 1 ff; Amartya Sen, 'Food and Freedom' (1989) 17 *World Development* 769; Amartya Sen, *Inequality Reexamined* (Harvard University Press 1995); Amartya Sen, *Poverty and Famines: An Essay on Entitlement and Deprivation* (OUP 1982).

18 OECD (n 14) 22.

19 ibid 27.

20 Häberli (n 7). See also T Josling and others, 'Understanding International Trade in Agricultural Products: One Hundred Years of Contributions by Agricultural Economists' (2010) 92 *American Journal of Agricultural Economics* 424; Stefan Wager, 'International Agricultural Trade Liberalization and Food Security: Risks Associated with a Fully Liberalized Global Marketplace' (2009) 64 *Aussenwirtschaft: Schweizerische Zeitschrift für Internationale Wirtschaftsbeziehungen/The Swiss Review of International Economic Relations* 139.

21 UNCTAD, *Investment Policy Framework for Sustainable Development* (United Nations 2012).

22 William D Schanbacher, *The Politics of Food: The Global Conflict between Food Security and Food Sovereignty* (ABC-CLIO 2010) viii.

23 Matias E Margulis, 'The Regime Complex for Food Security: Implications for the Global Hunger Challenge' (2013) 19 *Global Governance* 53–67.

and economic access to sufficient safe and nutritious food that meets their dietary needs and food preferences for an active and healthy life.'[24] This definition includes the dimensions of availability of food, accessibility and utilization for people's proper health. Also, a fourth requirement is the stability of the above-mentioned dimensions over time.

The proliferation of international institutions and concepts reveals a pattern of 'punctuated, rather than gradual growth'[25] when institutions such as the World Food Program (WFP) and the Food and Agriculture Council (FAC) appeared, followed by the Committee on Food Security (CFS), IFAD, World Food Council (WFC), and Consultative Group for International Agricultural Research (CGIAR) established in the 1970s. Then the 1996 World Food Summit and, after the food crisis, the United Nations (UN) High Level Task Force on Global Food Security (GFS) and the G8 Global Partnership on Agriculture, Food Security and Nutrition were created. Some of these institutions had structured mandates and complex structures involving State and non-State actors. Other later institutions developed voluntary guidelines and international codifying efforts creating a web of regulations in food security. This chapter focuses on the trade aspect regulated by such institutions with special attention to divergent approaches to the trade aspect and visions from WTO and the FAO.

Policy Responses According to Food Security Approaches

Regarding trade, the FAO states: 'open markets have a pivotal role to play in raising production and incomes. Trade enables production to be located in areas where resources are used most efficiently and has an essential role in getting product from surplus to deficit areas.'[26] It also points out that rapid income growth sustained for a long period actually leads to poverty reduction, food security, and nutritional improvement of the population. However, the FAO sees the problem in the fact that the link of growth to food security and nutrition may be weakened by unfavourable income distribution as well as limited access of the poor to some of the benefits of trade such as infrastructure, improved technology, and human capital formation. In this sense, the FAO considers in its policies that rising inequality, 'left unchecked', could even dampen subsequent growth and trade would actually produce negative consequences.[27] The reason is that some of the negative effects of trade liberalization would evidently be seen in some groups, specifically protected farmers. Liberalization would mean exposition to lack of competitiveness for protected exports and a price rise for the consumer.

Other movements support an extremist view that argues for protection to be limited only to small farmers in order to achieve food security. These views are based on the idea that because food security has not been achieved for hundreds of millions of the world's poor, then other models of food sovereignty should take centre stage in the fight against global malnutrition.[28] In their opinion, models, such as the *Via Campesina*, which promote food sovereignty, 'demonstrate how farming communities are founded on community gatherings, the exchange of knowledge, and social events that express the cultural traditions of an

---

24 World Food Summit (n 10).
25 Matias E Margulis, 'The Evolving Global Governance of Food Security' (2011) <http://papers.ssrn.com/sol3/papers.cfm?abstract_id=1823453> accessed 15 January 2015; Rosemary Rayfuse and Nicole Weisfelt, *The Challenge of Food Security: International Policy and Regulatory Frameworks* (Edward Elgar 2012).
26 FAO, *Panorama Food and Nutritional Security 2014 Executive Summary* (FAO 2014) 16.
27 FAO, *Poverty Alleviation and Food Security in Asia: Lessons and Challenges* (United Nations 1998) 2. See also Emmanuel Jimenez, *Development and the next Generation* (World Bank Publications 2006).
28 Schanbacher (n 23) ix.

agrarian livelihood'.[29] They see this as a way towards guaranteeing the human rights of peasants and farmers in order to provide them with food security.

As simplistic as this may seem, there is some sense to this thinking. There has been a strengthening of dispute resolution systems at a multilateral, regional and bilateral level, which means more protection for private interests, more protection for trade and more protection for economic interests. There has also been a strengthening of some human rights forums such as the creation of an International Criminal Court to punish genocide and other crimes against humanity. And yet, there is no system to punish massive violations of human rights when there is famine, hunger, and malnutrition or even to have the right to food recognized by international courts according to the international community in the ICESCR.[30] Moreover, within the international trade system, in the GATT there is no mention to the right to food or food security. Despite trade global regulations, global programmes and food aid, national food security is still at risk. Because of this, it is understandable how some authors go back to the concept of food sovereignty and subsistence economy because to them the international system has 'failed to deliver'.

Also promoting a higher input in local food systems, Olivier De Schutter calls 'for a reform of the international trade system', to 'strengthen agriculture', and to 'turn away from further liberalization'.[31] De Schutter, a former UN Special Rapporteur on the Right to Food, had the merit of bringing the concept of food security to various fields (such as trade) and drawing a connecting line, as well as promoting intensively the reform of regulations in the AoA. He also called to refrain from additional trade liberalization. De Schutter argued that WTO rules conflict with food security because current Green Box and domestic support rules are unbalanced; they provide more flexibility to developed country farmers than to developing country farmers.[32] In his thinking, the multilateral trade regime as well as regional and bilateral trade agreements must allow countries to develop and implement ambitious food security policies including public food reserves, temporary import restrictions, active marketing boards and safety net insurance schemes in support of the right to food.[33]

These two positions, the food sovereignty model and the milder position calling for a strengthening of the agricultural systems, have been criticized for not taking into account that income inequality plus rising prices for food cannot be solved by solely focusing on internal food systems, but need to be addressed with an integrative view that also considers trade and investment to be used as tools to contribute to food security. All groups – farmers, producers and consumers – need trade. However, even when taking into account the importance of trade, there is much criticism regarding imbalances present in the current trading system, hindering the real economic growth and poverty reduction strategies of developing countries. Below, some of these regulations in AoA and how they conform to a regime complex of multilevel regulations, which may translate into obstacles for food security, are mentioned.

29 ibid 9.
30 United Nations, International Covenant on Economic, Social, and Cultural Rights, New York, 16 December 1966, *United Nations Treaty Series*, vol 993, 3. There has been recognition though by the Interamerican Human Rights Court in the three cases against Guatemala.
31 De Schutter, 'The World Trade Organization and the Post Global Agenda Putting Food Security First in the International Trade System' (n 7).
32 ibid.
33 Olivier De Schutter, 'The FAO Must Do More to Promote Food as a Basic Human Right' *The Guardian* (London, 4 March 2013) <www.theguardian.com/global-development/poverty-matters/2013/mar/04/fao-food-basic-human-right> accessed 13 February 2014.

Apart from the WTO, two institutions have been effectively involved in food security regulation contributing not only to its discussion but also to the multilevel framework. In the case of the OECD, this forum deals with some food security matters. For instance, it has supported the respective presidencies of the G8/G20/AFSI (which has a food security multi-donor trust) sessions on issues related to food security, food price volatility and agricultural productivity. Additionally, it is involved in the UN High Level Task Force on the Food Security (HLTF) and it participates in the Global Donor Platform on Rural Development. In 2011 and 2012, the OECD held meetings at the Global Forum on Agriculture which focused on poverty reduction and policy coherence for food security in developing countries, and it published a series of documents on responsible agricultural investment. For the FAO, its involvement with food security is crucial since its main objective is 'raising levels of nutrition and standards of living of the people under their respective jurisdictions; securing improvements in the efficiency of the production and distribution of all food and agricultural products; bettering the condition of rural populations; and thus contributing towards an expanding world economy and ensuring humanity's freedom from hunger'.[34] Also, the CFS has been very active in drafting principles for responsible agriculture and for discussions of its improvement. Whereas the FAO deals directly with food security issues, the WTO deals with the trade aspect of it, especially within the discussion at the Doha Development Round and just recently in the Bali agenda.[35] Some of the provisions are analysed in the following sections.

The Role of WTO in Food Security Regulation and the Regime Complex

Food Security Regulation in the Agreement of Agriculture (AoA)

The AoA mentions in its preamble: 'commitments under the reform programme should be made in an equitable way among all Members, having regard to non-trade concerns, including food security and the need to protect the environment'. It is, however, the only mention of food security and does not provide guidelines on how to achieve it. Additionally, former WTO Director General Pascal Lamy referring to food security considered that ' . . . trade plays or can play a better role in addressing the rise in food prices and tackling food insecurity. Trade is part of the solution, and not part of the problem.'[36] His statement recognizes the fact that trade has an impact on food security and could contribute to it, but like the AoA he does not state how trade can be part of the solution and does not provide a roadmap to help achieve this goal. Moreover, he does not address some of the problems of the AoA that have consolidated the status quo of some countries but has left others without room, and he does not address the specific issues of developing and least developed countries.

At the Doha Development Round, discussions about development and trade took place in November 2011. Ministers supported the role of free trade in promoting economic development and alleviating poverty. Some of the subjects of discussion included trade in agricultural

---

34 For more information: <http://cic.nyu.edu/sites/default/files/page_global_governance_public_good.pdf> accessed 15 January 2015.

35 Christian Häberli, 'After Bali: WTO Rules Applying to Public Food Reserves' (2014) FAO Commodity and Trade Policy Research Working Paper no 46 <www.fao.org/3/a-i3820e.pdf> accessed 15 January 2015.

36 Pascal Lamy, 'Lamy on the Rise in Food Prices: "Trade Is Part of the Answer, Not Part of the Problem"' (Berlin Agriculture Ministers' Summit, 22 January 2011) <www.wto.org/english/news_e/sppl_e/sppl183_e.htm> accessed 15 January 2015.

products, trade and technological transfer, intellectual property, health and preferential treatment for developing country exports. However, the discussions did not transform into actual regulations and the AoA kept provisions that affect food security in developing countries. The Agreement required members to liberalize agricultural trade across the three main areas of market access, export subsidies and domestic support, including converting non-tariff import restrictions to tariffs, binding and reducing them. But many developing countries, because of lack of tarification, were not permitted to use the special safeguard mechanisms, which would have given them more room to act and protect sensitive agricultural products, which other developed nations were allowed to do. Scholars have criticized rules like these by stating that, in fact, the AoA institutionalized existing inequalities by prohibiting some countries from using these measures while it consolidated the situation of developed countries. Even though some developing nations now also use these mechanisms, and even though subsidies are also subject to criticism, the main problem is that the playing field is not the same for all. Therefore, trade liberalization opponents say that such measures actually have crowded out local producers and have caused price increases for importers. Later in 2013 in Bali, Ministers continued to discuss the development agenda and even included trade facilitation and food security issues according to some countries' interests, but again, no reforms have been included in the AoA yet.

Allowing for subsidies, the AoA consolidated the situation of large countries, which had a negative influence on food prices, and consequently, created price volatility. Moreover, it maintained obstacles in the form of technical barriers to trade and bureaucratic measures, which impact small-scale farmers and farmers from developing countries. Such subsidies have a negative impact on farmers, by artificially supporting them whereas other measures could lend support in long-term ways such as providing technology and education for a more competitive future.[37] Even so, subsidies are not the preferred measure in cases of small economies with competitiveness problems. But even if they were the only way to confront globalization, because of the ruling of the AoA, these small economies are not allowed to use them.[38] Furthermore, regulations on internal support and export competition pose unanswered questions in areas where there is much room for improvement. Countries have carte blanche to impose export restrictions even in cases of food aid, which some LDCs may depend on. Export restrictions may then lead to a shortage or even lack of food not only in the market but also where food aid is concerned.

Regarding the impact of trade distortion, according to the OECD in 2006 when prices were lower than today, 'the price depressing effects of OECD country policies caused cereal and meat prices to be 2–3% higher than they would otherwise be' and in the case of dairy products, '50% cuts caus[ed] prices to increase by 13%'.[39] In this sense, even though in other products the consequences were not as evident (because the effects are complex and vary by country), the main conclusion from this study was that OECD countries should reform primarily because of their own interest to do so.[40] On balance, the OECD's analysis concluded

---

37 Christian Häberli, 'Do WTO Rules Improve or Impair the Right to Food?' in Joseph McMahon (ed) *Research Handbook on the WTO Agriculture Agreement: New and Emerging Issues in International Agricultural Trade Law* (Edward Elgar 2012) 81. Also, on subsidies' impact on farmers, Kym Anderson, *Reducing Distortions to Agricultural Incentives: Progress, Pitfalls, and Prospects* (2006) World Bank Policy Research Working Paper 4092 <http://elibrary.worldbank.org/doi/pdf/10.1596/1813–9450–4092> accessed 15 January 2015.

38 This is when 'trade becomes part of the problem', Häberli, 'Do WTO Rules Improve or Impair the Right to Food?' (n 7) 90–98.

39 OECD (n 14) 72.

40 ibid.

that most developing countries would gain from OECD country liberalization. However, the gains would be relatively small compared to the benefits of reforming their own policies.[41]

To name some further difficulties, even measures that are found in the Amber Box, which is said to allow only minimal distortions, may have effects on global trade or on production. The same applies to the case of domestic support of food reserves. One of the unanswered questions is how big 'minimal' distortions would have to be before such distortions shift a measure into the Amber Box,[42] which has not been properly defined in the text of the AoA or in dispute resolution cases.[43] Additionally, the *de minimis* rule set a limit for contributions of 10 per cent approximately in developing countries and 5 per cent in developed countries. But, the *Developing Country Green Box* in article 6.2 is very limited. Some authors consider that this *de minimis* rule is in reality so limited that most developing countries cannot make use of it for poor producers in small economies,[44] whereas larger economies can. For those countries to make use of it, measures must be provided through a publicly funded government programme without the effect of providing price support to producers,[45] whereas subsidies provided by larger economies do have a bigger distortion potential than small subsidies given by small developing nations in times of crisis. There is evidence that even the Green Box support mechanisms may have a negative impact on farmers in developing countries without Amber Box support.[46] There is some evidence that export competition was one of the causes of the food crisis because it had an impact on net food-importing developing countries (NFIDC). Consumers were hit by high prices and small farmers did not have the response capacity to increase production. Also, given that export restrictions are mechanisms to disincentive production, they cannot improve food security. At the bare minimum, food aid purchases should be allowed without export restrictions.[47]

In short, the regulations in such a complex system and the contradicting, overlapping rules with different regulatory layers need to fulfil the minimum standard of 'do no harm',[48] meaning that international regulations should at least avoid negative spill-overs over national food security and vice versa. In this sense, the starting point is that any trade reform should be directed towards doing 'no harm' to developing and least developed countries in their pursuit towards food security.

Multilevel Governance of Food Security Regulation

The different layers of governance and international bodies dealing with food security matters only at international level – not to mention the national ones – not only constitute a system of multilevel or multilayered governance,[49] but also result in what some authors call a 'regime

---

41 ibid.
42 Häberli, 'Three "Bali Deliverables" for More Food Security' (n 9) 22.
43 ibid.
44 ibid.
45 Art 6 Agreement on Agriculture.
46 Kym Anderson, 'Reducing Distortions to Agricultural Incentives: Progress, Pitfalls, and Prospects' (2006) 88 *American Journal of Agricultural Economics* 1135.
47 Häberli, 'Three "Bali Deliverables" for More Food Security' (n 9) 22.
48 Sandra Polaski, 'Agricultural Negotiations at the WTO: First, Do No Harm' (2005) *Policy Outlook*, Carnegie Endowment for International Peace <http://carnegieendowment.org/files/PO18.polaski.FINAL.pdf> accessed 15 January 2015.
49 Thomas Cottier and Maya Hertig, *The Prospects of 21st Century Constitutionalism* (2003) 7 *Max Planck Yearbook of United Nations Law* 261; Thomas Cottier, The Prospects of International Trade Regulation (CUP 2014) 30. See also Thomas Cottier, 'Poverty, Redistribution, and International Trade Regulation' in Krista Nadakavukaren Schefer (ed), *Poverty and the International Economic Legal System: Duties to the World's Poor* (CUP 2013) 50.

complex'[50] of food security precepts. Regime complexes are an 'indirect, unintentional outcome as a result of institutional proliferation at the global level, rescaling of authority from the state to the transnational-level, and a tendency for mission creep among existing institutions to expand into new policy domains'.[51] The problems arising from a regime complex are among others the interlocking of governance, its diffusion making it difficult to define the roles of each institution, policy making problems, ruling complexities, the overlapping of rules, difficulties in finding the hierarchy of international bodies in the subject, problems in resolving conflicts, and lastly the proliferation of different, sometimes incoherent definitions and objectives according to each institution's own agenda and mandate.

So, although some may think that food security is actually insufficiently regulated, others may see this multilevel ruling system as an obstacle hindering the real precepts that are needed to ensure food security at an international and national level, or consider some of the initiatives as 'soft law'[52] that lacks real implementation and enforcement. However, soft law instruments serve not only as a means of interpretation, but also as the basis for enforceable rules to be drafted and *lacunae*, for instance, in areas such as investment law and investor–state arbitration.[53] In an ideal regulatory system, institutions have a coherent language with connecting points that allow them to integrate other organizations' regulations. For this, food security should be regarded as the end of the avenue where a series of roads, traffic lights and trains are connected and designed carefully by pairing the regulations and avoiding any harm on other ones. Only this way can a regime complex find coherence. As seen above, the special trade aspect of food security should have a similar goal and approach to integrate different views and solutions. Clearly, trade is not the only solution to food insecurity, but neither is the opposite of trade, the Via Campesina movement. Trade can facilitate food security if the regulation is right, but attention should also be given to national food security and education, and alternatives should be given to farmers who cannot cope with liberalization and globalization.

Below is an example of the interaction of multilevel governance regulations, which shows how policies at different levels have an effect on food security, including multilateral, regional and national rules.

The Example of Rice in Costa Rica: Multilateral Systems – DR-CAFTA – Internal Food Security Policies, and Results

Regulatory Framework for Rice

As discussed above, food security approaches are diverse at the levels of governance within the international order and among institutions as well when they collide at the multilateral,

---

50 Margulis (n 24) 57. The Regime Complex is defined as an 'array of partially overlapping and non-hierarchical institutions governing a particular issue-area', Kal Raustiala and David Victor, 'The Regime Complex for Plant Genetic Resources' (2004) 58 *International Organization* 277.

51 Margulis (n 26) 3, and Margulis (n 24) 57.

52 See for example Kenneth W Abbott and Duncan Snidal, 'Hard and Soft Law in International Governance' (2000) 54 *International organization* 421; Gregory Shaffer and Mark Pollack, 'Hard Versus Soft Law in International Security' (2011) 52 *Boston College Law Review* 1147.

53 Andrea K Bjorklund and August Reinisch, *International Investment Law and Soft Law* (Edward Elgar 2012); and about sources in general, Moshe Hirsch, 'Sources of International Investment Law' *International Investment Law and Soft Law* (Edward Elgar 2012).

regional and national layers. In some cases, overlapping institutions may add to the discussion in the field; in others, the result is an incoherent regulatory system. It does contribute when precepts are coherent; the field is levelled among countries, and when such approaches are adopted as part of a food security strategy. This case exemplifies such policies at various levels and shows how both the international and national system would benefit from greater coherence. The rice case serves to identify these different regulations and their outcomes.

In order to understand rice, it is important to know that according to the National Income and Expenditure Survey, rice is not only an essential product in the daily diet of Costa Ricans but it is also one of the most important products for the lowest income quintiles. Rice cultivation accounts for 3.9 per cent of total value added of agricultural, livestock and fisheries production in Costa Rica, according to Secretaria Ejecutiva de Planificacion Sectorial Agropecuaria (SEPSA) 2012. Micro and small farmers represent 80 per cent of the total rice production but cultivate only 20 per cent of the total rice crops.[54] National policies on rice are based on a combination of tariffs, a performance requirement for the import of paddy rice, and a price fixing mechanism. The level of distorting subsidies resulting from the minimum producer price in Costa Rica is five times the level stipulated in WTO commitments, which has already led to consultations at the WTO.[55] Also, several studies have specifically assessed the policies. For instance, Umaña[56] states that import protection and price controls for rice have not increased yields, but have created significant rents for rice millers by transferring income from consumers to producers and by maintaining local prices above international prices for years. In this study, it was found that since most mills are vertically integrated, they have favoured imports over having to deal with rice farming. Gains from trade thus have benefited millers who receive rent from lower international prices, but they have not benefited 300,000 consumers living in poverty.[57] Other authors[58] conclude that the pricing scheme does not contribute to important policy objectives, nor does it increase productivity or improve access to consumers. In this sense, producers receive lower rates compared to the fixed price due to the difference in rice quality. However, even though consumers pay prices above international prices, productivity does not increase, but the fixed pricing actually increases inputs and services used in rice production. Petrecolla[59] estimates that income transfers from consumers to the rice industry reached 396.4 million from 1996 to 2005, from which only 20 per cent went to farmers.

However, in order to fully understand this policy one needs to look at the historical background. In the year 1949, the government of Costa Rica passed bills to create more food security in a time of national crisis. With rice being the main staple and with international prices for rice threatening to increase, the government created a fixed price for rice that was adjustable

---

54 Source: Ministry of Agriculture of Costa Rica. See the latest statistics at: Ministerio de Agricultura, 'Censo Nacional' (2015) 21 <www.mag.go.cr/bibliotecavirtual/a00338.pdf> accessed 15 January 2015.

55 WTO, 'Trade Policy Review Report by the Secretariat Costa Rica', 6 August 2013, WT/TPR/S/286 <www.wto. org/english/tratop_e/tpr_e/tp386_e.htm> accessed 15 January 2015.

56 Víctor Umaña, 'Food Policy Coherence for Sustainable Development: The Case of the Rice Sector in Costa Rica' (2011) 8 *ATDF Journal* 41.

57 ibid.

58 Nelson Arroyo, Rudolf Lücke and Luis Rivera, 'Análisis sobre el Mecanismo Actual para la Estimación y Determinación de los Precios del Arroz Bajo el Contexto de la Cadena de Comercialización' (Instituto de Investigaciones en Ciencias Económicas Editorial Universidad de Costa Rica 2013) 86–94.

59 Diego Petrecolla and Marina Bidart, 'Condiciones de Competencia en cadenas agroalimentarias claves de América Latina y el Caribe: desafios y oportunidades' (Instituto Interamericano de Cooperación para la Agricultura IICA 2009) 25–55.

to inflation.[60] At the time, this fixed price was important for rice producers to survive the crisis and for poor consumers to be able to afford their staple food. After the crisis in the 1980s, a time when rice was highly subsidized in the United States,[61] importers started importing rice to Central America at very low prices – lower than the fixed price from the Costa Rican government – but sold to the consumer at the fixed price. This situation caused most of the small farmers difficulties, and the country's rice production to disappear.[62] Some farmers became rice traders and others were forced to diversify into other products. With the negotiation and implementation of the free trade agreement between the Dominican Republic, Central America and the United States (DR-CAFTA), the situation was consolidated in a contingent of rice from the US that could enter Costa Rica without any tariffs.[63] Therefore, it became clear that rice production was not going to be an option anymore. Rice fields were not suitable for other crops, so they were sold, used for real estate developments or just as natural landscape, which provided an income source for the short term. For instance, between the harvests of 2000–2001 and 2005–2006, Costa Rica experienced a downward trend in paddy rice yields. They fell annually by 2.2 per cent, reaching only 3.35 metric tons during the 2005–2006 harvests.[64] According to the FAO, average yields in metric tons in the period of 2008–2011 were much higher in several other countries including Uruguay, Argentina, China and Nicaragua. In the same period, the average yield of rice in the United States was much higher.[65] Costa Rican rice was just not competitive anymore.

The quota under DR-CAFTA, which escalated throughout the years, is big enough to satisfy internal rice consumption.[66] For instance, according to CONARROZ, the consumption of rice in 2011–2012 was estimated at 247,892 metric tons of milled rice, which is equivalent to the per capita consumption of 53,71 kg. This was the largest amount of rice consumed in Costa Rica, which was due to the increase in population. According to the liberalization annexes of the DR-CAFTA, namely the Notes in Annex 3.3 concerning Costa Rica, there is a contingency of rice to the US that enters without taxes, which will become unlimited after 20 years.[67]

Results of Multilevel Regulation in the Costa Rican Rice Case and the Way Forward

All of this has resulted in decreasing rice production throughout the years, which has an impact especially on small farmers and their families. However, with subsidized rice

60 Poder Ejecutivo, 'Decreto No 37699-MEIC' (2013) <www.elfinancierocr.com/economia-y-politica/Decreto-arroz-MEIC_ELFFIL20130520_0002.pdf> accessed 21 July 2014.
61 Rebecca P Judge, 'US Prices and Rice Production in Costa Rica' (2004) <http://documents.apec.umn.edu/RJudgeEnvSp04.pdf> accessed 6 October 2014.
62 Kym Anderson and Alberto Valdés, *Distortions to Agricultural Incentives in Latin America* (World Bank 2008); Umaña-Alvarado, 'Welfare Effects of a Change in the Trade Policy Regime for Rice in Costa Rica' in *Trade Policies, Household Welfare and Poverty Alleviation* (United Nations 2014) 197.
63 Tratado de Libre Comercio entre Estados Unidos, Republica Dominicana, y Centroamerica, Notas y Anexos (DR-CAFTA Agreement Notes and Annexes): <www.sice.oas.org/tpcstudies/USCAFTAChl_s/CAFTADR_S/TLC_EEUU_DRCAFTA_Capitulo_3_ListasDesgravacion_anexo3-3-CR-notas.pdf> accessed 15 January 2015.
64 The decrease was not only a result of the regulatory situation but also due to an acarus that affected rice crops.
65 FAOSTAT (2014) <http://faostat.fao.org/site/339/default.aspx> accessed 15 January 2015.
66 'Costa Rica Milled Rice Domestic Consumption by Year (1000 MT)' <www.indexmundi.com/agriculture/?country=cr&commodity=milled-rice&graph=domestic-consumption> accessed 6 October 2014.
67 Poder Ejecutivo, 'Decreto No 37699-MEIC' (n 62). It should be noted that this should be close to year 8 of the ratification of the treaty for Costa Rica. However, some of the provisions have already been put in place. For more information: <http://unctad.org/en/PublicationChapters/gds2014d3_06_CostaRica_en.pdf> accessed 15 January 2015.

coming from the US, farmers had no chance to compete, especially given the fact that the contingent will become unlimited by year 20 of the DR-CAFTA agreement. But instead of implementing national food security policies to ensure technology and education to remaining farmers, or diversification of production, the government put in place a measure that benefits rice traders. Therefore, a regulatory advantage is given for rice traders who are able to import rice at a low price from the US and sell it in the national market at the fixed price for a profit. By now, given that rice production has not increased in the country, the fixed price is causing imbalances in the possible benefits from trade. It is important to mention that the Trade Policy Review from the WTO pointed out that several governments have tried to deal with the situation and there is a law to change the fixed price policy for rice. However, it was not possible to achieve this change in the last two governmental periods.[68] This is an example of how incoherent food security policy is, by lack of coordination and lacking the proper regulation at the national level.

In sum, at this point it would be better to take advantage of the DR-CAFTA by removing the price fixation and letting consumers pay less for rice.[69] Traders will lose subsidies but may continue as rice importers, and millers will continue to import rice from the United States using the performance requirement applied for the DR-CAFTA quota to keep the mills operating.[70]

Concluding Remarks

For food security concerns and the challenge of feeding the world by 2020, it is important to note that farmers and consumers have different interests, which leads them to support different agendas in trade liberalization. While farmers and traders could benefit from high prices in food, poor consumers applaud policies for price reduction and even price support, or else they call for more jobs and higher incomes. Under these circumstances, precepts are to be found in different levels of governance. Parts of the policies contribute to food security but some may actually appear as obstacles. Important is that such layers of governance are taken into account when drafting public policies. In balance, trade regulation plays a crucial role that should be considered when drafting public policies across the governance layers. Also, important is to respect the principle of 'no-harm' meaning that policies should not harm food security, even if they do not contribute to food insecurity as effectively In this regard, the minimum to be expected is that national regulations do not harm food security at any level in a particular multilateral and regional setting. Neither should international regulations limit the options for national food security or consolidate disparities between larger and smaller countries. Even though regulations cannot benefit all groups equally, the minimum principle would be that they do not expressively harm other groups by creating situations of disadvantage as seen in the Costa Rican rice case. For instance, the WTO aims to have a balanced playing field for all member countries, where countries that 'have the means' to subsidize are given stronger limits and countries that do not have the means are given more flexibility.

---

68 Poder Ejecutivo, 'Decreto No 37699-MEIC' (n 62). For a short commentary describing how rice has now become a political and not a technical matter, see the former Vice Minister of Trade Fernando Ocampo 'Asunto Político, No Técnico', *La Nación* (San José, 7 February 2015) <www.elfinancierocr.com/opinion/Opinion-Fernando_Ocampo-arroz-salvaguarda-OMC-Conarroz_0_679132111.html> accessed 20 April 2015.

69 The news report that Costa Rican rice is the seventh most expensive rice in the world, Marvin Barquero, 'Precio Del Arroz En Costa Rica Es El Sétimo Más Caro En El Mundo', *La Nación* (San José, 5 May 2014) <www.nacion.com/economia/agro/Arroz-nacional-setimo-caro-mundo_0_1412658734.html> accessed 25 June 2014.

70 Umaña (57) 41.

The WTO also recognizes that liberalization is not the only avenue towards food security and that it will not automatically lead to a recovery of the food production in poor countries,[71] but that liberalization should be accompanied by other internal policies, especially those concerning income distribution and farmer support without bias. National production and investment policies are also important to food security. Trade is just one part of the solution. In this sense, regulations in the AoA are what authors call 'a job half done',[72] and other policies at various levels should take this into account. In the example of Costa Rican rice, the situation is now that poor consumers are affected and the only way forward would be to transform national food security policies that are obsolete. Since subsidies are present in other economies and even the closest deals at trade development rounds have not come to a good port, then national policies are meant to cope with this imbalance and take advantage of the free trade agreements in place, so that benefits can reach all groups with a strong national food security strategy. Given the actual situation, then for the case of Costa Rica and in order to take advantage of rice prices, free trade and consumers' food security, price liberalization seems to be the way forward. For other cases it may be more complex, but then at least, some urgent reforms to the AoA should take place if countries are to take food security objectives seriously in the future. Countries, then, should take seriously the task of drafting a national food security policy without bias for some groups and take into account the layers of governance and each country's current situation.

---

71 'Trade liberalization alone won't lead to automatic recovery of domestic production in poor countries or more investment in food crops', Häberli (n 7) 165. See also Kym Anderson, *Trade Liberalization, Agriculture, and Poverty in Low-Income Countries* (2003) WIDER Discussion Papers, World Institute for Development Economics (UNU-WIDER) no 2003/25 <www.econstor.eu/bitstream/10419/52862/1/369105362.pdf> accessed 15 January 2015; Steve McCorriston and others 'What Is the Evidence of the Impact of Agricultural Trade Liberalisation on Food Security in Developing Countries?' (2013) EPPI Centre, Social Science Research Unit, Institute of Education, University of London, Report 2105, 7 ff.

72 Christian Häberli, 'God, the WTO and Hunger' in Krista Nadakavukaren Schefer (ed), *Poverty and the International Economic Legal System: Duties to the World's Poor* (CUP 2013) 103.

13 WTO and Renewable Energy

Lessons from the Case Law[*]

Paolo Davide Farah[**] and Elena Cima[***]

Introduction

Climate change is probably the most relevant problem to be tackled by contemporary world. Investment in renewable energy is one of the core strategies to address the adverse effects of climate change. The support that governments give to the renewable energy sector covers a wide variety of measures[1] that range from taxes on carbon emissions to measures aimed at transferring an economic advantage to firms and companies investing in renewables or

* This chapter was previously published by the authors in (2015) 49(6) *Journal of World Trade*. This scientific result is part of the West Virginia University Energy Institute and Multidisciplinary Center for Shale Gas Utilization (WV, USA). The research leading to these results has received funding from the People Programme (Marie Curie Actions) of the European Union's Seventh Framework Programme (FP7/2007–2013) under REA grant agreement no 269327 Acronym of the Project: EPSEI (2011–2015) entitled 'Evaluating Policies for Sustainable Energy Investments: Towards an Integrated Approach on National and International Stage' and gLAWcal – Global Law Initiatives for Sustainable Development (United Kingdom). Corresponding author email address, Professor Paolo Davide Farah: paolofarah@yahoo.com. An earlier draft of this paper was presented at the International Conference 'The Reform of International Economic Governance' organized by the Research Project 'International Law and the New Governance after the Economic Crisis' and the Department of Public International Law, University of Granada, Spain, 9–10 Oct. 2014. A special thanks should be addressed to the participants in the above mentioned event as well as Chi Carmody (University of Western Ontario, Faculty of Law), Andrew Lang (London School of Economics, Department of Law) Friedl Weiss (University of Vienna, Faculty of Law), Matthias Goldmann (Max Planck Institute for Comparative Public Law and International Law – Heidelberg).

** Paolo Davide Farah: West Virginia University, Department of Public Administration within the Eberly College of Arts and Sciences and College of Law (WV, USA). Research Scientist and Principal Investigator at gLAWcal – Global Law Initiatives for Sustainable Development (United Kingdom). Dual PhD in International Law at Aix-Marseille University (France) and at Università degli Studi di Milano (Italy). LLM College of Europe, Bruges (Belgium), JD (*Maitrise*) in International and European Law, Paris Ouest La Defense Nanterre (France). Visiting Scholar (2011–2012) at Harvard Law School, EALS – East Asian Legal Studies (USA). EU Commission Marie Curie Fellow (2009–2011) at Tsinghua University School of Law, THCEREL – Center for Environmental, Natural Resources & Energy Law in Beijing (China) and at the CRAES – Chinese Research Academy on Environmental Sciences in Beijing (China). Fellow at the IIEL – Institute of International Economic Law (2004–2005) at Georgetown University Law Center (USA). A special acknowledgment should be addressed to the East Asian Legal Studies at Harvard Law School who hosted me as Visiting Scholar and provided an excellent academic and research environment.

*** Elena Cima: PhD candidate at the Graduate Institute of International and Development Studies, Geneva (Switzerland). LLM 2014, Yale Law School (USA); LLB 2010, University of Milan (Italy). Substantial parts of this chapter were written when I was EU Commission Marie Curie Fellow at Tsinghua University School of Law, THCEREL – Center for Environmental, Natural Resources & Energy Law in Beijing (China) and Research Fellow at Università del Piemonte Orientale 'Amedeo Avogadro', Disei – Dipartimento di Studi per l'Impresa e il Territorio (Italy).

1 See Miguel Mendonca, David Jacobs and Benjamin Sovacool, *Powering the Green Economy: The Feed-in Tariff Handbook* (Earthscan 2010); Luca Rubini, 'The Subsidization of Renewable Energy in the WTO: Issues and Perspectives' (June 2011) Working Paper 2011/321.

to consumers that buy them, such as grants, loans, tax incentives or pricing support (like feed-in tariffs).[2] Governmental support to alternative and renewable energy industry represents a fairly common choice for governments in need to comply with the commitments that bind them within the international framework for climate change.[3] Besides being a *common* choice, renewable energy subsidies represent an *effective* one: according to the Intergovernmental Panel on Climate Change (IPCC):

> one of the most effective incentives for fostering GHG reductions are the price supports associated with the production of renewable energy, which tend to be set at attractive levels. These price supports have resulted in the significant expansion of the renewable energy sector in OECD countries due to the requirement that electric power producers purchase such electricity at favorable prices.[4]

One might even say that public support is not just preferable but rather necessary in the specific case of measures intended to fight climate change: according to economic analysis, public support is needed whenever the market fails to tackle specific externalities or to provide consumers with the goods and services they ask for.[5] This seems to be the case when it comes to global warming, if we believe that climate change may be the 'greatest and widest-ranging market failure ever seen', as stated in the Stern Report.[6] The real problem, when it comes to promoting the use and diffusion of renewable energy, lies in the fact that neither the benefits of the deployment of such energy nor the true costs of fossil fuels are included in their prices. This makes fossil fuels relatively cheap and renewable goods and services relatively expensive. The standard economic reaction to this situation is the introduction of governmental provisions as well as pigovian taxes[7] or subsidies intended to redress economic injustices or imbalances.

At the other hand of the spectrum, it is generally recognized that subsidies often produce harmful effects on free trade and production rather than equitable results, and international trade law has taken into account all these concerns in drafting specific rules on subsidies. In this chapter, we are going to draw the attention on the effects of renewable energy subsidies, distinguishing subsidies which are necessary for desirable and acceptable purposes from those that are nothing but disguised protectionist measures and that might trigger international trade

---

2 On feed-in tariffs see generally Mario Ragwitz, Claus Huber and Gustav Resch, 'Promotion of Renewable Energy Sources: Effects on Innovation' (2007) 2 *International Journal of Public Policy* 35.

3 The international commitments on climate change and global warming are enshrined in the text of the Kyoto Protocol, which was adopted in 1997. The Protocol sets explicit emission targets for certain signatory countries: each of these countries was to reduce its greenhouse gas (GHG) emissions so that its total emissions, when converted to a carbon-equivalent basis, did not exceed a specified percentage of its base period emissions. On the other hand, developing and least developed countries were not addressed with any specific commitment, but could benefit from certain flexible mechanisms provided for in the Protocol and thus contribute to the global emission reduction. After the end of the first commitment period (2008–2012), the emission targets were reaffirmed for a second commitment period (2013–2020).

4 Sujata Gupta and others, 'Policies, Instruments and Co-operative Arrangements' in Robert Howse and Petrus van Bork (eds), *Options for Liberalising Trade in Environmental Goods in the Doha Round* (International Centre for Trade and Sustainable Development 2007).

5 See Rubini (n 1) 5.

6 Nicholas Stern, *The Economics of Climate Change: Stern Review* (CUP 2007).

7 A pigovian tax is a tax applied to an economic activity that generates negative externalities.

remedies. In particular, the case law of the World Trade Organization (WTO) on the matter is very relevant as it shows the existing approach – as well as its shortcoming and room for improvement – towards environmental subsidies. This case law involves measures challenged to be inconsistent with the Agreement on Subsidies and Countervailing Measures (ASCM), which initially divided all potentially distorting subsidies into three categories: prohibited, actionable and non-actionable.[8] While *prohibited* subsidies[9] (described in article III and including both export subsidies and local content requirement subsidies) are trade-distorting per se and therefore totally unacceptable,[10] actionable subsidies[11] are only *potentially* trade-distorting, which means that the complaining country has to show that the subsidy has an adverse effect on its interests. If not prohibited or actionable, the subsidy is permitted. Initially, a third category of subsidies existed under the ASCM – the so-called *non-actionable* subsidies.[12] This category, which included subsidies that did not create any trade-distorting effects, was introduced on an experimental basis for a five-year period, which expired in 2000 without being renewed.[13]

This chapter is divided in three sections. The first one offers an overview of WTO disputes involving subsidies in the renewable energy sector, the second one focuses on the recent decisions in the *Canada – Renewable Energy* and *Canada – Feed-in Tariff Program* disputes and on some important issues they raise, while in the last one we draw our conclusions.

Overview of WTO Disputes Involving Subsidies in the Renewable Energy Sector

So far, the Dispute Settlement Body (DSB) of the WTO has been presented with a few disputes regarding renewable energy, while none has been presented in relation to measures

---

8   For a general overview of the regulation of subsidies provided in the WTO, see Patrick FJ Macrory, Arthur E Appleton and Michael G Plummer, *The World Trade Organization: Legal, Economic and Political Analysis* (Springer 2005) 687–734; Jeffrey Waincymer, *WTO Litigation: Procedural Aspects of Formal Dispute Settlement* (Cameron May 2002) 765–69; RK Gupta, *Anti-dumping and Countervailing Measures: The Complete Reference* (Sage 1996); Michael J Trebilcock and Robert Howse, *The Regulation of International Trade* (Routledge 2005) 268–73; Andreas Lowenfeld, *International Economic Law* (OUP 2003) 234–41; Alan O Sykes, 'The Economics of WTO Rules on Subsidies and Countervailing Measures' in P Macrory, A Appleton and M Plummer (eds), *The World Trade Organization: Legal, Economic and Political Analysis* (2005); Gary N Horlick and Peggy A Clarke, 'WTO Subsidies Discipline During and After the Crisis' (2010) 13 *Journal of International Economic Law*, 859. For a thorough analysis of the historical evolution of GATT and WTO negotiations on subsidies, see Andrew L Stoler, 'The Evolution of Subsidies Disciplines in GATT and the WTO' (2010) 44 *Journal of World Trade* 797; Gary N Horlick, 'A Personal History of the WTO Subsidies Agreement' (2013) 47 *Journal of World Trade* 447. For a focus on the current Doha negotiations, see Debra P Steger, 'The Subsidies and Countervailing Measures Agreement: Ahead of its Time or Time for Reform?' (2010) 44 *Journal of World Trade* 779.
9   WTO Agreement on Subsidies and Countervailing Measures (ASCM) pt II arts 3–4.
10 Most developing and least developed countries see both export and local content subsidies as crucial to their industrialization and development, while industrialized nations have always considered this particular category of governmental support as severely and inherently trade-distorting, see Debra P Steger (n 8) 787.
11 ASCM pt III arts 5–7.
12 ASCM pt I art 1. For a detailed analysis of ASCM art 1, *see* Edwin Vermulst and Folkert Graafsma, *WTO Disputes. Anti-dumping, Subsidies and Safeguards* (Cameron May 2002) 281–305; Pierre Didier, *Les Principaux Accords de l'OMC et leur Transposition dans la Communaute Europeenne* (Bruylant 1997) 193.
13 Alan O Sykes (n 8).

supporting fossil fuels – and especially oil.[14] On the other hand, several disputes concerned export and local content subsidies (thus 'prohibited' under the ASCM). The findings and conclusions reached by WTO Panels and the Appellate Body in these cases can surely help clarify the WTO approach towards such types of governmental support. What can be concluded from the analysis below is that both the Panel and Appellate Body have interpreted the rules quite narrowly, so as to not leave much space to States' policies in favour of renewables. This, despite the inarguable evolution of the WTO case law toward its deep and final objectives represented by the WTO preamble when it comes to assessing the relationship between trade and non-trade concerns, and especially the environment.[15]

The first two disputes relate to the Canadian renewable energy generation sector: *Canada – Feed-In Tariff Program* and *Canada – Renewable Energy*.[16] In both disputes, the Canadian measures challenged, respectively, by the European Union (EU) and Japan, as well as the WTO provisions, whose violation is complained of, are the same. Both the EU and Japan challenged the FIT Program established by the Canadian province of Ontario in 2009 providing for guaranteed, long-term pricing for the output of renewable energy generation facilities that contained a defined percentage of domestic content. The complainants deemed this programme to be inconsistent with – among others – articles 3.1(b)[17] and 3.2[18] of the ASCM because of the local content requirement present in the feed-in tariff system.[19] The panels circulated their Reports on 19 December 2012, rejecting the complainants' claim that the challenged measures were to be considered 'subsidies' according to the ASCM.[20] As we will

---

14 The *US – Gasoline* dispute deals with a petroleum-derived product, and specifically concerns a US measure providing imported and domestic gasoline with different treatments. While it certainly offers incredible insights on the interpretation of several GATT rules, it does not address the central theme of our chapter – the specific role played by energy in the WTO framework.

15 The first time the relevance of environmental concerns vis-à-vis free trade was subject of debate was in the context of the GATT Tuna I case. In this occasion, the Panel gave an extremely narrow approach of the GATT so to leave no room for environmental measures. See *United States – Restrictions on Imports of Tuna from Mexico* (1993) GATT BISD 39S/155 (Tuna I) (report not adopted by the GATT Contracting Parties). After Tuna I, the evolution towards an increasing acceptance of environmental concerns is exemplified in the decisions of the following disputes: Appellate Body Report *United States – Standards for Reformulated and Conventional Gasoline*, 29 April 1996, WT/DS2/AB/R; Appellate Body Report *EC – Measures Affecting Meat and Meat Products*, 16 January 1998, WT/DS26/AB/R; Appellate Body Report *United States – Import Prohibition of Certain Shrimps and Shrimp Products*, 12 October 1998, WT/DS58/AB/R; Appellate Body Report *EC – Measures Affecting the Prohibition of Asbestos and Asbestos Products: Report of the Appellate Body*, 12 March 2001, WT/DS135/AB/R; Appellate Body Report *Brazil – Measures Affecting Imports of Retreated Tyres*, 3 December 2007, WT/DS332/AB/R See John H Jackson, 'Comments on Shrimp/Turtle and the Product/Process Distinction' (2000) 11 *EJIL* 303; Robert L Howse and Donald H Regan, 'The Product/Process Distinction – An Illusory Basis For Disciplining 'Unilateralism' In Trade Policy' (2000) 11 *EJIL* 249.

16 Panel Report *Canada – Measures Relating to the Feed-In Tariff Program*, 19 December 2012, WT/DS426/R; Appellate Body Report *Canada – Measures Relating to the Feed-In Tariff Program*, 6 May 2013, WT/DS426/AB/R; Panel Report *Canada – Certain Measures Affecting the Renewable Energy Generation Sector*, 13 September 2010, WT/DS412/R; Appellate Body Report *Canada – Certain Measures Affecting the Renewable Energy Generation Sector*, 19 December 2012, WT/DS412/AB/R.

17 Art 3(1)(b) ASCM reads: 'Except as provided in the Agreement on Agriculture, the following subsidies, within the meaning of art 1, shall be prohibited . . . (b) subsidies contingent, whether solely or as one of several other conditions, upon the use of domestic over imported goods.'

18 According to art 3(2) ASCM, 'A Member shall neither grant nor maintain subsidies referred to in para 1.'

19 The other claims regarded the alleged violation of art 2(1) of the Agreement on Trade Related Investment Measures (TRIMS) and art III(4) GATT.

20 The Panel's rejection of the complainants' claim regarding the violation of arts 3(1)(b) and 3(2) ASCM is based on the fact that, according to the Panel, the complainant could not prove that a 'benefit' was conferred through the

see in the following paragraphs, the Report circulated by the Appellate Body on 6 May 2013, casts doubt on the accuracy of the panels' reasoning.[21]

In 2010, another dispute was initiated, this time by an investigation carried out by the United States Trade Representative (USTR) on 15 October 2010, which covered a broad variety of Chinese policies and practices affecting trade and investment in the wind power technology sector.[22] As a follow-up to this investigation, the United States (US) held WTO consultations with China on 16 February 2011.[23] However, such consultations did not cover all the issues raised in the investigation but rather focused on subsidies. The US made clear the view that the subsidies provided to Chinese wind turbine manufacturers under the Special Fund programme – through which Chinese manufacturers of wind turbines and of components of wind turbines can receive multiple grants – were prohibited because they were conditioned upon the use of domestic over imported goods (and therefore 'prohibited' according to article 3 of the ASCM Agreement). Following those consultations, China took action formally revoking the legal measure that had created the Special Fund programme.

Two new requests for consultation have been presented in 2012 and 2013: European Union and Certain Member States – Certain Measures Affecting the Renewable Energy Generation Sector[24] and India – Certain Measures Relating to Solar Cells and Solar Modules.[25] In the first case, China requested consultations with the EU, Greece, and Italy regarding certain feed-in tariff (FIT) programmes implemented by a number of EU Member States in the renewable energy sector, while in the second, the US challenged Indian measures relating to domestic content requirements under the Jawaharial Nehru National Solar Mission ('NSM') for solar cells and solar modules.

---

measures at issue and therefore could not prove the existence of a benefit according to art 1 ASCM. The reasons underlying such a ruling will be analysed further on in the ch when dealing with subsidies. On the other hand, the other claim – regarding the violation of art 2(1) TRIMS and art III(4) GATT – was accepted, Panel Report *Canada – Measures Relating to the Feed-In Tariff Program* (n 16); Panel Report *Canada – Certain Measures Affecting the Renewable Energy Generation Sector* (n 16).

21 Appellate Body Report *Canada – Measures Relating to the Feed-In Tariff Program* (n 16); Appellate Body Report *Canada – Certain Measures Affecting the Renewable Energy Generation Sector* (n 16).

22 The USTR investigation was based on a petition filed on 9 September 2010 by the United Steel, Paper and Forestry, Rubber, Manufacturing, Energy, Allied Industrial and Service Workers International Union, AFL-CIO CLC (USW). C Moyer, J Wang and TP Stewart, on behalf of the USW, *China Policies Affecting Trade and Investment in Green Technology*, Petition for Relief under S 301 of the Trade Act of 1974 as amended before the United States Trade Representative (USTR), vol 1 of 9: Petition and Exhibits s 1 (9 September 2010) 208. The text of the petition is available on: <www.wyden.senate.gov/download/section-301-petition_-chinas-policies-affecting-trade-and-investment-in-green-technology-volume-1?download=1> accessed 10 July 2015. The United States has then requested a consultation with the WTO Dispute Settlement Body: *China – Measures Concerning Wind Power Equipment* WT/DS419. The challenged policies were the following: (a) quotas imposed on the export of several raw materials necessary to produce wind turbines; (b) subsidies contingent on export performance and on the use of domestic products over imported ones, allegedly inconsistent with art 3(1) ASCM and with para 10(3) of China's Accession Protocol; (c) local content requirement, deemed to be inconsistent with art III(4) GATT and para 3(a) of China's Accession Protocol; (d) trade-distorting subsidies, violating arts 5–6 ASCM; and (e) technology transfer requirements for investors, found to be inconsistent with paras 1(2) and 7(3) of the Accession Protocol.

23 *China – Measures Concerning Wind Power Equipment* (n 22).

24 Request for Consultations by China, *European Union and Certain Member States – Certain Measures Affecting the Renewable Energy Generation Sector*, 5 November 2012, WT/DS452/1.

25 Request for Consultations by the United States, *India – Certain Measures Relating to Solar Cells and Solar Modules*, 6 February 2013, WT/DS456/1.

The Disputes Involving Canada and Renewable Energy

All the disputes briefly described above involve subsidies accorded to renewable energy enterprises, considered prohibited according to article 3 of the ASCM because of the 'local content requirement' they prescribe.[26] While in the *China – Wind* dispute, the official position of the Panel is unknown because China removed the measure at stake after consultations with the US, and the last two disputes are still at a request-for-consultations stage, the Panel and Appellate Body Reports on *Canada – Feed-In Tariff Program* and *Canada – Renewable Energy*, offer interesting insights on the problems of subsidies in the renewable energy sector. In order to decide whether subsidies – generally prohibited – might be permitted because of their 'green' nature, we will answer two questions: are measures supporting renewable energy to be considered as 'subsidies' according to the ASCM? And secondly, if they are, can they still be justified?

Do Measures Supporting Renewable Energy Qualify as 'Subsidies' According to the ASCM?

The ASCM provides a definition of 'subsidies' in article 1: a subsidy exists whenever a financial contribution is made by a government or any public body within the territory of a member, which confers a benefit. Moreover, according to article 1(2), only a measure that is a 'specific subsidy' as defined in Part I of the ASCM is subject to the WTO's subsidies discipline. In order to verify whether measures adopted to support trade in renewable energy fall within the scope of the ASCM, two requirements need to be analysed: (a) the existence of a financial contribution of public nature; and (b) the existence of a benefit.

The Existence of a Financial Contribution

Article 1 of the ASCM contains a detailed and exhaustive list of governmental measures that qualify as 'financial contribution', thus providing for a high degree of certainty and predictability.[27] Such measures range from grants, loans and equity infusions (government practices which involve a direct transfer of funds), to fiscal incentives (government revenue that is otherwise due is foregone or not collected), and provision of goods or services as well as purchase of goods. According to the same provision, such measures do not need necessarily to be of public nature: as a matter of fact, when entrusted or directed by the government, measures carried out by private entities still qualify as 'financial contribution'.[28] Moreover the aforementioned measures are not to be considered *alternative* but they might even be cumulative. As a matter of fact, the Appellate Body in the *Canada – Renewable Energy* and *Canada – Feed-In Tariff Program* disputes, quoting a previous dispute,[29] stated that 'a

---

26 Art 3(1)(b) ASCM identifies the following subsidies as prohibited: 'subsidies contingent, whether solely or as one of several other conditions, upon the use of domestic over imported goods'.

27 Debra P Steger (n 8) 781, 784.

28 Art 1 ASCM: 'For the purpose of this Agreement, a subsidy shall be deemed to exist if: (iv) a government makes payments to a funding mechanism, or entrusts or directs a private body to carry out one or more of the type of functions illustrated in (i) to (iii) above which would normally be vested in the government and the practice, in no real sense, differs from practices normally followed by governments.'

29 Request for Consultation by the European Communities, *United States – Measures Affecting Trade in Large Civil Aircraft* (6 October 2004) WT/DS317/1.

transaction could be covered by more than one subparagraph' because – for example – there is 'no 'or' included between the subparagraphs'.[30] In this specific case, Japan had initially claimed that Ontario's FIT Program would qualify as both 'direct transfer of funds' and 'purchase of goods,' under article 1(a)(1)(i) and 1(a)(1)(iii) ASCM. The Panel considered the FIT Program as a 'purchase of goods,' ruling out the second possible qualification based on the assumption that such finding would infringe '[the] principle of [effective treaty interpretation],' thus considering the subparagraphs of article 1 as alternative. The Appellate Body reversed the Panel's findings declaring the possibility for a measure to fall under two or more subparagraphs. However, it found that the arguments advanced by the claimant on this matter were not sufficient and therefore ruled out the qualification of the measure at stake as 'direct transfer of funds'.

When assessing the type of financial contribution, the Panels and the Appellate Body considered the FIT Program implemented by the Government of Ontario as involving a 'purchase' according to article 1(a)(1)(iii), based on several legal arguments. One of the main arguments used by the Panel is that the 'Government of Ontario takes possession over electricity and therefore "purchases" electricity.'[31] According to the Panel, what is required by the term 'purchase' is just the mere 'payment (usually monetary) in exchange for a good:'[32] (a) it does not require the entity purchasing the good (in this case, the government) to be supplied for its own use; (b) nor it implies *physical* possession over the good purchased. In particular, as far as electricity is concerned, physical possession would be inherently impossible, being 'an intangible good that, in general, cannot be stored and must be consumed almost at the same time it is produced'.[33]

The Existence of a Benefit

As stressed by the Panels in *Canada – Renewable Energy* and *Canada – Feed-In Tariff Program* – and previously noted by both the Panel and Appellate Body on other occasions[34] – to assess the existence of a benefit, the analysis should not focus on whether the recipient is better off than its competitors but rather whether it is better off than it would have been without the financial contribution.[35] This approach might allow measures adopted to support renewable energy producers. As a matter of fact, we need to consider that, as we emphasized previously, the prices of neither fossil fuels nor renewable energies include the negative externalities of the former and the positive ones of the latter. This creates a condition of disadvantage for renewable energy producers. Thus, if we need to just consider whether the

30 Appellate Body Report *Canada – Measures Relating to the Feed-In Tariff Program* and *Canada – Certain Measures Affecting the Renewable Energy Generation Sector* (n 16) para 5.122.
31 Panel Report *Canada – Measures Relating to the Feed-In Tariff Program* and *Canada – Certain Measures Affecting the Renewable Energy Generation Sector* (n 16) para 7.224.
32 Panel Report *Canada – Certain Measures Affecting the Renewable Energy Generation Sector* (n 16) para 7.227.
33 ibid para 7.229.
34 Appellate Body Report *Canada – Measures Affecting the Export of Civilian Aircraft*, 21 July 2000, WT/DS70/AB/R, para 157.
35 Whether the subsidy affects competition needs to be analysed later and separately when assessing the actual effects of the subsidy (and so this analysis will take place only when it is proved that the specific financial contribution falls within the scope of art 1 ASCM), Sadeq Z Bigdeli, 'Incentive Schemes to Promote Renewables and the WTO Law of Subsidies' in Sedaq Z Bigdeli, Thomas Cottier and Olga Nartova (eds), *International Trade Regulation and the Mitigation of Climate Change* (CUP 2009); Luca Rubini (n 1) 24, 25. See also Appellate Body Report *Canada – Measures Affecting the Export of Civilian Aircraft* (n 34) para 149.

recipient of the financial contribution is better off than absent the contribution itself – without considering the impact on competition – in this case we might say that the subsidy is not conferring an advantage but rather compensating a disadvantage faced by the producer.[36]

In order to compare the position of the recipient with and without the financial contribution, one must identify the specific marketplace and use it as a benchmark:[37] as stated by the Appellate Body, 'that a financial contribution confers an advantage on its recipient cannot be determined in absolute terms, but requires a comparison with a benchmark, which, in the case of subsidies, derives from the market'.[38] However, the Panel concluded that the marketplace identified by the complainants – the wholesale electricity market that currently exists in Ontario – could not be used as a 'reliable' indicator because it was not competitive enough: if the absolute nonexistence of government intervention is not required, on the other hand, a government's involvement as a provider of a particular good which makes it impossible to determine whether a recipient is 'better off' absent the financial contribution, rules out the possibility to use that particular marketplace as a benchmark.[39] This evaluation led the Panel to conclude that the existence of a benefit had not been proved. The Appellate Body found two main problems with the panels' analysis of the relevant market for the purpose of the benefit comparison. According to the Appellate Body, not only the panels did not follow the right sequence of steps in the benefit analysis – they should have started, rather than concluding,

36 Since renewable energy producers face costs significantly higher than those faced by producers of fossil fuels, these kinds of support measures 'simply reimburse or compensate the enterprise for taking some action that it would otherwise not take, and the enterprise has not necessarily acquired any competitive advantage over other enterprises that neither take the subsidy nor have to perform these actions', see Robert Howse, *Climate Change Mitigation Subsidies and the WTO Legal Framework: A Policy Analysis* (International Institute for Sustainable Development 2010) 13.

37 As stated by the Appellate Body in *Canada – Aircraft*, 'the marketplace provides an appropriate basis for comparison in determining whether a "benefit" has been "conferred", because the trade-distorting potential of a "financial contribution" can be identified by determining whether the recipient has received a "financial contribution" on terms more favorable than those available to the recipient in the market', Appellate Body Report *Canada – Measures Affecting the Export of Civilian Aircraft* (n 34) para 157. See also Panel Report *Canada – Export Credits and Loan Guarantees for Regional Aircraft: Report of the Panel*, 28 January 2002, WT/DS222/R para 7.343; Panel Report *United States – Tax Treatment for 'Foreign Sales Corporations' (art 21.5 – EC)*, 20 August 2001, WT/DS108 para 7.278–77.296. The same conclusion was reached by the Panels in *Canada – Renewable Energy* and *Canada – Feed-in Tariff Program*. Here, the Panels stressed that the importance of the marketplace in this analysis is further supported by art 14 ASCM, which sets some rules for calculating the amount of the subsidy in terms of the benefit to the recipient and which has been proved to be 'relevant context in interpreting art 1(1)(b).' According to this provision, for the government purchase of goods to confer a benefit, it needs to be made for 'more than adequate remuneration,' and the adequacy of this remuneration must be evaluated in relation to the 'prevailing market conditions' for the good in question in the country of purchase. Panel Report *Canada – Measures Relating to the Feed-In Tariff Program* (n 16) para 7.274; Appellate Body Report *Canada – Measures Affecting the Export of Civilian Aircraft* (n 34) 155–58.

38 Appellate Body Report *Canada – Measures Relating to the Feed-In Tariff Program* and *Canada – Certain Measures Affecting the Renewable Energy Generation Sector* (n 16) para 5.164.

39 Appellate Body Report *United States – Final Countervailing Duty Determination with Respect to Certain Softwood Lumber from Canada*, 19 January 2004, WT/DS257/AB/R, 93. Several authors argue that this is a problem affecting energy in general: the energy market is extremely distorted because of the heavy public intervention, especially in support of fossil fuels. Luca Rubini, *The Definition of Subsidy and State Aid: WTO and EC Law in Comparative Perspective* (OUP 2009) 226–33; Rubini (n 1) 24; Daniel Peat, 'The Wrong Rules for the Right Energy: The WTO SCM Agreement and Subsidies for Renewable Energy' (2012) 24 *Environmental Law and Management* 3; Robert Howse, *World Trade Law and Renewable Energy: The Case of Non-Tariff Barriers* (United Nations Conference on Trade and Development 2009) 11. The following WTO dispute deal with this specific issue: *Canada – Measures Affecting Dairy Exports* DS113.

with the definition of the relevant market – but the analysis itself was inaccurate. As a matter of fact, the panels should not have limited their analysis to the benchmarks that were part of the complainants' argument in a situation where the evidence and the arguments presented by the complainants may have allowed them to take into account several additional factors (such as the type of contract, the size of the customer, and the type of electricity generated).[40] This might have led to a different conclusion and to the identification of a market that could have been used as benchmark. Unfortunately, the insufficient findings in the Panel Report made it impossible for the Appellate Body to complete the legal analysis.[41]

Are 'Subsidies' on Renewable Energy Justified?

The complainants in the *Canada – Renewable Energy* and *Canada – Feed-In Tariff Program* disputes were not able to prove the existence of a benefit for the recipient of the government measure, and therefore there was no violation of the ASCM by the Government of Ontario. It might be nevertheless interesting to conduct a purely theoretical reasoning over the possibility to justify measures supporting renewable energy if they were to be found to be 'prohibited subsidies' according to articles 1 and 3 ASCM. In particular, we would like to address an issue which has proved to be extremely controversial: the possibility to apply the general exceptions set out in article XX GATT to the ASCM, since the latter lacks its own exceptional clause.

Can we apply article XX GATT to a subsidy, which goes beyond the scope of the Agreement? In other words, can article XX GATT integrate the provisions of the SCM Agreement? Various arguments can be made against such applicability. First of all, one might stress the fact that in order for article XX GATT to apply, the ASCM should explicitly recall it, as it happens in the Agreement on Sanitary and Phytosanitary Measures (SPS Agreement), which makes express reference to article XX(b) GATT in articles 1 and 2.4.[42] Furthermore, not only does the ASCM not mention such provision but, in article 3.1, on prohibited subsidies, it specifically excludes from the scope of the provisions what is 'provided in the Agreement on Agriculture.' Finally, the Agreement on subsidies used to have its own exception, enshrined in article 8, now no longer in force. The existence of a provision similar to article XX but designed exclusively for the SCM Agreement could be seen as a sign of the inadequacy and eventually inapplicability of article XX GATT.[43]

On the other hand, a few arguments have been proposed in favour of the applicability of article XX GATT to the ASCM: the first one relates to a general principle of international law, the second one is the result of a purely logical reasoning, and the last one is based on the WTO case law. First, we need to consider the hierarchy of the different agreements belonging to the WTO legal framework. As a matter of fact, the principle of *lex specialis derogat*

40 Appellate Body Report *Canada – Measures Relating to the Feed-In Tariff Program* and *Canada – Certain Measures Affecting the Renewable Energy Generation Sector* (n 16) paras 5.170–78, 5.214–15.215.
41 Appellate Body Report *Canada – Certain Measures Affecting the Renewable Energy Generation Sector* (n 16) para 5.224.
42 According to art 1 SPS Agreement, Members desire 'to elaborate rules for the application of the provisions of GATT 1994 which relate to the use of sanitary or phytosanitary measures, in particular the provisions of art XX(b),' while art 2(4) reads as follows: 'Sanitary or phytosanitary measures which conform to the relevant provisions of this Agreement shall be presumed to be in accordance with the obligations of the Members under the provisions of GATT 1994 which relate to the use of sanitary or phytosanitary measures, in particular the provisions of art XX(b).'
43 Rubini (n 1) 35.

legi generali, widely applied by international courts and tribunals, is a broadly accepted customary international law principle of treaty interpretation.[44] The GATT applies as soon as trade in goods is affected, and can be therefore classified as *lex generalis*, while the SCM Agreement – as well as other agreements such as the SPS Agreement, the Technical Barriers to Trade (TBT) Agreement, the Agreement on Agriculture (AoA), and so on – has a specific scope of application and therefore qualifies as *lex specialis*. This means that, while the provisions of the ASCM – as *lex specialis* – take precedence over those of the GATT – *lex generalis* – in case of conflict, the GATT remains always applicable to fill in possible gaps, where the ASCM does not specifically contemplate otherwise. The second argument is purely logical. It stems from the analysis of the different measures covered by the two agreements (GATT and ASCM) and from the consideration that denying the applicability of the exceptions set out in article XX GATT to subsidies would create irreversible and unjustified policy inconsistencies. As a matter of fact, the GATT covers measures – such as total bans and quotas – which are widely known as more restrictive and trade-distorting than subsidies. Needless to say that such an approach would end up allowing more distorting measures and banning less distorting ones.[45] Finally, the last argument is based on the WTO case law. In the *China – Publications and Audiovisual Products*[46] dispute, the Appellate Body agreed that article XX of the GATT could apply to China's Protocol of Accession (in particular to article 5.1),[47] and for the first time it showed a positive attitude towards the idea that such provision might be applicable beyond the scope of the agreement.[48] There is still a crucial difference between China's Accession Protocol and the SCM Agreement: the latter – like the other WTO Agreements – does not include a general 'without prejudice clause' as written in China's Accession Protocol. Whether this obstacle could be overcome or not based on the legal relationship between the ASCM and GATT provision, is still debated.[49]

It follows that the WTO treaty structure is complex and the relationship between the provisions of the WTO Agreements is not at all clear. On the one hand, WTO Panels and the Appellate Body are not likely to agree to the application of article XX to the ASCM provisions, since, in the interpretation of WTO Agreements, they have often adopted a quite narrow approach that appears to apply the rules of the Vienna Convention on the Law of Treaties (VCLT) rather mechanically.[50] On the other, the recent ruling in the aforementioned *China –*

---

44 With specific reference to this principle in the context of the WTO, see Joost Pauwelyn, *Conflicts of Norms in Public International Law: How WTO Relates to Other Rules of International Law* (CUP 2003) 385. See also Tim Graewert, 'Conflicting Laws and Jurisdictions in the Dispute Settlement Process of Regional Trade Agreements and the WTO' (2008) 1 *Contemporary Asia Arbitration Journal* 287.

45 See Robert Howse (n 36) 13; Rubini (n 1) 35.

46 Appellate Body Report *China — Measures Affecting Trading Rights and Distribution Services for Certain Publications and Audiovisual Entertainment Products*, 21 December 2009, WT/DS363/AB/R.

47 ibid paras 205–33.

48 In this dispute, the United States challenged a variety of provisions within various Chinese measures as inconsistent with para 5(1) of China's Accession Protocol, related to the regulation of the right to import the specific products at stake into China. China invoked art XX(a) GATT as a defence, especially relying upon the introductory clause of para 5(1) of its Accession Protocol, which reads: 'without prejudice to China's right to regulate trade in a manner consistent with the WTO Agreement.' Rubini (n 1) 36; Joost Pauwelyn, 'Squaring Free Trade in Culture with Chinese Censorship: The WTO Appellate Body Report on "China – Audiovisuals"' (2010) 11 *Melbourne Journal of International Law* 119.

49 Pauwelyn (n 48).

50 Julia Ya Qin, 'Pushing the Limits of Global Governance: Trading Rights, Censorship and WTO Jurisprudence – A Commentary on the China–Publications Case' (2011) 10 *Chinese Journal of International Law* 271, 292; Julia Ya Qin, 'The Challenge of Interpreting "WTO-PLUS" Provisions' (2010) 44 *Journal of World Trade* 127, 132.

Publications and Audiovisual Products case represents a 'welcome development in WTO jurisprudence'.[51] Undoubtedly, however, allowing article XX GATT to be used to justify any WTO violation – even beyond the list of objectives mentioned therein – would confer considerable power to the Panels and the Appellate Body, increasing the discretion they already exercise in the 'weighing and balancing' activity required under article XX.[52]

Conclusions

The goal of this chapter was to highlight some unresolved issues and tensions that characterize the way the WTO deals with renewable energy subsidies. These tensions include, first, the inherent lack of coherence and coordination among different WTO Agreements and the insufficiency of current interpretive tools. Second, the non-inclusion of 'energy' or 'renewable energy' in any WTO agreement makes it hard for WTO rules to fully acknowledge and value the specific obstacles faced by renewable energy producers and consumers. It is necessary to weigh the positive externalities of renewable energy use against the negative ones created by fossil fuels when evaluating national policies, and the WTO still lacks a suitable mechanism to achieve this goal. Third, the need to condemn local content requirement should be balanced with the necessity, for developing countries and emerging economies, to develop or improve their own domestic renewable energy industry, and a subsidy programme completely void of a local content requirement would hardly help the country develop its own domestic production and market. One possible solution could be to include a period of transition, provided for in the Protocol of Accession, where the local content requirements are accepted by the WTO until a certain level of development is reached. All these tensions show the fundamental inadequacy of existing WTO rules in this area. It is now indisputable that climate change is one of the most relevant problems to face contemporary world and it has to be addressed with new instruments, which, in the framework of the WTO, would require a change of course – leaving the current judicial status quo behind with the adoption of a more flexible interpretation of WTO Agreements toward sustainable development and the protection of the environment.

51 Ya Qin, 'Pushing the Limits' (n 50) 293.
52 Pauwelyn (n 48).

Part IV

Investment

14 Economic Crises, Sovereign Debt Restructurings and the Shifting Landscape of International Investment Law

Catharine Titi[*]

Introduction

For about half a century, investment promotion and protection have been the alpha and omega of the international investment law system and international investment agreements' (IIAs) principal reason of existence. Concluding these agreements, States have offered investors safeguards such as fair and equitable treatment, full protection and security, protection in case of expropriation, most-favoured-nation treatment, and guarantees of free capital transfers, in tandem with the possibility of recourse to investor-State arbitration. Strengthening investment protection, States started to confine their policy space and their capacity to adopt measures for the protection of the public interest, including in situations of crisis. The system's limitations were made evident in the aftermath of arbitrations initiated against Argentina concerning measures taken by the South American State in order to tackle its economic and financial crisis of 2001. This, in conjunction with industrialized countries' own experience with investor-State arbitration under the North American Free Trade Agreement (NAFTA), seems to have brought to attention the urgent need for reform.[1] The United States and Canada were the first to consider ways in which to protect their regulatory freedom and circumscribe the interpretative leeway of arbitral tribunals by addressing their right to pursue specific public policy goals, including their ability to respond to situations of economic and financial crisis.[2]

At the time that the North American attempts at reform took place, the probability that EU Member States would be faced with analogous problems seemed quite remote. In contrast with the NAFTA model, EU Member State investment treaties were concluded with developing countries whose investors had minimal investment in Europe. Where economic crises were concerned, there was an apparent unlikelihood of a crisis similar to Argentina's confronting Europe. But a decade later, the situation is radically different. The EU is currently negotiating investment agreements with industrialized partners, such as the United States,[3] and recent investment claims registered against EU Member States as a result of the

* Catharine Titi is a Research Scientist at the French National Centre for Scientific Research (CNRS) and Member of the CREDIMI, Law Faculty of the University of Burgundy. She may be contacted at cathy_titi@hotmail.com.

1 eg. see KJ Vandevelde, A Comparison of the 2004 and 1994 U.S. Model BITs: Rebalancing Investor and Host Country Interests, in Sauvant, KP (ed), *YB on Int'l Inv L & Pol 2008–2009* (OUP 2009) 290–92.

2 Catharine Titi, *The Right to Regulate in International Investment Law* (Nomos and Hart Publishing 2014) 19.

3 For the negotiations on the EU-US Transatlantic Trade and Investment Partnership (TTIP) see <http://ec.europa.eu/trade/policy/in-focus/ttip/> accessed 20 September 2014. On EU negotiations in general see Marc Bungenberg and Catharine Titi, Developments in International Investment Law, in C Herrmann, M Krajewski and JP Terchechte (eds) *European Yearbook of International Economic Law* (Springer 2014).

economic and financial crisis in Europe – notably, the *Ping An*[4] and *Marfin*[5] cases against Belgium and Cyprus respectively arising out of nationalizations in the banking sector and the *Cyprus Popular Bank*[6] and the (rejected on jurisdictional grounds) *Poštová banka*[7] claims against Greece in relation to that State's 2012 debt restructuring – demonstrate all too well that even industrialized countries are not immune to investment arbitration. The adjudication of disputes arising out of economic crises and sovereign debt restructurings has become in the last few years a political issue whose importance stretches beyond the initial cases involving the Argentine crisis. It is not astonishing that mentalities in Europe are changing and, even if this is not wholly due to the crisis, the reform of international investment law is now being led by the European Union in ways not previously envisaged.

The chapter will aim to explore this very reform of international investment law in the light of, inter alia, economic crises. Focusing on the post-crisis EU-led reform, it will examine in turn novel formulations of substantive and procedural standards, including provisions and policy Statements explicitly referring to the financial sector and economic crises, in order to better understand the new face of international investment law and the new generation of international investment agreements.

Reform of International Investment Law in Light of Economic Crises and Sovereign Debt Restructurings

In general, economic crises seem to have brought about considerations related to either broad measures taken in times of economic and financial turmoil, including prudential measures, or sovereign debt restructurings. The analysis that follows will briefly consider these in turn, using the Argentine crisis disputes as a case study.

The several cases launched against Argentina in the immediate aftermath of its economic and financial crisis of 2001 and the 'pesification' of its economy brought to light the need to safeguard State capacity to deal with situations of severe economic and financial downturns.[8] Economic crises are in principle considered to affect a State's essential security interests[9] and so one avenue of response in this respect is the introduction of exceptions allowing derogations from investment treaty provisions where a State adopts measures necessary for the protection of its essential security interests.[10] Exceptions relating to essential security interests predate the onset of the said disputes, some of which were decided on the basis of the Argentina–United States bilateral investment treaty (BIT) of 1991 which contained such a clause.[11] So much the interpretation of the clause by some of the first Argentine crisis tribunals,[12] the criticism addressed to them by the annulment

---

4 *Ping An Life Insurance Co of China, Limited and Ping An Insurance (Group) Co of China, Limited v Belgium*, ICSID Case No ARB/12/29, registered 19 September 2012.

5 *Marfin Investment Group Holdings S.A., Alexandros Bakatselos and others v Cyprus*, ICSID Case No ARB/13/27, registered 27 September 2013.

6 *Cyprus Popular Bank Public Co Ltd v Greece*, ICSID Case No ARB/14/16, registered 16 July 2014.

7 *Poštová banka, a.s. and ISTROKAPITAL SE v Greece*, ICSID Case No ARB/13/8, Award, 9 April 2015.

8 More than 50 cases have been initiated against Argentina, which corresponds to around one tenth of all known investment treaty claims. See UNCTAD, Recent Developments in Investor-State Dispute Settlement (ISDS), *IIA Issues Note* No 1 (Revised) May 2013 <www.unctad.org/diae> 29, Annex 2.

9 Titi (n 1) 82 ff.

10 On these exceptions, ibid 206 ff.

11 Art XI Argentina–US BIT. For the disputes see Titi (n 1) *passim*. See further Catharine Titi, 'Investment Arbitration in Latin America: The Uncertain Veracity of Preconceived Ideas' (2014) 30 *Arbitration International* 357, 369 ff.

12 These are especially the *CMS Gas Transmission Co v Argentina*, ICSID Case No ARB/01/8, Award, 12 May 2005; *Sempra Energy International v Argentina*, ICSID Case No ARB/02/16, Award, 28 September 2007;

committees[13] and the discussion around the State's margin of appreciation in that context[14] as the interpretation of the treaties that did not contain such an exception[15] raised the question of the necessity of drafting an essential security interests exception in order to safeguard a modicum of the state's regulatory flexibility in dealing with a crisis situation.[16]

By the time the disputes were born, the United States had already moved a step further, enshrining its essential security interests exceptions in self-judging language and thus rendering the State more or less the sole judge of whether the measures adopted are necessary for the protection of its essential security interests.[17] This shift in US treaty practice took place after the interpretation of an essential security interests exception by the International Court of Justice (ICJ) in its 1986 *Nicaragua* Judgment[18] and was reflected in the 1992 US–Russia BIT (not in force), the 1999 US–Bahrain BIT and the 1992 US Model BIT.[19] But the expansion of the exception and of its formulation as a self-judging clause outside the North American treaty model follows the adjudication of the Argentine crisis disputes and the (variety of) jurisprudential solutions that were adopted in that context.

The facts that triggered the cases are well documented. The deepening of Argentina's economic recession in 2001 precipitated a severe economic and political crisis[20] that resulted in violent demonstrations, deaths and a succession of five presidents in less than a fortnight.[21] In order to deal with a situation that was slipping out of control, stabilize the economy and restore confidence in the economy among the population,[22] Argentina adopted a series of measures, including the freezing of bank accounts to prevent a run on the banks with Decree No. 1570/01,[23] known as the *Corralito*,[24] and the abandonment of the currency board system that had pegged the Argentinean peso to the US dollar with the Emergency Law of

---

and *Enron Creditors Recovery Corporation (formerly Enron Corporation) and Ponderosa Assets, L.P. v Argentina*, ICSID Case No ARB/01/3, Award, 22 May 2007.

13 See *CMS Gas Transmission Co v Argentina*, ICSID Case No ARB/01/8, Decision on Annulment, 25 September 2007; *Sempra Energy International v Argentina*, ICSID Case No ARB/02/16, Decision on annulment, 29 June 2010; and *Enron Creditors Recovery Corp and Ponderosa Assets, L.P. v Argentina*, ICSID Case No ARB/01/3, Decision on the Application for Annulment, 30 July 2010.

14 For example William W Burke-White and Andreas von Staden, 'Investment Protection in Extraordinary Times: The Interpretation and Application of Non-Precluded Measures Provisions in Bilateral Investment Treaties' (2007–08) 48 *Virginia Journal of International Law*, *passim*.

15 See Titi (n 1), 290–93.

16 ibid.

17 UNCTAD, 'The Protection of National Security in IIAs', *UNCTAD Series on International Investment Policies for Development* (United Nations 2009) 91. On self-judging clauses, see Titi (n 1) 195 ff; Burke-White and von Staden (n 13) 376 ff.

18 *ICJ, Military and Paramilitary Activities in and against Nicaragua (Nicaragua v United States of America), Merits, Judgment, ICJ Reports 1986*.

19 See *LG&E Energy Corp, LG&E Capital Corp and LG&E International Inc v Argentina*, ICSID Case No ARB/02/1, Decision on Liability, 3 October 2006, paras 211, 213; *CMS Gas Transmission Co v Argentina*, ICSID Case No ARB/01/8, Award, 12 May 2005, paras 339, 368; Enron Award (n 11) para 327; *Sempra Energy International v Argentina*, ICSID Case No ARB/02/16, Award, 28 September 2007.

20 *BG Group plc v Argentina*, UNCITRAL, Final Award, 24 December 2007, paras 54 ff; *LG&E Decision on Liability* (n 18) para 54.

21 *El Paso Energy International Co v Argentina*, ICSID Case No ARB/03/15, Award, 31 October 2011, para 91; *BG Group* (n 19) paras 60, 72; *CMS Gas Award* (n 11) para 64; *LG&E Decision on Liability* (n 18) paras 63, 235–36.

22 Burke-White and von Staden (n 13) 309.

23 Argentina: Decreto 1570/2001, BO 3 December 2001, No 29787, 1.

24 *El Paso* (n 20) para 91; *LG&E Decision on Liability* (n 18) para 63; *BG Group* (n 19) paras 56, 70 ff. The word *corralito* is the diminutive of *corral*, which refers to a corral, an animal pen or enclosure, thus making reference to the restrictive effect of the measures. See *BG Award*, ibid fn 38.

January 2002.[25] These measures had an impact on foreign investors protected under bilateral investment treaties concluded by the South American State. While broadly similar (all of them old generation agreements), these treaties were nonetheless not identical. Notably, as already mentioned, the bilateral investment treaty concluded between Argentina and the United States in 1991 contains a (non-self-judging)[26] essential security interests' exception, allowing the host State to digress from any obligation assumed under the treaty if such digression is necessary for the protection of its essential security interests.[27] By contrast, its counterparts concluded between Argentina, on the one hand, and France and the United Kingdom, on the other, do not contain an equivalent exception, thereby prioritizing, through the absence of any wording indicating the contrary, investment protection over the State's essential security interests.[28]

It is remarkable that in the case of the disputes born on the basis of the Argentina–US BIT, and despite the presence of an essential security interests exception that rendered recourse to customary international law inappropriate before examination of the exception,[29] some tribunals turned to the necessity defence as enshrined in the International Law Commission's Articles on Responsibility of States for Internationally Wrongful Acts (hereinafter ILC Articles).[30] The plea of necessity as encapsulated in the ILC Articles requires the presence of a number of criteria, which, as interpreted in arbitral jurisprudence, raise the threshold for successful invocation of the defence so high that the latter becomes unavailable in practice.[31] This unavailability of the customary law defence of the State of necessity may have encouraged States to incorporate essential security interests exceptions in their newer treaties in order to reserve for themselves what customary law does not grant, to wit the possibility to digress from their investment treaty obligations to protect their security.[32]

Moving beyond the initial Argentine crisis disputes, a new chapter in the adjudication of economic crises by arbitral tribunals has started to be written with disputes involving Argentina's sovereign debt restructuring. Following its economic and financial crisis, Argentina defaulted on its debt in December 2001. Some time later, in early 2005, an attempt was made to restructure and the State secured the acceptance of at least 75 per cent of its creditors,[33] which permitted the restructuring of over US$100 billion debt.[34] This first attempt

---

25 Ley 25.561, Emergencia Pública y Reforma del Régimen Cambiario, BO 7 January 2002. See further *BG Group* (n 19) para 73; *Enron Award* (n 11) paras 71 ff; *El Paso* (n 20) para 95; *LG&E Decision on Liability* (n 18) paras 64 ff.

26 The issue of whether the said exception in the treaty was self-judging or not triggered an intense rift between the Argentinean Government and the claimants in the disputes that arose. Unanimously, the tribunals found that the exception was not self-judging. For a discussion of this topic, see Titi (n 1) 195 ff.

27 Art XI of the US–Argentina BIT (1991).

28 See Titi (n 1) 290–91.

29 See generally *CMS Gas Decision on Annulment* (n 12).

30 See *Draft Arts on Responsibility of States for Internationally Wrongful Acts*, Report of the International Law Commission on the work of its fifty-third session (23 April – 1 June and 2 July – 10 August 2001), UN GAOR, 56th Sess, Supp No 10, UN Doc A/56/10 (2001).

31 See Titi (n 1).

32 For examples see ibid.

33 See Karen Halverson Cross, 'Arbitration as a Means of Resolving Sovereign Debt Disputes' (2006) 17 *American Review of International Arbitration* 335. According to a 2009 survey, Argentina appeared to have been an exception among recent sovereign debt restructurings in obtaining a relatively low creditor participation, see Ugo Panizza, Federico Sturzenegger and Jeromin Zettelmeyer, 'The Economics and Law of Sovereign Debt and Default' (2009) 47 *Journal of Economic Literature* 672, 683.

34 See Halverson Cross (n 32) 335.

at restructuring was followed by a new offer in 2010 targeting the holdout investors of the 2005 restructuring. Following the restructurings, holdout investors deposited claims against the Latin American country and the disputes born have subsequently raised the question of the necessity of according policy space to a State wishing to restructure its debt.[35] The country faced a new default in 2014 and the number of sovereign defaults beyond those involving Argentina indicates the topic's wider implications: in early 2012, Greece launched the largest ever sovereign debt restructuring relating to €205 billion in debt, and, as mentioned above, two ICSID cases were registered against it, while other recent sovereign debt restructurings include those of Belize (twice since 2007), Ecuador (2009) and Jamaica (twice since 2010),[36] opening the way for further future claims.

Judicial resolution of disputes is not foreign to sovereign debt restructuring. As a rule, sovereign debt instruments provide for *litigation* of such disputes although they remain silent on the potential for *arbitration*.[37] The latter is a new phenomenon and one that has raised heated questions. Notably, it has been debated whether sovereign bonds constitute covered 'investment' so much within the meaning of investment treaties as within the meaning of the ICSID Convention, and whether States have consented to the arbitration of mass claims,[38] the latter issue arising in particular with respect to the *Abaclat, Ambiente Ufficio*[39] and *Alemanni*[40] cases.

However, it should be noted that although the latter tribunals accepted jurisdiction over the claims brought before them, the most recent decision relating to sovereign debt restructuring at the time of writing, the *Poštová banka* award, found differently. Although the *Poštová banka* tribunal did not openly disagree with its predecessors, it considered, inter alia, that the Greece–Slovakia BIT under interpretation included a definition of investment that was considerably different from the one that led the Argentine debt restructuring tribunals to conclude that sovereign bonds were protected as covered investment.[41] The tribunal remarked that although the BIT established that investment 'means any kind of asset', it qualified this by noting 'and in particular, but not exclusively, includes' and incorporating a list of the assets non-exclusively included. In other words, the broad definition of investment ('any kind of asset') was followed by the specification that 'the term applies especially to a specific group or category'.[42] The latter, the tribunal considered, are broad

35 UNCTAD, 'Sovereign Debt Restructuring and International Investment Agreements' *IIA Issues Note No 2* (United Nations, July 2011) 3.

36 International Monetary Fund, *Sovereign Debt Restructuring – Recent Developments and Implications for the Fund's Legal and Policy Framework*, 26 April 2013, 6.

37 Brazil appears to be an exception to this rule, whose debt agreements have regularly provided for arbitration of disputes. See Halverson Cross (n 32) 339, 341 ff.

38 Catharine Titi, 'The Arbitrator as a Lawmaker: Jurisgenerative Processes in Investment Arbitration' (2013) 14 *Journal of World Investment & Trade* 835–38; Kevin P Gallagher, 'The New Vulture Culture: Sovereign debt restructuring and trade and investment treaties' *IDEAs Working Paper Series* Paper No 02/2011, 15 ff.

39 *Abaclat and others v Argentina*, ICSID Case No ARB/07/5, Decision on Jurisdiction and Admissibility, 4 August 2011; *Ambiente Ufficio S.p.A. and others v Argentina*, ICSID Case No ARB/08/9, Decision on Jurisdiction and Admissibility, 8 February 2013.

40 *Giovanni Alemanni and others v Argentina*, ICSID Case No ARB/07/8, Decision on Jurisdiction and Admissibility, 17 November 2014.

41 *Poštová banka, a.s. and ISTROKAPITAL SE v Greece*, ICSID Case No ARB/13/8, Award, 9 April 2015, paras 298 ff, 304 ff.

42 ibid para 314. An apparent contradiction exists between this Statement and another Statement in para 313, where there the group or category of assets is described as 'not closed, or limited or restrictive'.

but not unlimited.[43] Unlike the Italy–Argentina BIT applicable in the *Abaclat* case, the list of covered investments in the Greece–Slovakia BIT 'does not contain any reference to "obligations" or to "securities," much less to *public* titles or obligations'.[44] The latter treaty does not contain any language to 'suggest that the State parties considered, in the wide category of investments of the list of article 1(1) of the BIT, public debt or public obligations, much less sovereign debt, as an investment under the treaty'.[45] References to bonds in the BIT were limited to bonds issued by companies.[46] The tribunal equally rejected the claimants' argument that bonds constituted loans, covered by the BIT[47] and their interpretation in connection with 'claims to money'.[48] It concluded that there was no investment and the claimants were not investors within the meaning of the BIT, and therefore the tribunal lacked jurisdiction *ratione materiae* to hear the merits of the dispute.[49] In an *obiter dictum*, since it had already determined that it did not have jurisdiction under the BIT, the tribunal examined whether sovereign bonds constituted investment under the ICSID Convention. In that case, the majority found that, if it were to accept the 'objective' test ('contribution, duration, risk'), the claimants did not have an investment and the tribunal did not have jurisdiction.[50] This latter part of the award is particularly important, because the tribunal, although narrowing its interpretation to the claims at hand, clearly distanced itself from the Argentine sovereign debt restructuring tribunals and considered that sovereign debt is not investment for the purposes of the ICSID Convention.

In parallel with these jurisprudential developments, negotiators have started to rethink the formulation of some relevant investment agreement provisions. Concretely, newer treaties sometimes preclude sovereign debt restructuring from the purview of their arbitration clause. Although this had also been the case with older treaties that do not cover portfolio investments,[51] significantly for the point discussed here some new treaties explain that 'public debt operations' do not constitute an investment[52] or that such operations are not subject to the treaty's investment protection provisions,[53] or they exclude the possibility of raising claims related to sovereign debt restructurings.[54] Other possible avenues States could take in the future would be to ensure that agreements prevent arbitration of mass claims, make explicit that sovereign crises come within the scope of an essential security interests exception[55] and

43 ibid para 313.
44 ibid para 331.
45 ibid para 332.
46 ibid para 335.
47 ibid paras 336 ff.
48 ibid paras 341 ff.
49 ibid para 350.
50 ibid paras 360 ff.
51 Art 1(1)(b) Denmark-Poland BIT (1990).
52 Art I Colombian Model BIT (2007), art 838, fn 11, Canada–Colombia FTA, art I Colombia–UK BIT (2010), art I Colombian Model BIT (2007). For a relevant discussion, see also República de Colombia, Departamento Nacional de Planeación, 2002, Documento Conpes 3197, 'Manejo de los Flujos de Endeudamiento en los Acuerdos Internacionales de Inversión Extranjera', Bogotá DC, 26 August 2002 <www.dnp.gov.co/Portals/0/archivos/documentos/Subdireccion/Conpes/3197.PDF.> accessed 15 January 2015. See also José Antonio Rivas, Colombia, in Chester Brown (ed), *Commentaries on Selected Model Investment Treaties* (OUP 2013) 203.
53 Annex 10-A United States Dominican Republic–Central America Free Trade Agreement (US–DR–CAFTA).
54 See Annex 10-F United States–Colombia Free Trade Agreement (US–Colombia FTA).
55 See also Gallagher (n 37) 27, and Kevin P Gallagher, 'Mission Creep: International Investment Agreements and Sovereign Debt Restructuring' (*Investment Treaty News*, 12 January 2012) <www.iisd.org/itn/2012/01/12/mission-creep-international-investment-agreements-and-sovereign-debt-restructuring-3/> accessed 15 January 2015.

provide waivers in contracts associated with sovereign debt.[56] Other recent treaties include a so-called 'filter' mechanism for a *renvoi* to the contracting parties of the issue whether pruden-tial measures exceptions apply in a given case.[57] Investment law is therefore changing even if in apparently incremental ways in response to host States' experience with claims arising out of financial and sovereign debt crises. The discussion will now turn to the elaboration of the EU's investment policy in light of the recent financial and economic crisis.

EU-Led Reform

The entry-into-force of the Treaty of Lisbon in 2009 constitutes an important turning point in the elaboration of international investment law norms in the European Union with poten-tially deep ramifications for the drafting of international treaty standards around the globe. Pursuant to article 207 of the Treaty on the Functioning of the European Union (TFEU), foreign direct investment, whose protection at the post-establishment stage was until then Member State competence, has become part of the Union's common commercial policy and therefore an exclusive EU competence. This transfer of competence, from the Mem-ber States to the Union, born out of a desire to offer a solid basis for the Union's external economic action in order to enhance its role in the elaboration of international investment treaty norms,[58] means that the EU is currently negotiating the first EU-wide international investment agreements.[59]

The elaboration and refining of the EU's international investment policy marks a distinct break with the traditional European treaty model, in other words, with what has become known as the 'best practices'[60] or the 'gold standard'[61] of the Member States. Instead, the EU is setting its own standard.[62] This standard is in principle close to the post-2004 North Amer-ican treaty model and reflects the new generation of investment agreements, which generally allows host economies ampler policy space than its predecessors.[63] But the EU wishes to fur-ther reform international investment law, and its policy is being designed against a

---

56 SI Strong, 'Rogue Debtors and Unanticipated Risk' (2014) 35 *University of Pennsylvania Journal of Interna-tional Law*; Catharine Titi, 'Institutional Developments in Investor-State Dispute Settlement and Arbitration under the Auspices of the International Centre for Settlement of Investment Disputes' in C Herrmann, M Kra-jewski and JP Terchechte (eds) *European Yearbook of International Economic Law*, 2015, Springer.

57 See UNCTAD, *World Investment Report 2015*, New York and Geneva, UN, 2015, p. 149.

58 See Marc Bungenberg and Stephan Hobe, 'The Relationship of International Investment Law and European Union Law' in M Bungenberg et al (eds), *International Investment Law: A Handbook* (Beck/Hart/Nomos 2015); Bungenberg and Titi (n 2).

59 On the status of the EU negotiations, see <http://ec.europa.eu/trade/policy/accessing-markets/investment/> accessed 30 September 2014.

60 See for example, European Parliament Resolution of 6 April 2011 on the future European international invest-ment policy, 2010/2203 (INI), [2012] OJ C296 E/05, 2 October 2012, paras 9, 18, 19; European Commission, Communication, 'Towards a Comprehensive European International Investment Policy' COM (2010) 343 final, Brussels, 7 July 2010, 9, 11.

61 Nikos Lavranos, 'In Defence of Member States' BITs Gold Standard: The Regulation 1219/2012 Establishing a Transitional Regime for Existing Extra-EU BITs – A Member State's Perspective' (2013) 10 *Transnational Dispute Management*.

62 Catharine Titi, 'Investment Law and the European Union: Towards a New Generation of International Invest-ment Agreements' (2015) 26 *European Journal of International Law* 3; Catharine Titi, 'Full Protection and Security, Arbitrary or Discriminatory Treatment and the Invisible EU Model BIT' (2014) 15 *Journal of World Investment & Trade* 534, 536 ff.

63 See Titi (n 37) 843 ff.

multifaceted background which, apart from North American influences, comprises a 'constitutional obligation'[64] to respect the principles that guide its external action,[65] a complex institutional power structure between EU institutions and the Member States, recent denunciations of first generation BITs, namely those by South Africa[66] and Indonesia,[67] and the negotiation of comprehensive investment treaties with developed countries.[68] Most notably, for the purposes of the present discussion, the EU is exercising its competence in the aftermath of a severe economic and financial crisis and with the hindsight of the arbitrations relating to the Argentine crisis and debt restructurings. It is therefore not astonishing that in its investment agreements the Union expressly wishes to safeguard the host economy's right to regulate in the face of economic crises. In the public consultation on the Transatlantic Trade and Investment Partnership negotiations with the United States, the Union clearly demonstrated its intention not only to guarantee host economies the right to take measures for prudential reasons, 'including measures for the protection of depositors or measures to ensure the integrity and stability of [their] financial system', but also more globally to allow measures 'taken in time of crisis in order to protect consumers or to maintain the stability and integrity of the financial system'.[69] It is noteworthy that the Union remarks in the same document that such provisions are 'in line with other EU agreements', thus making reference to free trade agreements (FTAs) the Union has previously concluded.

EU investment policymaking, and the new economic crisis-specific provisions, form part of the new *platinum* standard of the European Union[70] that, given the latter's weight in investment negotiations, presents a real opportunity for the Union 'to set a new agenda for investment protection and investor State [*sic*] dispute settlement provisions'.[71] The EU wishes to improve its investment agreements in a twofold approach targeting both substantive and procedural standards. The analysis that ensues will briefly consider the two in turn.

Substantive Standards

With its new investment policy, the Union seeks to achieve a 'better balance' between the State's right to regulate and investment protection and to design 'clearer and better standards'.[72] The two objectives go hand in hand and the Commission considers that investment protections must be clearly defined and leave no room for 'interpretative ambiguity', an issue considered particularly important where it is question of the 'State's right to regulate

---

64 Marc Bungenberg, 'Preferential Trade and Investment Agreements and Regionalism' in Rainer Hofmann, Stephan Schill and Christian J Tams (eds), *Preferential Trade and Investment Agreements: From Recalibration to Reintegration* (Nomos 2013) 284.

65 Art 21 of the Treaty on European Union (TEU).

66 See <http://investmentpolicyhub.unctad.org/IIA/CountryBits/195#iiaInnerMenu> accessed 30 September 2014.

67 UNCTAD, *World Investment Report 2014*, 114; Michael Ewing-Chow and Mr Junianto James Losari, Letter, 'Indonesia is letting its bilateral treaties lapse so as to renegotiate better ones' *Financial Times* (London, 15 April 2014); Ben Bland and Shawn Donnan, 'Indonesia to terminate more than 60 bilateral investment treaties' *Financial Times* (London, 26 March 2014).

68 For example EU negotiations with Canada and the United States.

69 European Commission, 'Public Consultation on Modalities for Investment Protection and ISDS in TTIP', 2014 <http://trade.ec.europa.eu/doclib/docs/2014/march/tradoc_152280.pdf> accessed 15 January 2015.

70 On the platinum standard, see Titi 'Full Protection' (n 60) 536 ff.

71 European Commission Fact sheet, 'Investment Protection and Investor-to-State Dispute Settlement in EU agreements', November 2013, 3 <http://trade.ec.europa.eu/doclib/docs/2013/november/tradoc_151916.pdf> accessed 15 January 2015.

72 European Commission (n 69) 3; European Commission (n 67) Introduction and text accompanying Question 5.

for public policy objectives'.[73] The relevance of measures affecting the financial sector and dealing with economic crises is obvious in this respect and the European Commission has emphasized that the 'principle' of the right of the States to pursue legitimate public policy objectives as enshrined in EU FTAs will apply to the investment protection provisions of the new EU agreements.[74]

In accordance with these Statements, the draft EU–Canada Comprehensive Economic and Trade Agreement (CETA) incorporates an essential security interests exception[75] and an exception for prudential measures.[76] Not dissimilarly to Canada's Model BIT,[77] the CETA prudential exception specifies that nothing in the agreement shall prevent the parties 'from adopting or maintaining reasonable measures for prudential reasons', such as for the protection of investors and depositors, the maintenance of the safety, soundness or integrity of financial institutions or in order to ensure 'the integrity and stability of a Party's financial system'.[78] The same agreement further incorporates an exception relating to safeguard measures, where, in exceptional circumstances, capital movement may 'cause or threaten to cause serious difficulties for the operation of the economic and monetary union of the European Union'[79] and an exception for balance-of-payments problems where 'Canada or a Member State of the European Union that is not a member of the European Monetary Union experiences serious balance-of-payments or external financial difficulties'.[80]

In seeking, among others, to achieve a 'balance' between investment protections and the host economy's right to regulate, the European Commission has stressed that treaty standards must be drafted in a 'detailed and precise manner'.[81] In this respect, the new EU approach targets particularly investment law's two most important standards, the fair and equitable treatment and expropriation.[82] Although the particular new formulation of the fair and equitable treatment has little direct or explicit bearing on the financial system,[83] the drafting of the expropriation standard may be introducing an important new element in this respect, at least for European agreements. Like US and Canadian BITs before it,[84] the CETA embraces the police powers doctrine and States that 'except in the rare circumstance where the impact of the measure or series of measures is so severe in light of its purpose that it appears manifestly excessive, non-discriminatory measures of a Party that are designed and applied to protect legitimate public welfare objectives, such as health, safety and the environment, do not constitute indirect expropriations'.[85] Significantly, an element of proportionality seems to have been

---

73 European Commission (n 69) 6. See also European Parliament resolution of 9 October 2013 on the EU–China negotiations for a bilateral investment agreement, 2013/2674(RSP) para 41.

74 European Commission (n 69) 7.

75 Art X.05: National Security, Chapter on Exceptions, CETA, version of 26 September 2014.

76 Art 15.1: Prudential Carve-out, Financial Services Chapter, CETA, version of 26 September 2014. See also art 20: Investment Disputes in Financial Services and Annex XX of the same Financial Services Chapter.

77 Art 18(2) of Canada's Model BIT (version of 2012).

78 Art 15.1, Financial Services Chapter, CETA, version of 26 September 2014.

79 Art X.03: Temporary Safeguard Measures with regard to Capital Movements, Exceptions Chapter, CETA, version of 26 September 2014.

80 Art X.04: Restrictions in Case of Balance of Payments and External Financial Difficulties, Exceptions Chapter, CETA, version of 26 September 2014.

81 European Commission (n 69) 7.

82 See also Titi, 'Investment Law and the European Union' (n 60).

83 See art X.9: Treatment of Investors and of Covered Investments of CETA's Investment Chapter, version of 26 September 2014.

84 See the US and Canadian Model BITs' respective annexes on Expropriation.

85 Annex X.11: Expropriation, para 3, of CETA's Investment Chapter, version of 26 September 2014.

introduced in the aforecited provision, although the draft agreement falls short of incorporating a provision equivalent to that of article 1 of Protocol One of the European Convention on Human Rights.[86] The Annex on Indirect Expropriation makes further explicit that, although the economic impact of a measure is one of the factors to be taken into account when determining whether there has been an indirect expropriation 'the sole fact that a measure or series of measures of a Party has an adverse effect on the economic value of an investment does not establish that an indirect expropriation has occurred'.[87] The Commission has explained that it wants to ensure that investors shall not be compensated 'just because their profits have been reduced through the effects of regulations enacted for a public policy objective'.[88] Although measures taken in times of financial crises are not directly cited in CETA's Annex on Indirect Expropriation, it is argued that such measures adversely affecting investors could fall under the scope of such a clause.

Investor-State Dispute Settlement

Substantive standards aside, the EU wishes to improve the modalities of the functioning of investor-State dispute settlement (ISDS), focusing on 'building a modern, transparent and efficient ISDS system'.[89] Although this target does not bear directly on economic crises, it is worth considering since, at least in part, it has come about as a response to critiques of international investment law that arose acutely in the aftermath of the adjudication of sovereign crises by arbitral tribunals.

The EU's first policy goal in this respect has been to increase transparency in ISDS. For the European Commission, improvement of investment arbitration is not conceivable without transparency.[90] It is worth noting that the EU participated in the elaboration of the UNCITRAL Transparency Rules[91] and, upon EU initiative,[92] the latter have been introduced in the current version of the CETA text.[93] Of course, the concern with transparency has been prominent already in the NAFTA context. The NAFTA Free Trade Commission's (FTC) 2001

---

86 During a 'Right to regulate' roundtable organized by the Dutch Ministry of Economic Affairs, Agriculture and Innovation on 13 July 2012, the majority of participants favoured the incorporation of an ECHR-like provision on expropriation in future EU investment treaties. Such a provision also existed in Norway's Draft Model BIT of 2007.

87 Annex X.11: Expropriation, para 2, of CETA's Investment Chapter, version of 26 September 2014.

88 European Commission (n 69) 8; European Commission, 'Investment protection does not give multinationals unlimited rights to challenge any legislation', Brussels, 20 December 2013 <http://trade.ec.europa.eu/doclib/press/index.cfm?id=1008> accessed 15 January 2015.

89 European Commission, 'Public consultation on modalities for investment protection and ISDS in TTIP', 2014, 3 <http://trade.ec.europa.eu/doclib/docs/2014/march/tradoc_152279.pdf> accessed 15 January 2015.

90 On transparency, see Federico Ortino, 'Transparency of Investment Awards: External and Internal Dimensions' in Junji Nakagawa (ed), *Transparency in International Trade and Investment Dispute Settlement* (Routledge 2013) 119; Catharine Titi, 'International Investment Law and Good Governance' in Marc Bungenberg, Jörn Griebel, Stephan Hobe and August Reinisch (eds), *International Investment Law: A Handbook* (2015); Séverine Menétrey, *L'amicus curiae, vers un principe commun de droit procédural?* (Dalloz 2010); Séverine Menétrey, 'La transparence dans l'arbitrage d'investissement' (2012) *Revue de l'Arbitrage* 33; Andrew Newcombe and Lluís Paradell, *Law and Practice of Investment Treaties* (Kluwer Law International 2009); Friedl Weiss and Silke Steiner, 'Transparency as an Element of Good Governance in the Practice of the EU and the WTO: Overview and Comparison' (2007) 30 *Fordham International Law Journal* 1545.

91 European Commission (n 69) 8.

92 See art 11 of the EU–Canada Free Trade Agreement Investor-to-State Dispute Settlement Text, Investor-to State Dispute Settlement text after discussions on 28–30 January 2013, 1 February 2013.

93 Art X.33 Transparency of Proceedings of CETA's Investment Chapter, version of 26 September 2014.

Notes of Interpretation of Certain Chapter 11 Provisions highlighted the absence of a general duty of confidentiality imposed on the disputing parties[94] and a FTC Joint Statement on a 'Decade of Achievement' in 2004 welcomed the fact that Mexico has 'joined Canada and the United States in supporting open hearings for investor-State disputes'.[95] All NAFTA awards are public[96] and express provisions on transparency figure in the US and Canadian Model BITs and treaties concluded on their basis.[97] But the provisions on transparency remain new in the EU context and the incorporation of the UNCITRAL Transparency Rules is novel, given that the latter were only adopted in 2014. Another recently signed treaty to have included the UNCITRAL Transparency Rules is the 2014 bilateral investment treaty concluded between Colombia and France.[98]

Other amendments to the investor-State dispute settlement system include preventing investors from engaging in multiple or frivolous claims, in order to both ensure that investors may not 'win twice' and discourage 'long shot' claims.[99] This is a concern especially in light of the fact that even a successful respondent State may be liable to pay its arbitration costs.[100] The EU further aims to incentivize investors to launch their claims in local courts or resort to amicable settlements or other alternative dispute resolution methods.[101] Concretely, the draft CETA introduces procedural requirements for the submission of claims to arbitration[102] and it regulates the situation where claims are brought concurrently under the investment agreement and another international agreement.[103] Possibly inspired by a 2006 ICSID Convention amendment, the same agreement contains provisions on the rejection of claims that are manifestly without legal merit[104] and those 'unfounded as a matter of law'.[105]

Another novel EU suggestion concerns the introduction of a code of conduct for arbitrators, including specific provisions to address conflicts of interest.[106] Further proposals include binding guidance by the parties on the interpretation of a treaty provision after the agreement has been concluded and the introduction of an appeals mechanism in order to increase consistency in ISDS.[107] While some treaties, such as the US Model BIT, envisage the possibility

---

94 NAFTA Free Trade Commission (FTC) Notes of Interpretation of Certain Ch 11 Provisions, 31 July 2001 <www.sice.oas.org/tpd/nafta/Commission/CH11understanding_e.asp> accessed 30 September 2014.

95 See NAFTA FTC, Joint Statement on 'Decade of Achievement', San Antonio, 16 July 2004 <www.interna tional.gc.ca/trade-agreements-accords-commerciaux/agr-acc/nafta-alena/JS-SanAntonio.aspx?lang=eng> accessed 30 September 2014.

96 See Ortino (n 77) 124.

97 For example see art 29 US Model BIT (2012), arts 31–32 Canadian Model BIT, art 10.20 of the US–Chile FTA, art 10.21 of the US–DR–CAFTA.

98 Art 15 of the Colombia–France BIT (2014).

99 European Commission (n 69) 8; European Commission (n 67).

100 ibid.

101 European Commission (n 67).

102 Art X.21 of CETA's Investment Chapter, version of 26 September 2014.

103 ibid.

104 Art X.29 of CETA's Investment Chapter, version of 26 September 2014.

105 Art X.30 of CETA's Investment Chapter, version of 26 September 2014. See further European Commission (n 67).

106 The Code of Conduct is included in Annex 1 (Dispute Settlement) Rules of Procedure and Code of Conduct of the CETA, version of 26 September 2014. See further European Commission (n 69) 8–9; European Commission (n 87) 3–4. European Commission (n 67). See also European Parliament (n 71) para 42.

107 European Commission (n 69) 8–9; European Commission (n 87) 3–4. European Commission (n 67). See also European Parliament (n 71) para 42.

of a future appellate system, the TTIP at least at some stage was expected to create such a mechanism.[108]

More interestingly for the topic under discussion, EU investment agreements may leave outside the scope of their arbitration clause measures adopted 'in times of crisis in order to protect consumers or to maintain the stability and integrity of the financial system'.[109] The CETA contains in a lengthy annex an Understanding between Canada and the EU relating to prudential measures and disputes in financial services.[110] Article 20 (Investment Disputes in Financial Services) of CETA's Financial Services Chapter functions as a *lex specialis* amending the Investment Chapter's arbitration clause and introduces a filtering mechanism for investment disputes in the financial sector. This provision is to be interpreted in line with the aforementioned Understanding between Canada and the EU. The European Commission's all too recent informal text proposal to the United States (US) for the negotiations on the investment chapter of the Transatlantic Trade and Investment Partnership (TTIP) of 16 September 2015, proposes the exclusion of multi-party proceedings.[111]

Conclusions

International investment law has been on a trajectory of reform especially in this last decade. Reform has often been the outcome of critiques levelled at the system which have threatened or threaten the existence of the international system of investment protections. Part of these critiques but also part of the reason for reform have been recent economic crises and, in Europe, the recent global downturn, seen in light of arbitral cases involving Argentina's economic and financial crisis and debt restructurings. Although it is difficult to identify the extent to which these specific factors have encouraged the drafting of particular provisions, it is doubtless that new exceptions in EU treaties relating to measures taken in situations of economic crisis and prudential measures play a restrictive role vis-à-vis investment tribunals' interpretive leeway and allow a host economy more freedom when dealing with such situations without violating an investment agreement. In this sense, the new formulations of substantive standards and accompanying exceptions introduce a measure of balance and are to be welcomed. Likewise, provisions aimed at improving the functioning of the investor-State arbitration system, including those that may leave out of the treaty's scope measures taken in times of crisis, reflect the new sensitivity about safeguarding the public interest, and indirectly about the State's capacity to deal with situations of crisis. As cases relating to Argentina's debt restructurings and the most recent financial crisis are yet to be decided, it remains to be seen how tribunals will deal with the new issues, including in the near future with the novel treaty provisions, and how investment policy will respond to these adjudications.

---

108 European Commission (n 67).
109 ibid.
110 Annex XX of CETA's Financial Services Chapter, version of 26 September 2014.
111 Article 6(5) of section 3 of the European Commission's draft TTIP text on investment, 16 September 2015. The draft proposal is available at http://europa.eu/rapid/press-release_MEMO-15-5652_en.htm <last accessed 16 September 2015>.

Index

Printed and bound by CPI Group (UK) Ltd, Croydon, CR0 4YY
08/05/2025
01864327-0012